ATLAN

West Point Lighthouse, Prince Edward Island, ©Andrew Penner/iStockphoto.com

Editorial Director   Cynthia Clayton Ochterbeck

THE GREEN GUIDE ATLANTIC CANADA

Editor	Gwen Cannon
Contributing Writer	Bruce W. Bishop
Researcher	Pamela Delaney
Production Manager	Natasha G. George
Cartography	Mapmobility Corp., Peter Wrenn
Photo Editor	Yoshimi Kanazawa
Proofreader	Claiborne Linvill
Layout & Design	Nicole D. Jordan
Cover Design	Laurent Muller, Ute Weber

Contact Us:

The Green Guide
Michelin Maps and Guides
One Parkway South
Greenville, SC 29615
USA
www.michelintravel.com
michelin.guides@us.michelin.com

Michelin Maps and Guides
Hannay House
39 Clarendon Road
Watford, Herts WD17 1JA
UK
☏ (01923) 205 240
www.ViaMichelin.com
travelpubsales@uk.michelin.com

Special Sales:

For information regarding bulk sales,
customized editions and premium sales,
please contact our Customer Service
Departments:
USA   1-800-432-6277
UK   (01923) 205 240
Canada 1-800-361-8236

Note to the Reader
While every effort is made to ensure that all information printed in this guide is correct and up-to-date, Michelin Apa Publications Ltd. accepts no liability for any direct, indirect or consequential losses howsoever caused so far as such can be excluded by law.

One Team...
A Commitment to Quality

There's just one reason our team is dedicated to producing quality travel publications—you, our reader.

Throughout our guides we offer **practical information**, **touring tips** and **suggestions** for finding the best places for a break.

Michelin driving tours help you hit the highlights and quickly absorb the best of the region. Our descriptive **walking tours** make you your own guide, armed with directions, maps and expert information.

We scout out the attractions, classify them with **star ratings**, and describe in detail what you will find when you visit them.

Michelin maps featured throughout the guide offer vibrant, detailed and easy-to-follow outlines of everything from close-up museum plans to international maps.

Places to stay and eat are always a big part of travel, so we research **hotels and restaurants** that we think convey the essence of the destination and arrange them by geographic area and price. We walk you through the best shopping districts and point you towards the host of entertainment and recreation possibilities available.

We **test**, **retest**, **check and recheck** to make sure that our guidebooks are truly just that: a personalized guide to help you make the most of your visit. And if you still want a speaking guide, we list local tour guides who will lead you on all the boat, bus, guided, historical, culinary, and other tours you shouldn't miss.

In short, we remove the guesswork involved with travel. After all, we want you to enjoy exploring with Michelin as much as we do.

The Michelin Green Guide Team

PLANNING YOUR TRIP

INTRODUCTION TO ATLANTIC CANADA

Sandra Phinney/Michelin

©iStockphoto.com/Nick Free

CONTENTS

DISCOVERING ATLANTIC CANADA

HOW TO USE THIS GUIDE

PLANNING YOUR TRIP

The blue-tabbed PLANNING YOUR TRIP section at the front of the guide gives you **ideas for your trip** and **practical information** to help you organize it. You'll find tours, ideas for recreation in the great outdoors, a calendar of events, information on shopping, sightseeing, childrens' activities and more.

INTRODUCTION

The orange-tabbed INTRODUCTION section explores **Nature** from topography to flora and fauna. The **History** section spans early settlement to the present. The **Art and Culture** section covers art, literature, music and cinema,

Sidebars

Throughout the guide you will find peach-colored text boxes (like this one) with lively anecdotes, detailed history and background information.

while **Atlantic Canada Today** delves into contemporary aspects.

DISCOVERING

The green-tabbed DISCOVERING section features Atlantic Canada's Principal Sights, arranged geographically by province, featuring the most interesting local **Sights**, **Walking Tours**, nearby **Excursions**, and detailed **Driving Tours**.

Contact information, admission charges, hours of operation, and a host of other **visitor information** are given wherever possible. Admission prices shown are normally for a single adult.

STAR RATINGS★★★

Michelin has given star ratings for more than 100 years. If you're pressed for time, we recommend you visit the ★★★ or ★★ sights first:

★★★	Highly recommended
★★	Recommended
★	Interesting

Address Books - Where to Stay, Eat and more....

WHERE TO STAY

We've made a selection of lodgings and arranged them within the cities by price category to fit all budgets (*see the Legend on the cover flap for an explanation of the price categories*). For the most part, we've selected accommodations based on their unique regional quality, their regional feel, as it were. So, unless the individual lodging embodies local ambience, it's rare that we include chain properties, which typically have their own imprint.

See the back of the guide for an index to the accommodations featured throughout the guide.

WHERE TO EAT

We thought you'd like to know the popular eating spots in Atlantic Canada. So, we selected restaurants that capture the regional experience—those that have a unique regional flavor (*see the Legend on the cover flap for an explanation of the price categories*). We're not rating the quality of the food per se; as we did with the lodgings, we selected restaurants for many towns and villages, categorized by price to appeal to all wallets.

See the back of the guide for an index to the restaurants featured throughout the guide.

MAPS

- Regional **Driving Tours** maps.
- Atlantic Canada map with the **Principal Sights** highlighted.
- Maps for major **cities** and **villages**.
- **Local tour** maps.

All maps in this guide are oriented north, unless otherwise indicated by a directional arrow. The term "Local Map" refers to a map within the chapter or Tourism Region. A complete list of the maps found in the guide appears at the back

of this book, as well as a comprehensive index and list of restaurants and accommodations.

See the map Legend at the back of the guide for an explanation of map symbols.

ORIENT PANELS

Vital statistics are given for each principal sight in the DISCOVERING section:

- **Information:** Tourist Office/Sight contact details.
- **Orient Yourself:** Geographic location of the sight with reference to its local core as well as surroundings, towns and roads.
- **Parking:** Where to park.
- **Don't Miss:** Unmissable things to do.
- **Organizing Your Time:** Tips on organizing your stay; what to see first, how long to spend, crowd avoidance, market days and more.
- **Especially for Kids:** Sights of particular interest to children.
- **Also See:** Nearby PRINCIPAL SIGHTS featured elsewhere in the guide.

SYMBOLS

Spa	Spa Facilities		Tours
Kids	Interesting for Children	P	On-site Parking
	Also See	▶	Directions
	Tourist Information	✕	On-site eating Facilities
	Hours of Operation		Swimming Pool
	Periods of Closure	△	Camping Facilities
	Closed to the Public		Beaches
	Entry Fees		Breakfast Included
	Credit Cards not Accepted		A Bit of Advice
	Wheelchair Accessible		Warning

Contact - Addresses, phone numbers, opening hours and prices published in this guide are accurate at the time of press. We welcome corrections and suggestions that may assist us in preparing the next edition. Please send your comments to:

UK
Michelin Maps and Guides
Hannay House
39 Clarendon Road
Watford, Herts WD17 1JA
travelpubsales@uk.michelin.com
www.michelin.co.uk

USA
Michelin Maps and Guides
Editorial Department
P.O. Box 19001
Greenville, SC 29602-9001
michelin.guides@us.michelin.com
www.michelintravel.com

Cabot Trail on the western coast of Cape Breton, Nova Scotia
Wally Hayes/Nova Scotia Tourism, Culture and Heritage

PLANNING YOUR TRIP

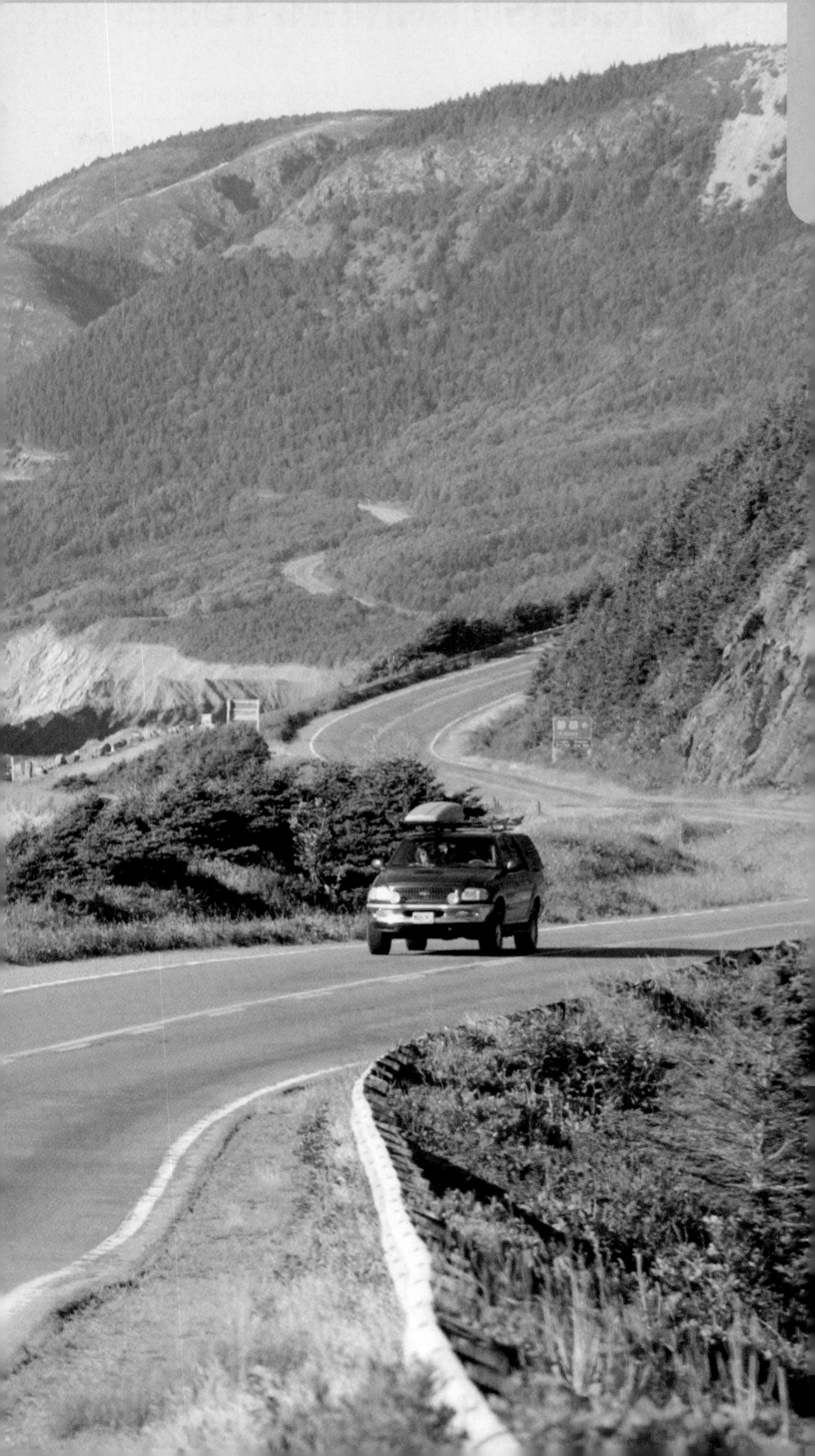

MICHELIN DRIVING TOURS

Driving allows travellers to appreciate the stunning coastlines of Atlantic Canada and the ruggedness of the interiors. The following two fast-paced tours, 22 and 12 days respectively in duration, are intended as planning tools, not as fixed routes.

1 Maritime Provinces

Round-trip of 4,235km/2,632mi (not including ferries) from Halifax. Time: 22 days. This tour of the three Maritime provinces is an interesting blend of seascapes, rocky headlands, sandy beaches and the high tides of the Bay of Fundy, with historical highlights such as the French fortress of Louisbourg, Halifax and its citadel, the Acadian country and the important port of Saint John.

DAYS/ ITINERARY/ SIGHTS

1–2 Halifax★★★
3 **Halifax – Antigonish** (261km/162mi); Sherbrooke★
4 **Antigonish – Sydney** (212km/132mi); Louisbourg Fortress★★★

5 **Sydney – Ingonish** (127km/79mi); Glace Bay (Miners' Museum★★), Cabot Trail★★ (described in opposite direction), Ingonish
6 **Ingonish – Baddeck** (233km/145mi); Cabot Trail★★, Cape Breton Highlands National Park★★, Chéticamp, Baddeck★
7 **Baddeck – Charlottetown** (263km/163mi and ferry); Prince Edward Island, Charlottetown★★
8–9–10 800km/500mi (maximum) Prince Edward Island Scenic Drives
11 **Charlottetown – Miramichi** (259km/161mi and ferry)
12 **Miramichi – Campbellton** (301km/187mi); Shippagan★, Village Historique Acadien★★
13 **Campbellton – Woodstock** (311km/193mi); Saint John River Valley★★ (described in opposite direction), Grand Falls★★, Hartland★
14 **Woodstock – Fredericton** (101km/63mi); Kings Landing★★
15 **Fredericton – Saint John** (109km/68mi); Fredericton★★
16 Saint John★★
17 **Saint John – Alma** (143km/89mi); Fundy National Park★★

18 **Alma – Truro** (254km/158mi);
Hopewell Cape★★, Moncton,
Fort Beausejour★★, Springhill★

19 **Truro – Annapolis Royal**
(243km/151mi); Truro,
Annapolis Valley★★ (described
in other direction)

20 **Annapolis Royal – Yarmouth**
(131km/81mi); Annapolis Royal★★,
Port Royal Habitation★★

21 **Yarmouth – Lunenburg**
(311km/193mi); Yarmouth★★,
South Shore★★ (described in
opposite direction), Liverpool,
Ovens Natural Park★,
Lunenburg★★

22 **Lunenburg – Halifax**
(176km/109mi); South Shore★★,
Peggy's Cove★★

2 Newfoundland

Round-trip of 2,046km/1,268mi (not
including ferries) from North Sydney,
Nova Scotia. Time: 12 days. This tour
of Canada's most easterly province
enables visitors to discover the scenic
wonders of Gros Morne, the French
island of St.-Pierre and the old port
city of St. John's.

DAYS/ ITINERARY/ SIGHTS

1 **North Sydney – Port aux
Basques** by ferry (🚢it is advisable
to spend the previous night in
Sydney)

2 **Port aux Basques – Wiltondale**
(298km/185mi)

3 Gros Morne National Park★★

4 **Wiltondale – Gander**
(336km/208mi)

5–6 **Gander – Trinity** (182km/113mi);
Terra Nova National Park★, Cape
Bonavista★, Trinity★★

7 **Trinity – Grand Bank**
(333km/206mi); Burin Peninsula,
Grand Bank

8 **Grand Bank – St.-Pierre** (by ferry
from Fortune); St.-Pierre★

9–10 **St.-Pierre – St. John's**
(362km/224mi); St. John's★★★

11 **St. John's – Cape Shore**
(175km/109mi); Placentia (Castle
Hill★), Cape St. Mary's★

12 **Cape Shore – North Sydney**
(by ferry from Argentia operating
mid-Jun–Sept three times weekly,
🚢call to confirm schedule; reserve
ferry well in advance of your trip).

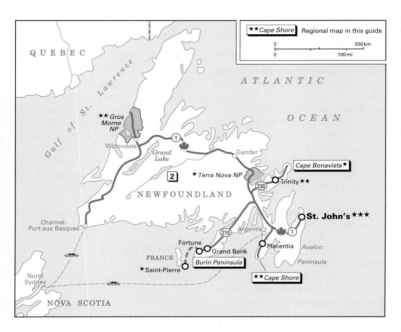

WHEN AND WHERE TO GO

When to Go

CLIMATE

Atlantic Canada's climate is varied and sometimes extreme in Newfoundland and Labrador. In some parts of the region, winter lasts longer than summer; yet the latter, when it comes, can be very warm. One major factor influencing climate is the proximity to large bodies of water: chiefly, the Atlantic Ocean. The Atlantic tends to make winters warmer and summers cooler. Regions distant to them are inclined, therefore, to have much colder winters and hotter summers. *See also Climate in the Introduction.* Daily weather reports and 5-day forecasts by Environment Canada are available at www.weatheroffice.ec.gc.ca, as well as on television and radio and in newspapers. Other useful websites are www.weather.com and www.theweathernetwork.com. For weather for specific cities covered in this guide, visit the websites, if available, listed within the *Discovering Atlantic Canada* section.

SEASONS

Atlantic Canada's main **tourist season** extends from the Monday on or before May 24 (Victoria Day) to the first Monday in September (Labour Day). Many attractions lengthen the season to the Thanksgiving weekend (second Monday in October). In mid-size to large cities, sights are usually open year-round.
Except in Labrador and northern parts of Newfoundland, visitors can enjoy fairly comfortable daytime temperatures but chilly nights from mid-April to mid-May in **spring;** in a few areas, spring skiing is still possible. New Brunswick celebrates the harvest of maple syrup with sugaring-off parties. Most visitors come to Atlantic Canada during the **summer** season, extending from the last weekend in May to early September. July and August are considered peak season and are ideal for outdoor activities such as sailing, kayaking, canoeing or hiking. Comfortably warm but rarely humid days with temperatures ranging from 18°-28°C/64°-82°F can be enjoyed throughout most of this region. May and September are pleasant months, whereas June, particularly in Nova Scotia, can be quite rainy. However, many attractions have curtailed visiting hours, so phone ahead. The western region of New Brunswick as well as Cape Breton Island in Nova Scotia offer spectacular displays of **fall** colours from mid-September until early October.
The Atlantic Canadian winter, from mid-November to mid-March, offers opportunities to enjoy **winter** activities such as downhill and cross-country skiing, skating, snowshoeing and snowmobiling. New Brunswick experiences heavier snowfall than its Maritime neighbours. Main highways are snowploughed, but vehicles should be winterized and snow tires are recommended.

WHAT TO PACK

Year-round, it is advisable to have a raincoat or hooded coat, in view of the coastal weather in this region. Warmer wear is necessary in early spring, late autumn and winter, when heavy top coats and layers of clothing are essential. In summer it can be cool in the evenings in many places, so taking some warmer clothes is recommended. Comfortable footwear is essential, especially for sightseeing.

Where to Go

See Sightseeing p24

KNOW BEFORE YOU GO

Useful Websites

Tourism New Brunswick
www.tourismnewbrunswick.ca

**Newfoundland and
Labrador Tourism**
www.newfoundlandlabrador.com

Nova Scotia Tourism
www.novascotia.com

Prince Edward Island Tourism
www.gentleisland.com

Canadian Tourism
www.canada.travel
(The official site of the Canadian
Tourism Commission)

Tourist Offices

🚷 *Also see Information under the
entry headings within each province in
Discovering Atlantic Canada.*
Tourist offices operated by provincial,
municipal and regional agencies dis-
tribute road maps and brochures that
provide information on points of interest, seasonal events, accommodations
and recreational activities. All publications are available free of charge. Local
tourist offices (telephone numbers,
addresses and websites listed under
the entry headings in this guide)
provide information about accommodations, shopping, entertainment,
festivals and recreation. On the maps
in this guide, information centres are
indicated by the symbol 🛈.

International Visitors

In addition to tourism offices, visitors
from outside Canada may obtain information from the nearest Canadian
embassy or consulate in their country
of residence. Embassies of other countries are located in Canada's capital,
Ottawa. Most foreign countries maintain consulates in Canada's provincial
capitals. For further information on
all Canadian embassies and consulates abroad, contact the website of
**Foreign Affairs and International
Trade Canada:** *www.international.
gc.ca.* For a complete list of Canadian
embassies and consulates abroad, go
online to www.voyage.gc.ca.

SELECTED CANADIAN
CONSULATES AND EMBASSIES

US
1175 Peachtree St. NE, 100 Colony
Square, Suite 1700, Atlanta,
GA 30361-6205, ☎404-532-2000.
www.atlanta.gc.ca
1251 Avenue of the Americas,
Concourse Level, New York, NY
10020-1175, ☎212-596-1628.
www.newyork.gc.ca
550 South Hope St., Los Angeles,
CA 90071-2627, ☎213-346-2700.
www.losangeles.gc.ca

Australia
Level 5, Quay West Bldg., 111
Harrington St., Sydney, NSW 2000,
☎9-364-3000.
www.international.gc.ca/australia

Germany
Leipziger Platz 17, 10117 Berlin,
☎30-203120. www.berlin.gc.ca

United Kingdom
38 Grosvenor St., Macdonald House,
London W1K 4AA, ☎020 7258
6506. www.london.gc.ca or
www.canada.org.uk

ENTRY REQUIREMENTS

All travellers need a valid passport,
Air NEXUS card or other valid travel
document to visit Canada and return
to the US by air. As of January 31, 2008,
Canadian and US citizens must present
a passport, or both a government-
issued photo ID (such as a driver's
license) and a birth certificate, to

cross the Canada/US border by land or sea. Parents bringing children into Canada are strongly advised to carry birth certificates. Parents taking children under 18 years of age into the US, or returning to the US after visiting Canada, must present a birth certificate for them. As of June 2009, or earlier, only a passport or other appropriate secure document will be accepted for anyone, including US citizens, to enter the US. Check the websites www.canada.travel or www.travel.state.gov (US government site) for the most recent updates. All other visitors to Canada must have a valid **passport** and, in some cases, a visa (see list of countries at www.cic. gc.ca/english/visit/visas.asp). No vaccinations are necessary. For entry into Canada via the US, all persons other than US citizens or legal residents are required to present a valid passport. Check with the Canadian embassy or consulate in your home country about entry regulations and proper travel documents.

CUSTOMS REGULATIONS

Non-residents may import personal baggage temporarily without payment of duties. Persons of legal age as prescribed by the province (&see provincial introductions) may bring into Canada duty-free 200 cigarettes, 50 cigars and some other forms of **tobacco. Alcohol** is limited to 1.14 litres (40 imperial ounces) of wine or spirits, or 24 bottles (355ml or 12 ounces) of beer or ale. All **prescription drugs** should be clearly labelled and for personal use only; it is recommended that visitors carry a copy of the prescription. For more information, call **Border Information Service** ☎800-461-9999 (within Canada) or ☎204-983-3500; or visit **Canada Border Services** Agency online at www.cbsa-asfc.gc.ca.
Canada has stringent legislation on firearms. A firearm cannot be brought into the country for personal protection while travelling. Long guns may be imported by visitors 18 years or older only for hunting or sport-

ing purposes. Certain **firearms** are prohibited entry; restricted firearms, which include handguns, may only be imported with a permit by a person attending an approved shooting competition. For further information on entry of firearms, contact the **Canadian Centre for Firearms** (284 Wellington St., Ottawa, ON K1A 1M6; ☎800-731-4000; www.cfc-cafc.gc.ca). Most animals, except domesticated dogs and cats, must be issued a Canadian import permit prior to entry into Canada. **Pets** must be accompanied by an official certificate of vaccination against rabies from the country of origin. Payment of an inspection fee may be necessary. For details, contact the **Canadian Food Inspection Agency** (59 Camelot Dr., Ottawa, ON K1A 0Y9; ☎613-225-2342; www.inspection.gc.ca).

CURRENCY EXCHANGE

&See Money in Basic Information.

HEALTH

Before travelling, visitors should check with their health care insurance to determine if doctor's visits, medication and hospitalization in Canada are covered; otherwise supplementary insurance may be necessary. **Manulife Financial** offers reimbursement for expenses as a result of emergencies under their Visitors to Canada Plan. The plan must be purchased before arrival, or within five days of arrival, in Canada. For details, contact **Manulife Financial** (2 Queen St. East, Toronto, ON, M5W 4Z2; ☎800-268-3763; www. coverme.com). You may also be able to arrange travel insurance through your national automobile association, such as the American Automobile Association.

Accessibility

Full wheelchair access to sights described in this guide is indicated in admission information by the symbol &. Most public buildings and many attractions, restaurants and hotels provide wheelchair access. Disabled parking is provided and the law is strictly enforced. For details contact the provincial tourist office (*see provincial introductions*).

Many national and provincial parks have restrooms and other facilities for the disabled (such as wheelchair-accessible nature trails or tour buses). For details about a specific park, call ☎888-773-8888 or visit *www.pc.gc.ca*. Additional information is available from **Easter Seals Canada** *(90 Eglinton Ave. East, Suite 208, Toronto, ON M4P 2Y3; ☎416-932-8382; www.easterseals.ca)*.

Passengers who need assistance should give 24-48hrs advance notice; also contact the following trans-portation providers to request their informative literature for riders with disabilities:

Via Rail
☎888-842-7245
Special Needs Services:
☎800-268-9503 (TDD)
www.viarail.ca

Greyhound Canada
☎800-661-8747 (Canada)
☎800-397-7870 (TDD)
www.greyhound.ca

Reservations for hand-controlled cars at rental companies should be made well in advance.

GETTING THERE AND GETTING AROUND

See also the Practical Information section for each province.

By Plane

American carriers offer **air** service to Atlantic Canada's major airports, such as Halifax International. Air Canada *(☎888-247-2262 Canada/US; www.aircanada.com)* flies from larger US cities and all Canadian cities.

Air Canada offers service from some European cities to Atlantic Canada, as well as from some destinations in the Caribbean, Asia and the Pacific. Domestic air service is offered by Canada's national airline **Air Canada** *(☎888-247-2262 or 800-361-8071 TDD)* as well as its affiliated regional airlines and by Calgary-based **WestJet** *(☎800-538-5696 or 877-952-0100 TDD)*. For specifics, contact the provincial tourist office (*see provincial introductions*).

Major airports in Atlantic Canada serviced by international airlines are listed in the Practical Information section of each province. Many smaller regional airlines serve the provinces and territories. Air service to remote areas is provided by several charter companies. Check with the regional tourist offices regarding your specific destination.

Note: Upon departure from some Canadian cities, travellers should be prepared to pay a $10 or higher Airport Improvement Fee before boarding the aircraft.

By Ship

Canada maintains an extensive ferry-boat system within Atlantic Canada. Ferry service from the US (Bar Harbor and Portland in Maine) connects to Yarmouth, Nova Scotia. Contact the provincial tourist offices for information and schedules (*see provincial introductions for details*).

By Train

Amtrak offers daily **rail** service to Montreal from Washington, DC and

New York City, as well as from New York City to Toronto. From Toronto and Montreal, travellers can continue on a VIA Rail train to New Brunswick and Nova Scotia. Aside from these direct routes, connections are offered from many major US cities. For schedules in the US, access ☎800-872-7245 or www.amtrak.com. **VIA Rail,** Canada's national passenger rail network, traverses the country with 18 major routes from coast to coast. First-class, coach and sleeping accommodations are available on transcontinental, regional and intercity trains. Amenities offered are dome cars, dining cars and lounges, baggage handling (including bicycles), reservation of medical equipment, wheelchairs and preboarding aid with 24hr minimum notice. Train travel within the Atlantic provinces is inadequate, so buying unlimited train travel passes is not recommended. Special rates are offered for students with an ISIC card, for youth and for senior citizens. Reservations should be made well in advance, especially during summer months and on popular routes like Toronto to Halifax. For information and schedules in Canada, contact the nearest VIA Rail office or call ☎888-842-7245 (US and Canada); www.viarail.ca. The Travel Planner section of the Via Rail website lists overseas sales agents.

By Coach/Bus

Bus travel from the US is offered by **Greyhound.** For information and schedules www.greyhound.ca or call the local US bus terminal. It is advisable to book well in advance when travelling during peak season. **Greyhound** offers Canada Travel Passes, which are sold internationally. Unlimited travel from 7 days up to 60 days is available. Peak season rates range from $329 to $750 (reduced rates available in off-season and for senior citizens). For fares and schedules, call Greyhound: ☎800-661-8747 (Canada), ☎800-231-2222 (US); or go online to www.greyhound.ca.

Other regional companies supplement Canada's extensive motorcoach service (see the yellow pages of local telephone directories).

By Car

🚗See also the Practical Information section for each province.
Given Atlantic Canada's size, it is best not to try to cover all of the provinces during one visit. 🚗See Driving Tours for suggested 12- and 22-day itineraries. The Maritime provinces have an extensive system of well-maintained major roads. In the northern regions (such as in rural Newfoundland and Labrador) and off main arteries, however, many roads are gravel or even dirt. 🚗Extreme caution should be taken when travelling these roads, especially in winter or during bad weather.

DOCUMENTS

Foreign **driver's licenses** are valid for varying time periods depending on the province. Drivers must carry vehicle **registration** information and/or rental contract at all times. Vehicle **insurance** is compulsory in all provinces (minimum liability is $200,000). US visitors should obtain a Canadian Non-Resident Inter-Province Motor Vehicle Insurance Liability Card **(yellow card)**, available from US insurance companies. For additional information contact the Insurance Bureau of Canada (777 Bay St., Suite 2400, Toronto, ON M5G 2C8; ☎416-362-2031; www.ibc.ca).

GASOLINE AND ROAD CONDITIONS

Gasoline is sold by the litre (1 gallon = 3.78 litres); prices vary from province to province. All distances and speed limits are posted in kilometres (1 mile = 1.6 kilometres). During winter it is advisable to check road conditions before setting out. **Snow tires** and an **emergency kit** are strongly recommended. Studded tires are allowed in winter in some provinces; for seasonal limitations, contact the regional Ministry of Transportation (check the blue pages in the local telephone directories).

ROAD REGULATIONS

Unless otherwise posted, the speed limit on rural highways is 100km/h (65mph) and in urban areas 50km/h (30mph). Service stations that are open 24 hours can be found in large cities and along major highways. The use of **seat belts** is mandatory for all drivers and passengers. Most provinces prohibit **radar detection** devices in vehicles. Traffic in both directions must stop (except on divided roads) for a yellow school bus when signals are flashing. Unless otherwise indicated, **right turns on red** are allowed after coming to a complete stop. Information on highway conditions in each province can be obtained by contacting the regional Ministry of Transportation (check the blue pages in the local telephone directories).

IN CASE OF ACCIDENT

If you are involved in an accident resulting in property damage and/or personal injury, you must notify the local police and remain at the scene until dismissed by investigating officers. There are detachments of the Royal Canadian Mounted Police (RCMP) in Newfoundland and Labrador (☎709-772-5400), Prince Edward Island (☎902-566-7112), Nova Scotia (☎902-490-6883) and New Brunswick (☎506-452-3400). Highways are patrolled by the Royal Canadian Mounted Police (www.rcmp. ca/traffic/index_e.htm) as are other areas not served by municipal police. There is always the option of dialing 911 initially, as most areas are covered by this emergency line. Hospitals are indicated by square blue signs carrying a white H.

CANADIAN AUTOMOBILE ASSOCIATION (CAA)

This national member-based organization (1145 Hunt Club Rd., Ottawa, ON K1V 0Y3; ☎613-247-0117; www.caa.ca) offers services such as travel information, maps and tour books, accommodations reservations, insurance, technical and legal advice, and emergency roadside assistance. These benefits are extended to members of other international affiliated clubs (proof of membership is required). The CAA maintains for its members a **24hr emergency road service** ☎**800-222-HELP** (🕭 see provincial introductions for CAA listings).

CAR RENTAL

Most major rental car agencies have offices at airports and in large cities in Atlantic Canada. (Typically, rates are higher when renting a car from an airport location.) Minimum age for rental is usually 25. To avoid a large cash deposit, payment by credit card is recommended. More favourable rates can sometimes be obtained by making a reservation before arriving in Canada, but be aware of drop-off charges.

- ◆ **Avis:** ☎800-331-1212. www.avis.com
- ◆ **Hertz:** ☎800-654-3131. www.hertz.com
- ◆ **Budget:** ☎800-268-8900. www.budget.com
- ◆ **National/Tilden:** ☎800-227-7368. www.nationalcar.ca
- ◆ **Thrifty:** ☎800-847-4389. www.thrifty.com

Barrett and MacKay/New Brunswick Tourism

Coastal drive in Fundy National Park

WHERE TO STAY AND EAT

Hotel and Restaurant listings fall within the Address Books of each province. For prices categories, ⚓ see the Legend on the cover flap.

Where to Stay

⚓ *For a selection of accommodations, see the green boxes titled* **Address Books** *within the major cities and areas described in this guide. Lodgings in this guide can also be found in the Index under the heading* **Where to Stay.** Atlantic Canada offers accommodations suited to every taste and pocketbook. Luxury **hotels** generally are found in major cities, while **motels** normally are clustered on the outskirts of towns. **Bed-and-breakfast inns** (B&Bs) are found in residential areas of cities and towns, as well as in communities, villages and more secluded natural areas. Many properties offer special packages and weekend rates that may not be extended during peak summer months *(late May–late Aug)* and during winter holiday seasons, especially near ski resorts. Most resort properties include outdoor recreational facilities such as golf courses, tennis courts, swimming pools and fitness centres. Activities—hiking, mountain biking and horseback riding—often can be arranged by contacting the hotel staff. Many cities and communities levy a **hotel occupancy tax** that is not reflected in hotel rates. Provincial and regional tourist offices offer free publications and maintain websites listing accommodations by location and type (⚓ *see provincial introductions for addresses*). Government tourist offices supply listings (free) that give locations, phone numbers, types of service, amenities, prices and other details. The Atlantic provinces cover quite a large area, and in less populated regions it may be difficult to find accommodations, especially at the end of a long day's drive. Advance reservations are recommended, particularly during the tourist season *(Victoria Day to Labour Day)*. During the off-season, establishments outside urban centres may be closed; it is therefore advisable to telephone ahead. Guaranteeing reservations with a credit card is recommended.

HOTELS

Rates for hotels vary greatly depending on season and location. Expect to pay higher rates during holiday and peak seasons. For deluxe hotels, plan to pay at least $300-$500/night per standard room, based on double occupancy in peak season. Moderate hotels usually will charge $90-$200/night. When making a reservation, ask about packages including meals, passes to local attractions, etc. Typical amenities at hotels include televisions, alarm clocks, in-room phones, smoking/non-smoking rooms, restaurants and swimming pools. Suites and in-room efficiency kitchens are available at some hotels. Always advise the reservations clerk of late arrival; unless confirmed with a credit card, rooms may not be held after 6pm.

MOTELS

Along major highways or close to urban areas, motels such as Comfort Inn, Quality Inn and Choice Hotels (☎877-424-6423), Best Western *(in NB, NS and PEI; ☎800-780-7234)* and the locally-owned Wandlyn Inns in NB and NS (☎800-561-0000) offer accommodations at moderate prices ($70–$115), depending upon the location. Amenities include in-room television, alarm clock and telephone. Smoking and non-smoking rooms, restaurants and swimming pools are often available on-site. Some in-room efficiency kitchens may be available. Family-owned establishments and small, independent guest houses that offer basic comfort can be found in Atlantic Canada.

BED AND BREAKFASTS AND COUNTRY INNS

Most B&Bs and country inns are privately owned; some are located in historic structures in residential sections of cities or small towns. In rural areas lodgings are a rustic cabin or a farmhouse. At B&Bs the room rate includes complimentary breakfast ranging from continental fare to a gourmet repast; some offer afternoon tea and evening sherry or light snacks. Guests are invited to use the sitting room and garden spots. Country inns are larger establishments, some with more than 10 rooms and dining facilities. Private baths are not always available, and often there is no phone in individual rooms. Smoking indoors may not be permitted. Reservations should be made well in advance, especially during peak seasons and holidays. Ask about minimum stay requirements, and cancellation and refund policies. Most establishments accept major credit cards, but some B&Bs may not. Rates vary seasonally ($75-$200) for a double room per night. Rates may be higher when amenities such as hot tubs, private entrances and scenic views are offered. In Atlantic Canada, there are a few associations of innkeepers and bed and breakfast owners, but each has different criteria for joining. Often there is no central reservation service; each accommodation acts independently. Phone ahead or look at the websites to judge what is best. **New Brunswick Bed & Breakfast Association** (☎888- 678-7678); **Nova Scotia Association of Unique Country Inns** (www.uniquecountryinns.com); **Inns of Distinction of Prince Edward Island** (www.innsofpei.com); **Newfoundland and Labrador B&Bs** (www.bbcanada. com/newfoundland).

RESERVATIONS SERVICES

Numerous organizations offer reservation services for B&Bs and country inns. Many services tend to be regional, but the **Professional Association of Innkeepers International** (☎856-310-1102; www.paii.org) and **Wakeman & Costine's North American Bed & Breakfast Directory** (☎828-387-3697; www.bbdirectory. com) include properties for Canada as a whole. The **Independent Innkeepers' Assn.** publishes an annual register that includes Canadian B&Bs and country inns; ☎269-789-0393 or 800-344-5244 or book online: www. selectregistry.com. For a complete listing, search the Internet using the keyword "bed and breakfast" or ask your travel agent.

HOSTELS

Hostelling International Canada, affiliated with the International Youth Hostel Federation, offers a network of budget accommodations from coast to coast. A simple, no-frills alternative to hotels and inns, hostels are inexpensive dormitory-style accommodations (blankets and pillows are provided) with separate quarters for males and females. Many have private family/couples rooms that may be reserved in advance. Amenities include fully equipped self-service kitchens, dining areas, common rooms and laundry facilities. Rates average $15–$25 per night for members (higher for non-members). Hostels often organize special programs and activities for guests. Advance booking is advisable during peak travel times, but walk-ins are welcome. Membership is $35/year, but non-members are also admitted. When booking, ask for available discounts at area attractions, rental car companies and restaurants. For information and a free directory, contact **Hostelling International Canada** (400-205 Catherine St., Ottawa, ON K2P 1C3; ☎613-237-7884 or 800-663-5777; www.hihostels.ca).

UNIVERSITIES AND COLLEGES

Most universities make their dormitory space available to travellers during summer vacation (May–Aug). Rooms are sparse; linens are provided. Bathrooms are communal and there are no in-room telephones. Rates average $20–$35/day per person. Reservations are accepted. When booking, ask about on-campus parking and food service. For more information contact the local tourist office or the university directly.

CAMPING AND RV PARKS

Atlantic Canada has excellent campgrounds that are operated privately or by the federal and provincial governments. Government sites are located in the many national and provincial parks. Fees are nominal. These campgrounds are well equipped and fill up quickly. Most park **campgrounds** are open mid-May through Labour Day, and usually operate on a first-come, first-served basis. Dates are subject to change: visitors should check with park visitor centres for rates and maximum length of stay. Some parks offer reservation services; some offer winter camping. Campsites often include a level tent pad, picnic table, fireplace or fire grill with firewood, and parking space near a potable water source. Most have toilet buildings and kitchen shelters. Some campgrounds are for tents only; others allow recreational vehicles; most do not have trailer hook-ups, although many have sewage disposal stations. Many accommodate persons with disabilities. For a list of campgrounds contact the provincial tourist office (*see provincial introductions*). Advance reservations are recommended, especially during summer and holidays. In most parks and forests, campgrounds are available on a first-come, first-served basis.

NATIONAL AND PROVINCIAL PARKS

Campgrounds are relatively inexpensive but fill rapidly, especially during school holidays. Facilities range from simple tent sites to full RV hook-ups (reserve 60 days in advance) or rustic cabins (*reserve one year in advance*). Fees vary according to season and available facilities (picnic tables, water/electric hook-ups, used-water disposal, recreational equipment, showers, restrooms): camping & RV sites $8–$21/day; cabins $20–$110/day. For all Canadian national park reservations, contact the park you are visiting or **Parks Canada** (*888-773-8888; www.pc.gc.ca*). For **provincial parks,** contact the provincial or local tourism office for information (*see Provincial Parks in the index*). As well as 8 national parks, throughout Atlantic Canada there are some 70 **provincial parks.**
For more information, contact Parks Canada (above).

PRIVATE CAMPGROUNDS

Commercial campgrounds offer facilities ranging from simple tent sites to full RV hook-ups. They are slightly more expensive (*$10–$60/day for tent sites, $20–$25/day for RVs*) but offer amenities such as hot showers, laundry facilities, convenience stores, children's playgrounds, pools, air-conditioned cabins and outdoor recreational facilities. Most accept daily, weekly or monthly occupancy. During the winter months (*Nov–Apr*), campgrounds in northern regions may be closed. Reservations are recommended, especially for longer stays and in popular resort areas. There are also camps throughout Atlantic Canada that are accredited and provide short-term accommodation for children and/or people with special needs. In all of Atlantic Canada, there is only one private campground dedicated to naturists or nudists: located In PEI, it is called The Oasis (*www.theoasisresort.com*).For details on private campgrounds, contact: **Camping Association of Nova Scotia** (*902-425-5454 ext. 431, www.campingns.ca*); camps in PEI are members of the Camping Association of Nova Scotia; **New Brunswick Camping Committee** (*506-853-3507, www.nbcamping.ca*); **Newfoundland & Labrador Camping Association** (*709-576-6198*).

Where to Eat

*For a selection of restaurants, see the green boxes titled **Address Books** within Discovering Atlantic Canada. Restaurants in this guide can also be found in the Index under the heading **Where to Eat**.*

Canada's regional cuisines encompass traditional comfort foods as well as novel creations. Atlantic Canada is no exception, and locals are proud of their **seafood.** Newfoundland and Labrador is famed for oysters, mussels, clams and other fruits of the sea. Lobster fishing is a huge industry in southwestern Nova Scotia. Lobster pound workers will gladly show visitors the largest, the oldest, the oddest (some are found blue in colour or even rarer, half-red and half-green). Summertime brings clam bakes on the beach, or large boiling pots of mussels mixed with other shellfish. Restaurants compete to make the best **crab cakes** (or fish cakes, made with local haddock), and homemade **seafood chowder** (with or without shellfish and sometimes simply haddock, potatoes and onions) is a staple in every Atlantic Canadian home.

Nova Scotia's annual food promotion, **"Taste of Nova Scotia,"** is offered at over 45 dining establishments, inviting patrons to sample the province's specialties. Boutique wineries in Nova Scotia are receiving raves from sommeliers in California and France: estate wineries can be found in the Annapolis Valley. Prince Edward Island is famous in summertime for village **lobster suppers,** be they held in a church hall or in an upscale location overlooking the water. Halifax and Saint John's, both known for their university populations, are great "pub" cities, where inexpensive dinners lure students to spend the evening enjoying draught beer and often, traditional live Celtic music. On the southwestern shore of Nova Scotia, the scallops harvested in the Bay of Fundy off Digby are a daily delight. **Digby scallops** are juicier and larger than bay scallops found in most North American inland cities. Now that cod has largely been removed from the menu in Newfoundland and Labrador, arctic char, lobster, salmon, snow crab and halibut are favourite dinners; **squid burgers** are an island peculiarity there. When on the island or in Labrador, tasting **screech,** a dark rum seemingly more potent than others, is a must. Game in Atlantic Canada includes caribou steaks and even moose. Blueberries, partridgeberries and yellow bakeapples (raspberry-like in appearance, but with a rich, distinctive taste) are among the fruits of the region. New Brunswick **fiddleheads** (an edible fern) are considered a culinary delicacy. **Dulse,** a dried edible seaweed, often takes an aquired taste, but it is sold next to potato chips in many corner stores.

WHAT TO SEE AND DO

Outdoor Fun

CANOEING AND KAYAKING

Offering circuit canoe trips, sea kayaking (Malpeque Bay, PEI), white-water rafting, accessible routes in Nova Scotia's Kejimkujik Park ("Keji" for short) and lodge-based paddles of tranquil lakes, Atlantic Canada is a paddler's heaven. Lifejackets are mandatory in Canada and it's illegal to drink and boat. For trip planning and information about the sports in the area, visit www.paddlingcanada.com, www.canoekayakcanada.ca. For leaving no trace travel, go to http://lnt.org. Some national and provincial parks offer canoe rentals.

FISHING

Atlantic Canada's abundant lakes and rivers offer a variety of fishing spots for anglers; **deep-sea fishing** is possible in the Maritime provinces, where boats can be chartered. Among highlights for inland fishing are Cape Breton's Margaree Valley and New Brunswick's Miramichi Valley. Licences are required for **fishing** and can be obtained from national and provincial park offices, designated sporting goods stores or other retail businesses. Some parks offer boat and canoe rentals. **Hunting** is not permitted within the national parks.

HIKING

Hiking in the Atlantic provinces is primarily enjoyed in national and provincial parks. Hikers should ask park officials about trail conditions, weather forecasts and safety precautions. Overnight **hikers** in backcountry areas are required to register at the park office before setting out and to deregister upon completion of the trip. Trail distances are given from trailhead to destination, not round-trip, unless otherwise posted. Topographic maps and a compass are indispensable for backcountry hiking; Gem Trek Publishing *(☎250-380-0100 or 877-921-6277; www.gemtrek.com)* and Federal Maps, Inc. *(☎416-607-6250 or 888-545-8111; www.fedmaps. com)* are two sources for obtaining detailed topographic maps.

SKIING AND BOARDING

Atlantic Canada does not have as many skiing and snowboarding areas as other parts of Canada, but these sports can be enjoyed. Downhill ski areas include Marble Mountain in Newfoundland, Sugarloaf in New Brunswick and Mactaquac Provincial Park in New Brunswick maintains trails for cross-country skiers. Check *www.skicanada.org* for packages, resorts, ski and snowboard organizations in Atlantic Canada; for snowboarding: *www.out-there.com*.

WILDLIFE WATCHING

In the Atlantic Provinces, wildlife is best observed in the provincial and national park systems. **Whales** can be seen *(especially Aug and Sept)* off the coasts of Newfoundland, New Brunswick and Nova Scotia. **Bird** watching is popular, particularly at the Kejimkujik Seaside and Newfoundland's three seabird colonies: Cape St. Mary's, Witless Bay and Funk Island. When watching or photographing wildlife, respectful distance is crucial. Stiff fines are given in parks for feeding and otherwise habituating wildlife: never feed, pet or disturb wild creatures of any kind. For more information, visit the Canadian Wildlife Federation's website: www.hww.ca.

Hiking at Cape Chignecto Provincial Park, Nova Scotia

Bruce Bishop/Michelin

Spas ⚓

Wellness and spas go hand in hand, particularly when married to idyllic, spectacular nature. In eastern Canada, you can be pampered with a massage beside the Atlantic Ocean, soak in a hot tub overlooking the Bras d'Or Lakes, or enjoy treatments at a heritage estate. Day spas, destination spas (which serve spa cuisine and offer lifestyle improvement), resort spas, mineral and medical spas are thriving. Browse *www.leadingspasofcanada. com* to see what Atlantic Canada has to offer.

Activities for Children Kids

In this guide, sights of particular interest to children are indicated with a Kids symbol. Many of these attractions offer discounted admission to visitors under 12 years of age as well as special children's programs designed for all ages. Canada's national parks usually offer discount fees for children. In addition, many hotels and resorts feature special family discount packages, and most restaurants offer children's menus.

Calendar of Events

Atlantic Canada has a wide variety of fairs, festivals and celebrations throughout the country, many based on historic events. *See Principal Festivals in the Practical Information section of each province.*

Shopping

BUSINESS HOURS

Business hours in Atlantic Canada are, for the most part, Monday to Friday 9am–5pm. In general, retail stores are open Monday to Friday 9am–6pm (until 9pm Thursday and Friday), Saturday 9am–5pm. Sunday shopping is a relatively recent phenomenon in the region; Prince Edward Island has limited shopping on that day. Many small convenience stores in gas stations may be open longer hours.
For banking hours, see Money in the Basic Information chapter.

GENERAL MERCHANDISE

Downtown areas provide opportunities for shopping at department stores, national chains, specialty stores, art galleries and antique shops. Major department stores in Atlantic Canada include Hudson's Bay Co. (known locally as "The Bay") and Sears. Revitalized historic districts, such as the Historic Properties in Halifax, house boutiques, art galleries and restaurants. Large **shopping malls** are generally located outside downtown areas. Bargain hunters will want to look for **outlet malls** that offer savings of up to 70% at brand-name factory stores. In Nova Scotia and Prince Edward Island, Frenchy's stores sell used and new clothing that originates from the US at bargain prices. Recreational **outerwear** companies, such as Mountain Equipment Co-op enable visitors to equip themselves from head to toe before setting out on hiking or fishing trips.

ARTS AND CRAFTS

Hooked rugs, mats and other **Acadian crafts** can be found at the gift shops at the Acadian Museum in Cabot Trail's Chéticamp and at Grand-Pré National Historic Site east of Wolfville. Tartans, kilts and other **Scottish attire** are for sale in Nova Scotia, particularly along the Cabot Trail. In the outports of Newfoundland, handknit items such as mittens, scarves and hats can be purchased at local historical museums. In many parts of eastern Canada, **native arts** and crafts are plentiful; museums, and cultural centres on tribal lands, exhibit and sell baskets, carvings, jewellery and other handiwork. Homemade preserves and pickles are the predominant offerings at the Prince Edward Island Preserve Company, which are exported around the world.

Gilbert's Cove Lighthouse, Digby County, Nova Scotia

FARMERS' MARKETS

Prince Edward Island is known for its potato harvests, and Nova Scotia's Annapolis Valley produces fruit and vegetables, beef and dairy products. Charlottetown's lively farmers' market gives islander craft and food vendors a place to display their wares. During harvest time, many farmers sell produce at roadside stands as well as at farmers' markets. Visitors can pick their own fruits and vegetables (for a small fee) at farms that are open to the public.

WINERIES

There are several boutique and estate wineries in Nova Scotia's Annapolis Valley; most wineries welcome visitors with guided tours that include free wine tastings. Many wineries will sell their vintages to the public; these same wines are not often found in provincial liquor stores, as the price mark-up would normally be too high. During the fall harvest season, check with area visitor centres to find out about wine-related festivals and special events.

Sightseeing

TRACING THE PAST

Genealogy is popular in Atlantic Canada, especially in Nova Scotia. Local museums, schools and universities, genealogical societies and churches have archival facilities for tracing one's roots. Many towns and special interest groups have their own heritage societies, such as the Annapolis Heritage Society *(www.annapolisheritagesociety.com)*, the Windsor Hockey Heritage Society *(www.birthplaceofhockey.com)*, the Nova Scotia Railway Heritage Society *(www.novascotiarailwayheritage.com)* and one for those interested in Fortress Louisbourg *(www.fortress.uccb.ns.ca/historic/heritage.html)*. For information, contact the **Genealogical Association of Nova Scotia** *(www.chebucto.ns.ca/recreation/gans/)* or the **Nova Scotia Genealogy Network Association** *(http://nsgna.ednet.ns.ca/)*.

HISTORIC SITES

All four Atlantic provinces are diligent in preserving their past, showcased in some 44 national historic sites. Nova Scotia boasts more historic sites than any province in Canada except Quebec. Designed for daytime visits, most sites are open from Victoria Day to Labour Day, with reduced hours in the early spring and fall. Most charge a nominal admission fee and at many, interpretation centres and costumed guides provide insight into area history and cultural heritage. Visit the websites of each province for details.

ORGANIZED TOURS

Two principal tour operators offer escorted trips throughout the Atlantic region, many tailor-made to specific interests, such as travelling to the two UNESCO parks in Newfoundland: Ambassatours *(www.ambassatours. com)* based in Halifax, and Maxxim Vacations *(www.maxximvacations. com)* based in St. John's. Both companies offer trips of varying durations throughout Atlantic Canada. In addition, Natural Habitat Adventures (www.naturalhabitatadventures.com) offers trips to see harp seals on ice floes in the Gulf of St. Lawrence and whales and seabirds in Newfoundland.

NATIONAL PARKS AND RESERVES

Atlantic Canada's national parks and national preserves offer the visitor spectacular scenery, a wealth of flora and fauna and recreational opportunities.

General Information

Most points of interest are in the southern national parks, accessible by car. Well-marked hiking trails permit outdoor enthusiasts and novices alike to enjoy the backcountry. Parks are open year-round; however, some roads may be closed during the winter. Daily entry or use fees range from $2.50 to $6 per adult. Discounts are offered at some parks to senior citizens (25%) and children (50%). Additional fees are charged for camping, fishing and guided programs. **Visitor centres** (⏲*open daily late May–Labour Day; reduced hours the rest of the year)* are usually located at park entrances. Staff are available to help visitors plan activities. Trail maps

and literature on park facilities, hiking trails, nature programs, camping and in-park accommodations are available on-site free of charge. Interpretation programs, guided hikes, exhibits and self-guided trails introduce the visitor to each park's history, geology and habitats. ✐*For park activities, see specific parks in each province.*
A good reference for planning a visit to Canada's national parks is Roberta Bondar's **Passionate Vision: Discovering Canada's National Parks** *(Douglas & McIntyre, Ltd., 2000).*

WORLD HERITAGE SITES

Atlantic Canada boasts four UNESCO World Heritage sites. **L'Anse aux Meadows** contains the remains of an 11C Viking settlement. In western Newfoundland, **Gros Morne National Park** provides the coastal lowland, alpine plateau, fjords, glacial valleys and sheer cliffs of a spectacular wilderness. The old town of **Lunenburg,** on the south shore of peninsular Nova Scotia, has survived its 1753 roots as a planned British colonial settlement. The **Joggins Fossil Cliffs** in Joggins, Nova Scotia, became a World Heritage Site in mid-2008. ✐*For details, see the entries within the Discovering section.*

DISCOUNTS

For Students and Youths
Student discounts are frequently available for travel, entertainment and admissions. Age eligibility varies: child rates usually apply for up to 12 years old; youth rates from 12–17. With a valid student card, any student 12 years and older can obtain an International Student Identity Card for discounts on rail travel and more (available at many ViaRail stations, or online from www.isic.org).

For Senior Citizens
Many attractions, hotels, restaurants, entertainment venues and transportation systems offer discounts to visitors age 62 or older (proof of age may be required). Canada's national parks usually offer discount fees for seniors.

Visiting seniors should feel free to ask specific businesses if such a discount is available.

Books

Anne of Green Gables. Lucy Maud Montgomery (1908)
This Canadian classic recounts the adventures of a precocious orphan girl adopted by an elderly brother and sister who had expected to adopt a boy. The setting is a farm in Prince Edward Island.

Barometer Rising. Hugh Maclennan (1941)
Part of most Maritime schools' curriculum, this highly regarded novel tells the story of the tragic Halifax Explosion of 1917 when two munitions ships collided in the harbour, decimating most of the city's north end and killing thousands.

The Shipping News. E. Annie Proulx (1993)
This Pulitzer prize-winning novel (made into a Hollywood movie in 2001) focuses on a hack journalist from New York who emigrates to Newfoundland and begins to find himself as well as love in the local community.

Fall on Your Knees. Anne-Marie MacDonald (2002)
Some say this epic novel of four sisters from Cape Breton Island is the quintessential description of the island's unique habitat and complicated lifestyle. It is an engrossing, detailed family drama with touches of high comedy.

When the Earth Was Flat. Raymond Fraser (2007)
This Fredericton author has written memoirs, essays and sketches on a variety of subjects, including Leonard Cohen, Alden Nowlan, New Brunswickers in Hollywood, and assorted eccentrics met during his career.

Nova Scotia: A Traveller's Companion. Lesley Choyce, ed. (2007)
Three hundred years of travel writing about Nova Scotia by the famous and not so famous make this compilation an engrossing read. Essays include impressions of the province from Joseph Howe, Thomas Chandler Haliburton, Charles Dickens, Rudyard Kipling, Archibald MacMechan and many others.

Films

Titles listed below represent films from Atlantic Canada that can be rented or purchased from larger video retailers.

Anne of Green Gables (1985)
The TV movie of this beloved classic set in Prince Edward Island is still eminently suitable for the whole family.

Margaret's Museum (1995)
A bittersweet love story set in the coal mining town of Glace Bay, Nova Scotia, starring Helena Bonham-Carter. A British-Canadian co-production with a parental advisory.

The Shipping News (2001)
This film version of the Annie Proulx novel (🌐 *see Books above*), directed by Lasse Hallström and starring Kevin Spacey and Judy Dench, shows Newfoundland's scenic beauty and the extremes of its weather.

Shattered City: The Halifax Explosion (2003)
This movie from the Canadian Broadcasting Corporation explores the 1917 explosion in Halifax harbour that killed more than 2,000 people and injured some 9,000.

Open Heart (2004)
This TV movie depicts the drama among the staff and the serious medical shortcomings of a fictitious Saint John, New Brunswick, hospital.

Poor Boy's Game (2007)
Filmed in Halifax, this contemporary drama deals with the issues of violence and racism in the darker neighbourhoods of a Maritime city. Stars Danny Glover.

BASIC INFORMATION

Electricity

120 volts, 60 cycles. Most small American appliances can be used in Atlantic Canada. European appliances require an electrical transformer, available at electric supply stores.

Emergencies

Most Atlantic Canadian cities and many of its rural areas have **911** telephone service for emergency response. When 911 is dialled from any telephone in a served area, a central dispatch office sees the dialling location and can redirect the call to the appropriate emergency response agency—fire department, police or ambulance. Some of rural Atlantic Canada is not within range of cellular telephone service, and although coverage extends along most major highways, service can be unreliable in remote regions. Public Safety Canada maintains extensive links to information and services on public safety: www.safecanada.ca.

Mail/Post

Post offices across Atlantic Canada are generally open Monday to Friday 8am–5:30pm; extended hours are available in some locations. Sample rates for first-class mail (letter or postcard; up to 30 grams): within Canada, 52 cents; to the US, 93 cents; international mail, $1.55. Mail service for all but local deliveries is by air. Visitors can receive mail c/o "General Delivery" addressed to Main Post Office, City, Province and Postal Code. Mail will be held for 15 days and has to be picked up by the addressee. Some post offices have fax services, and all post offices offer international courier service. Postal facilities may be located at selected Canadian retailers. For information regarding postal codes or locations of facilities call ☎866-607-6301; *www.canadapost.ca.*

Metric System

Canada has adopted the International System of Units popularly known as the metric system. Weather temperatures are given in Celsius (C°), milk and wine are sold by millilitres and litres, and grocery items are measured in grams. All distances and speed limits are posted in kilometres (to obtain the equivalent in miles, multiply by 0.6). Some examples of metric conversions are:

  1 kilometre (km) = 0.62 miles
  1 metre (m) = 3.28 feet
  1 kilogram (kg) = 2.2 pounds
  1 litre (L) = 33.8 fluid ounces = 0.26 gallons (1 US quart = 32 fluid ounces)

Money

Canadian currency is based on the decimal system (100 cents to the dollar). Bills are issued in $5, $10, $20, $50, $100, $500 and $1,000 denominations; coins are minted in 1 cent, 5 cents, 10 cents, 25 cents, $1 and $2. Exchange money at banking institutions for the most favourable exchange rate. ATM machines are available in many cities; most ATMs dispense cash in increments of $20. Most merchants accept debit or credit cards, except in remote areas. Self-serve gas and parking lots and even store checkouts are somewhat common. It is best to carry a few "loonies" or "toonies" (the $1 and $2 coins) for parking meters, tips and snacks. Most public telephones accept calling cards at no charge, but local calls cost 25–50¢ (one or two quarters).

BANKS

Banking institutions are generally open Monday to Friday 9am–5pm. Some banks may be open on Saturday morning. Banks at large airports have foreign exchange counters and extended hours. Some institutions may charge a fee for cashing traveller's cheques; ask in advance. Most principal bank cards are honoured at affiliated Canadian banks. ⊘Use bank branded ATM machines to avoid the higher fees charged by private operators.

CREDIT CARDS AND TRAVELLER'S CHEQUES

The following major credit cards are widely accepted in Atlantic Canada: Discover, MasterCard/Eurocard and Visa. Most banks will cash traveller's cheques and process cash advances on major credit cards with proper personal identification. Bank fees for cashing traveller's cheques may be high; ask in advance.

CURRENCY EXCHANGE

The most favourable exchange rate can usually be obtained at branch offices of a national bank. Some banks charge a small fee for this transaction. Private exchange companies generally charge higher fees. Airports and visitor centres in large cities may have exchange outlets as do some hotels. The Canadian dollar fluctuates with international exchange rates. Exchange facilities tend to be limited in rural and remote areas. If arriving in Canada late in the day or on a weekend, visitors may wish to exchange some funds prior to arrival (a few banks are open on Saturday mornings in major cities, however).

⊘You can use ATMs to withdraw Canadian currency from your home account, but check with your bank first to see if it has reciprocal arrangements with a Canadian bank for a lower fee.

TAXES

Canada levies a 5% Goods and Services Tax (GST) on most goods and services. The Harmonized Sales Tax (HST) of 13%, which includes the GST, applies in the provinces of New Brunswick, Nova Scotia and Newfoundland and Labrador. Referred to as zero-rated goods and services, certain items, such as groceries and prescription drugs, are taxable at a rate of 0%. A limited number of goods and services are exempt from the GST/HST. In Prince Edward Island, the total tax is 15%: 5% is the federal GST and 10% is the provincial tax.

Public Holidays

⊘For provincial holidays see provincial introductions. The following holidays are observed in Atlantic Canada. Most banks, government offices and schools are closed:

New Year's Day: January 1
Good Friday: Friday before Easter Sunday
Easter Monday: Monday after Easter Sunday
Victoria Day: Closest Monday to May 24
Canada Day: July 1
Labour Day: 1st Monday in September
Thanksgiving: 2nd Monday in October
Remembrance Day: 2nd Wednesday in November
Christmas Day: December 25
Boxing Day: December 26

Smoking

All Canadian provinces and territories have enacted comprehensive smoke-free legislation, and municipal bylaws are commonplace. Smoking is banned from aircraft, buses, trains and most offices, but restrictions for other public spaces vary among municipalities. Smoking in public places is increasingly unacceptable.

Telephones

To call long distance within Canada and to the US, dial 1+ area code + number. For overseas calls, refer to the country codes in most telephone directories, or dial "0" for operator assistance. Some operators speak French as well as English. Collect calls and credit card calls can be made from public pay phones. For local directory assistance, check the white pages of the phone directory or dial 411; outside the local area code dial 1+ area code + 555-1212. Telephone numbers that start with **800, 866, 877** or **888** are toll-free *(no charge)*. A local call costs 25 to 50 cents. Be aware that many hotels place a surcharge on all calls.

EMERGENCY NUMBERS

911 service is operative in major cities; otherwise dial "0" for the operator and ask for the police. In most provinces a Tourist Alert Program is operated by the Royal Canadian Mounted Police from June until September. If you see your name in the newspaper or hear it on the radio, contact the nearest RCMP office immediately.

Time

Canada spans six time zones, but the coast-to-coast time difference is only 4hrs 30min because Newfoundland time is 30min in advance of the Maritime provinces, which are on **Atlantic Time.** Except for the area on the coast from L'Anse au Clair to Cartwright which operates on **Newfoundland Time,** Labrador observes Atlantic Time (½ hour behind Newfoundland). Daylight Saving Time (clocks are advanced 1 hour) is in effect from the second Sunday in March to the first Sunday in November (*see provincial introductions for details*).

Tips

Tips or service charges are not normally added to a bill in Atlantic Canada. However, it is customary to give a tip (a small gift of money) for services received from food servers, porters, hotel maids and taxi drivers. In restaurants and for taxi drivers, it is customary to tip 10-15% of the total amount of the bill. At hotels, porters should be tipped $1 per bag, and maids $1 per night.

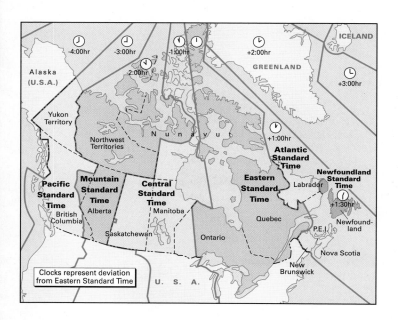

Iceberg watching at Cape Twillingate, Newfoundland

NATURE

Battered by the Atlantic Ocean on one side and washed by the calmer Gulf of St. Lawrence on the other, Canada's four Atlantic seacoast provinces (New Brunswick, Nova Scotia, Prince Edward Island, and Newfoundland and Labrador)—also known as Atlantic Canada—lie on the eastern side of the continent. They share the pervasive influence of the sea, which has moulded, in great measure, their economic, political and cultural development.

Geographical Features

ECOZONES

There are two ecozones here: New Brunswick, Nova Scotia and Prince Edward Island are in the Atlantic Maritime Ecozone, which applies to only 2% of all of Canada; Newfoundland and Labrador share the Atlantic and Northwest Atlantic Ecozone with the province of Quebec.

Barren and rocky by the sea while densely forested inland, the landmasses possess some fertile areas—the Saint John River Valley, the Annapolis Valley and Prince Edward Island. Their indented coastlines are studded with bays, inlets, cliffs and coves. The Bay of Fundy produces a phenomenal tidal bore. The highest recorded tide in the world occurred at Burncoat Head on the Nova Scotia shore: a difference of 16.6m/54ft between high and low tides.

APPALACHIAN MOUNTAINS

About 200 million years ago, these mountains, which stretch from Alabama in the US to Newfoundland, were the first to be folded on the edges of the continent. Since then, extensive erosion by ice, rivers and sea has reduced them to mere stumps of their former heights. Today the region is a series of generally flat to rounded uplands, with few sharp peaks rising to no more than 1,280m/4,200ft. Parts of the region,

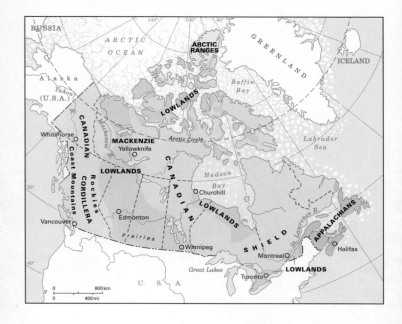

notably northern New Brunswick and Cape Breton Island, are hilly, lying near the end of the Appalachian Mountain chain. In the western part of Newfoundland, the Long Range Mountains (average height 610m/2,000ft) are part of this chain. Prince Edward Island, and the Annapolis, Ristigouche and Saint John River valleys are notable areas of plains where ancient glacial lakes have left fertile soil.

WILDLIFE AND VEGETATION

Seven national parks in Atlantic Canada help preserve the coastline. They are Terra Nova, Kouchibouguac, Fundy, Prince Edward Island, Cape Breton Highlands, Kejimkujik and Gros Morne. Within the parks, one will experience the shifting sands of the seashore; walk in boreal and primeval forests, and marvel at the rugged cliffs. These parks are home to many species of birds and wildlife, some of which are endangered.

Atlantic Canada's varied landscape hosts several species of animals typical of regional fauna. The forests provide habitat for **white-tailed deer, black-tailed deer** and **mule deer**. The largest of the deer family is a distinctively Canadian animal, the **moose,** which inhabits the forests of Newfoundland and Cape Breton Island in Nova Scotia. Also distinct is the Canada **lynx,** previously located throughout the country but now surviving in the northern mainland and in Newfoundland. Trapped nearly to extinction, **beavers** once again thrive across Canada, occupying the streams and ponds of forested regions. Over 30 species of **whales** ply Canada's coastal waters, including the humpback and fin (off Newfoundland, New Brunswick and Nova Scotia).

Atlantic Canada's bird population ranges from the Canada goose, Atlantic puffin and piping plover to the **bald eagle** that breeds in parts eastern Canada. Although most species are migratory, over 400 species of birds have been documented as breeding in Canada.

In New Brunswick, at the Atlantic Canada Conservation Data Centre, 40,000 observation records of extremely rare to uncommon plants and animals in the Atlantic region have been noted, with over 8,000 for New Brunswick, 6,000 for Nova Scotia, 2,000 for Prince Edward Island, 6,500 for Newfoundland and 60 for Labrador.

Atlantic Canada is positioned south of the tree line, where the **boreal forest** of spruce, tamarack and other conifers gradually begins. It is interspersed with innumerable bogs, marshes and other wetlands. Broadleaf trees such as birch, aspen and poplar appear, and some wetlands, especially in Nova Scotia, support commercial cranberry and blueberry farms. Unfortunately, wetlands are in retreat in Canada, with 65% already gone due to agricultural expansion into the coastal marshes. More deciduous trees are found until **mixed forest** predominates.

In eastern Canada, forestry, agriculture and urbanization have left only isolated pockets of old-growth forest. Hardwoods such as maple, birch and beech compete for well-drained soils with commercial stands of conifers like spruce and pine.

Climate

The sea largely determines the climate of this region. Moving south down the Atlantic coast, the cold **Labrador Current** enters the Gulf of St. Lawrence by the Strait of Belle Isle. Meeting warmer air currents moving in off the continent to the west, the cold waters of the current can cause fog banks along Newfoundland's and Nova Scotia's coasts.

Winters are stormy along the Atlantic but milder than inland. Summers are cooler and less humid than in Ontario and Quebec at the same latitude. The coast is cooler than inland.

In general, precipitation is evenly distributed throughout the year. Snow falls in all the provinces, but is heaviest in northwestern New Brunswick. Labrador experiences a more severe climate with more extreme temperatures but less precipitation.

HISTORY

Immigration and exploration have shaped Atlantic Canada's history. Vikings settled briefly in Newfoundland 1,000 years ago. Reports of abundant natural resources from French and English explorers led Europeans to establish temporary settlements as they fished the rich Gulf of Saint Lawrence some 500 years ago. Claims to North America led to nearly two centuries of war among France and England and the indigenous peoples. In the 19C fear of American takeover ultimately led to Canadian Confederation—New Brunswick and Nova Scotia were among the founding provinces. Soon thereafter, Prince Edward Island joined Confederation; Newfoundland held out until the mid-20C.

Past to Present

NATIVE CULTURES

Before the arrival of Europeans, the Atlantic provinces were inhabited by Indians of the **Eastern Woodlands** culture: **Mi'kmaq** in New Brunswick, Nova Scotia and Prince Edward Island lived by hunting and fishing; **Maliseets** cultivated the land in southern New Brunswick like their Iroquoian brothers in Ontario; and the **Beothuk** in Newfoundland also fished and hunted. The Beothuk's belief that all goods were held in common increased hostilities with the early European fishermen who frequently found their supplies missing.

Mass murder and European diseases diminished these people greatly. The last known surviving Beothuk died in St. John's in 1829.

EUROPEAN CLAIMS

Although he is credited as the first European arrival, **John Cabot** (1450-98)—an Italian navigator on a 1497 voyage of discovery for England's Henry VII—was not the first European to set foot in the region. Archaeological remains prove that the Norse settled on the Newfoundland coast about the year 1000. There is reason to believe the **Irish** reached the province's shore in the 6C, and it is possible that **Basques** fished the North

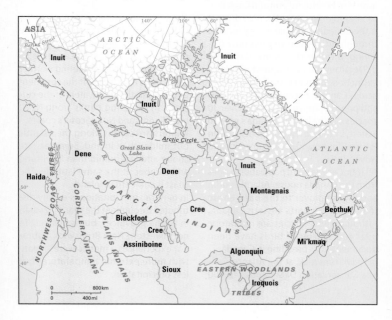

Atlantic as early as the 15C. At Red Bay in Labrador, archaeologists have discovered the presence of a large 16C Basque whaling port. Cabot's importance lies in his publicizing the region's rich fisheries. The Basques, English, French, Portuguese and Spanish came for the cod, especially abundant off Newfoundland's Grand Banks.

In 1583 Newfoundland was proclaimed the territory of Elizabeth I at St. John's. **Jacques Cartier** had claimed Prince Edward Island for France in 1534, renaming it Île-St.-Jean. Sieur de Monts and **Samuel de Champlain** established **Port Royal** in Nova Scotia in 1605.

In 1621 James I granted present-day Nova Scotia, Prince Edward Island and New Brunswick to **Sir William Alexander** to establish a "New Scotland" there (both men were Scots)—hence the Latin name *Nova Scotia* used on the original charter. In 1632 Charles I returned the region to the French.

Acadie (Acadia) was what the French called a vague area covering pockets of Nova Scotia, Prince Edward Island, New Brunswick and Maine. The Acadians are descendants mainly of 17C French colonists, who, in the 18C, did not feel loyalty to either the feuding English or French. The English Crown granted a few charters in the 17C for colonies on Newfoundland, but authority for local law and order, granted in 1634 by Charles I, belonged largely to the **fishing admiral**—master of the first British ship to enter a harbour. French claims to the region ended in 1713 when, by the Treaty of Utrecht, France retained **Saint-Pierre** and **Miquelon,** islands off southern Newfoundland.

THE ACADIANS

The Treaty of Utrecht gave Acadians the choice of leaving British territory or becoming British subjects. The Acadians stated they would take the oath with exemption from military service. Then, in 1747, nearly 100 New England soldiers billeted in the village of Grand Pré were killed, as they slept, in a surprise attack by a French force from Quebec. Treachery among the Acadian inhabitants was suspected. Fear of future attacks hardened the British toward the Acadians, especially after 1749 when Halifax was founded with 2,500 English settlers who could provision the army. In 1755 Gov. **Charles Lawrence** delivered his ultimatum—take an unqualified oath of allegiance or be removed from Nova Scotia. When the Acadians refused, Lawrence quickly issued the Deportation Order. Over the next eight years, 14,600 Acadians were forcibly deported. Unwelcome in the colonies, the Acadians were able to establish a new community only in Louisiana and as **Cajuns,** survive to this day. Some escaped to Saint-Pierre and Miquelon. Others fled to Île-St.-Jean until 1758, when the island was captured by a British expedition under **Lord Rolo,** and later annexed by Nova Scotia. Left untouched was a small settlement in the Malpeque area, the origins of Prince Edward Island's French-speaking population today. When peace was restored between England and France in 1763, most exiles returned to settle mainly in New Brunswick, and southwestern Nova Scotia, where their descendants live to this day.

EXPANDING POPULACE

The population of the future confederation of Canada was overwhelmingly French at this time. A few settlements in Newfoundland and Halifax were the only English-speaking exceptions. This imbalance was not to endure. The aftermath of the American Revolution brought thousands of **Loyalists** to the remaining British colonies (Nova Scotia, Prince Edward Island and Lower Canada, later named Quebec) and led to the creation of two more colonies—New Brunswick and Upper Canada (later Ontario).

After Deportation the British offered free land to anyone willing to settle in Nova Scotia. New Englanders from the south, groups from the British Isles and from the German Rhineland, and Scottish Highlanders accepted the offer.

After 1776, when revolution erupted in the American colonies, Nova Scotia was transformed by 30,000 Loyalists who fled the new US. A separate administration was set up in 1784 and called New Brunswick for the German duchy of Braunschweig-Lüneburg, governed at that time by England's George III. Other Loyalists settled in Prince Edward Island, named in 1799 in honour of the father of Queen Victoria.

CONFEDERATION

Fear of American takeover encouraged the small groups of British colonists to unite for common defence. In September 1864, representatives of Nova Scotia, New Brunswick and Prince Edward Island met with a delegation from Canada (then only Ontario and Quebec) to discuss British union in North America. This historic conference, held in Charlottetown on Prince Edward Island paved the way for Confederation in 1867 when their actions helped to propel the British Parliament into ratifying the **British North America Act.** The resulting new political entity, initially composed of four founding provinces—**Ontario, Quebec, New Brunswick** and **Nova Scotia**—adopted a parliamentary system of government and separation of federal and provincial powers. **Prince Edward Island** joined its sister Maritime provinces in Confederation in 1873. Newfoundland chose not to join, holding out until 1949, when it became Canada's 10th province. An amendment to Newfoundland's Terms of Union in 2001 made a name change from the province of Newfoundland to the province of **Newfoundland and Labrador.**

Time Line

PRE-COLONIAL PERIOD

c. AD 1000 — Norse reach Newfoundland.
1497 — **John Cabot** explores east coast of Canada.

NEW FRANCE

1534 — **Jacques Cartier** claims Canada for France.
1583 — Sir Humphrey Gilbert claims Newfoundland for England.
1605 — Samuel de **Champlain** establishes **Port Royal.**

1713 — Treaty of Utrecht is signed. France cedes Acadia to Britain.
1719 — France begins to build **Fortress Louisbourg** as a fortified town that was completed on the eve of the first siege in 1745.
1755 — Acadian Deportation from Nova Scotia begins.
1756-63 — Seven Years' War.
1763 — **Treaty of Paris** is signed. France cedes New France to Britain.

BRITISH REGIME

1749 — **Halifax** is built by the British as a garrison town.
1758 — A proclamation calls for election of a General Assembly in Nova Scotia, the beginnings of parliamentary democracy in Canada.
1761 — **Yarmouth,** NS founded by Massachusetts settlers as a shipbuilding port.
1783 — American colonies gain independence from Britain. **Loyalists** migrate to Canada; many settle in southern New Brunswick and the south shore of Nova Scotia.
1784 — New Brunswick is created by the partition of Nova Scotia.
1798 — St. John's Island changes its name to Prince Edward Island.
1841 — **Act of Union** creates the United Province of Canada.
1847 — **Responsible government** system is implemented in Canada.

CANADIAN CONFEDERATION

1864 — Prince Edward Island hosts the Charlottetown Conference, the first meeting leading to the Articles of Confederation.
1867 — British North America Act establishes Canadian Confederation.
1873 — Prince Edward Island enters Confederation.

1912 — Famous ship *Titanic* sinks
on her maiden voyage.
Many victims buried in
Halifax cemetery.

1914-18 — World War I.

1917 — Collision between two
munitions ships in the harbour causes an explosion
that decimates the north
end of Halifax.

1927 — Britain's Dominion of Newfoundland awarded Labrador,
claimed by Quebec, in settlement of 25-year dispute.

1928 — **Pier 21** opens in Halifax,
beginning the processing of
1.5 million immigrants into
Canada until 1971.

1939-45 — World War II. Canada
receives large numbers
of European immigrants.
Thousands come through
Halifax's Pier 21.

1949 — **Newfoundland** enters
Confederation.

CONTEMPORARY ATLANTIC CANADA

1961 — Canadian government
pledges $25 million to
reconstruct **Fortress
Louisbourg**. Work con-
tinues to this day with the
largest reconstructed 18C
French fortified town in
North America.

1962 — Trans-Canada Highway is
completed.

1977 — The federal government
intervenes to protect the
Atlantic fishery by extending the offshore limit to
370km (200 nautical mi)
off Newfoundland and
Labrador.

1992 — The federal government cur-
tails cod fishing off eastern
Newfoundland and Labrador
indefinitely.

1996 — Canada's last census of the
century. The country's population stands at 28.8 million.

1997 — New Confederation Bridge
links Prince Edward Island
to the mainland.

THE NEW MILLENNIUM

2000 — Newfoundland commemorates Norse landing 1,000
years earlier.

2001 — Newfoundland adds "and
Labrador" to its official
provincial name. A nation-
wide **census** confirms a
population of 29.5 million
in Canada.

2002 — Canadian troops join
international peacekeeping
mission in Afghanistan with
many Atlantic Canadians
leading the way.

2005 — The Acadian communities in
Nova Scotia, New Brunswick
and Prince Edward Island
celebrate the 400th anni-
versary of the first French
settlement at Port Royal
in Canada.
The White Rose offshore
oil and gas field, located
350km east of Newfound-
land, begins development.

2006 — Elections held in **Nunatsiavut**, a large portion of Labrador, to determine self-government among the Inuit.

2007 — Robert Ghiz becomes
premier of Prince Edward
Island, the youngest pro-
vincial leader (b.1974) in the
country, followed by Nova
Scotia's Rodney MacDonald
(b.1972) and New Bruns-
wick's Shawn Graham
(b. 1968). Newfoundland
and Labrador's Danny Wil-
liams isn't that much older
(b. 1950).

2008 — Nova Scotia recognizes
250 Years of Parliamentary
Democracy in Canada with
celebratory events.
Re-enactment of second
British siege (1758) of
Fortress Louisbourg to cel-
ebrate 250-year anniversary.

2009 — Extension of Trans-Labrador
Highway from Cartwright
to Happy Valley-Goose Bay
scheduled for completion.

ART AND CULTURE

Atlantic Canadian culture is rooted in a blend of British, French, and Aboriginal traditions. American media and entertainment do not dominate here as much as in Ontario or western Canada. Various federal government programs and laws attempt to support Canadian cultural initiatives. The federally funded Canadian Broadcasting Corporation (CBC) provides countrywide television and radio coverage; the National Film Board provides funding and distribution support for film; and other federally funded programs support art, music and dance.

Newfoundland and Labrador, the last province to join Confederation, has retained much of its British and Irish roots. Some of its native sons and daughters have become nationally known musicians, comedians, artists and novelists. Nova Scotia claims a musical legacy that has become known around the world.

Art

NATIVE EXPRESSIONS

Over centuries, Atlantic Canada's indigenous peoples have developed diverse modes of artistic expression that bear witness to their distinctive lifestyles and beliefs. Most of the Atlantic region's aboriginals (notably Maliseet, Passamaquoddy, Mi'kmaq, Montagnais and Innu) are descended from nomadic peoples, who excelled in the art of beadwork (shell, bone, rock or seed) and embroideries (porcupine quills and moose or caribou hair). Caribou-hide vests and moccasins and various birchbark objects were often adorned with geometric incisions and drawings. Elaborate belts of wampum (beads made from shells) feature motifs illustrating significant events in native history. Wampum was exchanged at peace ceremonies and during the signing of treaties. Mi'kmaq art and crafts can be purchased at aboriginal cultural centres throughout Nova Scotia.

Inuit Art

Art forms developed over centuries have brought no small renown to the inhabitants of Canada's Arctic regions.

In Labrador and the eastern region of peninsular Quebec live the Innu people, formerly known as the Naskapi-Montagnais Indians. Algonquian-speaking, their culture featured exceptionally made animal skin clothing, much of which was highly decorated with painted or woven designs. With the decline of traditional lifestyles resulting from increased contact with nonindigenous peoples, sculpture and other forms of arts and crafts gradually lost their magic or religious significance and provided a new source of income to the aboriginal population.

PAINTING AND SCULPTURE

17C-18C

The arrival of French and British colonists in the early 17C introduced European aesthetics and forms to the artistic landscape. Religion dominated life in what was then New France; thus, church decoration was the focus of early Canadian art. Art was also the means of depicting topography. British army officers were sent to Nova Scotia and Quebec to paint topographic views of the colonies for military purposes. Some of these works, inspired by the romantic ideals of late 18C England, are best exemplified by the carefully executed watercolours of officer Thomas Davies (1737-1812).

19C

Throughout the 19C, the arrival of European artists had a decisive impact on Canadian painting. **Paul Kane** (1810-71), born in Ireland, came to Canada as a child. He travelled the country extensively; his detailed portraits of native peoples (*The Death of Omoxesisixany* c.1856) are of significant historical interest today. In 1887, **Anna Leonowens** (1834-1915), known primarily as the inspiration for the British governess portrayed in the *Anna and the King of Siam* book and musical, found herself in Halifax. At this time, she became an instrumental founder of the Nova Scotia College of Art and Design. One of its most famous principals was to be **Arthur Lismer,** a member of Canada's famous Group of Seven landscape painters.

Early 20C
Robert Harris (1849-1919) left Prince Edward Island to train in Paris, but returned to execute perhaps the most prestigious commission in Canada, *The Fathers of Confederation* (1883); thereafter, Harris became one of Canada's eminent portraitists.

POST-WAR ERA

After World War II, no single school of thought prevailed over the inspirational and creative effervescence of contemporary art. Throughout Canada, artists strove to develop their own highly personal styles, like the scenes of his native New Brunswick of **Jack Weldon Humphrey** (1901-67). Nova Scotian **Maud Lewis'** (1903-70) folk art of happy scenes and brightly coloured landscapes belied the turmoil of her personal life and mobility impairments.

THE CONTEMPORARY SCENE

In recent years, Canadian art has evolved alongside major international currents; it has distanced itself from traditional painting while emphasizing more diversified forms and techniques. Although born in Toronto, **Alex Colville (**b. 1920) is closely associated with Nova Scotia, where he moved at the age of nine. His works are suffused with clear maritime light; his representational or "hyper-realist" style often reveals itself in scenes reflective of his personal life (*To Prince Edward Island,* 1965). The surrealist works of Nova Scotian artist **Brian Porter** (b. 1949) hang in galleries around the country. St. John's born artist **Christopher Pratt** (b. 1935) and his wife, New Brunswicker **Mary West Pratt** (b. 1935), have each contributed much to the art world with their individual painterly visions. Pratt designed the provincial flag for Newfoundland and Labrador.

Literature and Language

LITERATURE

Throughout the era of exploration and colonization, the literature of Atlantic Canada was limited to travel memoirs (Cartier, Champlain), stories, and historical missives known as the **Relations,** written by Jesuit missionaries, who recorded their lives and work in the New World. In large measure, Atlantic Canadian literature resonates with a rich sense of place. Whether in the diaries and novels of 19C immigrant settlers or the poems and literary works of the 20C and 21C, writers grapple with what it means to be "from down east".

Regional Literature
Canadian Confederation, in 1867 In Prince Edward Island, engendered confidence: Canada became a nation and its writers found their voice. The anthropomorphism of wild animals, à la Beatrix Potter, characterized some books by **Charles G.D. Roberts,** while his contemporary **Lucy Maud Montgomery** began her enduring *Anne of Green Gables* series set in Prince Edward Island.

In Nova Scotia, at the turn of the 19C, poets such as Francis Sherman, Bliss Carman and Sir Charles G.D. Roberts (who also wrote popular fiction) had many fans.

Urbanization and the trauma of World War II resulted in greater introspection among Canadian writers as they questioned the established order. In the 1940s and 50s, two Nova Scotian novelists gained national prominence: Thomas Raddall (1903-94) was known for his prolific output of historical fiction; **Hugh MacLennan** (1907-90) wrote evocative tales about the Halifax Explosion of 1917 (*Barometer Rising,* 1941) and the English-French situation in Quebec (*Two Solitudes,* 1945). Newfoundland and Labrador's best-selling author **Farley Mowat** (b. 1921) (*Never Cry Wolf, Sea of Slaughter)* remains Canada's champion of the environment, with his compelling recountings of humanity's destructive impact.

Contemporary Currents

Newfoundlander **Michael Harris** (*Unholy Orders: Tragedy at Mount Cashel*), Nova Scotian **Anne Marie MacDonald** (*Fall on Your Knees*) and New Brunswick's **Antonine Maillet**, among others, have won international acclaim with their entertaining and sometimes controversial books.

LANGUAGE

Considered to be the **"founding nations,"** the British and the French are the largest populations in Canada (37 and 32 percent respectively). To reflect this composition, federal services (e.g. the postal system) are officially bilingual. The province of New Brunswick is also officially bilingual; approximately 35 percent of the population speaks French. All road signs are in English and French. Nova Scotia and Prince Edward Island are not officially bilingual, but pockets of Acadian French villages are found in both provinces; however the majority of Acadians speak English. (On Nova Scotia's Cape Breton Island, it is said more residents there speak Gaelic than in present-day Scotland.) In Newfoundland and Labrador, English is officially used, although that province has many expressions, words and colloquialisms that are not found elsewhere in the country. Labrador's native population is predominantly Innu, an Algonquian-speaking people, many of whom also speak English.

> "Canada could have enjoyed:
> English government, French culture,
> and American know-how.
> Instead it ended up with:
> English know-how, French government, and American culture."
>
> John Robert Colombo,
> *Oh Canada*, 1965

Music and Dance

MUSIC

It may have all started in 1605, when Samuel de Champlain decreed that his infant settlement at Port Royal have music and laughter during the harsh winters. So began his "Order of Good Cheer," which has prevailed to this day in the region. Atlantic Canadians are never at a loss for live music, whether in their kitchens or at a concert hall.

From Acadian folk songs to classical music and rock, Atlantic Canada's multifarious musical genres hum with creativity. Each of the four provinces boasts its own form of **traditional music,** whether the Gaelic rhythms of Cape Breton Island, the Irish-influenced rock in Newfoundland, the Acadian fiddle music found in New Brunswick and mainland Nova Scotia, or the folksy tones of native Prince Edward Islanders. Today pop-rock Irish groups like **Great Big Sea** continue to popularize songs of Newfoundland's seafaring past. Halifax is known for its international **buskers'** festival every summer. A popular pub scene is fueled by the student populations of the city's five universities.

Canada's **classical music** tradition was under way in colonial times, with concert announcements appearing in newspapers as early as 1751. Halifax audiences were delighted by performances of the music of Handel, Bach and Mozart. The 1840s exposed Canadians to international touring performers such as singer Jenny Lind. Local and regional musical societies—the precursors of today's philharmonic orchestras—sprang up around the country.

Atlantic Canada's **folk music** boasts a varied tapestry of prominent singer-songwriters: Stan Rogers (1949-83) and Prince Edward Island's **Lennie Gallant** (b. 1955) and **Stompin' Tom Connors** (b. 1936), Cape Breton Island's Barra MacNeils and members of the **Rankin Family** have all successfully moved their folk, country or Celtic melodies to mainstream. **Rita MacNeil** (b. 1944), another Nova Scotian, charms audiences with her local ballads about Maritime life and the mining traditions of Cape Breton. The quintessential Maritime fiddle music of **Don Messer** (1909-73) and his Islanders was a staple on Canadian television and radio from the 1940s through the 1960s, and helped launch the careers of singers Catherine MacKinnon (b. 1944), John Allan Cameron (1938-2006) and

Courtyard, Confederation Centre of the Arts, Charlottetown, PEI

Bruce Bishop/Michelin

internationally renowned **Anne Murray** (b. 1945). Another well known and loved Maritime musician was **Denny Doherty** (1940-2007) who became famous as one of the quartet in the American pop group The Mamas and the Papas.

DANCE

There are at least 20 dance organizations who are members of the umbrella group **Dance Nova Scotia,** including three devoted to Scottish highland dancing, and one to Polish folk dancing. In Moncton, New Brunswick, the **Atlantic Ballet Theatre of Canada** has gained ground, touring in Europe for the first time in 2008.

In Prince Edward Island, the **College of Piping & Celtic Performing Arts of Canada** features, among other varieties, highland, jig and step dancing during summer school sessions. In Newfoundland and Labrador, Irish dancing remains king, and some companies, like **iDance** in St. John's, have toured in Iceland and the US. The troupe exhibits the province's unique hybrid of Irish dance touched with English, Portuguese, Scottish, Basque and French influences. Throughout Atlantic Canada, dance is a popular cultural recreation that can be professional or designed for the amateur.

Cinema

Canadian locations are frequently chosen for their lower production costs and visual similarity to certain parts of the US. Atlantic Canada is high on Hollywood's list. Along with Vancouver and Toronto, Halifax hosts domestic and international production companies that employ a variety of local personnel in TV movies, co-productions and films.

Examples of US-made movies include Jody Foster and Richard Harris in *Echoes of a Summer* (1976), shot in Chester, NS, and *The Scarlet Letter* with Demi Moore (1995), filmed in Shelburne, NS.

Noted Atlantic Canadian **directors** include Thom Fitzgerald, whose first feature, *The Hanging Garden*, about a dysfunctional Cape Breton family, won national critical acclaim in 1997. **Michael Donovan,** an independent producer from Halifax, teamed with US-documentary filmmaker Michael Moore and ended up with an Oscar for *Bowling for Columbine* in 2003. Actors from the Atlantic Provinces include newcomer Ellen Page (*Juno*, 2007) and veteran **Gordon Pinsent** (*The Rowdyman*, 1972; *Away from Her*, 2006). The Atlantic Film Festival, now approaching its 30th year in 2010, showcases Atlantic Canadian filmmakers (shorts and features) every September in Halifax.

ATLANTIC CANADA TODAY

The Economy

The following is a very general account of economic activity in Atlantic Canada. Statistics Canada provides electronic publications for readers seeking detailed information (fees may apply): www.statcan.ca. Another source is the Canadian government's website http://canada.gc.ca, which provides links to all government publications.

FISHING

For centuries **fishing** was one of Canada's primary industries. Today, Canada is still a leading exporter of fish in the world, although the country's east and west coasts have seen declines in fish stocks in recent years. The Atlantic coast supplies the vast majority of fish.

In the late 1990s cod stocks on the **Grand Banks** off Newfoundland collapsed due to overfishing, and the Canadian government in 2002 declared a moratorium on cod fishing, ending a 500-year-old industry. Due to this ban, Newfoundlanders and Labradorians now fish for **snow crab** and **northern shrimp,** whose catches require fishing farther from shore and in deeper waters. This change has opened new markets and new processing plants, enabling more than half of the 30,000 fishers who had lost their jobs to be re-employed.

The most valuable catches for Nova Scotia are **lobster** and **scallops,** although fishing haddock and herring, as well as **aquaculture,** are becoming increasingly important. Prince Edward Island is famous for **mussels** and Malpeque **oysters.** In New Brunswick, **aquaculture** focuses on the cultivation of mussels, clams and oysters. This province is clearly leading the salmon aquaculture industry in the Bay of Fundy, boasting annual sales in excess of $270 million in processed and unprocessed products. All three provinces also harvest cod, grey sole, flounder and redfish. Newfoundland and Labrador's seal hunt is not without its share of controversy from abroad, but it survives under annual strict regulations regarding harvesting—and quotas set by the federal government.

AGRICULTURE

Agriculture is the backbone of Prince Edward Island, famous for its **potatoes.** Agriculture is equally important in New Brunswick's St. John River Valley and in Nova Scotia's **Annapolis Valley,** with a focus on dairy products, livestock, poultry and eggs. Apple orchards and estate wineries abound, fed by the rich fertile soil. The Christmas tree market, and to some extent, maple-syrup processing, have become more important to the Maritime economy. Farms exist in Newfoundland on the **Avalon Peninsula** and in **Codroy Valley,** but they supply local markets only. The extensive forests of New Brunswick and Nova Scotia supply timber for many pulp and paper plants, and the forestry industry in New Brunswick alone directly employs about 17,000 people and indirectly employs an additional 6,000. In late 2007, the Atlantic Canada Opportunities Agency provided $12 million to invest in the beef processing facilities of New Brunswick, Nova Scotia and Prince Edward Island.

RICHES BENEATH LAND AND SEA

Although in decline in some parts of the country, mining has played an important economic role in every region of Canada. New Brunswick is one area that produces zinc and lead. Antimony is mined near Fredericton, and two potash mines are situated near Sussex. Coal continues to be extracted at Minto-Chipman. New Brunswick's electric power resources are significant. A nuclear power station is located at Point Lepreau on the Bay of Fundy. The **iron ore** mines of the Labrador Trough in western Labrador are the major source of Canada's iron ore products. The discovery in 1993 of nickel in Voisey Bay, Labrador, opened a new source of wealth. Copper and gold are also mined in Newfoundland. In Nova Scotia coal, gypsum (the most productive gypsum mining region in the world). and salt are mined. **Coal** mining on Cape Breton Island has 300-year-old roots in Nova Scotia. That province's tidal power plant at Annapolis Royal supplies 20 megawatts at peak production. The Point Lepreau Nuclear Generating Station in New Brunswick is also a significant electric power resource.

But it is the Atlantic Ocean that may enable Atlantic Canadians to compete in the future in the global marketplace. Offshore **oil** and **gas** discoveries are generating high optimism: Hibernia and Terra Nova, in Newfoundland, have been producing oil since 1997 and 2002; and a third major project, White Rose, began production in 2005. Hibernia, located 315km/196mi east of St. John's, holds an estimated three billion barrels of oil underneath the Grand Banks—some 80m/262ft below the water surface. By the year 2000, Hibernia was responsible for 12 percent of the country's oil output. Hibernia also has a large reserve of natural gas, which may be extracted in the future.

Labrador's **hydroelectric** potential is enormous. Virtually all the power produced by the huge generating station at **Churchill Falls** goes to the province of Quebec.

The importance of provincial **oil** and **natural gas** is seen in the huge Sable Offshore Energy Project (Canada's first) off Nova Scotia. Over 17 million cubic metres/600 million cubic feet of gas are produced every day. In New Brunswick, oil and gas have been produced since the early 20C. The Irving Oil Refinery at Saint John is Canada's largest.

TRANSPORTATION

Because of Atlantic Canada's geography, transportation has always been of prime importance. People and cargo still move by water among the Atlantic Provinces: between Nova Scotia and New Brunswick, Maine and Newfoundland; from New Brunswick to Prince Edward Island; and from Newfoundland to the French islands of St. Pierre and Miquelon. Transport of fresh seafood to the US market is heavily dependent on the ferries that make their way among the Atlantic provinces.

Aviation plays an important role in the region, although domestic air travel can be cost-prohibitive and/or difficult. Some smaller airports such as the one in Yarmouth, Nova Scotia, are waiting to be re-opened to commercial traffic. There is rail service from Toronto and Montreal to points in New Brunswick and to Halifax, but the rail links within Atlantic Canada are sparse compared to what they were in the last century. Highways are good throughout the region, and there are several bus lines and smaller shuttle buses that make their way throughout Atlantic Canada.

Bruce Bishop/Michelin

Domaine de Grand Pré, Grand Pré, Nova Scotia

MANUFACTURING AND THE NEW ECONOMY

The food sector dominates Atlantic Canada's manufacturing. Some 300 companies engage in pharmaceutical and medical research, telecommunications and advanced technologies such as satellite remote sensing and ocean-mapping. Music, filmmaking, and the plastic arts are also growing industries. Environmental industries, especially in New Brunswick, complement traditional industries.

INFORMATION AND COMMUNICATIONS TECHNOLOGIES

With a highly educated workforce between the ages of 18 and 35, Atlantic Canada has become increasingly attractive to ICT (Information and Communications Technologies). The region's infrastructure supports today's global businesses with a world-class, high-speed digital telecommunications network. Approximately 1,800 ITC companies and 20,000 workers generate more than $4 billion in annual revenue. Call centres of US-based companies abound in the four provinces, for example, perhaps because of many employees being bilingual, but Atlantic Canada's labor costs (i.e., salaries, wages, and benefits) are also 21 percent lower than average US labor costs. Bell Aliant operates in the region and is one of the continent's largest regional telecommunications providers. The CGI Group Inc., in New Brunswick, is Canada's biggest IT supplier. Finally, the University of New Brunswick's Computer Science Department is recognized as being a national leader in IT.

AEROSPACE AND DEFENCE

Surprisingly perhaps, the aerospace and defence industry is growing quickly in Atlantic Canada, with each of the four provinces containing centres of expertise and specialization. The province with the most companies devoted to the aerospace industry is Nova Scotia, where 40 firms are engaged in advanced engineering, IT systems, component manufacturing, and related work. Summerside, Fredericton and Moncton also house aerospace companies. Throughout the Atlantic region, the Department of National Defence and the Canadian Forces employ over 24,000 people. This military presence alone contributes some $1.25 billion to Atlantic Canada's economy annually.

Government

Each of the four Atlantic Provinces has its own Legislative Assembly of elected representatives who control regional affairs (such as education, health care and highways). In Nova Scotia and Newfoundland and Labrador, the Legislative Assembly is called the House of Assembly. The Premier leads the provincial government and chooses the MLAs (members of the legislature) to serve as ministers in the Cabinet. (In Newfoundland and Labrador, the Premier would choose MHAs, members of the House of Assembly.) The Cabinet sets government policy and introduces laws for the Legislative Assembly to consider. Since Canada continues to be part of the British Commonwealth, each province has a Lieutenant-Governor, who Is appointed by the Premier. He or she serves as the Queen's representative in the province. The central government in **Ottawa,** the federal capital, assumes responsibility for such matters as defence, foreign affairs, transportation, trade, commerce, money and banking, and criminal law.

Population

According to 2007 government statistics, more than 2.3 million people live in the Atlantic provinces. Nova Scotia is the most populous province (935,106), followed by New Brunswick (750,851). Prince Edward Island has the lowest population (139,103). The most homogeneous of any province, Newfoundland and Labrador sustains a population of 507,475 with 98 percent declaring English as their mother tongue. The French-speaking minority (largely Acadians) is concentrated on Prince Edward Island and Nova Scotia (between 5 and 10 percent of the population) and New Brunswick (33 percent). Nearly 30 percent of Nova Scotia's population is of Scottish origin. The Mi'kmaq are the most populous of the First Nations in Newfoundland, New Brunswick and Nova Scotia. Inuit and Innu are found primarily in Northern Labrador. The African-Canadian population, less than 1 percent of the region's inhabitants, is concentrated primarily in the towns of Nova Scotia and New Brunswick.

Food and Drink

Atlantic Canada has many regional specialties. The provinces produce a variety of fruits, such as apples, peaches, cherries, and in the Annapolis Valley, wine. In New Brunswick, Nova Scotia and Prince Edward Island, the Acadians' French heritage enriches local communities with a fine culinary tradition: many area restaurants serve traditional foods such as pork dishes, meat pie *(tourtière)*, and potato/meat pie called **rappie pie** *(patates râpées)*. All of the Atlantic provinces offer a **seafood** cornucopia, especially oysters, lobster, scallops, and mussels. In Newfoundland, try **screech,** a heady dark rum, or one of the region's fine **beers;** both are popular with meals. The wines of Nova Scotia have become note-worthy to oenophiles but are sometimes difficult to find, since many are sold only at the wineries. **Jost, Grand Pré, Blomidon** and **Gaspereau** are respected Nova Scotian wineries. New Brunswick is famous for **fiddleheads,** the new shoots of ferns available fresh in May and June, and for **dulse,** an edible seaweed. In Newfoundland and Labrador, foods unusual to the rest of the country may include Colcannon, dough-boys, pea soup, salt fish and brewis, toutons, and **cod tongues.** In New Brunswick, the Miramichi River is the spawning grounds of Atlantic salmon: fresh salmon is found on the menus of many fine-dining restaurants.

Traditional feasts of seafood—particularly salmon, clams, oysters and lobster—or of the earth's bounty ("corn boils," strawberry fests, "spud days" and even a Brussels sprout festival) are staged in the province from May through October. Generations have enjoyed hot **Hodge Podge,** a mix of new potatoes and vegetables in milk. Acadian **potato and clam pie,** a Loyalist dish of fish chowder, and buckwheat pancakes topped with maple syrup are old-time favourites.

Not surprisingly, cod—eaten fresh, dried or salted—has traditionally been the staple of the Newfoundland diet. Fish and brewis, a mixture of boiled salt cod and hardtack (a hard, dry biscuit) soaked overnight, is a traditional dish. Fried cod tongues is a dish that should be prepared only with fish caught the same day. Squid burgers are an island peculiarity. Game includes caribou steaks and even moose. Traditional **Jigg's Dinners** are a hearty meat and potatoes plate piled high with carrots, cabbage and peas pudding. Fruits of the region include partridgeberries and yellow **bakeapples,** raspberry in appearance but with a distinctive taste. **Figgy Duff** (steamed pudding à la the 16C) is a popular dessert.

In Nova Scotia, traditional dishes—Acadia's **rappie pie,** Cape Breton lamb, Scottish oat cakes and the "truly Nova Scotian" **blueberry grunt**—tempt visitors to partake of a regional cookery harking back to Samuel de Champlain's gourmandize. The gastronomy of his Order of Good Cheer endures in the province's formalized food promotion, "Taste of Nova Scotia," offered at nearly 100 member dining establishments.

Prince Edward Island is known for its **potatoes,** more than 50 varieties of them. The four basic types characterize Island potatoes: long, round white, red, and yellow. Yukon gold is a popular yellow potato here; Red Pontiac and Chieftain are varieties of the red potato; and Superior and Kennebec are whiteskinned varieties of round potatoes. Shepody and several Russet varieties make up PEI's long potatoes.

Cape Forchu near Yarmouth, Nova Scotia

Sandra Phinney/Michelin

NEW BRUNSWICK

POPULATION 750,851 – MAP INSIDE FRONT COVER

Of the three Maritime Provinces, New Brunswick possesses the largest landmass. From its northernmost town of Campbellton to its southern port city of Saint John, the province extends 466km/290mi. Its western edge borders the US; Quebec lies to the north. The continental gateway to the Atlantic provinces, New Brunswick is linked to Nova Scotia by the Isthmus of Chignecto, but separated from Prince Edward Island by Northumberland Strait. However New Brunswick and the island have been connected by the Confederation Bridge since 1997. From the small western community of Hartland, near the US border, across to the eastern side and the city of Moncton, the province measures 285km/177mi wide. Fredericton, the provincial capital, is situated centrally, on the banks of the Saint John River, which runs two-thirds the length of the province, emptying into the Bay of Fundy. The northeast corner is heavily Acadian, a string of French-speaking villages, like Caraquet, savouring their cultural and maritime heritage. In fact, New Brunswick is officially bilingual: about 35 percent of the population speaks French. Originating primarily with Loyalists fleeing the US, the province's British heritage is evident, particularly in Fredericton and Saint John. These linguistic-cultural traditions coexist peacefully, enriching the provincial character as a whole.

- **Information:** Tourism and Parks, Campbellton. ☎800-561-0123. www.tourismnewbrunswick.ca.
- **Don't Miss:** Fort Beauséjour, Fundy National Park, Hopewell Cape and St. Andrews.
- **Organizing Your Time:** Allow one week to visit New Brunswick. If arriving by car from Quebec, spend 2 days making your way south to Fredericton, Moncton, Saint John and then St. Andrews, possibly departing on the Saint John ferry for Digby, Nova Scotia. If arriving from the US by ferry into Yarmouth, Nova Scotia, drive to Digby and take the ferry to Saint John; then take a similar route north through New Brunswick. If arriving by air, Moncton is a good terminus; then choose what directions to explore in the province.
- **Especially for Kids:** Acadian coast beaches, Moncton's zoo and two amusement parks.

Church and graveyard near Caraquet

Sandra Phinney/Michelin

Practical Information

GETTING THERE

BY AIR

Air Canada and its affiliates provide direct air service to Saint John, Moncton and Fredericton (☎902-429-7111 or 888-247-2262 Canada/US. www.aircanada.com).
Continental Airlines has daily direct flights from Moncton to Newark (☎800-523-3273 Canada/US. www.continental.com).
Corsair offers service from Paris to Moncton (website in French only: www.corsair.fr).
Delta has daily direct flights from Boston to Fredericton (☎800-241-4141. www.delta.com).
WestJet provides service from Ottawa and Hamilton to Moncton (☎800-538-5696. www.westjet.com).

BY TRAIN

VIA Rail services Moncton via Montreal, with connecting bus service to Saint John (☎506-842-7245 or 888-842-7245. www.viarail.ca). Service between Montreal and New Brunswick daily except Tuesday.

BY SHIP

Government-operated ferries (free) provide service in the lower Saint John River area and to islands in the Bay of Fundy. Ferries (toll) connect the province with Nova Scotia and Quebec. For information, contact New Brunswick Tourism (☾see below).

GENERAL INFORMATION

ACCOMMODATIONS AND VISITOR INFORMATION

The official tourist office publishes an annual travel guide giving information on history, attractions and scheduled events, which you can order or download from the Internet. Government-inspected hotels and motels, bed-and-breakfast lodgings and country inns, farm vacations and campgrounds are also listed. Contact **New Brunswick Tourism,** Tourism and Parks, PO Box 12345, Campbellton, NB, E3N 3T6. ☎800-561-0123. www.tourismnewbrunswick.ca

LANGUAGE

New Brunswick is officially bilingual; approximately 35 percent of the population speaks French. All road signs are in English and French.

ROAD REGULATIONS

The province has good paved roads. Speed limits, unless otherwise posted, are 80km/h (50mph) on provincial highways and 50km/h (30mph) in cities. **Seat belt** use is mandatory. **Canadian Automobile Assn. (CAA)** 378 Westmorland Rd., Saint John NB, E2J 2G4. ☎506-634-1400 or 800-561-8807 www.caa.maritimes.ca.

TIME ZONE

New Brunswick is on Atlantic Standard Time. Entering from the US or Quebec, set your watch ahead 1hr. Daylight Saving Time is observed from the 2nd Sunday in March to the first Sunday in November.

TAXES

In New Brunswick, the national GST has been combined with the provincial sales tax to form a Harmonized Sales Tax (HST). The HST for New Brunswick is levied at a single rate of 14% (some items are exempt). Nonresidents may be entitled to a rebate on certain goods taken out of the country within 60 days of purchase.

LIQUOR LAWS

The legal drinking age is 19. Liquor is sold in government stores. Some privately owned stores sell liquor as agencies for the provincial liquor corporation.

PROVINCIAL HOLIDAY

New Brunswick Day: 1st Monday in August

RECREATION

Miles of sand dunes are part of New Brunswick's Kouchibouguac National Park, and **hiking** trails abound in Fundy National Park, Mactaquac Provincial Park and Mt. Carleton Provincial Park. The Northumberland Strait, in the vicinity of Shediac's Parlee Beach

Provincial Park, has surprisingly warm waters for watersports enthusiasts, and on the beautiful Saint John River, houseboats can be rented by the week. Even **windsurfing** is enjoyed on the Eel River Bar of the province's Restigouche region and also off the Acadian Peninsula. For sports fishers, Atlantic salmon is found in the Miramichi and Restigouche valleys. Whale watching is popular from Deer Island, Grand Manan Island and St. Andrews, and Grand Manan is also big with birders, having attracted James Audubon to its shores to sketch its many species. The province boasts some 40 **golf courses,** including signature greens such as the Algonquin Hotel's in St. Andrews, Kingwoods in Fredericton and Fox Creek in Dieppe; for details, access www.golfnb.ca. Downhill **skiing** is popular at Sugarloaf Provincial Park; Mactaquac Provincial Park and Fundy National Park have cross-country trails. Contact the local tourist offices for details.

PRINCIPAL FESTIVALS

Jul **Loyalist Days Festival:** *Saint John*
   Lobster Festival: *Shediac*
   Irish Festival: *Miramichi*
Jul–Aug **Foire Brayonne:** *Edmundston*
   Bon Ami Festival Get Together: *Dalhousie*
Aug **Festival Acadien:** *Caraquet*
Sept **Harvest Jazz and Blues Festival:** *Fredericton*

A Bit of Geography

An extensive coastline faces Chaleur Bay in the north, the Gulf of St. Lawrence to the east, and the Bay of Fundy in the south, with its **Fundy Islands**. The 73,436sq km/28,354sq mi interior consists of mountainous uplands reaching 820m/2,690ft in the northwest, central highlands of hills 610m/2,000ft above sea level, the nearly L-shaped Saint John River Valley, and a sloping plain extending east to Chaleur Bay. The **Saint John River** flows 673km/418mi from northern Maine along the US/New Brunswick border to empty into the Bay of Fundy. Between Edmundston and Grand Falls, rural villages intersperse the farmed river valley. Turbulent at Grand Falls gorge, the river cascades over 25m/76ft cataracts and 18m/59ft at Beechwood—both sites of hydroelectric dams. After the provincial capital of **Fredericton,** the river gradually broadens, traversing picturesque farmland. Fertile soil in its upper and lower regions sustains extensive cultivation, particularly the north's thriving **potato industry.** At the city of its namesake, the river is thrown back by the mighty Fundy tides in a slim gorge called **Reversing Falls.** Today the river carries little except pleasure boaters and sailing enthusiasts who find its wide expanses and deep waters a paradise.

A Bit of History

Pre-Loyalists and Loyalists built ships of timber cut from the region's forests, especially New Brunswick's. Beginning as mast making for British naval vessels, the industry grew, particularly at Saint John, a great **shipbuilding** centre in the mid-19C. Two brothers who opened a shipyard in Chatham (now Miramichi) founded the **Cunard line**. Skilled craftsmen perfected clipper ships, schooners, brigs and barques, as shipyards sprang up along the coasts of Nova Scotia and Prince Edward Island. By Confederation in 1867, New Brunswick was wealthy, and by the late 19C, the province was the most prosperous in Canada. Yet, by 1900 steam had replaced sail power and steel hulls superseded wooden ones. However, the sea remains the provincial breadwinner. New Brunswick's extensive coastline still provides income for the fishing and shipping industries. Saint John remains a major port, servicing oil tankers and cruise ships alike, while Shippagan claims New Brunswick's largest commercial fleet. The social fabric of New Brunswick was woven by a diverse population of Mi'kmaq and Maliseet Indians, New England Loyalists, Acadians, Scots, Irish, Germans, Danes and Dutch. The richness of place names, such as Kouchibouguac, Memramcook, Shediac and Richibucto, stems from original Indian designations.

SOUTHEAST COAST

Facing its sister province of Prince Edward Island, New Brunswick boasts sandy beaches, dunes, lighthouses and villages along the southeast coast. Just inland lies the city of Moncton. National historical sites like Fort Beauséjour and Monument Lefebvre testify to a stormy provincial past: France and Britain's battles for the New World, the trials of the Acadians, and the struggles for religious freedom, to name a few. Natural phenomena are here as well, such as the tidal bore at Moncton, and the rock formations at Hopewell Cape. Jutting into Northumberland Strait, Cape Jourimain is New Brunswick's entry point to the 13km/8mi Confederation Bridge that joins the province with Prince Edward Island. Today, historical remnants and nature's creations co-exist happily with modern amusement parks, high-tech businesses and fast-food chains.

Fort Beauséjour★★

MAP INSIDE FRONT COVER

Overlooking the Cumberland Basin (an arm of Chignecto Bay), the Missiguash River Valley and the Tantramar Marshes, this former French fort is exceptional for its impressive **panorama**★★ of the surrounding country (*fog or rain may hamper visibility*). The fort stands on the Chignecto Isthmus, a narrow strip of land joining New Brunswick and Nova Scotia, which once marked the division between French and British lands. The scant remains of the mid-18C outpost testify to its turbulent history during the Anglo-French conflict in the New World.

- **Information:** Fort Beauséjour-Fort Cumberland National Historic Site, 111 Fort Beauséjour Rd., in Aulac. ☎506-364-5080. www.pc.gc.ca.
- **Orient Yourself:** The fort is situated in Aulac near Nova Scotia border, just off Trans-Can Hwy., Exit 550A. It stands on the Chignecto Isthmus, a narrow strip of land joining New Brunswick and Nova Scotia, southeast of Moncton.
- **Also See:** MONCTON, FUNDY NATIONAL PARK, PASSAMAQUODDY BAY

A Bit of History

In 1672 the Acadians first settled in this area, which they called Beaubassin, reclaiming it from the sea by an extensive system of dikes. After the Treaty of Utrecht ceded mainland Nova Scotia to Britain in 1713, they found themselves in the middle of a border conflict. The British built Fort Lawrence on their side of the isthmus; the French built Fort Beauséjour on their side. Captured in 1755 by a British force under Col. **Robert Monckton,** Fort Beauséjour was renamed Fort Cumberland. The Acadians were removed under the Deportation Order of that same year. Strengthened by the British, the fort withstood an attack in 1776 by New England settlers sympathetic to the American Revolution. Although manned during the War of 1812, the outpost saw no further military action. In 1926 the fort, rechristened Fort Beauséjour, was designated a national historic site.

Visit

♿⏰*Open Jun–mid-Oct daily 9am–5pm. 🎫$4.* ☎*506-364-5080. www.pc.gc.ca.* The **visitor centre** houses displays that depict the military and civilian history of the time. The restored ruins are accessible by a trail that takes visitors into one of the fort's underground casemates. Three restored underground casemates can be visited, and the earthworks are in good repair. A museum shop in the visitor centre features a good selection of local books.

Moncton

POPULATION 64,128 – MAP P 54

Set on a bend of the Petitcodiac River, Moncton is famous for its tidal bore, which rushes up the river from the Bay of Fundy. Named after Robert Monckton, the British commander in the capture of Fort Beauséjour, the city is generally considered the capital of Acadie. The first settlers in the area were German and Dutch families from Pennsylvania, but they were joined by Acadians returning to British territory after Deportation. Today one-third of the population is French-speaking. The city is an important business centre and rail hub. It is home to two universities, Université de Moncton and Atlantic Baptist University.

- **Information:** Tourism Moncton, City Hall, 655 Main St. ☎506-853-3590 or 800-363-4558. www.gomoncton.com.
- ▶ **Orient Yourself:** Main Street runs through Moncton's **downtown** roughly from Vaughan Harvey Blvd. on the west to King St. on the east. Highfield Square is a popular shopping centre on Main Street. East of Moncton lies **Dieppe,** a municipality within the Greater Moncton Area: the airport and Crystal Palace Amusement Park are located here, as is Champlain Place (next to Crystal Palace), with some 160 stores. Site of the zoo and large man-made attractions, **Magnetic Hill** rises northwest of downtown Moncton, off the Trans-Can Highway. Its age-old claim to fame is a hill that creates the illusion of causing vehicles to move "uphill" (ask local residents to explain).
- **Parking:** Moncton has electronic meters, fed by coin or by a card purchased at city hall. Finding a space is not generally a problem.
- ◷ **Organizing Your Time:** Moncton's sights can be seen in a couple of days, but take an extra day for a trip to Hopewell Cape. For the Bay of Fundy tidal bore at Moncton, check www.waterlevels.gc.ca for the tides, which can be predicted a year in advance. From Moncton, you are only an hour from Prince Edward Island or Nova Scotia.
- **Kids Especially for Kids:** The zoo and both amusement parks.

A Bit of History

Before Canada became a dominion, a railway link between the Maritime colonies and the Province of Canada was begun in 1858. By 1871 a connection to Moncton was complete, and the community became the headquarters for the **Intercolonial Railway's** maintenance shops. This development led to re-incorporation as a town in 1875. Even in the present day, all rail lines to and from the Maritimes go through Moncton. Once reliant on railway and government sectors, Moncton's economy has diversified in recent times: electronic commerce, transportation and distribution, food processing and light manufacturing play important roles. Its bilingualism has fostered rapid growth in the telecommunications industry.

Sights

Tidal Bore★

In the open ocean, the ebb and flow of the tide is barely noticeable, but in certain V-shaped bays or inlets, the tide enters the broad end and literally piles up as it moves up the bay. This buildup occurs in the **Bay of Fundy**, 77km/48mi wide at its mouth, narrowing and becoming shallower along its 233km/145mi length. Thus, the tide is squeezed as it travels the bay, a ripple increasing to a wave, known as a "bore," several feet high as it enters the river emptying into the bay. At Moncton the bore varies from a few inches to nearly two feet. The highest bores occur when the earth, moon and sun are aligned.

Musée acadien, Université de Moncton

Permanent exhibition The Acadian Adventure, Acadian Museum

Bore Park

Off Main St. at the corner of King St. Bore schedules available from the tourist office at city hall or from the website. Arrive 20min prior to view lowest level and return 1hr later to see high tide. ♿☎506-853-3590. www.gomoncton.com.

The tidal bore and changing levels of the Petitcodiac River are best viewed from the park. At high tide the river widens to 1.6km/1mi and the water level increases by up to 7m/23ft.

Thomas Williams House★

103 Park St. ⬤⬤ ✗ ♿ (first floor only). ◷ Open Jul-Aug Mon–Sat 10am–4:30pm Sun 1pm–4:30pm. Victorian Tearoom open for lunch Mon–Sat 11am–2pm; for tea Sun 2pm–4pm. ⬤ Contribution requested. ☎506-857-0590. www. gomoncton.com.

A fine example of Second Empire architectural style, this 12-room Victorian house (built in 1883) was a private dwelling until 1983, when it was donated to the city of Moncton. Thomas Williams and his wife, Analena, had 11 children; he began serving as treasurer of the Intercolonial Railway in 1875 when a link to Moncton was completed. Architecture and gardens buffs will find this home a relaxing delight on warm summer days. The tearoom is open for lunch and afternoon tea (ⓒ *see hours above; reservations suggested).*

Moncton Museum and Free Meeting House

20 Mountain Rd. ✗ ♿ (first floor only) ◷ Open year-round Mon–Sat 9am– 4:30pm, Sun 1pm–5pm; extended summer hours. ⬤Contribution requested. ☎506-856-4383. www.gomoncton.com.

A National Historic Site since 1990, the Free Meeting House, built in 1821, was originally designed as a home for all religious groups until they could afford to build their own churches. The City of Moncton completed the last stages of the building's restoration between 1987 and 1990. Note that there is no steeple, bell or cornerstone, as was the custom of New England meeting halls.

Next door, the small Moncton Museum holds permanent displays that explore the history of the city from pre-European settlement to the present. Genealogical records can be found here, as well as photographs and census records.

Graveyard enthusiasts should take a look at the adjacent cemetery, where headstones as far back as 1816 have been preserved.

Acadian Museum★

Université de Moncton, 165 Massey Ave. ◷Open Jun–Sept Mon–Fri 10am–5pm, weekends 1pm–5pm. Rest of the year Tue– Fri 1pm–4:30pm, Weekends 1pm–4pm. ⬤$4. ☎506-858-4088. www.umoncton. ca/maum (in French only).

Founded in 1963, the Université de Moncton claims the first law school

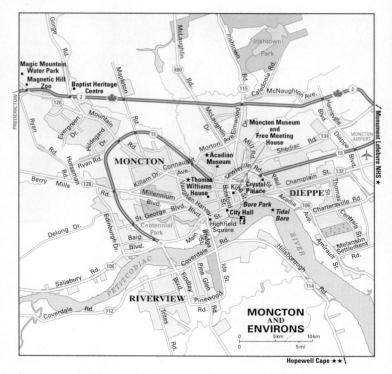

Hopewell Cape ★★ \

in the world teaching common law in the French language. The university's permanent collection of Acadiana dates from 1604 to the present and is a testament to the resilience of the Acadian people, their language and culture. Interiors of 18C houses are featured, as well as traditional dress, footwear and tools. Note the preserved book written by Acadia's founder, French explorer Samuel de Champlain.

Baptist Heritage Centre

Atlantic Baptist University, 333 Gorge Rd. ⚷ ◷ *Open year round, daily 9am–9pm.* ☎ *506-858-8970. www.abu.nb.ca.*
Known for its academic excellence, Atlantic Baptist University has grown from a small Bible college in 1968 to a full-fledged university offering degrees in a variety of disciplines. The Heritage Centre features displays on this Protestant denomination's 200-year old history in the region. Some 300 objects in the collection range from church furniture to musical instruments.

Additional Sights

Magnetic Hill Zoo

Kids *Magnetic Hill area, Exit 450 off Hwy. 2, 10km/6mi northwest of downtown Moncton.* ⚹ ⚷ ◷ *Open Apr–mid-May Mon–Fri 10am–4pm, weekends 10am–6pm. Mid-May–late Jun daily 9am–7pm. Late Jun–early Sept daily 9am–8pm. Early Sept–late Oct Mon–Fri 10am–6pm, weekends 9am–6pm. Guided tours daily 10am & 12:30pm.* ☞ *$9.50.* ☎ *506-877-7718. www.moncton.org/zoo.*
More than 400 birds, mammals, reptiles and fish live safely in this 40-acre park just outside Moncton. You'll see jaguars, camels, zebras and Arctic wolves. Emphasis is placed on education, especially about endangered species.

Magic Mountain Water Park

Kids *Magnetic Hill area, Exit 450 off Hwy. 2, at 2875 Mountain Rd.* ⚹ ◷ *Open mid-Jun–early Sept daily 10am–6pm (late Jun–late Aug til 7pm).* ☞ *$23.* ☎ *506-857-9283 or 800-331-9283. www.magic mountain.ca.*

Billed as "Atlantic Canada's largest water park," Magic Mountain has eight water slides, a wave pool, splash pads, and tube sliding and matting, as well as kiddie pools to keep the young ones happy. Exhausted parents can relax in the giant hot tub. Two 18-hole miniature golf courses are on-site *(admission charged)*.

Crystal Palace Amusement Park

Kids *499 Paul St., in Dieppe.* Kids X &. Open *Jul–Aug daily 10am–10pm. Rest of the year Mon–Fri noon–8pm (Fri til 9pm), Sat 10am–9pm, Sun 10am–8pm. March Break Sun–Thu 10am–8pm, Fri–Sat 10am–9pm.* $16. 506-859-4386. *www.crystalpalace.ca.*

Eastern New Brunswick's changeable winter weather ensures that this indoor amusement park, with its 8-cinema complex, hotel and small retail area, stays busy throughout the year. Kids will enjoy the various rides from a roller coaster to a carousel, and older folks might try the 18-hole mini-golf course or climbing wall.

Excursions

Monument Lefebvre National Historic Site★

480 Rue Centrale, in Memramcook. 20km/12.5mi southeast by Rte. 106 in St.-Joseph. &. Open Jun–mid-Oct daily *9am–5pm.* $4. 506-758-9808 (summer). www.pc.gc.ca.

Located in the Lefebvre Building of the **College St.-Joseph,** the first Acadian institution of higher learning, the site chronicles the history of the French-speaking culture. Founded by Father Camille Lefebvre in 1864, the college is now part of the Université de Moncton. The small museum features displays on the Memramcook Valley, where the Acadians maintained continuous settlement, despite Deportation. A recent exhibit traces the Acadians' odyssey from 1755 to today.

Hopewell Cape★★

35km/22mi south of Moncton by Rte. 114. Follow signs en route. Be sure to climb stairs at the posted time to avoid the 10m/32ft tides.

Near this little village overlooking Shepody Bay there remains an interesting phenomenon known as **The Rocks.** Sculpted by tidal action, wind and frost, these red sandstone formations, as high as 15m/50ft, stand on the beach. Tiny tree-covered islands at high tide, these shapes become "giant flowerpots" at low tide, their narrow bases widening to support balsam fir and dwarf black spruce at the top. Visitors can walk around them when the tide is out and look at crevices in the cliffs that, in time, will become new flowerpots.

Hopewell Cape's rock formations

J.-F. Bergeron/New Brunswick Tourism

CENTRAL NEW BRUNSWICK

Central New Brunswick is certainly the heartland of the province, almost bisected by two key rivers that have helped shape its history: the 673km/418mi-long Saint John and the 400km/249mi-long Miramichi. The latter is famed for its Atlantic salmon, which swim upriver to spawn, attracting anglers from around the world, including celebrities like Prince Charles. The river valleys that surround these bodies of water have given the province some of its most important natural resources: good soil for agriculture, forests for a pulp and paper industry, and mineral-rich deposits. Positioned in the lower central part of the province, the capital city of Fredericton sits on the banks of the Saint John River; the meandering river, lots of green spaces and stately brick buildings lend a relaxed atmosphere to the historic city of government. National and provincial historical sites are prevalent in this region as well, such as Fredericton's Military Compound.

Fredericton★★

POPULATION 50,535 – MAP P 57

Set on a bend in the placid Saint John River, opposite its junction with the Nashwaak River, this quiet, beautifully maintained city is the capital of New Brunswick. Filled with historic buildings and landscaped areas, downtown Fredericton overlooks the river. Greater Fredericton is home to half of the province's information technology, engineering, environmental and advanced training in technology industries. There is a youthfulness to this small city due, in large part, to its two universities (University of New Brunswick among them) and a variety of training colleges and institutes. Largely because of the munificence of a locally raised benefactor, Lord Beaverbrook (see below), Fredericton is an important cultural centre.

Information: Fredericton Tourism, 11 Carleton St., ☎506-460-2041, or 888-888-4768 or www.tourismfredericton.ca.

▶ **Orient Yourself:** The historic section, including the legislative building, lies on the south side of the river, along the area known as The Green. Just west, the Garrison District, off Queen Street, preserves the former British military compound. Bounded roughly by Queen, Church, Beaverbrook and Smythe streets, downtown is a bustling commercial district centred on King Street, with its Kings Place Mall.

P **Parking:** Visit the Tourism Centre at City Hall at 397 Queen St. for a free three-day visitors' parking pass. ☎506-460-2019.

Don't Miss: A daytime or evening visit to the Garrison District.

Organizing Your Time: Allow two days to leisurely appreciate Fredericton. The city can also serve as a base for visiting outlying sights.

Especially for Kids: Science East will hold the attention of children, especially those 8 years of age and older.

A Bit of History

In 1692 the French governor of Acadie constructed a fort at the mouth of the Nashwaak. Soon abandoned, the fort became an Acadian settlement, which survived until the Seven Years' War. However, Fredericton's true beginning came, like Saint John's, with the arrival of the Loyalists in 1783. Upon the formation of the province in 1784, the settlement they founded, complete with a college that is now the **University of New Brunswick,** was chosen as the capital. The more obvious choice, Saint John, was considered a less central site,

Lord Beaverbrook

Born William Maxwell Aitken in Ontario, and reared in Newcastle, New Brunswick, Lord Beaverbrook (1879-1964) was a successful businessman in Canada before leaving for England in 1910. After entering politics he was elevated to the peerage in 1917, adopting his title from a small New Brunswick town. Having established Beaverbrook Newspapers, he built a vast empire on London's Fleet Street. Influential in the government of **Winston Churchill,** he held several key cabinet posts during World War II. Although absent from the province most of his life, Beaverbrook never forgot New Brunswick. In addition to gifts to Newcastle, he financed, in whole or in part, an art gallery, a theatre and several university buildings in Fredericton.

vulnerable to sea attack. Named Fredericton after the second son of George III, the new capital soon became the social centre for the governor and the town's military garrison.

By the 20C most of the population worked for the provincial government or the university. The 21C, however, has seen more diversification, with rapid growth in the information technology industry in particular. Manufacturing, engineering and retail services and tourism are also major contributors to the city's economy. Proximity to key provincial and municipal policy makers is a factor in attracting businesses here.

Downtown

Stretching along the southern bank of the Saint John River is a strip of parkland known as **The Green**★. This grassy, tree-lined expanse provides a fitting setting for the city's historic buildings.

Beaverbrook Art Gallery★★

703 Queen St. ♿ ◷*Open Jul–mid-Sept daily 9am–5:30pm (Thu 9pm). Rest of the year Mon–Sat 9am–5:30pm, Sun noon–5.30pm.* ◷*Closed Jan 1, Dec 25.* ⬨*$8.* ☏*506-458-8545. www.beaverbrookart gallery.org.*

Works are rotated on a regular basis; those described below may not be on view.

Designed and financed by Lord Beaverbrook, the original structure was his gift to the people of New Brunswick. Opened in 1959 and expanded in 1983, the gallery features the donor's collection of British, European and Canadian art. The permanent collection now numbers more than 3,000 works, the signature piece of which is Salvador Dali's huge surrealistic canvas **Santiago el Grande,** depicting St. James on horseback being carried to heaven; the work is on permanent display.

The collection of **British art** is the most comprehensive in Canada. Paintings by Hogarth, Lawrence, Romney, Gainsborough and Reynolds are juxtaposed with works by Turner, Stanley Spencer, Augustus John and Graham Sutherland. Continental Europe is represented by paintings by Cranach, Botticelli, Delacroix, Tissot and Corneille de Lyon. The **Canadian Collection** features works by most of the country's best-known

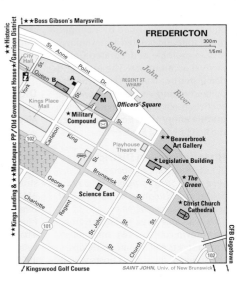

artists, including Cornelius Krieghoff and the Group of Seven. In 1995 a new gallery was added to showcase the works of major Atlantic Canadian artists, such as New Brunswick-born Miller Gore Brittain, Jack Weldon Humphrey and Fred Ross, as well as Alex Colville, who moved to Nova Scotia from Toronto as a boy.

Legislative Building★

♿ ⏲ *Open Jun–Aug daily 9am–5pm. Rest of the year Mon–Fri 9am–4pm. ⏲Closed major holidays.* ☎506-453-2527. *www.gov.nb.ca.*

Opposite the art gallery stands the stately Georgian seat of provincial government, with its classical dome and double-columned portico. Constructed of sandstone in 1882, this building replaced the old Province Hall, which was destroyed by fire.

Visitors are permitted to see the assembly chamber with its tiered balcony and to view **portraits** of Queen Charlotte and George III, replicas of paintings by Joshua Reynolds. The parliamentary library is reached by a striking wooden spiral staircase.

Christ Church Cathedral★

168 Church St. ⏲*Open Jul–Sept Mon–Fri 9am–6pm, Sat 10am–6pm, Sun 1pm– 5pm. Rest of the year Mon–Fri 9am– 4:30pm, Sat 9am–4pm, Sun 1pm–5pm.* ☎ 506-450-8500. *www.christchurch cathedral.com.*

Completed in 1853, this elegant stone church is distinguished by a copper-green spire and pointed arch windows. It is an example of decorated Gothic Revival architecture. The interior is dominated by a hammer-beam wooden pointed **ceiling.** At the entrance to the south transept stands a cenotaph with a **marble effigy** of the Rev. John Medley, the first bishop of Fredericton.

Historic Garrison District★★

571 Queen St., Officers' Square. ♿⏲*Open year round. $8 to participate in "Day in a Soldier's Life" (Jul–Aug).* ☎506-460-2041. *www.tourismfredericton.ca.*

This walkable area in Fredericton's downtown contains two small museums, a sports hall of fame and shops. In the summer, the district hosts various festivals and free nightly entertainment. Contemporary art enthusiasts may want stop at the Gallery Connexion, a non-profit artists-run centre where, in summer, a resident artist is on staff.

The highlight of the district is the **military compound**★, a National Historic Site. The central location of the former British military headquarters shows the importance of the infantry garrison in early Fredericton. Once stretching from Queen Street to the river, between York and Regent streets, the compound retains few of its original buildings. Now a pleasant park known as **Officers' Square,** the old parade ground is the site of the former **officers' quarters,** a three-storey stone building with white arches, constructed in 1839 with additions in 1851 *(changing of the guard Jul–Aug Tue–Sat, weather permitting).*

A few blocks west, the **Guard House (A),** built in 1827, stands adjacent to the **soldiers' barracks (B),** a stone building with wooden terraces. Both have been restored and furnished.

York-Sunbury Historical Society Museum (M)

In officers' quarters. ⏲*Open late Jun– Labour Day daily 10am–5pm. Apr–May & Sept–Dec Tue–Sat 1pm–4pm.* 🎟*$3.* ☎506-455-6041.

This museum provides a portrait of the area from its settlement by the Native American population to the present. Exhibits on the Loyalists and the garrison are included, and a World War I trench has been reconstructed. The mounted Coleman frog, which weighed 19kg/42 pounds, is on display.

Old Government House★

51 Woodstock Rd. ♿⏲*Open year round, May–Labour Day 10am–4pm, Rest of the year by appointment.* ☎506-453-2505. *www.gnb.ca/0184/index-e.asp.*

Sitting on the banks of the Saint John River, this sandstone building was constructed in 1826 to serve as the residence of New Brunswick's governors and lieutenant-governors. From 1867 to 1996, it functioned in several capacities such as a barracks, a hospital and a school. Renovations to the house were completed in 1998, and today tours of two floors take

Address Book

For price categories, see the Legend on the cover flap.

WHERE TO STAY

$$ Crowne Plaza Lord Beaverbrook Hotel – *659 Queen St.* ✕ ⚐ 🄿 ⌕
☎ *506-455-3371 or 866-444-1946.* *www.cpfredericton.com. 168 rooms.* Now a Crowne Plaza hotel, the Lord Beaverbrook, built in 1947, has an unbeatable location in the downtown core (the Beaverbrook Art Gallery is right next door). The spacious, if austere, guestrooms have all the modern amenities. Three on-site restaurants range in offerings from bar/snack food to upscale cuisine.

$$ The Colonel's Inn – *843 Union St.* 🄿 ⌁ ☎ *506-452-2802 or 877-455-3003.* *www.bbcanada.com/1749. html. 3 rooms.* Impeccably maintained, this 1902 residence is just across the river from downtown Fredericton, accessible by shuttle boat or a pleasant walking trail. Each of the three air-conditioned bedrooms has a private bath, phone and TV/VCR. Breakfast included.

$$ On the Pond Country Retreat – *20 Rte. 616, in Mactaquac.* 🄿 Spa ☎ *506-363-3420 or 800- 984-2555.* *www.onthepond.com. 8 rooms.* Just 21km/13mi northwest of Fredericton, this waterside retreat offers recreation and relaxation. Guest quarters in the English-cottage-style lodge are decorated in a woodland theme. Downstairs you'll find a cozy great room with stone fireplace. Spa packages include massages, whirlpool access and more.

$$ Very Best Victorian B&B – *806 George St.* ⌁ ☎ *506-451-1499.* *www.bbcanada.com/2330.html. 5 rooms.* This handsome 19C house is located in a quiet residential neighbourhood within walking distance of downtown. All the antique-filled bedrooms have modern amenities. Features include an outdoor pool, a cedar sauna and a pool table. Breakfast is served in the dining room or in the gazebo near the pool.

WHERE TO EAT

$ El Burrito Loco – *304 King St.* ⚐ ☎ *506-459-5626.* **Mexican.** Though housed in a former fast-food joint on a busy downtown intersection, this restaurant is renowned for its authentic Mexican fare. Once a restaurateur in Puerto Vallarta, the owner has transported his recipes northward to the delight of many customers.

$$ BrewBakers – *546 King St.* ☎ *506-459-0067. www.brewbakers.ca.* **International.** This well-frequented eatery contains dining rooms on several levels. The place still has enough nooks and hideaways to afford privacy and quiet to couples. The menu roams from pizza and pasta to steaks, sesame chicken and seafood.

$$ The Palate Restaurant & Café – *462 Street St.* ☎ *506-450-7911.* *www.thepalate.com.* **International.** This casual bistro boasts an open kitchen, local art on the walls, background jazz and menus leaning toward the eclectic such as Mexican-inspired pork, Thai chicken or lamb osso bucco. Enjoy your selections inside, or on the umbrella-shaded front patio.

$$ Racines Restaurant – *536 Queen St.* ☎ *506-474-1915. www.racinesrestaurant. ca.* **Contemporary.** Fredericton-born Joanne Gimblett and her chef husband, Thomas, opened this upscale dining spot opposite Officers' Square in 2005. Seafood stars in such creative concoctions as blackened Cajun haddock with spinach topped with mango ginger coulis or coconut-coated Atlantic snow crab with sweet chili sauce.

---

in the original office of the lieutenant-governor, a music room, library, a dining room and conservatories. Note that the drapery, carpets and walls in the main floor drawing room match what is seen in the 1835 painting *Indian Dance*.

Science East

Kids *668 Brunswick St.* ⚐ 🕐*Open Jun–Aug Mon–Sat 10am–5pm, Sun 1pm–4pm. Sept–May Mon–Fri noon–5pm, Sat 10am–5pm.* ⚏ *$6.* ☎ *506-457-2340. www.scienceeast.nb.ca.*

Downtown Fredericton boasts a science centre with 100 interactive exhibits housed in a restored former jailhouse (1842). Founded by volunteers, this innovative educational facility, opened in 1999, is popular with kids of all ages. Although Science East is geared to

New Brunswick Tourism

Changing of the Guard, Military Compound

inquisitive children, adults gravitate to the Energy and Climate Change Gallery as well as the basement's jail memorabilia and prisoner biographies.

Additional Sights

Boss Gibson's Marysville★★
20 McGloin St., off Rte. 8, 10km/6mi northeast of downtown Fredericton. & ⓒOpen *daily year-round.* ☎ *506-460-2129. www.tourismfredericton.ca. Self-guided walking-tour brochure available from Fredericton tourism office.*

A National Historic District since 2003, Marysville sits on the Nashwaak River. The 19C mill town preserves stores, churches, tenement houses and a sizable brick cotton mill—which, as Marysville Place today—has been converted to house government offices. Note the handsome wooden mansions of Knob Hill that were once home to the managers of the mill.

The village was started by Alexander "Boss" Gibson (1819-1913), a wealthy landowner who was one of the founders of the New Brunswick Railway, in 1862. Gibson sold his mill in 1908 and died a pauper five years later. Marysville is named in honour of his wife, Mary.

Kingswood
31 Kingswood Park, 2.5km/1.5mi south of downtown Fredericton via Hanwell Rd. (Rte. 640). ⚒ & ⓒOpen year-round *daily 9am–9pm (Fri–Sat 11pm).* ☜fees

vary. Golf $65 (early Jun–Sept); $50 (spring & fall). ☎800-423-5969. *www.kingswoodpark.com.*

Located on the south side of Fredericton, this comprehensive family-oriented recreation park includes a 9-hole and an 18-hole golf course, a state-of-the-art fitness club, gymnasium, ice rink and 80,000-sq ft bowling alley and food court with an indoor playground. Lessons are offered.

Excursions

Mactaquac Provincial Park★★
1256 Rte. 105, 24km/15mi west of Fredericton. ⚒△⚒&☜ⓒOpen *daily year-round.* ☜*$7/vehicle (Jun–Aug).* ☎506-363-4747 *www.tourismnewbrunswick.ca.*

This 1200-acre provincial park overlooks the Mactaquac Dam on the Saint John River. With 300 campsites *(ⓒ open mid-May–mid-Oct),* an18-hole golf course and pro shop, hiking trails, two supervised beaches, two marinas, picnic facilities and a recreation centre (equipment rentals), this provincial park is one of the best-equipped in Atlantic Canada. The lodge offers sit-down dining and a snack canteen.

Military Museum, CFB Gagetown
Rte.102, in Oromocto, 30km/18mi southeast of Fredericton. Follow signs to the main gate at Base Gagetown. Museum Building A-5. & ⓒOpen *Jun–Aug Mon–Fri 8am–4pm, weekends 10am–4pm. Rest of the year Mon–Fri 8am–4pm.* ☜*Contribution requested.* ☎506-422-1304. *www. museumgagetown.ca.*

Canadian Forces Base Gagetown is one of the most important training bases in the country. Stretching some 1100sq km/425sq mi, the terrain is ideal for training under various conditions: the small hills are conducive to mountain-warfare training; jungle warfare is replicated in the dense forests and swamps.

At the museum, indoor and outdoor displays, as well as Canadian and American weapons, uniforms and other artifacts depict the history of the military in New Brunswick since 1800. The story is told of Gen. Thomas Gage, commander of the British forces in the American Revolutionary War, who received, in 1765, a land grant that is now the site of Gagetown. Other exhibits include artifacts and weapons from the Yukon Field Force, the Boer War and World Wars I and II.

Miramichi Valley★

MAP INSIDE FRONT COVER

The name Miramichi has long been associated with fine salmon fishing. A major spawning ground for Atlantic salmon, the Miramichi River has two branches (the Southwest Miramichi and the Little Southwest Miramichi), which meet near the city of Miramichi and flow east to Miramichi Bay and into the Gulf of St. Lawrence. Towns in the valley include Boiestown and Doaktown in the central part of the province and Miramichi and Baribog Bridge near the river's mouth. The area is also lumber country. The city of Miramichi (formerly the towns of Newcastle and Chatham) is known for its shipbuilding past. Joseph Cunard, founder of the famous shipping line, lived in Chatham, where he owned several businesses.

- **Information:** ☎800-561-0123. www.tourismnewbrunswick.ca.
- ▶ **Orient Yourself:** The valley lies in central New Brunswick. Boiestown is 68km/42mi north of Fredericton by Rte. 8, Doaktown is 94km/58mi northeast of Fredericton by Rte.8.
- **Don't Miss:** The Atlantic Salmon Museum, with its fishing collections and lovely views of the river.
- **Organizing Your Time:** Allow 2 days to see the major sights.
- **Especially for Kids:** The aquarium at the Atlantic Salmon Museum.

Sights

Atlantic Salmon Museum★

263 Main St., in Doaktown. ♿◷*Open Jun–mid-Oct Mon–Sat 9am–5pm, Sun 1pm–5pm. Mid-Apr–May Mon–Fri 9am–5pm.* ⌷*$5.* ☎*506-365-7787 or 866-725-6662. www.atlanticsalmonmuseum.com.*
Overlooking a series of pools on the Miramichi River, this museum is devoted to the area's famed Atlantic salmon. Displays include boats, nets, flies and fishing rods, migration routes and predators. The theatre shows a video about salmon fishing; the small Kids aquarium contains specimens of the fish.

Central New Brunswick Woodmen's Museum

6342 Rte. 8, in Boiestown. ◷*Open mid-May–mid-Oct daily 9:30am–5pm.* ⌷*$5.* ☎*506-369-7214. www.woodsmen museum.com.*
This museum presents life in a lumber camp. On display is a sawmill with its original equipment and a range of tools from axes to chain saws. The recreated bunkhouse and cookhouse evoke the flavour of camp life. A small **train** *($2)* runs continuous tours around the site.

MacDonald Farm Provincial Historic Site

600 Rte. 11, Bartibog Bridge, 13km/8mi east of Miramichi on Rte. 11. ◷*Open mid-Jun–Labour Day daily 9:30am–4:30pm. Late May–mid-Jun Mon–Fri 9:30am–4:30pm.* ⌷*$2.50.* ☎*506-453-2324.*
Overlooking the Miramichi estuary, this old stone farmhouse (1820) has been restored to the period when Alexander MacDonald and his family lived in it. Beside the river a "net" shed houses fishing gear. Costumed guides perform traditional crafts. Visitors can participate in domestic chores, including feeding the farm animals.

Joseph Cunard

Joseph Cunard was born in Halifax in 1799 and died in Liverpool, England, in 1865 – but he became a larger-than-life lumbering, milling and shipbuilding magnate in Chatham. He and his brother Henry began their empire in the 1820s, backed by older brother Samuel. A physically imposing man, Joseph had a personality to match; he had many loyal employees and several enemies. Most of his 1,500 employees felt indebted to him, and he enjoyed an almost cult-like status in the Miramichi area. Returning from a transatlantic crossing, he would often be welcomed by a 13-gun salute. His mansion, which he bought after his marriage in 1833, had a ballroom, peacocks on the grounds, and a circular driveway where a coach with liveried footmen waited for his command. In 1847 his empire began to unravel due to economic depression and his financial recklessness. It took until 1850 to close all his businesses, and hundreds of once-loyal workers were left bitter, penniless and unemployed. He left for Liverpool with his family that same year and achieved financial success again in shipping. Although he is despised by many to this day in Chatham, his debts were resolved by his brother Samuel in 1871.

Excursions

Kouchibouguac National Park

45km/28mi south of Miramichi by Hwy.11; take Exit 75, then go east to Rte. 117. ◷*Open mid-Jun–Labour Day 8am–8pm. Mid-May–early Jun & rest of Sept–mid-Oct 9am–5pm.* ◉*$7.80.* ✕🄿⚠&*(trails)* ☎*506-876-2443. www.pc.gc.ca.*

Opened in 1969 on the Gulf of St. Lawrence, this 238sq km/92sq mi wilderness park is a haven for cyclists, walkers, birders and kayakers. At Kelly Beach *(supervised late-Jun–Aug),* the waters are warm enough to swim. The park's name [pronounced Koo-she-BOO-ju-whack] is of Mi'kmaq derivation, meaning "river of the long tides." Indeed, Kouchibouguac preserves tidal rivers, freshwater ponds, bogs, lagoons, salt marshes and forests of fir, pine and spruce. Its 25km/15mi of sand dunes are the scenic highlight, home to the endangered piping plover. A large colony of terns also calls the park home. Cycling is popular along 60km/37mi of trails. The **Salt Marsh Trail** *(.7km/.4mi)* offers good views of the dunes. At **Kelly Beach** children will enjoy the 🄺🄸🄳🅂 puppet theatre *(late-Jun–Aug Sun & Wed).* Kayaks and canoes can be rented at Ryans Recreation Centre near South Kouchibouguac campground.

Le Pays de la Sagouine★

57 Acadie St., in Bouctouche. 85km/53mi south of Miramichi by Rte. 11, Exit 32A or B. ◷*Open late-Jun–Aug 9:30am–5:30pm.* ↝*Guided tours daily in English 10am & 2:30pm.* ◉*$15.* ☎*506-743-1400 or 800-561-9188 www.sagouine.com.*

The distinctive curved boardwalk to the Island of Fleas (l'Île-aux-Puces) marks the entry to the engaging Country of Sagouine, a real-life Acadian village complete with theatre, music, comedy and dance. Inspired by the novel *La Sagouine* (1971) by Bouctouche-born Acadian Canadian writer Antonine Maillet (b. 1929), the hands-on attraction opened in 1992. Visitors can learn to cook Acadian dishes, use traditional fishing techniques; play musical instruments and watch artists at work. Musical performances and dinner theatre round out the fun. Incidentally, the boardwalk is curved to withstand ice and tidal forces.

Sandra Phinney/Michelin

Broadwalks at Kouchibouguac National Park

NORTHEAST COAST

During his voyage to the area in 1534, Jacques Cartier entered the Bay of Chaleur and is credited with naming it ("bay of warmth" in French). The peninsula jutting into the bay in this northeast corner of the province has been dubbed the Acadian Peninsula. Fleeing Nova Scotia during the Deportation, many Acadians settled here in the mid-18C to rebuild their lives. Today their descendants preserve the crafts, music, food, language and celebrations of their culture, clearly visible at the Village Historique Acadien, near Caraquet. They continue to earn a livelihood from the bounty of the land and the sea, evident in Lameque Island's peat-moss bogs and Shippagan's commercial fishing industry. The coastline also is a source of income: residents and tourists are attracted in season to the warm waters of the Gulf of St. Lawrence and the white, sandy beaches, especially at Miscou Island.

Acadian Peninsula★

MAP INSIDE FRONT COVER

Extending 13km/8mi along the Bay of Fundy's steep cliffs, this rolling parkland is interrupted by deep-cut rivers and streams in deep valleys. Created by 9m/29ft or higher tides, the vast tidal flats, explorable at low tide, contain a wealth of marine life. Besides watching the tides, visitors have a host of amenities and activities from which to choose. Camping, golf, fishing, boating (rentals available), swimming in the on-site pool, tennis, mountain biking, hiking and in winter, cross-country skiing and snowshoeing. There are children's playgrounds on the premises.

- ☐ **Information:** ☎800-561-0123. www.tourismnewbrunswick.ca.
- ▶ **Orient Yourself:** Route 11 connects the main towns of the peninsula, from Shippagan west to Bathurst. From there, Route 8 leads south to the Miramichi Valley.
- ⊚ **Don't Miss:** Village Historique Acadien.
- ◷ **Organizing Your Time:** Allow 2 days to see the towns (allow a half day for Village Historique Acadian) and a third day, if visiting in summer, to enjoy the beaches.
- Kids **Especially for Kids:** The seal pool at Shippagan's Aquarium.

Sights

Shippagan★
☎506-336-3907.
www.ville.shippagan.com.
This town at the tip of the Acadian peninsula has the largest commercial fishing fleet in the province. Local plants process lobster, crab, herring, scallops and other fish. Peat-moss processing plants are here, as is a campus of the Université de Moncton.
Along the harbour, a **boardwalk** stretches 1.6km/1mi, offering views of the wharves and boats. A causeway leads to Lamèque Island, with its peat-moss bogs. Peat forms when vegetation decays only partially and is composed of peat moss or sphagnum. When dried, peat can be used as a form of fuel; among other uses, it also helps soil retain moisture. From Lamèque Island a bridge crosses to Miscou Island, which has fine beaches on the Gulf of St. Lawrence.

Aquarium and Marine Centre★
Kids 100 Aquarium Dr. ✕ � ◷ Open mid-May–Sept daily 10am–6pm. ☞$8. ☎506-336-3013. www.tourismnewbrunswick.ca.
Devoted to the marine life of the gulf, this museum features exhibits on the

Caraquet

Just west of Shippagan lies the seaport town of Caraquet (www.ville.caraquet.nb.ca), settled by Acadians in 1758, and now known as a hub of Acadian culture. Try to catch a performance by the Théâtre populaire d'Acadie, which stages productions in French. You'll want to visit Caraquet in August, when the town hosts its annual Acadian festival, opened by a **blessing of the fleet,** symbolic of Christ's benediction to the fishermen of Galilee. As many as 60 fishing boats, decked with bunting, arrive from all over the province to be blessed by the bishop of Bathurst.

The town is home to the charming 1891 **Hôtel Paulin ($$$),** a grand three-storey wooden building with a mansard roof *(143 Blvd. Saint-Pierre West; ☎506-727-9981or 866-727-9981; www.hotelpaulin.com).* Located on the second and third floors, the guest rooms have a French country look, with patterned quilts, rustic furniture and wood floors. Downstairs features an open sitting area and a public **dining room ($$)**, where the focus is on local seafood, like the seasonal Bay of Chaleur rum-runner lobster, and upscale Acadian-style cuisine. Rates include breakfast and a four-course dinner at the hotel.

St. Lawrence River and New Brunswick's lakes and rivers. In a series of aquariums, outdoor seal pool and touch tank, fish native to these waters are on view. Visitors can enter the cabin of a reconstructed trawler to see the mass of electronic devices used to find and catch fish.

Village Historique Acadien★★

Kids *14311 Rte. 11, 47km/29mi west of Shippagan.* ✕&☾*Open Jun–Sept daily 10am–6pm.* ☞*$15.* ☎*506-726-2600 or 877-721-2200. www.villagehistorique acadien.com.*

This reconstructed village depicts the life of the Acadians from 1780 to 1890, after their return from Deportation. Visitors enter the village through the **visitor centre** *(centre d'accueil),* where a video (18min) on the history of the Acadians provides a good introduction. Staffed by Acadians wearing traditional costumes, the village extends along a road nearly 1.6km/1mi long. Houses moved from various parts of the province have been furnished to represent the period. Only the wooden church is a copy of an original building. A grist mill, blacksmith forge, school, and

Hotel Paulin, Caraquet

Sandra Phinney/Michelin

woodworking and printing shops can also be visited.

The new millennium saw two dozen structures added to the village, including an operational hotel, bringing the time represented up to 1939. In 2007 a 1936 service station, a houselike white building trimmed in red, and two petrol pumps—all donated by Irving Oil company—opened for visitor viewing. (Irving Oil's founder, Kenneth Colin Irving, was a native of the Acadian town of Bouctouche, in the southeastern part of the province.)

Over the village flies the **flag of Acadie,** the French red, white and blue tricolour with a star symbolizing the Virgin Mary at the top left corner.

Acadian flag

© World Pictures/Photoshot

Bathurst

Rte. 11, 103km/64mi west of Shippagan. ☎*506-548-0400. www.bathurst.ca. Visitor centre, 850 St. Anne St. (on the waterfront);* ☎*506-548-0410.*

The town of Bathurst lies along the mouth of the Nepisiguit River, where it empties into Chaleur Bay. Long dependent upon forests and shipbuilding for livelihood, the local economy continues to benefit from the pulp and paper industry, as well as mining, small manufacturing and tourism. In 2003, the Acadie-Bathurst area hosted the Canada Winter Olympics.

A walk along its **boardwalk** facing the bay can be rewarding. The marina *(Queen Elizabeth Dr.)* bustles with activity; here, visitors can rent small craft to enjoy some time on the water.

Excursion

Atlas Park

Kids *In Pointe-Verte (access from Rte.11, Exit 333), 48km/30mi north of Bathurst.* ✕☉*Open daily year-round.* ☎*506-783-3717. www.acadie-bathurst.com.*

The centrepiece of this park is a former quarry, 30m/98ft deep and now filled with water. In summer, the park is a veritable recreation hub.

There are rowboats and paddlevboats, picnic grounds and walking paths as well as an amusement park.

Activities include fishing and scuba diving. In winter the lake freezes, accommodating skating and even under-ice scuba diving. The park has trails for cross-country skiing and snowmobiling. A cafeteria and lounge area are open on the premises year-round.

SOUTHERN COAST

Maybe it's the proximity to Nova Scotia and the highest tides in the world in the Bay of Fundy that both provinces share; maybe it's the miles of beaches, the tranquillity of Passamaquoddy Bay, or even Saint John's cosmopolitan flavour that draw people to the Southern Coast. Whatever your interests, the south shore of New Brunswick holds something for everyone, whether it be a world-famous national park, a quick passage to the rest of the Maritimes, or its own laidback lifestyle that has had a striking appeal to tourists, locals, and even a beloved US president, for the past three centuries. At Fundy National Park besides watching the tides, visitors have a host of amenities and activities from which to choose: camping, golf, fishing, boating *(rentals available)*, swimming in the on-site pool, tennis, mountain biking, hiking and in winter, cross-country skiing and snowshoeing.

Fundy National Park★★

MAP INSIDE FRONT COVER

Extending 13km/8mi along the Bay of Fundy's steep cliffs, this rolling parkland is interrupted by deep-cut rivers and streams in deep valleys. Created by 9m/29ft or higher tides, the vast tidal flats, explorable at low tide, contain a wealth of marine life. There's also a wealth of human activities from which to choose.

- **Information:** ☎506-887-6000. www.pc.gc.ca.
- ▶ **Orient Yourself:** The park is located near Alma, along Rte.114, which follows the coast south of Moncton. This is not the spot for the famed Fundy tidal bore: that can be seen from Bore Park in Moncton.
- **Kids Especially for Kids:** Herring Cove's and Point Wolfe's tidal pools at low tide. There are children's playgrounds on the premises.

Visit

✕⚠♿🕐*Open daily year-round.* 🕐*Visitor centre (east entrance) open mid-Jun–Labour Day daily 8am–10pm. Mid-May–mid-Jun & Labour Day–early Oct daily 8am–4:30pm. Rest of the year daily 8:15am–4:30pm.* ✺*$7 entry fee.* ☎*506-887-6000. www.pc.gc.ca. Note: views described may be obscured by fog.*

Eastern Park Entrance

From the park gate there is a fine **view**★ of the tranquil Upper Salmon River, the hills to the north, the small fishing village of Alma, Owl's Head and the bay. To appreciate the contrast, visit at both low and high tides.

Herring Cove

11km/7mi from entrance. At the end of the road, there is a **view**★ of the cove from above and a display on the tides. A path leads down to **Kids** tidal pools brimming with limpets, barnacles, sea anemones and other life at low tide.

Point Wolfe★★

10km/6mi from entrance.
The road crosses Point Wolfe River by a covered wooden bridge, below which is a small gorge forming the river's entry into Wolfe Cove. To collect logs floated downstream, a dam was constructed. Schooners loaded the sawed wood at wharves built in the coves. Today only the bridge and dam remain. At the end of the road, a path leads to the cove, providing good **views**★★ on the descent.

Fundy National Park

©Nat Girish/iStockphoto.com

Passamaquoddy Bay/ Fundy Isles★★

MAP P 70

An inlet of the Bay of Fundy between Maine and New Brunswick, this body of water is dotted with islands and indented with harbours along its irregular shoreline, which includes the estuary of the St. Croix River. Among the famous who have owned summer homes here are William Van Horne, president of the Canadian Pacific Railway from 1888 to 1899 and US president Franklin D. Roosevelt. The popular resort is also famous for its lobster and an edible seaweed known as dulse, a regional delicacy that is served in a variety of ways. *Fog and chilly weather occur even in summer, particularly on the islands.*

🔲 **Information:** ☎800-561-0123. www.tourismnewbrunswick.ca, or www.standrewsnb.ca

▶ **Orient Yourself:** St. Stephen, the biggest town on the Canadian side, lies 115km/71mi west of Saint John. St. Andrews sits on a small peninsula about 29km/18mi southeast of St. Stephen. The nearby islands (easily accessible) of Ministers, Deer and Campobello are all interesting in their own right.

😊 **Don't Miss:** Campobello, home of Franklin D. Roosevelt.

🕐 **Organizing Your Time:** Allow 2 full days to enjoy the area, including half a day for the International Park. Plan your itinerary around ferry times. Ferries depart from Letete (♨*see Deer Island and Campobello Island below for ferry departure times*) and from Blacks Harbour (♨*see Grand Manan Island below*).

🔲 **Especially for Kids:** The HMSC Aquarium-Museum.

♨ **Also See:** SAINT JOHN

A Bit of History

According to Indian legend, one day the Mi'kmaq hero-god **Glooscap** saw wolves about to attack a deer and a moose. Using his magical powers, he turned the animals into islands. In 1604 Samuel de Champlain chose the bay as the site of his first settlement and wintered with his followers on St. Croix Island (today in Maine) in the estuary of the river of the same name. However, the bleak conditions forced them to move the next year across the Bay of Fundy to Nova Scotia.

Loyalists, arriving in 1783 from the US, settled the communities of St. Stephen, St. Andrews and St. George, and of Deer and Campobello islands.

St. Andrews★★

☎506-529-5120. www.townofstandrews. ca or www.standrewsnb.ca. Situated at the end of a peninsula that juts into the bay, this charming town is lined with tree-covered residential and commercial avenues. A resort centre for summer visitors, the town supports the **Algonquin Hotel** (♨*see Address Book*), one of the foremost hostelries of the province.

Founded by Loyalists, St. Andrews became a prosperous mercantile and fishing town. In the early 1800s, Irish immigrants arrived, but many died on the journey across the Atlantic. Near the downtown a Celtic cross stands in testament to these early settlers. In 1842 some of its century-old houses were floated intact across the estuary when the Webster-Ashburton Treaty declared the Canadian/US border to be the St. Croix River—and some Loyalists discovered they were on the "wrong" side of it. Many original buildings remain and the town is designated a National Historic District. Restaurants and gift shops sit beside whale-watching tour offices along Water Street. Some locals refer to the town as St. Andrews-by-the-

Algonquin hotel and grounds

Sea, a moniker developed in the early days of the Fairmont Algonquin Hotel.

HMSC Aquarium-Museum★

Kids *Huntsman Marine Science Centre at Brandy Cove.* ⏲*Open mid-May–Labour Day daily 10am–5pm. Rest of Sept Thu–Sun 10am–5pm.* ☞*$7.50.* ☎*506-529-1202. www.huntsmanmarine.ca.*
This interesting little aquarium has fish tanks and displays on the marine ecosystems of the Bay of Fundy and neighbouring Atlantic waters. The star attraction is a family of harbour seals, which performs for visitors. Films are shown regularly in the theatre.

St. Andrews Blockhouse

On Joe's Point Rd. ⏲*Open Jun–Aug daily 10am–6pm.* ☞*$1.* ☎*506-529-4270. www.pc.gc.ca.*
Constructed during the War of 1812, the square wooden structure stands guard over the harbour. Built to protect New Brunswick's western frontier from American invasion, it is the only blockhouse remaining of the original 14 erected. Inside there are displays on the settlement of the town and on the blockhouse itself.

Kingsbrae Garden★★

Kids *220 King St.* ✗ ♿ ⏲*Open mid-May–mid-Oct daily 9am–6pm.* ☞*$10.* ☎*506-529-3335 or 866-566-8687. www.kingsbraegarden.com.*

This spectacular 11ha/27-acre estate opened in 1998 and features more than 2,500 different varieties of trees, shrubs and plants. Highlights are the children's fantasy garden, the cedar maze, and the scents and sensitivity garden that allows the visually and hearing impaired to smell and touch plants. A functional, scaled down Dutch windmill is on-site.

Charlotte County Courthouse★

123 Frederick St. ⏲*Open Apr–May & Oct–Nov Tue–Fri 1pm–4pm. Jun Mon–Fri 9am–5pm. Sept Mon–Fri 9am–4pm. Jul–Aug Mon–Sat 9am–5pm. Dec–Mar by appt.* ☎*506-529-4248. www.ccarchives. ca/courthouse.html.*
A National Historic Site since 1983, this 1840 courthouse was built in the Greek Revival style. A portico of six columns supports a massive tympanum containing the county seal. The county archives are stored next door in the Old Gaol, which was used as a place of incarceration from 1832, the year of its construction, to 1979. Some cells remain intact.

Ross Memorial Museum★

188 Montague St. ⏲*Open early Jun–early Oct Mon–Sat 10am–4:30pm; late Nov–early Dec Thu–Sun, call for hrs.* ☞*Contribution requested ($3 off-season).* ☎*506-529-5124. www.townsearch.com/ rossmuseum.*
Chestnut Hall, a two-story, redbrick Georgian-style house (1824), was pur-

Address Book

For price categories, see the Legend on the cover flap.

WHERE TO STAY

$$ Windsor House – *132 Water St.* ♿✗ ☎506-529-3330 *or 888-890-9463.* *www.innsite.com/inns/B010735.html 6 rooms.* This two-storey wood building, dating to 1798, is brightly painted and embellished with dormers and porch railings. It contains a parlour bar, billiards room and a **dining room ($$$)** that serves superb continental cooking with a contemporary twist. Spacious guest rooms have fireplaces, armoires or secretary desks, loveseats or settees and marble tiled bathrooms. Fancy but not fussy, Windsor House will make you feel right at home. Breakfast is included in the room rate.

$$$ Fairmont Algonquin – *184 Adolphus St.* ✗♿🅿Spa☒ ☎506-863-6310 *or 800-663-7575.* *www.fairmont.com. 234 rooms.* This sprawling 1889 Tudor-style railroad hotel rises from a carpet of lawn and trees on a bluff overlooking St. Andrews. The long lobby and adjoining front porch are perfect for idling; the cozy library is filled with volumes; and spa facilities, a beauty salon and a heated swimming pool encourage indulgence. The 18-hole golf course is one of the province's signature courses and offers sweeping bay views. Rooms are appointed with handsome fabrics and period reproduction or contemporary furniture. The **Passamaquoddy Dining Room ($$$)**, open May–Oct, is one of the town's best.

$$$$$ Kingsbrae Arms – *219 King St.* ✗🅿☒☎506-529-1897. *www.kingsbrae. com. 8 rooms.* A rambling 1897 shingled manor house, this upscale inn, furnished with fine art and antiques, is the only Relais & Chateaux property in the Maritimes. Bedrooms feature poster or canopy beds with down comforters; some rooms have gas-log fireplaces. Bathrooms feature whirlpool or cast-iron tubs and touch-control showers. After evening cocktails, guests dine around a massive table. Guests may also enjoy the Inn's parlour, library and lovely gardens, which are next door to Kingsbrae Garden.

WHERE TO EAT

$$ Niger Reef Teahouse – *1 Joe's Point Rd.* ☎506-529-8007. *Open mid-May–Oct.* **Contemporary.** This waterside (licensed) restaurant sits near the St. Andrews Blockhouse. The 1927 shingle and log structure retains its original Asian-style murals depicting New Brunswick's coastline. While best known for teas and creative sandwiches at lunch, Niger Reef offers a dinner menu featuring local seafood as well as steak kebabs and daily specials. On pleasant evenings, take a table on the rustic deck for great views of the bay.

$$ Rossmount Inn – *4599 Rte. 127.* ☎506-529-3351. *www.rossmountinn. com.* **Canadian.** *(Dinner only.)* This three-storey manor house, laden with antiques, is found 10 minutes north of St. Andrews' waterfront. The cheery dining room offers distant views of the northern bay. The menu changes seasonally, featuring seafood and fresh organic vegetables from the restaurant's garden and local farmers. With some main dishes under $20, the restaurant remains one of St. Andrews' better dining values.

---

chased by summer residents Henry Phipps Ross and Sarah Juliette Ross in 1938. Globe-trotters, art collectors and philanthropists, the American couple wanted a place to display their collection. Furnishings include Oriental rugs, paintings by Canadian artists, four-poster beds, and 19C pieces by cabinetmakers from the province.

The Islands

Ministers Island★

Access at the end of Bar Rd., twice daily at low tide. Tide schedules & tickets at 20 King St. in St. Andrews. ♿☉*Mansion open mid-May–mid-Oct.* ☒*$12.* ☎506-529-5081. *www.ministersisland.org.* Visitors drive across the ocean floor at low tide to Ministers Island to tour the former summer estate of Sir **William**

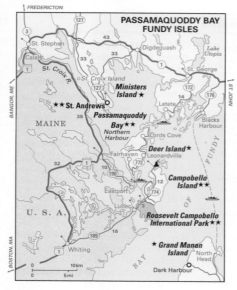

Van Horne

Van Horne (1843-1915). President of Canadian Pacific Railway for 11 years, Horne purchased the island in 1890 and built a 50-room sandstone mansion on a hill offering splendid **views** of the surroundings. The house, called Covenhoven, features furnishings of the period, and displays his landscape paintings. A large wooden barn holds equipment from Van Horne's working farm, which had vegetable gardens, fruit trees, horses and cattle. Family and friends used the turreted stone bathhouse after a visit to the beach. Hiking trails crisscross the 500-acre island, now a game reserve and home to deer.

Cottage at Roosevelt Campobello International Park

Deer Island★

Toll-free car ferry departs from Letete late Jun–mid-Sept daily 8:30am–7pm; ☎ 506-466-7340 or 888-747-7006; www.tourismnewbrunswick.ca. From Eastport, Maine Jul–Aug daily 9:30am–6:30pm, Jun & Sept daily 9:30am–5:30pm; $3 per person, $17/vehicle maximum; 🅿 ☎ 506-747-2159; www.eastcoastferries.nb.ca. Note: ferries operate on first-come, first-served basis. Lines form on weekends and at peak times.

Positioned so as to nearly enclose the bay, this Fundy island is a quiet place, inhabited primarily by fishermen. The world's largest lobster pound is located on its western side. A pleasant **trip**★ is the ferry ride to the island from Letete, among the smaller islands covered with birds. Swept by the tide in part of the narrow inlet of **Northern Harbour,** a corral where lobsters are kept year-round has been built with nets and fences. At the southern end of the island, a large whirlpool forms when the Fundy tides are running strong. Called **"Old Sow"** for the noise it makes, this vortex is visible from Deer Island Point or from the ferry to Campobello Island.

Campobello Island★★

Car ferry departs from Deer Island-Campobello Island late Jun–mid-Sept 8:30am–7pm; $3/person, $22/vehicle maximum; 🅿 ☎506-747-2159; www.eastcoastferries.nb.ca. Accessible by bridge from Lubec, Maine. Non-Americans need valid passport. See also Michelin GREEN GUIDE New England.

Known as the "beloved island" of US President **Franklin D. Roosevelt** (1882-1945), the site is a summer resort for vacationing Americans. Sandy beaches, picturesque coves, headlands, lighthouses and an international park named in Roosevelt's honour attract numerous visitors annually.

First settled in the 1770s, Campobello was named for **William Campbell,**

Van Horne Mansion, Ministers Island

the governor of Nova Scotia, and for its beauty (*campo bello* means "beautiful pasture" in Italian). By the end of the 19C, it had become a retreat for wealthy Americans. In 1883 one-year-old FDR first visited the island. Thereafter he spent summers on Campobello with his parents and later with his wife, Eleanor. He taught his five children to appreciate nature and took them fishing, boating and swimming—activities he had done as a child. Then, in 1921, FDR contracted polio and left the island for 12 years. In 1964 the Canadian and American governments jointly established the park to commemorate him.

Roosevelt Campobello International Park★★

 ♿ 🕔 *Grounds open year-round. Visitor centre open late May–Oct daily 10am–6pm (last 2 weeks Oct to 5pm). ☎506-752-2922. www.fdr.net.*
Preserved as a memorial to FDR, the southern part of the island is natural parkland—forests, bogs, lakes, cliffs and beaches—crisscrossed by several lovely **drives.** Note the view of Passamaquoddy Bay from Friar's Head *(turn right at picnic area sign just south of visitor centre)*, and of Herring Cove from Con Robinson's Point *(follow Glensevern Rd. East)*. Built in the Dutch Colonial style, the red-shingled, green-roofed

cottage *(same hours as visitor centre)* with 34 rooms belonged to FDR. Simply furnished, the rustic interior contains personal reminders of his days at Campobello. The west side rooms, especially the living room, have pleasant views of Friar's Bay. Films on the life of Roosevelt are shown in the **visitor centre.** North of the visitor centre, **East Quoddy Head Lighthouse** *(12km/7mi by Wilson's Beach and gravel road to the Point)* overlooks Head Harbour Island.

Grand Manan Island★

 ♿ 🕔 *Car ferry departs Blacks Harbour late Jun–mid-Sept daily 7:30am, 9:30am, 11:30am, 1:30pm, 3:30pm, 5:30pm & 9pm (no departure Sun 7:30am). Rest of the year approximately 4 crossings daily. 1hr 30min.* ⊜*$10.50/person, $31.40/vehicle. ☎506-642-0520. www.coastaltransport.ca.*
The largest of the Fundy islands, Grand Manan is noted for its rugged scenery that includes cliffs of 120m/400ft. A sizable **bird population** inhabits the island: about 230 species have been sighted. On the island's rocky west coast, **Dark Harbour** is a processing centre for **dulse,** which grows on submerged rocks in the Bay of Fundy. Collected at low tide and dried in the sun, dulse has a salty, tangy flavour. Rich in iron and iodine, it can be eaten raw or in soups.

Saint John ★★

POPULATION 68,043 – MAP P 75

The province's largest city, this industrial centre and port is fondly called "fog city" because of the dense sea mists that roll in off the Bay of Fundy. Its rocky, hilly site at the mouth of the Saint John River at the junction with the bay has resulted in a city with few straight roads and many culs-de-sac. The historic district fronts Saint John Harbour; vast Rockwood Park, home to the zoo, lies at its backyard. Despite suffering a devastating fire in 1877, Saint John is an important repository of Canada's 19C architectural heritage: some 6,000 structures here, in varying states of repair, qualify as historic properties. Definitely a working city, Saint John is a major port of call in the Maritimes for cruise ships. It is also the headquarters of Irving Oil, Canada's largest oil refinery: Irving's Canaport (1970) was the first deep-water terminal in North America; lying off Saint John harbour, it services supersize crude-oil carriers.

🛈 **Information:** ☎506-658-2855, 1-866-463-8639. www.tourismsaintjohn.com. Visitor centre in Shops of City Hall next to Market Square's east side.

▸ **Orient Yourself:** On the east side of the river sits the historic east side; opposite sprawls the industrial west side. The historic heart centres on King Square and comprises streets designed in a gridlike pattern; King Street, the main thoroughfare, ascends steeply from the waterfront. In the vicinity of Trinity Royal Church, the 20-block Trinity Royal Preservation Area (bounded by King, Prince William, Charlotte & Harding Sts.) contains many shops and several historic structures.

🅿 **Parking:** Parking is ample downtown, especially along Water and Prince William Streets: metered, in city lots and garages. Access www.uptownsj.com for a parking map.

😊 **Don't Miss:** Reversing Falls is so famous you have to see it.

Kids **Especially for Kids:** The New Brunswick Museum.

A Bit of History

Frenchman **Charles de La Tour** built a trading fort in 1630 on the site of present-day Saint John, which a compatriot burned down. The trade rivalry among the French in Acadia was compounded by the Anglo-French struggles. The area was ceded by the 1763 Treaty of Paris to the English. In 1783 some 14,000 Loyalists disembarked at the mouth of the river. Possessing few pioneering skills, they created a prosperous city of shipyards. From 1860 to 1880, however, Saint John began to decline: demand for wooden ships was decreasing and in 1877 half the city was destroyed by fire.

After a century of decline, the city began to revive in the 1960s. Today, high tech, oil and plastics industries are bringing prosperity. A new sports and entertainment venue, Harbour Station, has been constructed and the Imperial Theatre restored to its 1913 appearance. Both Symphony New Brunswick and Opera New Brunswick are based in the city. In 2005 construction began on a natural gas terminal within Canaport, Irving Oil's deep-water terminal; the new facility becomes operational in 2008.

Every July the city recalls its founding with a celebration known as **Loyalist Days.** Inhabitants dress in 18C costumes and re-enact the landing of 1783.

Downtown ★★

Saint John's downtown is commonly called Uptown by locals, since the district was built on a hill. It has been revitalized, making it a pleasant area for visitors to explore on foot (contact the tourist office for designated walks).

Address Book

For dollar-sign categories, see the Legend on the cover flap.

WHERE TO STAY

$$ Homeport Historic B&B – *80 Douglas Ave. 10 rooms.* [P] [≈] ☎*506-672-7255 or 888-678-7678. www.homeport.nb.ca.* Set on a rocky ridge that offers views across downtown to the bay, the Italianate manor dates to1858. Opened as a bed-and-breakfast inn in 1997, it has sizable guest rooms, furnished with Victorian-era antiques gleaned from local shops and auctions. Breakfasts include a hot dish, fresh fruit and homemade granola and preserves.

$$ Inn on the Cove & Spa – *1371 Sand Cove Rd.* [✗] [P] [Spa] [≈] ☎*506-672-7799 or 877-257-8080. www.innonthecove.com. 6 rooms.* All bedrooms offer unobstructed views of the Bay of Fundy. The **dining room (($$)** is run by owners who had their own TV cooking show *(reservations strongly suggested)*. With all that, plus a spa on the premises, guests may not be tempted to go into the city at all. Available for rent next door is a house that sleeps four, with a private entrance onto the beach.

$$ Mahogany Manor Bed & Breakfast – *220 Germain St.* [P] [≈] ☎*506-636-8000 or 800-796-7755. www.bbcanada.com. 5 rooms.* Tastefully decorated and furnished, this stately Queen Anne-style house was built at the beginning of the 20C. It is located on one of the nicest residential streets in Saint John, and has a lovely garden. Home-cooked breakfast specialties are stand-outs.

$$ Shadow Lawn Inn – *3180 Rothesay Rd., in Rothesay.* [P] [≈] ☎*506-847-7539 or 800-561-4166. www. shadowlawninn. com. 9 rooms.* Located in the outlying village of Rothesay, the inn is well worth the 10min drive from downtown Saint John. The elaborate house was built in 1870 as the summer home for a local

department store magnate. Rooms are furnished with a mix of antiques and period reproductions. Continental breakfasts are included in the rate. The inn's **restaurant ($$$)** serves seafood and Canadian fare in an upscale setting. Two suites are also available for accommodation.

WHERE TO EAT

$ Taco Pico – *96 Germain St.* ☎*506-633-8492. Closed Sun.* **Mexican.** Guatemalan immigrants opened this restaurant in 1994 and serve traditional black bean soup, soft tacos, fajitas and other Mexican staples. *Pepian,* a spicy Guatemalan-style beef stew, is a specialty. Also on the menu are scallops, shrimp, and mussels in green sauce.

$$ Billy's Seafood – *49-51 Charlotte St.* [占] ☎*506-672-3474.* **Seafood.** This attractive emporium operates as a fish shop by day and a classy, informal restaurant by night. Less pricey than the tourist-oriented eateries on the waterfront, Billy's specializes in seafood. You can order plain boiled lobster or pan-seared scallops, or something more complex, like the house bouillabaisse. Whatever you choose, it won't disappoint.

$$ Sebastian – *43 Princess St.* ☎*506-693-2005.* **International.** One of the newer, up-scale eateries, Sebastian offers light foods after the dinner hour. Comfortable leather couches and a martini list entice patrons to linger on for late-night socializing.

$$ Suwanna – *325 Lancaster Ave.* [占] ☎*506-637-9015. Closed Mon.* **Thai.** This highly popular restaurant, owned by a Swiss/Thai couple, has garnered raves for its Russian custard. It is the authentic Thai dishes, however, that keep diners coming back again and again. Reservations are a must.

Market Square Area★★

The square contains an attractive shopping mall with a central atrium and several levels, a hotel, convention centre and the New Brunswick Museum. Incorporated into the complex, a row of late-19C warehouses fronts a pleasant plaza around the **market slip** where Loyalists landed in 1783. In summer there are outdoor cafes and concerts in the plaza. The

1867 clapboard structure with ginger-bread decoration, **Barbour's General Store (A)** is a museum stocked with merchandise of the period (🅿️ 🕐 *open mid-Jun–mid-Sept daily 10am–6pm; ☎506-658-2939; www.tourismsaintjohn. com)*. Over St. Patrick Street a pedestrian bridge links the square with the Canada Games **Aquatic Centre** *(www.aquatics.nb.ca)* and **City Hall (B). Brunswick Square (C)** is a complex of shops, offices and a hotel.

New Brunswick Museum★ (M)

Market Square. ♿🕐*Open daily Mon–Fri 9am–5pm (Thu til 9pm), Sat 10am–5pm, Sun noon–5pm.* 🕐*Closed Mondays early Nov–mid-May & holidays.* ⊚*$6.* ☎*506-643-2300. www.nbm-mnb.ca.*

Devoted to the human, natural and artistic life of the province, this museum has excellent examples of Indian birchbark, quill- and beadwork. European settlement is traced from contact with native inhabitants to the lumbering and ship-building industries of the 19C. Fine and decorative arts from New Brunswick are on exhibit. The gallery of natural science features displays of the province's animal life and geological specimens. The Webster Canadiana Collection depicts the history of Canada to its late-19C expansion with maps, photographs, medals, documents and other materials; the art gallery is filled with paintings of historical figures and events from the country's past.

Loyalist House (D)

120 Union St. 🕐*Open Jul–mid-Sept daily 10am–5pm. May–Jun Mon–Fri 10am–5pm.* ⊚*$3.* ☎*506-652-3590. www. loyalisthouse.com.*

One of the oldest structures in the city, this house was built in 1817 by a Loyalist who fled New York state in 1783. One of the few buildings to escape the fire of 1877, the house has a shingled exterior on two sides and clapboard on the other. An expensive material at the time, clapboard was installed only on the north and east sides as weather protection. The plain exterior belies the elegant Georgian interior with its fine curved staircase and arches between rooms. Upon departure, note the solid rock foundations on the Germain Street side. All of Saint John is built on such rock.

King Square Area

Generally considered the centre of Saint John, this square has trees, flowerbeds arranged in the form of the Union flag and a two-storey bandstand. In one corner stands the old **city market (E)**, where a variety of New Brunswick produce can be bought, including dulse. On the other side of the square, the **Loyalist burial ground (F)** can be seen.

Saint John City Market

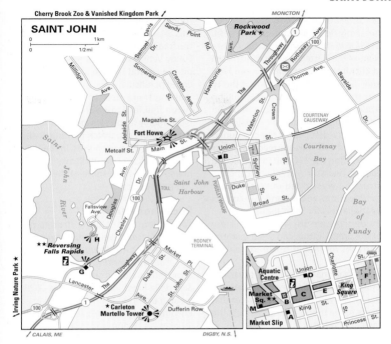

Cherry Brook Zoo & Vanished Kingdom Park /   MONCTON /

SAINT JOHN

/ CALAIS, ME   DIGBY, N.S. \

Additional Sights

Fort Howe Lookout

From Main St., go up Metcalf St., turn into a parking lot, go down Metcalf and turn left on Magazine St.

From this wooden blockhouse (o━┱) on a rocky cliff above the surrounding hills, there is a **panorama**★ of the docks, harbour, river and city.

Reversing Falls Rapids★★

Off Chesley Dr. (Rte. 100), south of downtown. To fully appreciate the rapids, visit at low tide, slack tide (🕐see below) and high tide. Check tide times online at www.tourismsaintjohn.com.

Where the Saint John River empties into the Bay of Fundy the tides are 8m/28ft high. At high tide when the bay water is more than 4m/14ft above river level, the water flows swiftly upstream. At low tide the bay is more than 4m/14ft below the level of the river, so the river rushes into it. As the tide rises, the rush of river water is gradually halted, and the river becomes as calm as a mill pond (slack tide) before gradually being reversed in direction. This reversal of the river current is marked just before the river—narrowing and curving around a bend in a deep gorge—enters the bay. The narrow bend creates rapids and whirlpools whenever the current is great in either direction, a phenomenon known as "reversing falls rapids."

Reversing Falls Bridge Lookout (G)

Parking at west end of bridge. Visitor centre ✕🅿🕐open mid-May–early Oct daily 8am–8pm; ☎506-658-2937; www.tourismsaintjohn.com. Take steps to roof. This lookout permits fine **views**★★ of the changing river current. Visitors unable to stay for the tidal cycle may enjoy the **film** *($2)*, which condenses the 24-hour event.

Falls View Park Lookout (H)

🅿*Parking at end of Falls View Ave.* The **views**★ of the rapids from the park are not as dramatic as those from the bridge.

Carleton Martello Tower★

454 Whipple St. West. From downtown, take Rte. 1 west to Exit 120 (for Digby Ferry); turn right on Duke St. W., left on

Lancaster Ave., right on Whipple. ⏱Open Jun–early Oct daily 10am–5:30pm. ⬤$4. ☎506-636-4011. www.pc.gc.ca.

None of the Martello towers constructed in British North America between 1796 and 1848 was ever attacked. Of the 16 constructed on the continent (including five in Halifax, Nova Scotia, and one in Saint John), 11 remain to this day. Built in 1813 as a defence for the city during the War of 1812, this Martello tower was used during the 19C and in both world wars. A two-storey steel and concrete structure was added in World War II to house anti-aircraft and fire-control headquarters for Saint John.

Inside, there are displays on the history of the area. Visitors can see a restored barracks room and restored powder magazine.

Now a National Historic Site, the tower provides a **panorama**★★ of the harbour, docks, rail yards and a breakwater that leads to Partridge Island, the bay, the river and the city.

Irving Nature Park★

Sand Cove Rd. From downtown, take Rte. 1 west to Exit 107; continue on Bleury St. to Sand Cove Rd., turn right and follow to end. ♿⏱Park open year round dawn–dusk. Information kiosk and auto loop open May–early Nov. ☎506-632-7777. www.ifdn.com/inp.

In 1992 J.D. Irving Limited—a large, diversified Atlantic Canada-based company that began as a sawmill in Bouc-

touche in the late 19C—established this 243ha/600-acre park to protect the fragile ecosystems along the Bay of Fundy. Vehicles are permitted seasonally on the coastal road that encircles the entire peninsula.

Walking trails, such as Seal Trail and Heron Trail, lead to areas where wildlife is commonly seen. From the observation deck, visitors can watch harbour seals, and maybe even porpoises, in the bay. A boardwalk has been built over the salt marsh for viewing some of the park's 250 bird species.

Rockwood Park★

Sandy Point Rd. Main entrance off Mount Pleasant Ave. From downtown, take Crown St. to Mount Pleasant Ave. ♿⏱Park open year-round daily 8am–dusk. Interpretation centre open May–Sept daily 10am–6pm. ☎506-658-2829. www. tourismsaintjohn.com.

Encompassing 870ha/2,200acres with 10 lakes, an 18-hole golf course, a campground, stables offering horseback rides, and a zoo, this urban park is unusual in Atlantic Canada, given its size and location within the city.

There are a dozen marked hiking trails, all a kilometre or less in length (downloadable trail map at www. tourismsaintjohn.com) and footpaths ideal for walking or jogging; one nature trail is paved for wheelchair access.

Lily Lake and the Fisher Lakes offer supervised swimming and sandy

Irving Nature Park

J.D. Irving Limited

beaches. The 18-hole golf course *(1255 Sandy Point Rd.; www.rockwoodparkgolf. com; ☎506-634-0090)* boasts the only aquatic driving range on Canada's east coast: balls hit into the water are later collected by boat. In winter horse-drawn sleigh rides are available.

Cherry Brook Zoo

Kids *901 Foster Thurston Dr., in Rockwood Park.* ♿️🕐*Open year round daily 10am– 6pm.* 🕐*Closed Dec 25.* ☜*$8.* ☎*506-634- 1440. www.cherrybrookzoo.com.*
This nonprofit zoo occupies 13ha/35 acres of land within Rockwood Park.

Aardwolves, marmosets, wildebeests, snow leopards and other exotic species live in natural, woodland settings. A boardwalk snakes through a wetlands habitat, permitting views of ducks, beavers and otters.

The Vanished Kingdom Park preserves lifesize replicas of extinct creatures, like the 10ft tall elephant bird, most of which disappeared within the past 100 years. The Endangered Species Awareness Centre displays illegal products confiscated at Canada's borders, such as those made from turtle shells.

WESTERN NEW BRUNSWICK

This part of the province has many attributes: its proximity to Maine, in the US, for day trips; the scenery of the Appalachian Mountains, where one can hike to the highest peak in the Maritime provinces; provincial parks that provide camping and other outdoor activities; and the province's longest river. The western border of New Brunswick is dominated by the Saint John River Valley, where the river runs two-thirds of its 673km/418mi course before curving east toward Fredericton. A major provincial attraction lies within this valley, Kings Landing Historical Settlement, and Hartland boasts the world's longest covered bridge. At Grand Falls gorge, the tranquil waterbody becomes turbulent, tumbling over 25m/76ft cataracts. Travellers who follow the river will not be disappointed: scenery ranges from farmland to mountains and forests—to say nothing of the beauty of the river itself.

Saint John River Valley★★

MAP INSIDE FRONT COVER

In the south the valley of this wide and scenic river is rolling and rural, supporting some of the richest farmland in New Brunswick. As travellers head north, the river traverses hilly, almost mountainous forests, the source of the province's substantial lumber industry. Settlements sprang up throughout the valley when some 4,000 of the Loyalists fleeing the US arrived here in 1783. In the 19C steamboats moved among these communities. Traffic took to the roads in the 1940s, but the valley remains the principal transportation, as the Trans-Canada Highway parallels it for much of its length in New Brunswick.

- ℹ️ **Information:** ☎800-561-0123. www.tourismnewbrunswick.ca.
- ▶ **Orient Yourself:** The Trans-Canada Highway parallels the river valley for 285km/177mi, from Fredericton to Edmundston, in the western part of the province, along its border with Maine.
- 😊 **Don't Miss:** Kings Landing and Grand Falls.
- 🕐 **Organizing Your Time:** Allow three full days to take the driving tour and do the sights of the valley justice.
- Kids **Especially for Kids:** Kings Landing has special programs for children, such as dressing up in 19C costumes and scavenger hunts.

Driving Tour

285km/177mi, from Fredericton to Edmundston.

Fredericton★★
♿*See FREDERICTON.*

▶ *Leave Fredericton on the Trans-Can Hwy. (Rte. 2).*

After traversing the provincial capital, the highway follows the river upstream to the Mactaquac Dam, New Brunswick's largest power project. The dam has created a reservoir, or head pond, about 150km/65mi long, affecting the valley as far as Woodstock. On the north bank of the head pond lies **Mactaquac Provincial Park** (♿*described in Fredericton chapter*), a haven for sports enthusiasts. The Trans-Canada Highway travels the south side of the pond with fine **views**★ as the country becomes increasingly rural.

Kings Landing Historical Settlement★★
Kids *37km/23mi. 20 Kings Landing Rd., in Kings Landing.* ✕◷*Open Jun–early Oct daily 10am–5pm.* ☞*$15.50.* ☎*506-363-4999. www.kingslanding.nb.ca.*
This restored village, which provides a glimpse of life from 1783 to 1900, has a beautiful **site** on the sloping banks

of the Saint John, beside a creek that joins the river via a small cove. Typical of the Loyalist riverbank settlements where lumbering, farming and some shipbuilding were principal occupations, the village provides an authentic glimpse of life in the river valley from 1783 to 1900.

After the American Revolutionary War, the land on which the village stands was given to veterans of the King's American Dragoons. When the Mactaquac dam project flooded their original sites, the houses and other buildings were moved here.

Apart from the well-restored farms with their fields of crops, the village has a church, school, forge, store and **theatre** with live entertainment (ask for details at the entrance). As they carry out routine chores, about 100 costumed interpreters explain aspects of 19C rural life.

Beside the millstream is an operating water-powered **sawmill.** Activated by a large waterwheel, a saw blade cuts through logs by moving along a wooden carriage. An example of a roadhouse of the period, the **Kings Head Inn** serves traditional refreshments. The commodious Morehouse residence stands near the elegant Ingraham house with its delightful garden overlooking the river.

Moored at the wharf (the "landing"), a half-size replica of a 19C **wood boat**

Kings Landing Historical Settlement

Brian Atkinson/New Brunswick Tourism

typifies vessels that transported lumber from sawmills and hay from farms to market.

Between Kings Landing and Woodstock, there are excellent **views**★★ of the Saint John River traversing lovely rolling country of farms and forests.

▶ *After Woodstock, leave Trans-Can Hwy. and take Rte. 103 to Hartland.*

Hartland★

120km/72mi. ☎*506-375-4357. www.town.hartland.nb.ca.*

Settled by Loyalists, this town in the centre of the potato-growing district is known for the longest **covered bridge** in the world. Completed in 1901 and rebuilt in 1920, the 391m/1,282ft bridge crosses the Saint John River in seven spans. Until 1960 the Trans-Canada Highway was routed over it, but today it links Routes 103 and 105.

As in other provinces, the first bridges built in New Brunswick were of wood, covered to protect the large timbers from weathering. These coverings could lengthen the lifespan of a bridge by 50 or 60 years.

Upon descending the hill on Route 103, note the good **view**★ of the bridge, which resembles a barnlike tunnel. The woodwork construction can be appreciated only from the interior *(cars can be driven through; no trucks).*

▶ *Take Rte. 105 on the east bank to Florenceville and Trans-Can Hwy. to Grand Falls.*

There are fine **views**★ from the highway of the river and farms of the agricultural area north of Florenceville. The Saint John gradually approaches the Maine border and enters the mountainous country of the north.

▶ *Leave Trans-Can Hwy. and enter Grand Falls.*

Grand Falls★★

219km/136mi. Falls and Gorge Commission: ☎*506-475-7769 or 877-475-7769. www.grandfalls.com.*

Built on a plateau above the river, this town is the centre of the potato belt.

Here the Saint John River changes suddenly and dramatically. The previously wide and tranquil river with gently sloping banks plunges over falls and, for about 1.6km/1mi, churns through a deep and narrow gorge. A power plant has diverted much of the water of the falls, but there are two good vantage points from which to see the gorge.

Falls Park

Accessible from Malabeam Information Centre on Madawaska Rd.; ✕&🕐*open Jul–Labour Day daily 9am–9pm; mid-May–late Jun & Labour Day–Oct daily 9am–6pm;* ☎*506-475-7788.*

This park offers a good **view**★ of the gorge and the falls below the power plant.

La Rochelle Centre★

In Centennial Park. Accessible from Malabeam Information Centre on Madawaska Rd. 🕐*Open daily late Jun–Labour Day 9am–9pm.* ▨*$3.* ☎*506-475-7766.*

Stairs descend into the gorge, which has walls as high as 70m/230ft in places. At the bottom, there are some deep holes in the rock called wells, but it is the **gorge**★★ that is impressive.

▶ *Continue north on Rte. 144.*

After Grand Falls the Saint John becomes wide and placid again, marking the Canadian/US border. The towns and villages seen across it are in Maine.

Edmundston

☎*506-737-1850 or 866-737-6766. www.ville.edmundston.nb.ca.*

Situated at the junction of the Madawaska and Saint John rivers, this industrial city, dominated by the twin-spired **Cathedral of the Immaculate Conception,** contrasts sharply with the rural landscape of the surrounding valley. Once called Petit-Sault ("little falls") to distinguish the rapids at the mouth of the Madawaska from those of Grand Falls, Edmundston was renamed in 1856 in honour of **Sir Edmund Head,** lieutenant-governor of New Brunswick from 1848 to 1854. The city's inhabitants are mainly French-speaking, although they claim Acadian, Quebecer, Indian,

Republic of Madawaska

Long contested among Ontario, Quebec, New Brunswick and the US, the land south of Lake Témiscouata in Quebec and New Brunswick, and the area north of the Aroostook River in Maine were once collectively called Madawaska. When bounderies were finally fixed, New Brunswick was left with the city of Edmundston and a thumb-shaped stretch of land. The long-standing dispute forged a spirited independence among the Madawaskans, who created for themselves a legend, rather than a political entity, a republic. Known as the Brayons because they crushed flax with a tool called a "brake," the Madawaskans have their own flag with an eagle and six stars (representing their different origins) and their own president, the mayor of Edmundston.

American, English and Irish origins. The **Madawaska Museum** presents the history of this region *(195 Herbert Blvd., at Trans-Can Hwy; ♿ ⏰ open daily 9am–8pm; ⌨$3.50; ☎506-737-5282)*.

Excursions

Mount Carleton Provincial Park

From Grand Falls, drive 17km/10.5mi north on Rte.2 to St. Leonard. From there, go 65km/40mi on Rte. 17 to St-Quentin. Exit on Rte.180 and take Rte. 385 to the park. ⚠ ⏰ Open mid-May—mid-Oct. Fee for campsites only. ☎506-235-0793. www.nbparks.ca.

Sited near the Nepisiguit River, within the Appalachian Mountain range, this 17,000ha/42,000-acre provincial park holds the highest peak in the Maritime provinces, Mount Carleton, which rises 820m/2,690ft; on its summit stands an old fire tower. A magnet for hikers, the park maintains some 62km/38mi of trails. Anglers are attracted to Atlantic salmon and trout in the Nepisiguit River, and bird watchers can search for up to 150 bird species. Canoeists will find a quiet paddle on Nictau and Nepisiguit lakes. And nature lovers should watch for moose and white-tailed deer. Camp-

ers come for the scenic beauty and isolation of the area *(the park's 88 campsites are unserviced, but toilets, showers and fresh water are available).*

Campbellton

From Grand Falls, drive 17km/10.5mi north on Rte.2 to St. Leonard. From there, go 157km/97mi on Rte. 17. Visitor centre, Salmon Blvd. (near bridge). ☎506-789-2367. www.campbellton.org.

The small city of Campbellton sits on the south bank of the Restigouche River at the western end of Chaleur Bay. Rising behind the town is Sugarloaf Mountain. Because of its proximity to the Quebec border, the community bills itself as the "gateway to the Maritimes." Officially opened in 1961, the huge Van Horn Bridge crosses the river to Quebec's Gaspesie Peninsula. Known as a salmon capital, Campbellton hosts the Restigouche Salmon Festival the first week of July. The waterfront features a **lighthouse** that doubles as a youth hostel in the summer *(Campbellton Light House, 1 Ritchie St.; ☎506-789-2773; www.hihostels.ca).*

Sugarloaf Provincial Park

596 Val D'Amour Rd., in Atholville. From Grand Falls, drive 17km/10.5mi north on Rte. 2 to St. Leonard. Go 157km/97mi on Rte. 17 and take Exit 415 at Campbellton. Open daily year-round. Ski centre open mid-Dec to mid-Apr. ⚠ ⏰ ☎506-789-2366. www.nbparks.ca.

Twelve downhill ski trails for novice to advanced skiers make this park especially popular in winter. Sugarloaf Mountain's vertical drop of 155m/507ft affords the longest run in the province (1,070m/3,510ft). In addition there are cross-country trails encircling Prichard Lake, snowmobile trails, a hill designated for toboggan rides, and skating on the park's pond. Summer brings a wealth of activities, like tennis and volleyball, mountain biking, and hikes through forested wilderness. Visitors can scale Sugarloaf's 305m/1,000ft summit for a view of nearby Campbellton and the Restigouche River. Paddleboats can be rented, and there's even an alpine slide. The campground has a children's playground.

For the best little places, follow the leader.

Looking for the latest news on today's best hotels and restaurants? Pick up the Michelin Guide and look for the Bib Gourmand and Bib Hotel symbols. With 45,000 addresses in Europe, in every category and price range, the perfect place to dine or stay is never far away.

NOVA SCOTIA

POPULATION 935,106 – MAP INSIDE FRONT COVER

Extending north to south, Nova Scotia consists of Cape Breton Island, and a 565km/350mi-long peninsula, 130km/81mi at its widest. Linked to New Brunswick by the Isthmus of Chignecto, the province is surrounded by the Gulf of St. Lawrence, Atlantic Ocean, Northumberland Strait and Bay of Fundy, with 7,460km/4,625mi of serrated coastline. At the southwestern end lies Yarmouth, terminus for ferries from the US. In the northeast, on Cape Breton, North Sydney accommodates ferries from Newfoundland and Labrador. Nova Scotia's westernmost town is Amherst, on the New Brunswick border, and Halifax, the provincial capital, dominates the eastern seaboard. Nova Scotia's principal industries are manufacturing, agriculture, fisheries and mining. It is the most populous of the four Atlantic provinces: the majority of its residents cluster in and around Halifax. Of Nova Scotia's 900,000-plus people, 11 percent are bilingual; the majority of Francophones live in the southwest part of the province and on Cape Breton Island's west coast; on the island's east coast, a decidedly Scottish influence can be seen. Nova Scotia's aboriginal people, primarily the Mi'kmaq, reside throughout the province, but mainly in 13 First Nations communities.

- **Information:** Tourism Nova Scotia, ☎902-425-5781 or 800-565-0000. www.novascotia.com.
- **Don't Miss:** Cape Breton Island and its Cabot Trail, Lunenburg, Halifax, Annapolis Royal.
- **Organizing Your Time:** In this book, Nova Scotia is divided into six sections: Halifax Region, South Shore, Southwest Nova Scotia, Fundy Coast and Annapolis Valley, Central Nova Scotia and Cape Breton Island. Cape Breton Island is a day's drive northeast from Halifax. Day trips from Halifax to towns along the South Shore can be leisurely accomplished in a week. Annapolis Valley can be enjoyed in 2 or 3 days. Central Nova Scotia can be explored in 3 to 4 days. To fully appreciate the province, 7 to 10 days should be allotted.
- **Especially for Kids:** Louisbourg Fortress and the beaches on the South Shore or along the Northumberland coast.

©Sandra Phinney/Michelin

Chestico Days boat parade, Port Hood, Cape Breton Island

Practical Information

GETTING THERE

BY AIR

Robert L. Stanfield International Airport Halifax (YHZ) is located off Exit 6 from Hwy. 102, near Enfield, 35km/22mi northeast of downtown Halifax. It is the only airport in Atlantic Canada that offers pre-clearance for US customs and immigration. ☎902-873-4422. www.hiaa.ca. **Air Canada** and **Air Canada Jazz** offer flights from Europe and the US and from various Canadian cities to Halifax, and connections within Atlantic Canada. ☎514-393-3333, 902-429-7111 or 888-247-2262 (Canada/US). www.aircanada.ca.

US airlines that stop in Halifax include American Airlines (☎800-433-7300), Delta (☎800-221-1212), Continental (☎800-231-0856), Northwest (☎800-225-2525), and United (☎800-241-6522). Zoom Airlines (☎866-359-9666) has seasonal flights to and from Europe, as does Icelandair (☎800-223-5500).

From Halifax airport, a frequent **shuttle bus** drops customers off at downtown hotels for under $20, but a **taxi** from the airport will cost approximately $55. Cab companies: Yellow ☎902-420-0000. Casino ☎902-425-6666.

Porter Airlines (☎888-619-8622) flies from Montreal, Ottawa and Toronto to Halifax (its planes land at Toronto Island Airport, close to the Toronto's downtown). **WestJet** (☎888-937-8538) has flights to other cities in Canada.

Sydney Airport (YQY) on Cape Breton Island has five flights daily to Halifax and points beyond on Air Canada Jazz. ☎902-564-7720. www.sydneyairport.ca.

Yarmouth Airport (YQI) is reserved for non-commercial aircraft and private jets only. ☎902-742-6484.

BY BUS AND TRAIN

Bus travel within the province is provided by **Acadian Lines** (SMT-Eastern) (☎902-453-8912, or 800-567-5151. www.smtbus.com). **Cloud Nine Shuttle** (☎902-742-3992 or 1-888-805-3335.

www.thecoudnineshuttle.com) has daily shuttle service from Yarmouth to Halifax and back, and its schedules usually provide for convenient airport, train station or ferry terminal pick ups or drop offs. **Campbell's Shuttle Service** (☎902-742-6101 or 800-742-6101. www.campbell-shuttle-service.com) also provides daily service from Yarmouth to Halifax and back. **VIA Rail** connects Nova Scotia through Montreal (☎888-842-7245 Canada/US. www.viarail.ca).

BY BOAT

Passenger and car ferry service connects **Bar Harbor,** Maine (3hrs), with **Yarmouth** NS and **Portland,** Maine (5hrs 30min), with **Yarmouth** NS (departure times May 30–2nd week Oct 8am and 4pm, but service alternates between Bar Harbour and Portland). Check schedules. No service 3rd week Oct–May. Reservations required. US$10 port and security fee each way. US$69/person Bar Harbor, US$99/person Portland. US$115/vehicle Bar Harbor, US$164/vehicle Portland. Fuel surcharge US$25/vehicle. ☎877-359-3760 (Canada/US). www.catferry.com

Saint John NB with **Digby NS** (departs daily year-round. One-way 2hrs 45min. Reservations required. $80/vehicle, $50/passenger plus $20 fuel surcharge).

For ferry schedules and reservations, contact Bay Ferries (☎800-249-7245, Canada/US. www.bayferries.com).

GETTING AROUND

BY CAR

Rental Cars

Major car-rental companies can be found at the Halifax and Sydney airports and at the Yarmouth ferry terminal (seasonal). Other cities or towns that have at least one car rental office include Halifax, Sydney, Yarmouth, Truro, Bridgewater, Westville (Stellarton), Port Hastings and Port Hawkesbury. Note that fees for car rentals from airport offices are generally higher than at a downtown location.

AvisCar – www.avis.com, Halifax Airport ☎902-429-0963, Reservations Canada: ☎800-879-2847, Reservations USA: ☎800-331-1212.

Budget – www.budget.com, Halifax Airport – ☎902-492-7551, Reservations – ☎800-268-8900

Enterprise Rent-A-Car – www.enterprise.com, Halifax Airport – ☎902-873-4700, Reservations – 800-261-7331

Hertz Canada – www.hertz.com, Halifax Airport – ☎902-873-2273, Reservations – ☎800-263-0600

National/Alamo – www.national.com, www.alamo.com, Halifax Airport – ☎902-873-3505, Reservations – National: ☎800-227-7368, Reservations – Alamo: ☎800-522-9696

Thrifty/Dollar – www.thrifty.com, www.dollar.com, Halifax Airport – ☎902-873-3527, Reservations – Dollar Rent A Car: ☎800-800-4000, Reservations – Thrifty Car Rental: ☎800-847-4389

GENERAL INFORMATION

VISITOR INFORMATION

For a free copy of a tourist guide and a map, contact Tourism Nova Scotia. PO Box 456, Halifax, NS, B3J 2R5, Canada. ☎902-425-5781 or 800-565-0000 (Canada/US). www.novascotia.com. There are visitor information centres throughout the province, specifically at Amherst, Digby, Halifax (2), Peggy's Cove, Pictou, Port Hastings and Yarmouth. There are also Nova Scotia Visitor Information Centres in Bar Harbor and Portland, Maine.

ACCOMMODATIONS

♿ *For a selection of lodgings, see the Address Books in the individual chapters in this guide.*

Nova Scotia Assoc. of Unique Country Inns www.uniquecountryinns.com

Canada Select ☎902-424-8929 www.canadaselect.com

RESERVATION SERVICES

Check In Nova Scotia arranges hotel, motel and B&B reservations throughout the province (and the rest of Atlantic Canada) at no charge and offers general tourist information. ☎800-565-0000. www.checkinnovascotia.com.

ROAD REGULATIONS

Nova Scotia has good paved roads; some interior roads are loose-surface. Speed limits, unless otherwise posted, are 100km/h (62mph) on the Trans-Canada Highway, 80km/h (50mph) on highways and 50km/h (30mph) in cities and towns. Right turns are permitted at red lights. Seat belt use is mandatory. Canadian Automobile Assn. (CAA), Halifax ☎902-443-5530; www.caa.ca.

TIME ZONE

Nova Scotia is on Atlantic Standard Time. Daylight Saving Time is observed from the 2nd Sunday in March to 1st Sunday in November.

TAXES

In Nova Scotia, the national General Services Tax (GST) has been combined with the provincial sales tax to form the Harmonized Sales Tax (HST). The HST for Nova Scotia is levied at a single rate of 13% (some items are exempt). There is no longer a federal or provincial rebate program for international visitors.

LIQUOR LAWS

The legal drinking age is 19. Liquor is sold in government stores and in some retail outlets, and is served in licensed bars and restaurants. Licensed vineyards may also serve wine and many special events have temporary liquor permits for the duration.

RECREATION

Nova Scotia offers a range of outdoor activities for exercise and adventure. Kejimkujik National Park is a large camping park in the southern interior with many lakes and rivers: **canoeing and kayaking** are popular there. A special national park licence for **anglers** is required, but there is ample opportunity for swimming, cycling, hiking and bird-watching, as well. At the other end of the province, Cape Breton Highlands National Park is known for its spectacular ocean scenery; camping and **hiking** its many trails is a must for the outdoor enthusiast. The beaches of the South Shore attract local **surfers,** even in winter, although waves only reach great heights in severe weather. Ocean swimming is not popular in Nova Scotia, due to the cool water temperature, but the beaches—some virtually empty even in mid-summer—are ideal for beachcombing, picnicking, walking or jogging. The province is blessed with lakes and rivers, and those, especially within the provincial parks, are best for swimming. Whale watching companies dot the narrow piece of land known as Digby Neck, and similar companies can be found on the west coast of Cape Breton. In Yarmouth, three **golf** courses within an hour's drive of each offer very reasonable green fees.

PRINCIPAL FESTIVALS

May–Jun **Apple Blossom Festival:** *Annapolis Valley*

Jul **Seafest** *Yarmouth and area*

Nova Scotia International Tattoo: *Halifax*

Metropolitan Scottish Festival and Highland Games: *Halifax*

Antigonish Highland Games: *Antigonish*

Gathering of the Clans and Fishermen's Regatta: *Pugwash*

Acadian Days: *Grand-Pré*

Festival acadien de Clare: *Meteghan*

Festival acadien international de Par-en-Bas: *West Pubnico*

Aug **Nova Scotia Gaelic Mod:** *St. Anns*

International Buskerfest: *Halifax*

Natal Day: *Province-wide*

Sept **Fisheries Exhibition & Fishermen's Reunion:** *Lunenburg*

Kentville Pumpkin People: *Kentville*

Oct **Octoberfest:** *Lunenburg*

Celtic Colours Festival: *Cape Breton*

Feb **Ice Wine Festival:** *Wolfville*

Savour Food & Wine Festival: *Halifax*

A Bit of Geography

The mainland is largely flat terrain, except for a rocky, indented eastern shore and a forested interior (maximum elevation of 210m/689ft). **South Mountain** forms the northern border of this upland interior. Stretching from Cape Blomidon to the tip of Digby Neck, the **North Mountain** range parallels South Mountain for 190km/118mi along the Bay of Fundy shore. Sheltered between them is the heart of the province's apple industry, the fertile Annapolis and Cornwallis river valleys. The cropped 300m/984ft **Cobequid Mountain** extends 120km/74mi over Cumberland County, which borders the Isthmus of Chignecto.

Northern Cape Breton Island is mostly a wooded plateau rising to 532m/1,745ft above sea level, a height that permits expansive views of the wildly beautiful, often mist-enshrouded coastline. At the northern end stretches **Cape Breton Highlands National Park,** with its celebrated driving route, the Cabot Trail. Culminating in the Strait of Canso, the south is predominantly a lowland. A vast inland sea 930sq km/359sq mi wide, **Bras d'Or Lake** nearly bisects the island.

Sandra Phinney/Michelin

Kayaks near Gilbert's Cove Lighthouse at St. Mary's Bay

A Bit of History

Earliest Inhabitants – Before the arrival of Europeans, Nova Scotia was inhabited by the **Mi'kmaq** people, who have called the province their ancestral home for millennia. These indigenous people were skillful hunter-gatherers who lived off the land and fished the rich coastal waters, lakes and rivers. Their language derives from the Algonquin family of languages. The Mi'kmaq call themselves *L'nu'k* ("the people"), and the word Mi'kmaq comes from the word *nikmak*, meaning "my kin-friends." Mi'kmaw is the singular form of Mi'kmaq. When the early French settlers began arriving in the area, the Mi'kmaq welcomed them, sharing their skills with these ancestors of the Acadians. Over the centuries, the Mi'kmaq survived conversion to Catholicism, treaties with Britain, and epidemics that greatly reduced their numbers. They continued friendly relations with the Francophone population. Intermarriage was not uncommon.

Of the province's estimated 24,000 indigenous people, more than 15,000 identify themselves as Mi'kmaq. Today they live in communities throughout the province, including Acadia First Nations the Annapolis Valley and Glooscap. Their intricate handiwork, especially basketry and quillwork, is highly prized and can be found in the Museum of Natural History in Halifax, the DesBrisay Museum in Bridgewater and the Rossignol Cultural Centre in Liverpool.

Acadie – In 1604 French explorers Sieur de Monts and **Samuel de Champlain** established **Port Royal** in Nova Scotia. The fort eventually was captured by the British in 1613 and held nearly 20 years before it was returned to the French, who called a vague area covering pockets of the province, as well as the other Maritimes *Acadie* (Acadia). French claims to the region ended in 1713, with the Treaty of Utrecht, which gave Acadians the choice of leaving British territory or becoming British subjects. Following a tragic event in 1747 at Grand Pré *(see Annapolis Valley)*, the British governor issued an ultimatum in 1755—take an unqualified oath of allegiance or be removed from Nova Scotia. For religious and other reasons, such as fear of having to fight other Frenchmen, the Acadians refused. Over the next eight years, 14,600 Acadians were forcibly deported in what has become known in provincial history as the **Deportation.** When peace was restored between England and France in 1763, most exiles returned to settle mainly in New Brunswick, and in southwest Nova Scotia, where their descendants live to this day.

The Arrival of the Loyalists – After Deportation the British offered free land to anyone willing to settle in Nova Scotia. New Englanders from the south, English immigrants from the British Isles, Germans from the Rhineland, and Scottish Highlanders accepted the offer. After the American Revolutionary War, as many as 100,000 Americans remained loyal to the British Crown but were not wanted there. Beginning in 1782, many of these "Loyalists" moved to Canada, a British territory, including many slaves who had fought on the side of Britain in the American colonies. This mass movement of loyal British subjects to Canada greatly shaped the country's development. Fishing, timber harvesting, shipbuilding and whaling became major occupations. Trade expanded from local ports to the distant shores of the West Indies and Europe.

Hauling in a catch

Sandra Phinney/Michelin

Seafaring Nation – One great industry established by the Loyalists was **shipbuilding.** Blanketed by virgin forest, little of which remains today, the province used its rich timber resources to bring prosperity to its inhabitants, especially during the Napoleonic Wars (1803-15) when Britain's need for wooden ships and ship parts was great. Along the south coast, Nova Scotia's schooners became legend, as did the sailors who manned them—universally called **Bluenoses,** an American term of derision for people who could survive the region's cold climate. More than a few fortunes were made from privateering: the east coast's plentiful coves and inlets, particularly around Liverpool, once concealed many an anchored pirate ship. Piracy diminished under threat of prosecution, and by 1900 the prominence of shipbuilding waned. Steam replaced sail power: steel hulls superseded wooden ones.

A Mix of Cultures – What began initially as a clash of European nationalities in the New World has slowly evolved into a largely harmonious mix of cultures in the province. Nova Scotia is peppered with the descendants of those early French, English Scottish and black settlers. Later arrivals included immigrants from Germany, Italy, Holland, and the Baltic countries. Today's newcomers hail from around the world, but there has been a marked increase in Irish, Asian, Arab and American immigrants to the province in recent years.

Traditional Dishes - Acadia's rappie pie, Cape Breton lamb, Scottish oat cakes and the truly Nova Scotian blueberry grunt tempt visitors to partake of **regional cookery** harking back to Samuel de Champlain's gourmandise. The gastronomy of his Order of Good Cheer endures in the province's formalized food promotion, **"Taste of Nova Scotia,"** *(www.tasteofnovascotia.com)* which has a membership of over 45 dining establishments, food producers and processors.

The province encourages **arts and crafts** through its design centre, and college of art and design in Halifax. Rug-hooking guilds, craft cooperatives and quilting groups are common across Nova Scotia. Acadian crafts are featured along the west coast of Cape Breton Island, and Gaelic wares abound along the east coast. Mi'kmaq baskets and moccasins are available in shops on Cape Breton Island as well as other locations.

Preserving the Past – Nova Scotia boasts more historic sites than any province in Canada except Quebec. Administered by the provincial museum system known as **Nova Scotia Museum,** some 27 historic sites from heritage houses to restored mills are open to the public. Since 1959 the Heritage Trust of Nova Scotia, a registered charity, has promoted the need for heritage preservation legislation. It also provides input on legislative policy to the municipalities and the provincial government, and has been able to designate more than 100 buildings throughout Nova Scotia with heritage status .

Genealogy is popular here: local museums, schools and universities, genealogical societies and churches have archival facilities for tracing one's roots. The migration of Nova Scotia's black population is chronicled in Dartmouth, New England's planter immigrants in Kentville. Descendants of Dutch, English, French, German, Greek, Hungarian, Irish, Italian, Lebanese and Polish settlers diversify the population.

Various cultural events and festivals preserve ancestral traditions, one of the largest being the International **Gathering of the Clans,** a tribute to the province's Scottish beginnings as "New Scotland" and a celebration of the culture, language and heritage of the Scots in Nova Scotia. Special events, the "gatherings," are held annually from April to August in many areas of the province. In southwest Nova Scotia, two summer **Acadian festivals** are held from mid-July to mid-August in Clare and Argyle, the *joie de vivre* of the Acadian people is celebrated with parades, concerts, talent shows, fishing competitions and theatre performances. Beginning in 2008, Cajun musicians from Louisiana were invited to perform at the festival in Argyle.

HALIFAX REGION

Located on the south coast of peninsular Nova Scotia, the Halifax Regional Municipality (coined locally as the "HRM") includes the capital city of Halifax and the city of Dartmouth. Encompassing 5,776sq km/2,153sq mi, with over 400km/250mi of coastline, it boasts the world's second-largest natural harbour, which also happens to be the deepest on earth that remains free of ice throughout the year. Incorporated in 1996, the municipality comprises an amalgamation of Halifax, Dartmouth, Bedford, Sackville and surrounding communities. More than one-third of Nova Scotians live in the HRM. Sister city to Halifax, Dartmouth sits across the harbour, accessible by two suspension bridges and the oldest continual saltwater ferry service in North America (1752). Dartmouth was incorporated as a town in 1873, but it wasn't until 1955 when the Angus L. MacDonald Bridge opened that the community began to thrive as a residential and commercial centre. The A. Murray MacKay Bridge opened in 1970, spurring further growth. The Halifax Regional Municipality has become Atlantic Canada's financial, cultural and tourism powerhouse. As a transportation hub served by rail, air and sea, the Halifax Region makes a good place to start an exploration of Nova Scotia as well as Canada's other eastern provinces.

Halifax★★★

POPULATION 359,183 – MAP P 96

Situated on the east coast at about the mainland's midpoint, the capital of Nova Scotia overlooks one of the finest harbours in the world. The deep outer inlet of the Atlantic Ocean narrows into a protected inner harbour called the **Bedford Basin.** Halifax is the largest city in the Atlantic provinces and the region's commercial and financial heart. Nova Scotia's administrative hub and an important centre for scientific research, Halifax is also a major seaport and serves as the Atlantic base of the **Canadian navy.** Lined with docks, oil refineries, a container terminal and grain elevator, the 6.5km/4mi-long harbour narrows before expanding into the Bedford Basin. The foot-shaped peninsula upon which the city was built is dominated by a hill, topped with a star-shaped citadel. These two factors—a natural harbour and a man-made fortress—were the basis of the city's founding. Halifax's hilly streets are stacked with colourful houses. Directly across the harbour lies Dartmouth, accessible by two bridges and regular ferry service. During the summer months, activities along Halifax's waterfront intensify: seaside restaurants and cafes bustle, vendors and live performers line the boardwalk, boats from nearby yacht clubs fill the harbour and large cruise ships linger in port. The harbour and citadel so crucial to Halifax's settlement continue to serve as centres of attractions for an ever-widening audience of admirers.

🛈 **Information:** Visitor Centres: Scotia Square, 5251 Duke St., and on the waterfront at Sackville Landing. Halifax Tourism ☎902-490-4000. www.halifaxinfo.com.

▶ **Orient Yourself:** 🕒*See map.* Downtown Halifax, with shops, hotels and restaurants, is bordered by Duke Street (north), Inglis Street (south), South Park Street (west) and Water Street and the harbourfront (east). The two main arteries are Barrington Street, running north to south, and Spring Garden Road, running west to east. If driving, be aware of one-way streets downtown, and slower traffic along the two main streets. Shops and restaurants, as well as the Historic Properties, Maritime Museum of the Atlantic and the Art Gallery overlook the harbour in and around Water Street. Above downtown is the Halifax Citadel. Many streets are hilly, sloping down from the hill on which the citadel is located. The MacDonald toll bridge connects downtown Halifax to downtown Dartmouth; it is the only bridge that accommodates pedestrians and bicycles. At the tip of Point Pleasant Park, in the south end, **North West Arm,** a narrow inlet of water, extends 3.5km/2mi along the peninsula's west side.

🅿 **Parking:** Downtown Halifax is quite congested and parking is difficult. Meters are colour-coded to indicate the maximum time you may park: red means 30min, grey 1hr, green 2hrs and yellow 5hrs; the rate is $1/hr. There are also public and private lots. The A. Murray MacKay Bridge and the Angus L. MacDonald Bridge are toll bridges: 75 cents per crossing.

😊 **Don't Miss:** The citadel and a harbour cruise.

🕐 **Organizing Your Time:** You will need at least 3 days to see Halifax. It is a good base from which to tour the area, in which case, allow a minimum 5 days.

🄺🄸🄳🅂 **Especially for Kids:** The Maritime Museum of the Atlantic and the Museum of Natural History.

👣 **Also See:** FUNDY COAST AND ANNAPOLIS VALLEY

A Bit of History

Early History – Halifax came into being because of the Fortress of Louisbourg. New Englanders had successfully captured the French fortress in 1745, only to see it later returned to France. Their anger prodded the British government to build a fort as a counterweight to the Louisbourg. In 1749 Halifax was founded with 2,500 English settlers who could provision the army. They constructed a fortified settlement on the site of the present-day city. From its inception Halifax was a military stronghold filled with soldiers and sailors.

The Royal Princes – Forbidden by their father to remain in England, two scapegrace sons of **George III** made Halifax their home. The future **William IV** spent his 21st birthday in wild revels off the port. His brother **Edward,** Duke of Kent, and later the father of Queen Victoria, served as commander in chief in Halifax from 1794 to 1800. Spending a fortune on defences, he made Halifax a member of the famous quadrilateral of British defences, which included Gibraltar and Bermuda. He installed the first telegraph system in North America by which he could relay orders to his men.

The City Today – As a major port city, Halifax is expected to welcome some 220,000 cruise ship passengers in 2008. In 2007 the Halifax Port Authority handled 12 million tonnes of cargo, the bulk of the container ships arriving from Europe and Asia. Thanks to

Ferry to Dartmouth in Halifax Harbour

Bruce Bishop/Michelin

Practical Information

AREA CODES

Halifax Regional Municipality (HRM) shares the same area code (902) with all of Nova Scotia. Locals calls can be made by dialling the seven-digit local number only; long-distance calls within Nova Scotia will require the addition of the 902 area code. For more information: ☎800-665-6000 or www.aliant.ca.

GETTING AROUND

BY PUBLIC TRANSPORTATION

The municipality operates a public transit system, Metro Transit, of buses and ferries within HRM (Halifax, Dartmouth, Bedford). Hours of operation: **Buses** Mon–Sun 6am–1am. **Ferries** run frequently, with increased frequency during rush hours (a 12min service between Halifax and Dartmouth), Mon–Sat 6am–midnight, Sun 6am–6:30pm. Cash **fare** for an adult is $2.50 (pre-paid fare is $2). Bulk ticket purchase: 20 for $32. Tickets are available at most drug stores, bookstores (including universities), bus terminals, Lotto booths and Sobey's grocery store. System maps & timetables available free of charge. Route information ☎902-490-4000 or 800-835-6428 or www.halifax.ca/metrotransit.

*Downtown Halifax merchants offer a service called FRED (**free rides** everywhere downtown) early July to late October to accommodate tourists in the city. Routes and stops are specifically labeled; for details ☎902-423-6658 or www.downtownhalifax.ns.ca.*

ACCESSIBILITY

Throughout the municipality, visitors with mobility concerns can use **wheelchair-accessible** bus and taxi service ($24; Need-a-Lift Transportation Services; ☎902-222-5438; www.needalift.ca) or Access-a-Bus (☎902-490-6999; www.halifax.ca/metrotransit); hearing-impaired travellers can access an interpreter: ☎902-429-5752; www.deafliteracynovascotia.ca); and those with vision problems can get audio versions of printed materials from www.voiceprintcanada.com.

BY CAR

Two bridges connect Halifax and Dartmouth, and tend to be very busy during weekday rush hours. Downtown Halifax is small enough to park the car and walk virtually everywhere; public parking facilities are marked with a green P-in-a-circle sign; private lots may be marked differently. There is no central information system for parking lots and street spaces, but information about specific locations may be obtained by accessing ☎902-490-4000 or 800-835-6428 or www.halifax.ca.
Car rentals: Avis ☎902-492-2847. Discount ☎902-468-7171. Enterprise ☎800-736-8222. Budget ☎902-492-7500.

BY TAXI

Taxi stands are located at high-traffic buildings downtown, but hailing or flagging a cab on a busy street is a rarity. It's best to call ahead one of the several taxi companies available. From the **airport,** a frequent shuttle bus drops customers off at downtown hotels for under $20, but a taxi from the airport will cost approximately $55. Cab companies: Yellow ☎902-420-0000. Casino ☎902-425-6666.

GENERAL INFORMATION

VISITOR INFORMATION

Visitor Centres: Scotia Square, 5251 Duke St., and on the waterfront at Sackville Landing. ☎902-490-4000. www.halifaxinfo.com.

ACCOMMODATIONS

For a listing of suggested hotels, ⌖see the Address Book. For **hotels/motels** contact **Destination Halifax** (☎877-422-9334; www.destinationhalifax.com). Hotels, motels, inns and bed & breakfasts can be booked through **Check In Nova Scotia** ☎800-565-0000, a free reservations service.

LOCAL MEDIA

Daily: *Halifax Chronicle Herald* (www.thechronicleherald.ca) and *Globe and Mail* (www.globeandmail.ca); *The Metro* is a free local daily. **Weekly:** *The Coast* (www.thecoast.ca). **Monthly:** *Where Halifax* (www.where.ca/Halifax) magazine, and free guides to entertainment, shopping, and restaurants.

The **Canadian Broadcasting Corporation** (CBC) has both TV and radio studios in downtown Halifax, transmitting local, national and international news and programming to Nova Scotians. CBC-Halifax also hosts the taping of its popular weekly comedy show, "This Hour has 22 Minutes."

SPORTS

Although no major league sports teams hail from the city, **hockey** and **baseball** are near and dear to Haligonians. The Halifax Mooseheads, Halifax Wolverines and Halifax Thunder excite their respective hockey fans, while the Halifax Pelham Canadians and the Dartmouth Moosehead Dry baseball teams attract their own admirers. Varsity sports are big between rivals Saint Mary's and Dalhousie universities. **Huskies Stadium** (923 Robie St.; www.stmarys.ca) on Saint Mary's University campus and the **Halifax Metro Centre** (Argyle St.; ☎902-421-1302) at the convention centre are the largest venues in the area for football and hockey games.

ENTERTAINMENT

Nightly live music is almost de rigueur at downtown lounges and pubs; coffeehouses and bookstores abound; cultural pursuits at Dalhousie's Cohn Auditorium, the Maritime Museum of the Atlantic, and various art galleries, including the Art Gallery of Nova Scotia are frequent and year-round.

Consult the arts and entertainment supplements in local newspapers for schedules of cultural events and addresses of principal theatres and concert halls. Tickets are available from Ticket Atlantic ☎902-451-1221. Tickets for the Rebecca Cohn Auditorium direct ☎902-494-3820 or 800-874-1669 or www.artcentre.dal.ca/cohn.html. Tickets for The Music Room and Chamber Music Society ☎902-429-9467 or www.themusicroom.ca.

Performing Arts

Neptune Theatre – 1593 Argyle St. ☎902-429-7070 or 800-565-7345. www.neptunetheatre.com. For 45 years, this theatre has delighted thousands of patrons with professionally staged musicals, dramas and comedies. A showcase for maritime talent, the Neptune balances fresh compositions by new artists with traditional favourites. Many productions have been written by regional playwrights and performed by local actors and dancers as well as international stars. Operating seasonally (Sept–May, sometimes to Jul), the Neptune allots most shows a month and-a-half run, although the first regional production of the popular Les Miserables extended well beyond that. Initially built as a vaudeville house and later used as a cinema, the structure was converted in 1963 to a playhouse. In 1997a multimillion-dollar transformation resulted in virtually a new complex with improved seating, air-conditioning, an expanded backstage area and intimate studio space.

The Cohn (Rebecca Cohn Auditorium at Dalhousie University) – 6101 University Ave., ☎902-494-3820. This auditorium is Halifax's premiere venue for showcasing local, national and international musical/theatrical talent. From classical and gospel to country and comedy, there is always a good show at The Cohn.

Tours

Alexander Keith's Nova Scotia Brewery – 1496 Lower Water St. ☎902-455-1474. www.keiths.ca. Brewery tours can be boring, but this tour of the place that makes the province's most famous beer is quite entertaining. "Employees" in period costume recount the brewery's history (Keith was a Scot who made a fortune brewing ale in Halifax starting in 1863) and then usher visitors into a tasting room, where the hosts' vocal chords get a workout on pub songs and Gaelic ballads. After the tour visitors may opt to dine at the on-site **restaurant ($)**, which serves light fare.

McNabs Island – Guided history and nature tours of McNabs Island in Halifax Harbour. McNabs Island Ferry operates year-round. Call for tour times: ☎902-465-4563 or 800-326-4563. www.mcnabsisland.com.

Nightlife

The Dome – 1726-1740 Argyle St., ☎902-422-5453. www.thedome.ca.

Open Wednesday through Saturday nights, this large nightclub is an old favourite among Haligonians. Local and visiting DJs are featured, and the six bars stay open as late as 3:30am.

The Maxwell's Plum – *1600 Grafton St.,* ✕ ☎*902-423-5090. www.themaxwells-plum.com.* This friendly Halifax pub has 60 beers on tap and serves cheap and pleasant eats. Available from 11am to 3pm, the weekend brunch is hearty and relaxing.

Reflections Cabaret – *5184 Sackville St.,* ☎*902-422-2957.* This busy night spot appeals to a wide range of club-goers who have in common the desire to have fun dancing or watching everything from drag contests to talent shows. It attracts a mixed-age crowd of 20 somethings to those in their mid-50s, depending upon the night.

The Split Crow – *1855 Granville St.,* ✕ ☎*902-422-4366.* This very popular pub is frequented by rockers, CEOs and university kids. Live "east coast" music nightly adds to the party atmosphere.

USEFUL NUMBERS ☎

- **Police 911 (emergency). Police 902-490-5016 (non-emergency)**
- **Halifax Train Station** (VIA Rail) 1161 Hollis St. VIA Rail 1-888-842-7245 or www.viarail.ca
- **Halifax (Robert Stanfield) Inter-national Airport** 902-873-4422 or 866-207-1690. www.hiaa.ca

- **Canadian Automobile Assn.** 3514 Joseph Howe Dr. 902-443-5530
- **CAA Emergency Road Service** (24hr) 416-222-5222
- **Shoppers Drug Mart** (24hr pharmacy) *various locations* 902-429-2400
- **Post Office** (locations in virtually all drug stores)
- **Road Conditions** Dial 511 or www.theweathernetwork.ca
- **Weather** (24hr) www.halifax.ca (click on "Visitors")

SHOPPING

High-end and eclectic shops offering fashions, antiques and home decor can be found along **Spring Garden Road** and **Barrington Street** in downtown Halifax. **Scotia Square** is an indoor shopping centre *(Duke and Barrington Sts).* More tourist-oriented shops are clustered on the waterfront in the **Historic Properties;** fine art galleries are here. Nova Scotia has many local artists and artisans, and the galleries showcase their works. The **Hyrdostone Market** area is a small, funky shopping district that offers boutiques, specialty food shops and interesting gift stores. Numerous malls dot the suburban landscape, such as **Mic Mac Mall** in Dartmouth. Sunday shopping has only recently become legal in Nova Scotia. Sunday hours for general merchandise shops are commonly noon to 4pm; stores are closed on major holidays.

Address Book

♿*For dollar sign categories, see the Legend on the cover flap.*

WHERE TO STAY

$ Fountain View Guest House – *2138 Robie St.* ☎*902-422-4169 or 800-565-4877. www.angelfire.com/id/fountain-view. 8 rooms.* 🅿 Situated across from Halifax Commons and a short walk from Citadel Hill, this guest house lies close to restaurants and commercial services. Fountain View offers variously sized, clean rooms with shared bathrooms. For an extra charge, a light breakfast can be served in your room.

$ Fresh Start B&B – *2720 Gottingen St.* ☎*902-453-6616 or 888-453-6616. www. bbcanada. com/2262.html. 8 rooms.* 🅿 ☲ This restored two-storey Victorian house is located near Macdon-ald Bridge, about a mile from Citadel Hill. Clean, simply furnished rooms come with private or shared bathroom. Breakfast features fresh-baked pastries and fruit salad with eggs Benedict, ham and cheese casserole or hot egg salad on an English muffin.

$$ Four Points Sheraton – *1496 Hollis St. 177 rooms.* ✕♿🅿☲ ☎*902-423-4444. www.starwoodhotels.com.* Located within walking distance of many downtown attractions, this moderately sized hotel is friendly, clean and comfortable. Families with children appreciate the small indoor pool and hot tub; a modest but sufficient fitness centre adjoins it. Free wireless Internet and indoor passage to a shopping mall with a food court and bar/restaurant help make this property appealing to the budget-conscious traveller. Indoor parking available *(fee)*.

$$ Halliburton House Inn – *5184 Morris St.* ☎*902-420-0658 or 888-512-3344. www.halliburton.ns.ca. 29 rooms.* ✗🅿🛏 Housed in three contiguous early 19C town houses, this downtown hostelry has the charm of a country inn. A tasteful sitting room with wing chairs, oil portraits and a fireplace greets arriving guests. Rates include a light breakfast. Enjoy the garden courtyard in summer. **Stories ($$$)**, the hotel restaurant, is renowned for its inventive fusion-style entrées (caribou ravioli, ahi tuna with Asian tomato vinaigrette); it is open to non-guests by reservation (☎*902-420-0658)*.

$$ The Lord Nelson Hotel and Suites – *1515 South Park St.* ☎*902-423-6331 or 800-565-2020. www.lordnelsonhotel.com. 260 rooms.* ✗♿🅿 Recently overhauled, this 1928 landmark, built by the Canadian Pacific Railway, preserves its Edwardian ambience while offering 21C amenities. The spacious lobby has warm walnut panelling and a coffered ceiling. Renovated rooms are decorated in soothing colours; many overlook the Public Gardens. The English pub-style **Victory Arms ($)** restaurant, open to non-guests, serves three meals.

$$ Prince George Hotel – *1725 Market St.* ☎*902-425-1986 or 800-565-1567. www.princegeorgehotel.com. 203 rooms.* ✗♿🅿🛏 Situated in the heart of downtown near the Metro Centre (a hockey and entertainment venue) and six blocks from the waterfront, the Prince George features a fitness centre with state-of-the-art exercise equipment and a heated indoor pool. **Gio ($$$)** restaurant offers a sophisticated menu of contemporary cuisine accented with local products, such as sablefish with herb risotto, or lamb with roasted beets and blue potatoes to guests and non-guests alike (for reservations, ☎902-425-1987). For excursions, the hotel will pack a lunch for you.

$$ Waverley Inn – *1266 BarringtonSt.* ☎*902-423-9346 or 800-565-9346. www.waverleyinn.com. 34 rooms.* ♿🅿🛏 Guest rooms in this historic 1870s inn are richly furnished with Victorian antiques, massive wooden beds and modern amenities. Deluxe quarters feature feather duvets and whirlpool baths. A hospitality suite provides round-the-clock snacks as well as a complimentary breakfast.

WHERE TO EAT

$ Bluenose II Restaurant – *1824 Hollis St.* ♿ ☎*902-425-5092.* **Greek.** For over 25 years the Bluenose has been serving home-style food at wallet-pleasing prices at the corner of Duke and Hollis, near Historic Properties. Famous for milk shakes, clams and chips, and Greek staples like souvlaki and moussaka, the restaurant also offers vegetarian selections such as spinach lasagna, fettuccine Alfredo and veggie burgers. Its breads and pastries are house-made.

$ Cellar Bar & Grill – *5677 Breton Pl., off South Park St.* ☎*902-492-4412.* **Mediterranean.** This two-room establishment caters chiefly to a loyal clientele with its wood-burning fireplaces and knowledgeable staff. A variety of gourmet pizzas (smoked salmon and chèvre) and pastas (sausage and peppers; spinach and prosciutto; or curried chicken and shrimp) are offered along with entrées such as haddock, salmon, and jambalaya with grilled cornbread.

$ CUT Steakhouse & Urban Grill –*5120 Salter St., at Lower Water St.* ♿ ☎*902-429-5120. www.cutsteakhouse.ca.* **Mediterranean.** A pricey steak house **($$$$)**, the upstairs CUT is open for dinner only. USDA dry aged beef is the focal point of the menu, with a 22oz. Porterhouse steak vying for attention with a "True Kobe Burger" (100% wagyu beef). Open for lunch and dinner, the downstairs Urban Grill has items under $10 but the portions are smaller. Designed with a late-1960s-inspired decor, the Grill serves dishes like chicken Tikka with red onion relish, or Lobster poutine in hollandaise with halloumi cheese.

$ Tomavino's Ristorante – *5173 South St.* ☎902-422-9757. *www.tomavinos. ca.* **Italian.** Under the Tomasino's sign, this longstanding foodie institution sits across from the Westin hotel. The subterranean haunt features brick walls and flickering candles as a setting for gourmet pizzas and pastas. Chicken pesto fusili (chicken breast in pesto, tomatoes and cream sauce over fusilli) remains a popular dish, but the *filetto meli-melo* (beef striploin with shrimp on linguini in a green peppercorn sauce) is also a good bet.

$$ Chives Canadian Bistro – *1537 Barrington St.,* ☎902-420-9626. *www.chives.ca.* **Canadian.** *Dinner only.* Opened by two owner-chefs who attended culinary school together, Chives has attracted a devoted following. The menu changes seasonally, and all efforts are made to use only sustainable seafood, local produce and foodstuffs from Nova Scotia, or the Maritimes, like pan-fried haddock with asparagus or apple and maple sausage stuffed pork loin. Located in a former bank, the restaurant placed its wine cellar in the bank's vault.

$$ Economy Shoe Shop – *1661-1663 Argyle St.* ☎902-423-7463. *www. economyshoeshop.ca.* **International.** A neon sign from an old cobbler's shop inspired this odd name for a popular cafe. Today, 10 years after opening, the place has grown from a single cafe to several businesses in one. The **Shoe Shop** bar is frequented by artistic types. The **Backstage** restaurant caters to the after-theatre crowd in an interior dominated by a giant fake tree. Tapas, like butter pecan shrimp, pizzas and pastas are on the menu, as well as seafood, steaks and chicken.

$$ Il Mercato Ristorante – *5650 Spring Garden Rd.* ☎902-422-2866. *www.il-mercato.ca. Closed Sun.* **Italian.** Situated on a bustling shopping street, this lively restaurant exudes a European flair in its decor and cuisine. Fresh herbs and flavourful sauces highlight Italian and Canadian dishes. But it's pastas like ravioli filled with roasted chicken or penne with basil pesto and roasted pine nuts that bring patrons back.

$$$ 5 Fishermen – *1740 Argyle St.,* ☎902-422-4421. *www.fivefishermen. com.ca.* **Canadian.** A seafood tradition in Halifax since the 1970s, this restaurant sits within a restored former school and subsequent home of the Nova Scotia College of Art and Design (now NSCAD University). The menu continues to impress with its seafood, meat and chicken entrées, a comprehensive wine list, and "mussel bar." Nova Scotia lobster or the seared Digby scallops are sure to please. A more casual downstairs dining spot, **Little Fish ($)** includes an oyster bar (☎902-425-4025).

$$$ daMaurizio Dining Room – *1496 Lower Water St. Dinner only. Closed Sun.* ☎902-423-0859. *www.damaurizio. ca.* **Italian.** Haligonians consider this restaurant, located in the Alexander Keith brewery, one of the finest in the city. The dining room offers a menu that is imaginative and authentically Italian. Signature dishes include *agnello scottadito* (roasted rack of lamb with roasted garlic, lamb stock and red wine reduction).

the completion of the Fairview Cove Container Terminal in 1982, Halifax can now accommodate the world's largest container vessels. Halifax is still a key departure point for Canada's troops, many of whom leave for tour of duty in Afghanistan. Halifax is also the east coast home of the Canadian navy; the Department of National Defence is a significant employer in the area. The city hosts five well-regarded universities: Saint Mary's (SMU), Dalhousie, Technical University of Nova Scotia, Mount Saint Vincent and NSCAD University (formerly the Nova Scotia College of Art and Design).

Downtown

Halifax Citadel ★★

🕐 *Grounds open year-round. Citadel open Jul–Aug daily 9am–6pm; May–Jun & Sept–Oct 9am–5pm. Rest of the year grounds open without services.* 🕐 *Closed Dec. 25.* ▦$11 ($7.05 off-season). ✕ ▯ ☎902-426-5080. *www.pc.gc.ca.*

Situated on a hill overlooking the city, the citadel is the fourth of forts dating to 1749 to occupy this site. A National Historic Site, the star-shaped masonry structure is a repository of Halifax's military history. Begun in 1828 at the order of the Duke of Wellington, the fort was not completed until 1856. Although never attacked, the fortification served the British army until 1906 and the Canadian military until after World War II.

Easily approached from downtown, or driven around via the perimeter road, the citadel's site offers **views**★ of the city, harbour, Dartmouth, George's Island and the Angus McDonald suspension bridge. The **clock tower,** the symbol of Halifax, was completed in 1803 and restored in 1962; the original was ordered by Prince Edward with four faces and bells to ring out the hours.

Surrounded by a dry defensive ditch, the fort contains a central parade ground where soldiers in 19C uniforms perform military drills *(mid-Jun–Labour Day daily)*. The complex houses an orientation centre, barracks, powder magazines, a small museum and exhibits. Visitors can walk on the ramparts, look at guns that served as the citadel's main defence and visit the outer ditches and ravelins. An audiovisual presentation *(50min)* **Tides of History** covers the city's past and its defences. Precisely at midday every day, the **noon gun** is fired.

Historic Properties and the Harbour★
Off Upper Water St.
The pedestrian area between Duke Street and the Cogswell interchange is called the Historic Properties. Several 19C stone warehouses and wooden

The Brewery Market

buildings house shops, studios, restaurants and pubs.

From Historic Properties visitors can walk west through a series of restored buildings to the Granville Street Mall and Scotia Square. A **boardwalk** follows the harbourfront north around the Marriott Hotel and south past the Law Courts and the terminus of the Dartmouth passenger ferry to the **brewery market.** A former brewery, the complex now houses several restaurants, shops and a farmers' market *(Sat 7am–1pm)*.

Harbour Cruise★★ (A *on map)*
Departs from Cable Wharf mid-May–mid-Oct daily 10am & 2pm (also 6:30pm Mon–Wed in peak season). Round-trip 2hrs. ∾*$22. 1hr tour at 4:30pm $18. Murphy's on the Water Tours* ✕ ♿ 🅿 ☎ *902-420-1015. www.murphysonthewater.com.*
The *Haligonian* III cruise provides commentary on the Halifax shipyards with its huge grain elevator; the container terminal where giant gantry cranes load

The Halifax Explosion
During both world wars, Halifax's Bedford Basin was used as a convoy assembly point so ships could cross the Atlantic in the safety of numbers if German submarines were sighted. In 1917 a French munitions ship, the **Mont Blanc,** was carrying a lethal combination of picric acid, guncotton, TNT and benzola. It collided in the harbour with a Belgian relief ship, the **Imo.** Until the atom bomb was dropped in 1945, the explosion was the largest man-made cataclysm in history. Miraculously, the crews survived, having abandoned ship in time. However, 1,400 people were killed outright, an estimated 600 died later and another 9,000 were injured.

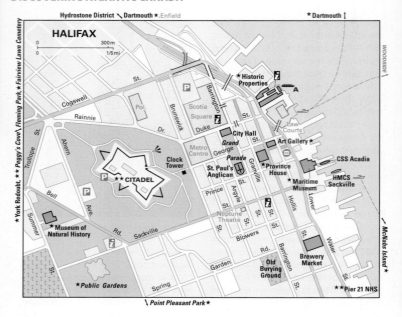

ships specially constructed to carry containers; and other points of interest that are seen on the tour.

The cruise rounds Point Pleasant and enters the **North West Arm,** a lovely stretch of water extending along the peninsula's west side and bordered by expensive homes and yacht clubs.

Maritime Museum of the Atlantic★

1675 Lower Water St. ◷*Open May–Oct daily 9:30am–5:30pm (Tue 8pm). May & Oct Sun 1pm. Rest of the year Tue–Sat 9:30am–5pm (Tue 8pm), Sun 1–5pm.* ◷*Closed Jan 1, Good Friday, Dec 25–26.* ◿*$8.50 ($4 Nov–Apr).* ♿ ☎*902-424-7490. http://maritime.museum.gov.ns.ca.*

Kids Located on the waterfront with a view of Halifax Harbour, this museum presents small craft, ship models, photographs and displays on maritime history. In the restored ship's **chandlery,** housed in an old warehouse, mariner's equipment is exhibited. Other highlights include a display on the *Titanic* and a recounting of the Halifax explosion. Sections are also devoted to the days of sail, the age of steam, and naval history. Outside, moored at the museum's wharf, the **CSS Acadia,** a steamship built in 1913

for the Canadian Hydrographic Service, can be boarded *(May–mid-Oct).*

Berthed at Sackville Landing, adjacent to the maritime museum, the restored **HMCS Sackville,** a World War II corvette that served in the Battle of the Atlantic, can also be boarded *(Jun–Oct.* ◿*$2.* ☎*902-429-2132).* Billed as Canada's "naval memorial," the site includes an interpretation centre, where a multimedia presentation *(15min)* is shown.

Province House★

1726 Hollis St. ◷*Open Jul–Aug Mon–Fri 9am–5pm, weekends & holidays 10am–4pm. Rest of the year Mon–Fri 9am–4pm.* ☛*To book a tour, call* ♿ ☎*902-424-4661. www.gov.ns.ca/legislature. Visitors must secure a pass from the front desk.*

Completed in 1819 this Georgian sandstone structure houses the Legislative Assembly of Nova Scotia, which has existed since 1758.

Visitors can see the **Red Chamber,** where the Legislative Council used to meet, with its portraits of King George III and Queen Charlotte at the head of the room. In the **assembly chamber,** visitors might witness debates when the body is in session. Once housing the provincial Supreme Court, the **legislative library** was the site, in 1835, of the self-defence of journalist **Joseph Howe** against a charge of criminal libel. His acquittal marked the beginning of a free press in Nova Scotia.

Art Gallery of Nova Scotia★

1723 Hollis St. ○Open daily 10am–5pm, Thu 9pm. ○Closed Dec 24-26 & Jan 1. ☞$12. ☞Tours daily 2:30 pm, Thu also 7pm. ✕ ૯ ☎902-424-7542. www.agns. gov.ns.ca.

Housed in the stately Dominion Building and the adjacent Provincial Building, this modern museum maintains a permanent collection of some 13,000 works of art, in particular the works of Atlantic Canada's foremost artists such as Alex Colville, Forshaw Day, Christopher and Mary Pratt and Francis M. Jones Bannerman. Exhibits including paintings of the **Group of Seven,** as well as international art. Regional **folk art**—painting, sculptures, paper and textiles—is a highlight, especially folk art by **Maud Lewis.** The museum possesses a small but excellent collection of **Inuit art.**

Grand Parade

Bordered by **City Hall** at one end and **St. Paul's Anglican Church** (*1749 Argyle St.; ☎902-429-2240; www.stpaulshalifax. org*) at the other, this pleasant square has been the centre of Halifax since its founding. Here the militia mustered, the town crier proclaimed the news,

and city dwellers hired sedan chairs; today the square is lined with benches under shade trees. Built in 1750 the small, timber-framed church is the oldest Protestant church in Canada (1750); a metal fragment from the *Mont Blanc* is embedded in its north end wall.

Museum of Natural History★

1747 Summer St. ○Open Jun–mid-Oct Mon–Sat 9:30am–5:30pm (Wed 8pm), Sun 1pm–5:30pm. Rest of the year Tue–Sat 9:30am–5pm (Wed 8pm), Sun 1pm–5pm. ☞$5.50 summer, $3.50 winter. Free Wed after 5pm. ૯ ▣ ☎902-424-7353. www.nature.museum.gov.ns.ca.

Kids This family friendly museum offers a comprehensive picture of Nova Scotia's land and sea by covering its geology, history, flora and fauna. **Mi'kmaq exhibits** include clothing, items made of birchbark, and splint baskets. Archaeological displays, natural-history dioramas and marine life, especially whales and sharks, can be viewed. Kids especially will enjoy the saltwater touch tank and re-created beehive, and at the **nature centre,** snakes, frogs and turtles.

Public Gardens★

Main entrance at corner of Spring Garden Rd. and South Park St. ○Open mid-Apr–mid-Nov daily 8am–dusk. ૯ ☎902-490-4894. www.halifaxpublicgardens.ca.

Opened to the public in 1867, this 7ha/17-acre park is a fine example of a Victorian garden, with weeping trees,

The bandstand in the Public Gardens in springtime

Pamela Delaney/Michelin

ponds, fountains, statues, formal plantings and an ornate bandstand. Note the massive wrought-iron entrance gate.

Old Burying Ground

Corner of Barrington St. & Spring Garden Rd. ⏱*Open year-round daily dawn–dusk.*
Best described as an outdoor museum, this downtown cemetery dates back to Halifax's founding in 1749. The earliest gravestone marks the death of a child in 1752, Malachi Salter, who was the son of a wealthy merchant. Erected in 1860, the large monument, the Welsford-Parker Monument, honours two Haligonians who died serving in the Crimean War (1853-56).

Pier 21★★

1055 Marginal Rd. ⏱*Open May–Nov daily 9:30am–5:30pm. Dec–Mar Tue–Sat 10am–5pm. Apr Mon–Sat 10am–5pm.* ⏱*Closed Dec 24-25.* 🎫*$8.50.* ♿🅿☎*902-425-7770. www.pier21.ca.*
This waterfront terminal is the last remaining immigration shed in the country. From 1928 until 1971 it was the premier entry point for newcomers to Canada, witnessing the arrival of a million immigrants and refugees, including 48,000 war brides (mostly British women married to Canadian soldiers stationed overseas) and their children. Today the former processing centre is a National Historic Site attracting visitors to its exhibits and families to its research facilities, where staff help people find relatives who passed through these portals.

Pier 21 replaced the deep-water Pier 2, which was heavily damaged during the 1917 Halifax explosion. In the ensuing years, the pier was the departure point for 495,000 Canadian soldiers en route to the battlefields of Europe. The post-war years on into the 1950s saw immigrants arrive from Europe, especially Holland, Italy, Hungary and the Baltics. In 1971 dwindling ship passage in favour of air transport led to Pier 21's closure. The building languished until local visionaries in the early 1980s decided to turn it into a museum. Canada's new Immigration Museum opened in 1999.

Restored to its 1920s appearance, the two-level building houses an exhibit hall where photographs, documents, artifacts and interactive displays detail the story of the largely European influx and a theatre shows a multimedia presentation *(30min)* evocating the immigrant experience. Children especially will enjoy the period 🄺🄸🄳🅂 **railway car.**

Additional Sights

Hydrostone District

Young St., between Isleville & Gottigen Sts. ☎*902-454-2000. www.hydrostone market.ca.*
Architecture aficionados will enjoy a visit to this 1920s planned community in the north end of Halifax. Patterned after an "English-style garden suburb," the neighbourhood grew from the ashes of the 1917 explosion. New buildings were constructed using "Hydro-Stone" concrete blocks. The area of richest architectural interest is known as **Hydrostone Market**. After a 1993 restoration, the one-block stretch of commercial buildings has blossomed into a retail hub of shops, restaurants and gardens.

Maritime Command Museum

CFB Stadacona, 2725 Gottigen St. ⏱*Open year-round daily 10am–3:30pm.* ♿☎*902-721-8250. www.pspmembers.com/ma commuseum.*
The history of the Canadian navy is recounted in **Admiralty House,** a two-storey Georgian mansion built in the mid-1800s. This, the largest of the National Defence Department's 55 museums, was opened in 1974 and is located on a military base in the north end of Halifax. Some 30 galleries hold displays illustrating aspects of Canada's military. Uniforms, service medals, model ships, historic photographs and presentation swords are on view.

Point Pleasant Park★

⏱*Closed to traffic; parking on Point Pleasant Dr., at Tower Rd., and near container terminal.* ⏱*Open year-round daily dawn–dusk.* ☎*902-490-4894. www.pointpleasantpark.ca.*
Situated at the southernmost point of the peninsula, this 75ha/186-acre park has fine **views**★★ of the harbour and the

North West Arm. For years the park was dominated by the military, which filled it with batteries and forts, the remains of which can still be seen. In 2003 an almost direct hit by a hurricane destroyed more than 75,000 trees in the park. Two years of public consultations led to a long-term plan to renew the park.

Prince of Wales Tower

🕐*Grounds open year-round. Tower open Jul–Labour Day daily 10am–6pm.* ☎*902-426-5080. www.pc.gc.ca.*
The prototype of what came to be called a **Martello tower,** this circular stone structure was the first of its kind in North America. Prince Edward ordered its construction in 1796, naming the tower for his brother—the future George IV. Its design was adapted from a tower on Mortella Point in Corsica that had proved almost impregnable. Such towers were built later in Canada and England to counter invasion by Napoleon's troops. Exhibits portray the tower's history, architectural features and importance as a defensive structure.

Fairview Lawn Cemetery★

West of downtown. Bordered by Bedford Hwy., Connaught Ave. and Windsor St. 🕐*Open year-round daily dawn–dusk.* ♿ *www.halifax.ca/history/tfairview.html.*
This would be a run-of-the-mill city cemetery, of interest only to locals, if the RMS *Titanic* had not sunk on April 15, 1912, off the southeast coast of Newfoundland. Of the 1,500 people who perished in the tragedy, 150 victims were buried in Halifax, in ceremonies held from May 3 to June 12, 1912. The majority of those (121) are interred in this cemetery. Each headstone at Fairview records the date and time of the sinking of the *Titanic.* Other victims are buried in Mount Olivet Catholic Cemetery and Baron de Hirsch Jewish Cemetery. Some 42 victims remain unidentified.

Excursions

McNabs Island★

Access by ferry from Halifax waterfront. For schedules ☎*902-465-4563 or 800-326-4563. www.mcnabsisland.com.*

Headstones of Titanic victims

Pamela Delaney/Michelin

Located in Halifax Harbour, east of Point Pleasant Park, the island attracts nature-lovers to its thick forests, colourful wild-flowers and large pond. Old roads serve as walking and cycling trails that lead to the remains of Fort McNab *(at the south end)*, sand beaches and good views, especially from the lighthouse. Sailing to NcNabs to anchor in a quiet cove or camp overnight is a popular outing.

Sir Sandford Fleming Park

5.5km/3mi by Cogswell St., Quinpool Rd. and Purcell's Cove Rd. (Rte. 253). 🕐*Open year-round daily 8am–dusk.* ♿ 🅿 ☎*902-490-4000.*
A peaceful haven in a residential suburb of Halifax, this park is a tribute to **Sir Sandford Fleming** (1827-1915), a prominent Scottish engineer. Instrumental in the construction of Canada's first continental railway, he also designed the nation's first postage stamp and urged the adoption of international standard time. Walking trails lead to Frog Pond off Purcell's Cove Road. The long stretch (3.5km/2mi) of narrow North West Arm can be seen in its entirety from **Dingle Tower** (🕐*open May–Oct daily 8am–5pm).*

York Redoubt★

11km/7mi by Cogswell St., Quinpool Rd. and Purcell's Cove Rd. (Rte. 253). 🅿 🕐 *Grounds open year-round.* ☎*902-426-5080. www.pc.gc.ca.*
Located on the bluffs above Halifax Harbour, this coastal fort played an integral

Pamela Delaney/Michelin

Pete's Frootique

Pete Luckett, a British entrepreneur from Nottingham, moved to Canada in 1979. A green grocer, he established his first store in Saint John. Before long, he was explaining the dos and don'ts of the world's most exotic fruits and vegetables to a national TV audience and in a newspaper column. Today his grocery stores stock fine foods, UK imports, locally made cheeses, and fresh produce. His Bedford store, just outside Halifax, also has over 700 wines for sale. The Halifax store often has live piano music in the background. *Two locations open daily 8am: 1515 Dresden Row, entrance off Birmingham St. ☎902-425-5700 (parking at City Centre Atlantic), and in Sunnyside Mall, 1595 Bedford Hwy. ☎902-835-4997 (free parking). www.petesfrootique.com.*

role in the city's defensive and warning systems. First constructed in 1793, the defences were strengthened by Prince Edward, who named the redoubt for his brother, the Duke of York. The martello tower Edward erected in 1798 was part of his signal communication system. During World War II, the redoubt became the centre for coordinating defence of the harbour and city against German attack.

At the north end, the remains of the stone tower can be seen. Gun emplacements face the harbour approach. At the south end, the **command post** contains displays on the defences and permits good **views**★ of the harbour.

Atlantic Canada Aviation Museum

20 Sky Blvd. at Halifax International Airport, 35km/22mi northeast of Halifax, near Enfield. Exit 6 off Hwy. 102. ○Open mid-May–mid-Oct daily 9am–5pm, winter by appointment. ◎$6. ❺✖☐☎902-873-3773. http://acam.ednet.ns.ca.

Kids Staffed entirely by volunteers, this museum recounts 100 years of Atlantic Canada's aviation history. Two dozen

aircraft are on display, in varying states of restoration, including a 1946 Ercoupe 415C and a CF-100 Canuck fighter. A new acquisition is a home-built helicopter donated by a native Nova Scotian; it is on view with two other helicopters in the Silver Dart Gallery, where most of the exhibits are located *(renovations to the Silver Dart Gallery are ongoing).*

Uniacke Estate Museum Park★

758 Main Rd., in Mt. Uniacke, 40km/25mi northwest by Rte. 7 and Rte. 1. ○Grounds open year-round daily dawn–dusk. House open Jun–mid-Oct Mon–Sat 9:30am–5:30pm, Sun 11am–5:30pm. ◎$3.25. ☐☎902-866-0032. http://museum. gov.ns.ca.

This fine example of plantation-style Colonial architecture, with its wide portico rising the two storeys of the house, stands on a peaceful lakeshore estate. Completed in 1815, it was the country home of Richard Uniacke, attorney general of Nova Scotia from 1797 to 1830. The interior looks today as it did in 1815, with the original furnishings of the Uniacke family.

Dartmouth★

POPULATION 70,000 – MAP INSIDE FRONT COVER

Site of a large naval dockyard and research centre, Halifax's sister city has a pleasant waterfront with shop-lined streets descending to it. Because of the presence of 23 lakes within its city limits, Dartmouth is called the City of Lakes. Settled in 1750, it attained official town status in 1873. Growth was gradual until the construction of the Angus L. MacDonald Bridge in 1955. The 1970 A. Murray MacKay Bridge, at the mouth of the Narrows, spawned additional development. Small, waterside Alderney Park features the **World Peace Pavilion** (94 Alderney Dr.), an outdoor exhibit of natural rocks and bricks from well-known sites such as China's Great Wall and the Berlin Wall. Connected to Halifax by two bridges, Dartmouth is serviced by the oldest continual **saltwater ferry** service (1752) in North America (⊙departs from Lower Water St. in Halifax daily; ⊙no service Jan 1, Good Friday, Easter Sunday & Dec 25; 12min crossing; ⊛$2; ♿🅿 ☎902-490-4000; www.region.halifax.ns.ca/metrotransit).

- **Information:** Scotia Square Visitor Centre, in Halifax. ☎902-490-4000.
- **Orient Yourself:** Dartmouth is a spread-out community with a small downtown core. Hwy. 111 runs in a semi-circle around downtown, beginning west at the McKay Bridge, then heading north and ending in a southeasterly direction. Halifax harbour lies south. Main west-east streets are Windmill Rd. (closest to the harbour), Wyse Rd. and Victoria Rd. When arriving from the MacDonald Bridge, the main south-north road is Nantucket Ave., which turns west onto Victoria Rd.
- **Don't Miss:** Shubenacadie Park just outside Dartmouth.
- **Organizing Your Time:** Allow a day to see the attractions of Dartmouth.

Sights

The Quaker House

57 Ochterloney St. ⚡Visit by guided tour only, early Jun–Labour Day Tue–Sun 10am–1pm & 2pm–5pm. ☎902-464-2253. www.dartmouthheritagemuseum.ns.ca. A short stroll from the ferry terminal, this heritage house is the sole survivor of 22 dwellings built for a group of Quaker whalers who moved to the province from New England in 1785. It was built for a tradesman who made barrels (a cooper).

Restored to the period, the house features a shingled exterior with paned windows typical of the houses constructed along the coast from Massachusetts to Nova Scotia in the 18C. Note the framed walls, off-centre front door, exposed beams and narrow winding staircase. An herb garden occupies the backyard.

Black Cultural Centre for Nova Scotia

1149 Main St. ⊙Open Jun–Sept Mon–Fri 9am–5pm, Sat 10am–3pm. Rest of the year Mon–Fri 9am–5pm. ⊛$6. ♿🅿 ☎902-434-6223 or 800-465-0767 (US/Canada). www.bccns.com.

This sizable museum, library and meeting hall complex opened in 1983 to foster understanding of the province's black history and culture. Exhibits cover early migration and settlement, military service, religion and community. There is a memorial to naval hero **William Hall** (1827-1904), the first Nova Scotian and first black to be awarded the Victoria Cross, the Commonwealth's military medal for exceptional courage.

Evergreen House/ Dartmouth Heritage Museum

26 Newcastle St. ⊙Open year-round Tue–Fri 10am–5pm, weekends 10am–1pm & 2pm–5pm. ⊛$2. ✗♿ ☎902-464-2916. www.dartmouthheritagemuseum.ns.ca/evergreen.

Built for a prominent judge during Canada's Confederation year (1867), this restored house is a typical example of a gentleman's home of the mid-Victorian era. Laden with antiques donated by area residents, the house was also the residence of the late Dr. Helen Creighton, a folklorist, whose book, *Bluenose Ghosts*, is a perennial bestseller in Atlantic Canada.

Fisherman's Cove

200 Government Wharf Rd., Eastern Passage. Rte. 111 south from either harbour bridge, then Rte. 322 south. Visitor Information Centre, Bldg 24. ☎902-465-8009. *www.fishermanscove.ns.ca.*

Situated on the Atlantic Ocean side of Dartmouth, this little cove is accessible by car. Fishing boats bob in the water along the wharf and painted huts resemble fishermen's quarters. Merchandise sold at wharf-side shops includes fine Nova Scotian artworks. A raised boardwalk leads through the sea grass near the water's edge. Fresh seafood, house-made chowders and sky-high lemon meringue pie are popular dishes at **Boondock's Dining Room ($$)**, known for its Devil's Island lobster stew *(200 Government Wharf Rd.;* ☎902-465-3474; *www.boondocksdining.ca).*

Shubenacadie Park★

Fairbanks Centre, 54 Locks Rd. (Rte. 111 south from either harbour bridge, take Waverley Rd. Exit, watch for signs). ☎902-462-1826. *http://shubie.chebucto.org.*

Over a century ago, the historic **Shubenacadie Canal** linked Halifax Harbour with the Bay of Fundy through a series of connected lakes and the Shubenacadie River running from Dartmouth to Cobequid Bay near Maitland. Today part of the canal route cuts through a lush, treed park, northwest of downtown Dartmouth, with walking and biking trails that edge Lakes Micmac and Charles. Although adjacent to a busy highway, the park provides a quiet retreat. Restored canal locks may be observed along the trails; Lock 3 can be seen at the Fairbanks Centre, headquarters for the canal system, where photographs, maps and artifacts are on display.

SOUTH SHORE

Winding 300km/186mi between Halifax and Yarmouth along the Atlantic Ocean, this coast is known for its surf-pounded shores, pretty fishing villages and tree-lined towns with elegant houses built from shipbuilding or privateering fortunes. The shore attracted settlers beginning with the French in 1632, who established LaHave. Germans founded Lunenburg in 1753, and British Loyalists fleeing the America Revolution came to the area in 1783. By 1787 Birchtown was home to some 270 families, mostly of free blacks. Peggy's Cove, a tiny, picturesque village, continues to be the subject of countless photographs—and ever-growing bus tours. The colourful town of Lunenburg, a UNESCO World Heritage Site, should not be missed. Liverpool is home to several museums, and Shelburne's waterfront has starred in a few movies.

Halifax to Barrington★★

MAP P 107

This 443km/275mi driving tour borders the Atlantic coast south of Halifax. The tour follows coastal rural routes that outline the heavily indented shoreline east of Highway 103, entering sleepy fishing villages and passing barren headlands washed by waves. Now that the provincial Highway 103 has been completed to Yarmouth, the former road, Route 3, is less crowded—and more scenic. The busy urban setting of Halifax is left behind for the wide-open landscape of sea and sky. Mid-summer to mid-fall is an ideal time to take the tour, although July and

Tranquil Peggy's Cove

August generally draw more visitors than the autumn months. For sea lovers and sailing enthusiasts, a seven-day cruise of the shore is available from Halifax (🕐 *for details, see sidebar below*).

🛈 **Information:** South Shore Visitors' Information Centre: *(mid-May–late Oct)* 109 Peggy's Point Rd., Peggy's Cove. ☎902-823-2253/2256.

▸ **Orient Yourself:** The drive traverses rural routes that leave Highway 103 from Halifax south to Shelburne en route to Yarmouth, the terminus of Highway 103. Route 3 takes longer to drive than the 103, but it is definitely more scenic. 🚗Fog is a big factor along the coast and can slow driving to a crawl. In general, mid-July to October are commonly free of fog, but it can occur anytime.

🚗 **Don't Miss:** The Fisheries Museum and a cruise on the *Bluenose II* in Lunenburg. The Rossignol Cultural Centre in Liverpool.

🕐 **Organizing Your Time:** Allow 3 days.

Kids Especially for Kids: The Ross Farm animals and wagon rides.

🕐 **Also See:** HALIFAX

Driving Tour

443km/275mi

Halifax★★★ (🕐*See HALIFAX*)

▸ *Leave Halifax by Rte. 3.*
Turn left on Rte. 333.

As the coast is approached, the landscape becomes almost desolate. Boulders left by retreating glaciers, and stunted vegetation give the area a lunar appearance.

Peggy's Cove★★

Immortalized by artists and photographers, this tiny village is set on a treeless outcropping of massive, deeply lined boulders. Its tranquil harbour, with colourful boats and fishing shacks built on stilts over the water, is indeed picturesque. Housing an operational post office *(seasonal)*, the **lighthouse** stands alone on a huge granite slab pounded by the Atlantic Ocean. 🚗*Sudden high waves and slippery boulders have resulted in tragedy. Use extreme caution when walking in this area.*

Upon departing, note the **carvings** of village residents done in the granite rock by William deGarthe (1907-83). A **memorial** to Swissair Flight 111, which crashed offshore on Sept 2, 1998, killing 229 passengers and crew, is located at The Whalesback, 1km/.5mi northwest of Peggy's Cove along Rte.333.

The road follows the coast with views of the villages on **St. Margarets Bay.**

▷ *Rte. 333 joins Rte. 3 at Upper Tantallon; follow Rte. 3 until Rte. 329 turns off after Hubbards. Tour the peninsula and rejoin Rte. 3 just before Chester.*

Chester★
Rte. 3, off Hwy. 103, 60km/37m from Halifax. ☎*902-275-3554. www.district. chester.ns.ca.*
Perched on cliffs rising out of Mahone Bay, this charming village has elm and chestnut trees and traditional New England frame houses. Founded by New Englanders in 1759, the prosperous community is a summer residence of Americans and a retirement spot for Canadians. **Pleasant Street,** the main thoroughfare, has shops and cafes. The village is home to yacht, tennis and golf clubs; a community playhouse; and an outdoor pool popular with locals.
The nearby **Graves Island Provincial Park** *(Rte. 3; open late Jun–early Sept;),* 3km/2mi east of Chester and linked to the mainland by a causeway, is ideal for a swim. Park activities include geo-caching, kite-flying and guided walks.

▷ *Take Rte. 12 North, 7km/4mi after Chester.*

Ross Farm Museum★
4568 Rte. 12, New Ross. 24km/15mi northwest of Chester via Rte. 12. ◷*Open May–Oct daily 9:30am–5:30pm. Rest of the year Wed–Sun 9:30am–4:30pm.* ▧*$6.* ☎*902-689-2210 or 877-689-2210. http:// rossfarm.museum.gov.ns.ca.*
Ⓚⁱᵈˢ Cleared from wilderness in 1816 by William Ross, this farm belonged to five generations of his family before acquisition by the Nova Scotia Museum Complex. Maintained as a living museum of 19C agrarian life, the farm features coopering (barrel making), candle making, forging, sheep shearing and other demonstrations. There are displays of plows and harrows, buggies and a well-stocked peddler's wagon. Horse-drawn wagon rides are offered. Berkshire pigs, oxen, Canadian horses, sheep, chickens and other heritage animals enliven the premises.

▷ *Return to Rte. 3.*

Mahone Bay★
Founded in 1754 by Capt. Ephraim Cook, the community was once a centre of piracy and privateering. Between 1756 and 1815 hundreds of small ships sailed from Nova Scotia ports to harass French, Spanish, Dutch and American vessels. These acts of piracy were carried out with royal blessing. After obtaining a license, a privateer could attack only enemy ships. All prizes had to be taken to Halifax, where the Court of Vice Admiralty decided their legality. Profits were enormous and coastal communities prospered.
Today this placid town is distinguished by three neighbouring churches lining the bay of the same name. Upon approaching the town, there is a **view**★ of their reflection in the water. The stores and cafes along **Main Street** are painted in a palette of colours; specialty shops and art galleries abound. A gazebo near the village's grocery store is the venue for Sunday evening concerts. **Jo-Ann's** *(9 Edgewater St.; open late-May–Oct daily 9am–7pm;* ☎*902-624-6305; www. joannsdelimarket.ca),* a delicatessen, market and bakery, is a good place to buy picnic supplies.

Mahone Bay Settlers Museum
578 Main St. ◷*Open Jun–Sept Tue–Sat 10am–5pm, Sun 1pm–5pm. Contribution suggested.* ♿ ☎ *902-624-6263. www.settlersmuseum.ns.ca.*
Housed in a cottage downtown, this museum serves as the repository of the town's past. Historic photographs, maps, charts, antiques and vintage furnishings of the 18C and 19C are on display; Wedgwood and Willow-patterned serving pieces are especially prized. Visitors interested in tracing their family tree can view ships' manifests, county cemetery listings and other documents in the museum's research facility.

▷ *Follow Rte. 3 south 10km/6mi.*

Lunenburg★★

Visitor Information Centre, Blockhouse Hill Rd. ☎902-634-8100 or 888-615-8305. ⏱Open May–Oct daily 9am–8pm.

Situated on a hilly peninsula with "front" and "back" harbours, picturesque Lunenburg is named for the northern German hometown (Lüneburg) of the first settlers, who arrived in 1753. Colourful historic houses, many with the "Lunenburg bump"—a five-sided second story dormer window overhanging the first floor—grace the street. **Old Town Lunenburg** was inscribed as a UNESCO World Heritage Site in 1995. Its civic design is considered the best example of a planned British colonial settlement in North America.

Brimming with 18C and 19C heritage properties, especially on Cumberland and Townsend streets, Old Town is bounded by Creighton, Kaulbach and Kempt streets and Bluenose Drive *(at the waterfront).* 🚶The area is hilly but walkable; interpretive signs are located at some intersections. Shops and galleries line Pelham and Montague streets. For a longer walk, the **Black Harbour Walking Trail** *(Lincoln & Falk Sts.)* follows Route 3 and then Route 332. 🚶For **views**★★ of Lunenburg's waterfront, drive to the picnic area across the harbour near the Bluenose Golf Club.

Once a pirates' haven, the town was sacked by American privateers in 1782. Known for its former shipbuilding industry, Lunenburg was the construction site of many schooners, including the **Bluenose,** winner of four international schooner races from 1921 to 1938. The *Bluenose II,* a replica, was built here in 1963. When in port *Bluenose II* offers seasonal **cruises** *(departs from Fisheries Museum: contact Lunenburg Marine Museum for schedule and reservations; ☎902-634-4794; ⬧$35; ♿🅿 Bluenose II Preservation Trust. ☎902-634-1963 or 800-763-1963 Canada/US; www.bluenose2.ns.ca).*

Fisheries Museum of the Atlantic★★

68 Bluenose Dr., Lunenburg harbour. ⏱Open Jul–Aug Tue–Sat 9:30am–7pm, Sun–Mon 9:30am–5pm. May–Jun & Sept–Oct daily 9:30am–5:30pm. Rest of the year Mon–Fri 9:30am–4pm. ⬧$9. ✕♿🅿☎902-634-4794 or 866-579-4909. www.fisheries.museum.gov.ns.ca.

🆒 Housed in a former fish-processing plant, this three-storey centre features exhibits ranging from the history of the Bluenose and the illicit "rum-running" trade during Prohibition to the development of the banks fishery. A sailmaker's workshop and a 1920s fish company office have been re-created, and ship models, tools and navigational equipment are on display. A theatre (regularly shown films), working dory shop and aquarium complete the museum.

Lunenburg's picturesque waterfront

Moored at the wharf, the **Theresa E. Connor,** one of the last saltbank schooners to fish the Grand Banks off Newfoundland, can be boarded. Built in 1938 the vessel has been refurbished to illustrate the dory-fishing era, when two-manned boats (dories) would haul in fish using trawl lines. The fish were salted on board a schooner, aptly called a "saltbanker," which served as a supply and delivery base. Characteristic of craft that replaced dory schooners, the steel-hulled side trawler **Cape Sable** can also be boarded. Built in Holland in 1962, this boat hauled trawl nets off Lunenburg until 1982. A replica of a shucking shed shelters equipment.

▶ *Follow Rte. 3 and turn left on Rte. 332 for 15km/9mi. Turn left at Felt-zen South and right on Ovens Rd.*

Ovens Natural Park★

🕐*Open mid-May–mid-Oct daily 8:30am–9pm. Rest of the year, call for hours.* 🚫*$8.* ✕ 🅿 ☎*902-766-4621. www.oven spark.com.*
Occupying 77ha/190acres along the coast, this privately owned park offers **views**★ across Lunenburg Bay to Blue Rocks. In the gold-rush fever of the 1860s, Ovens supported a mining town; In the small **museum,** visitors can see historic photographs and artifacts. Rent equipment *($6)* and pan for gold on Cunard's Beach, if there's any left. This land was the property of the Cunard family (founders of the famous shipping line), who had the beach dredged and the sand shipped to England to have its gold extracted.
A swimming pool, playground, Kids**petting zoo** *(Jul–Aug),* a path to the oven-like caves and **boat tours** *($23; late-Jun–early Sept)* are park activities. A **restaurant ($)** serves three meals a day. **Cabins ($)** are available for overnight stays.

▶ *Continue on Rte. 332 and then left on Rte. 3.*

The road follows the wide and tranquil estuary of LaHave River. Boats can be seen along this stretch of water lined with frame houses and trees. For cen-turies, the Mi'kmaq people made the banks of the river their home, fishing its waters and finding sustenance from area vegetation and animals.

Bridgewater

The river is crossed at this large, industrial town, first settled in 1812 and rebuilt in 1899 after a fire destroyed the downtown.

DesBrisay Museum

130 Jubilee Rd. 🕐*Open Jun–Sept Mon–Sat 9am–5pm, Sun 1pm–5pm.* 🚫*$3.* ☎*902-543-4033. www.desbrisaymuseum.ca.*
This modern brick building houses the community's history museum, which opened in 1902. Inside, exhibits illustrate the growth of Bridgewater. The muse-um's initial collections were amassed by Chester native Judge Mather DesBrisay (1828-1900), whose interests included natural history specimens from other parts of the world. The highlight of the displays is a **Morris cradle**★ with birch-bark panels adorned with Mi'kmaq motifs in intricate porcupine quillwork; it was crafted in the area c.1868.

▶ *Turn left on Rte. 331.*

The road passes the town of **LaHave,** mapped initially by Samuel de Cham-plain in the early 17C. Isaac de Razilly, lieutenant-governor of Acadie, built a fort here in 1632.
The road continues along the coast with many pleasant views of the sea and fish-ing villages, especially in the vicinity of **Medway Harbour.**

Liverpool

Founded in 1759 by New Englanders, Liverpool, like its great English name-sake, lies along the Mersey River. The river flows from the Annapolis Valley east through **Lake Rossignol,** Nova Scotia's largest freshwater lake. The privateering, fishing and ship repair of the town's past have largely been sup-planted by papermaking, fish processing and tourism today.
Bristol Avenue and Main Street (Rte. 3) are the central thoroughfares. In Liv-erpool's inner harbour, the **Fort Point Lighthouse** operated from 1855 to

1989. Visitors may try their hand at the "crank-held" foghorn; a small museum is on-site (& *Main St.;* ⏱ *open Jul–Aug 9am–8pm mid-May–Jun & Sept–mid-Oct 10am-6pm*).

Local son **Sherman Hines**, arguably Nova Scotia's best-known photographer, was instrumental in the creation of the Rossignol centre as well as his own photography museum. For country music fans, Liverpool's former railway station houses a museum devoted to the late **Hank Snow**, a local musician who made it big in Nashville (*148 Bristol Ave., at junction of Hwys. 3 & 8;* ⏱ *open mid-May–mid-Oct Mon–Sat 9am–5pm, Sun noon–5pm;* ⌖ $3; ☎ *902-354-4675. www.hanksnow.com*).

Perkins House Museum★

105 Main St. ⏱ *Open Jun–mid-Oct Mon–Sat 9:30am–5:30pm, Sun 1pm–5:30pm.* ⌖ *$2.* 🅿 ☎ *902-354-4058. http://museum. gov.ns.ca.*

This New England frame house, with odd-shaped corners and winding hidden stairs, was built in 1767 for Col. Simeon Perkins, a merchant and ship owner. Surrounded by other elegant residences, the house is set in fine gardens among tall trees.

On display next door in the Queens County Museum is a copy of the colonel's diary, which captures life in a colonial town from 1766 to 1812.

Sherman Hines Museum of Photography★★

Town Hall, 219 Main St. ⏱ *Open Jul–Aug Mon–Sat 10am–5:30pm, Sun noon–5:30pm. Mid-May–mid-Oct Mon–Sat 10am–5:30pm.* ⌖ *$4 contribution requested.* 🅿 ☎ *902-354-2667. www.shermanhinesphotographymuseum.com.*

This not-for-profit museum is **Sherman Hines'** homage to his profession. Housed in the former Town Hall (c.1902), the museum is the repository of a remarkable collection, not only of photographs by giants of the craft, but also of vintage cameras, tintypes, film boxes, magic lanterns, tripods and other equipment. The intimate **Victorian studio** replicates a working photographer's space with period props and furniture. Children will be intrigued by the 🄺 **camera obscura,** with its inverted projection of Liverpool's main street. In addition to images by Hines, the works of other practitioners are on view, such as the late portrait-photographer Yousuf Karsh of Ottawa, whose subjects included Georgia O'Keefe and Winston Churchill.

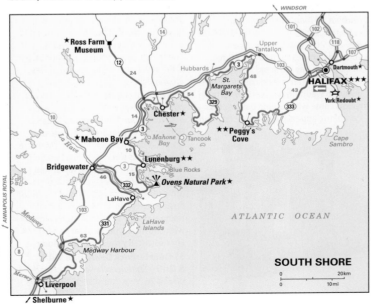

Address Book

♿For dollar sign categories, see the Legend on the cover flap. To overnight in offbeat accommodations, see the Rossignol Cultural Village in Liverpool.

WHERE TO STAY

$ The Sail Inn – *99 Montague St., Lunenburg. 4 rooms.* 🅿 ☎902-634-3537 *or 877-247-7075. www.sailinn.ca/index.htm.* Clean, comfortable and quiet, The Sail Inn has high-ceilinged, airy guest rooms with hardwood floors and handsome furnishings. Each suite has a spacious bath with a Jacuzzi or oversize tub and a kitchenette. High speed Internet is available and breakfast is included. A complimentary sail around the harbour aboard a 48' Ketch is included.

$$ Cooper's Inn – *36 Dock St. at Mason Lane, Shelburne. 8 rooms.* 🅿 ☎902-875-4656, *or 800-688-2011. www.thecoopersinn.com.* In this stately c.1784 shingled residence, with its hipped roof and widow's walk, guest quarters vary in size from a small room with queen-size bed to a suite that occupies the entire third floor. All have private bathrooms. Upon arrival, guests find a sample bottle of Jost wine in their room. Rates include an ample, hot breakfast in the cheery dining room.

$$ Oceanstone Inn & Cottages by the Sea – *8650 Peggy's Cove Rd., Indian Harbour. 10 rooms & suites; 7 beach cottages.* ✕🅿 Spa ☎902-823-2160 *or 866-823-2160. www.oceanstone.ns.ca.* Located minutes from Peggy's Cove, Oceanstone has attracted all types of travellers, from those on corporate getaways to wedding parties. Comfortable rooms come with private bathrooms. Part of the appeal is its seaside location,

but the contemporary cuisine at the **Rhubarb Grill ($$)** and even a small spa add to its popularity.

$$$ Oak Island Resort & Spa – *36 Treasure Dr., Western Shore. Exit 9 off Hwy. 103. Follow signs along Rte. 3. 106 rooms, 13 cottages.* ✕🅿 Spa ☎800-565-5075. www.oakislandresortandspa.com.* This large property is named for Oak Island, a privately owned island (⚬➤*not open to the public*) in Mahone Bay reputed to have buried treasure (excavations have been ongoing since 1795). Located near Chester, the resort may have a convention-atmosphere, but the recreational facilities, spa, and contemporary fare at **La Vista Dining Room ($$)** make a stay worthwhile.

WHERE TO EAT

$ Biscuit Eater Café & Bookseller – *16 Orchard St., Mahone Bay.* ☎902-624-2665. www.biscuiteater.ca. Closed Oct–May.* **Canadian.** In this funky, five-room cottage, used books, wi-fi, good coffee, home-baked goods and lunches are available every day *(open 8:30am, Sun 11am)*. Patrons can eat inside or on the outdoor patio. Readings and other literary events are offered regularly.

$ Magnolia's Grill – *128 Montague St., Lunenburg.* ☎902-634-3287. Closed Sun.* **International.** Reservations aren't accepted at this busy little 20-seat diner, but you can sign your name on a waiting list if you get there early. The spicy peanut soup is a standout, as is the key lime pie. Vegetarian dishes are a specialty.

$$ The Innlet Café – *249 Edgewater St., Mahone Bay.* ♿☎902-624-6363. www.innletcafe.com.* **Seafood and Steaks.** Somewhat of a local culinary institution, this cafe has been serving Mahone Bay residents since 1980 in a building that dates from 1799. The restaurant's unpretentious service and casual atmosphere (to say nothing of the food) ensure repeat visits. Mussels and all manner of fish are on the menu along with chowders, pasta, steaks and stews. For dessert, try the chocolate mud pie.

$$ Quarterdeck Beachside Villas & Grill – *Summerville Beach. Located off Exit 20, Hwy. 103.* ♿☎902-683-2998

Bruce Bishop/Michelin

Cooper's Inn

or 800-565-1119. www.quarterdeck. ns.ca. Closed Nov–Apr. **Seafood.** This restaurant on sandy Summerville Beach has been feeding hungry vacationers for 70 years; locals clearly enjoy the fare as well. Try the Neptune Caesar salad with scallops, shrimp and lobster, or the Atlantic planked salmon cooked in rum and butter over an open fire pit. Wash it all down with a Garrison Ale from the microbrewery in Halifax. Adjacent to the restaurant, a row of 15 **beachside units ($$$)** offers overnight lodging.

$$$ Charlotte Lane – *13 Charlotte Lane, Shelburne.* ☎*902-875-3314. Closed after Dec 25–mid-May.* **Contemporary.** Cheerfully decorated, this small restaurant has been a local and tourist favourite since it opened, as there are few fine-dining establishments along the South Shore. House specialities are typically a combination of local seafood, pastas and salads from the continent. Reservations are a must.

$$$$ Fleur de Sel – *33 Montague St., Lunenburg.* ☎*902-640-2121. Mid-Apr–May & mid-Oct–Dec Dinner Thu–Sat & Sun brunch. Jun–early Oct Dinner Mon–Sat & Sun brunch. www. fleurdesel.net.* **French.** People drive to Lunenburg from other parts of the province to enjoy dinner and brunch at Fleur de Sel. Exquisite French cuisine is presented in the intimate dining rooms of a bright Victorian house. Tasting menus are available, with or without wine pairings, and the Sunday brunch is a less-expensive but equally enjoyable repast. A dining experience not to be missed.

Rossignol Cultural Centre★★

205 Church St. ◷*Open year-round Mon–Sat 10am–5:30pm, Sun noon–5:30pm.* ☜*$4.* ☎*902-354-3067. www.rossignol culturalcentre.com.*

Opened in 2002, this complex consists of five museums, three art galleries, a library and a village of historic buildings. The centre is the creation of the aforementioned Sherman Hines, a gigantic showcase for his wide-ranging interests. The **Hunting and Mi'kmaq History Museum** contains a 1930s trapper's cabin, wooden canoes, arrowheads, snowshoes, decoys and Mi'kmaq crooked knives and baskets, among other artifacts. The 🅺🅸🅳🆂 **Wildlife Museum** displays preserved animals from Mongolia, Africa and North America such as a polar bear, leopard, warthog, muskox and buffalo. The **Folk Art Museum** spotlights Nova Scotian works in this genre, many with maritime themes. The whimsical **Museum of Outhouses** provides a look at these necessities from the past.

For romantic adventurers, unusual **lodgings ($$)** are available for overnight stays, including a sheep-herder's Mongolian ger, a Plains Indian teepee and a replica 18C British blockhouse appointed with museum exhibits.

▶ *Take Hwy. 103 about 20km/12mi southwest to Port Joli. Turn left at Port Joli and drive 5.5km/3.5mi on St. Catherines River Rd. (unpaved).*

Kejimkujik Seaside★

Entrance to park is marked with a sign. ◷ *Open mid-Jun–Labour Day daily 8:30am–9pm. Rest of the year daily 8:30am–4:30pm.* ◷ *Closed Dec 25.* ☜*$5.50.* 🅿 ☎*902-682-2772. www.pc.gc. ca.* ⊘*No fires, no camping, no bicycles.*

This coastal unit of **Kejimkujik National Park** *(70km/43mi inland)* encompasses a 22sq km/8.5sq mi expanse of spruce woodland, wetland and sand on a broad cape between Port Joli and the Western Channel. As far back as 1861, the site was known for sheep farms; at MacLeods Cove, the foundations of a farmhouse can be seen.

From the parking lot, two hiking trails with interpretive panels wind through

Piping plover

iStockphoto.com/Paul Tessier

Sailing Away But Not Far

A relaxing option for seeing the South Shore from the water is a seven-day cruise aboard the *Caledonia* that sails from Halifax. Snug on this 75m/245ft-long square-rigged barquentine (a sailing ship with three or more masts), passengers enjoy a leisurely sail southbound on the first overnight; an unhurried return passage to Halifax consumes the rest of the voyage. Passengers can go ashore at Port Mouton, Liverpool, LaHave, Lunenburg and Mahone Bay. Day excursions include hiking, kayaking or shopping and sightseeing. The on-board chef uses local ingredients and recipes to ensure a truly "Down East" experience; the wine list is international. Limited to 77 people. Cruises depart Sept–mid-Oct and start at $2,106 per person. ☎902-429-1474 or 877-429-9463. www.canadiansailingexpeditions.com.

The Caledonia sets sail

Courtesy of Canadian Sailing Expeditions

grassy terrain and low-lying shrubs to the coast. From the 1.2km/.74mi mark, hikers can continue on the **Harbour Rocks Trail** *(5.2km/3.2mi return)*, which leads to sandy beaches (*the water is very cold and not recommended for swimming due to dangerous currents and undertows; no lifeguards on duty)*. Farther along lies the park's largest beach, **St. Catherines River Beach,** nesting site of the endangered piping plover (*closed late Apr–early Aug during nesting season)*. The **Port Joli Head Trail** *(8.7km/5.4mi return)* takes visitors to a point where the full force of the ocean can be appreciated (*use caution: rogue waves may occur without warning)*. Alder, holly, witherod and huckleberry grow along the trails. In the peat-covered bogs, two varieties of orchid, dragon's-mouth and Calapogon's flowers, can be seen in summer. The park attracts seagulls, warblers, blue jays and sparrows as well as black bear, river otter, mink and deer. Seals might be seen basking offshore.

▶ *Return to Hwy. 103, drive south 35km/22mi and take Exit 25 for Rte. 3 to Shelburne.*

Shelburne★

Tourist bureau at corner of Dock and King Sts. ☎902-875-4547.
This small waterfront town sits at the mouth of the Roseway River, which emp-

ties into elongated Shelburne Harbour. Founded by Loyalists in 1783, the town was briefly one of the largest 18C cities in North America. At that time, the community's population swelled to an estimated 10,000 when additional British sympathizers sought sanctuary from the American Revolutionary War. The expansion was short-lived, since many settlers moved elsewhere. In 1995 Shelburne's waterfront was redesigned as a 17C Massachusetts village to serve as the setting for the Hollywood feature film, *The Scarlet Letter,* starring Demi Moore. Today weathered shingled houses, several dating to the 1780s, and commercial buildings dot Dock Street, former hub of the town's bustling mercantile activity. The **historic district** is bounded by Dock Street along the water's edge, King Street, Water Street and Anne Street. *A combination ticket ($8) provides admission to the Dory Shop, Shelburne County Museum, Ross-Thomson House and Muir-Cox Shipyard; individual admission is $3.*

Dory Shop Museum

11 Dock St. Open Jun–Sept daily 9:30am–5:30pm. $3; ☎902-875-3219. http://museum.gov.ns.ca.
Measuring 5m–7m/15ft–22ft in length, a **dory** is a small, shallow boat that revolutionized Grand Banks fishing in the 1850s. This museum is housed in one of seven dory-making shops dating from

1880 on the Shelburne waterfront at the time. Inside, visitors are shown how dories are made. Hand-made boats can even be ordered ($950 to $4000).

Shelburne County Museum

Corner Maiden Lane & Dock St. ○*Open Jun–mid-Oct daily 9:30am–5:30pm. Rest of the year weekdays 10am–noon & 2pm–5pm, Sat by appointment.* ⌾*$3.* ☎*902-875-3219. www.historicshelburne.com.*
This museum recounts Shelburne's Loyalist and shipbuilding past with local exhibits and artifacts. In the resource centre, Shelburne's 18C newspapers, court records and other town documents can be viewed on microfilm.

Ross-Thomson House Museum★

Charlotte Lane. ○*Open Jun–mid-Oct daily 9:30am–5:30pm.* ⌾*$3.* 🅿 ☎*902-875-3219. .*
Veterans of the West Indies trade, sons of a Scottish merchant opened this two-storey structure. By 1785 it was in use as a combination house, store and warehouse for items of international trade such as salt, molasses, cod and pickled herring. Though the store closed in 1880, the building remains, now restored to the 1820s period, as the oldest building in Shelburne that operated as a store. Note the roof shapes: gambrel and gable.
Visitors can tour the well-stocked interior of the old store.
Restored to the 1780s, the adjoining residence of brothers George and Robert Ross can also be visited.

Muir-Cox Shipyard

South end of Dock St., three blocks south of Anne St. ○*Open Jun–Sept daily 9:30am–5:30pm.* ⌾*$3.* ☎*902-875-1114. www.historicshelburne.com.*
This shipyard, one of the oldest in the province, was the construction site for barques, fishing boats, yachts and other vessels between 1820 and 1984. In the **interpretive centre,** shipwright's tools and exhibits on the area's shipyards are presented. At the **yacht shed,** an active boat-building facility, visitors are welcome to observe construction *(weekdays 8am–4pm).*

Sandy Point Lighthouse

10km/6mi south of Shelburne, via Hammond Dr. and Sandy Point Rd.
This 14m/47ft sentinel has stood guard over Shelburne's harbour since 1873, when it was originally built on a pier. Now sitting in a crib just offshore, the tapered-square, wooden lighthouse (⊶ *not open to the public)* is accessible on foot at low tide across a sand bar.

▶ *Take Rte.3 south 7km/4mi to Birchtown.*

Birchtown

This small rural community was notable in the 1780s as the first black settlement in eastern Canada.
To encourage emigration to its northern colonies, the British promised blacks loyal to the Crown freedom and land in Canada, once the American Revolutionary War ended. Birchtown briefly became the area's largest settlement of free blacks, established in 1783. After years of hardship, residents petitioned the Crown for productive land, not the poor soil many were given. As an optional solution, the British government offered free transport to Sierra Leone, a British colony in West Africa, where land and self-government were promised. Nearly half the area's blacks accepted the offer and left in 1792. Those who remained continued to push for justice and equality. Improvements were gradual. (In 2006 Mayann Francis became the first African Canadian lieutenant governor of Nova Scotia.)

Black Loyalist Heritage Site

98 Old Birchtown Rd. ○*Open early Jun–early Sept. Rest of the year by appointment.* ⌾*$2.50.* 🅿 ☎ *902-875-1606 or 888-354-0072. www.blackloyalist.com.*
The site comprises historic St. Paul's Anglican Church; a restored one-room 19C schoolhouse, containing a museum; a walkway with interpretive panels that recount the history of Birchtown's black families; and a government-sponsored plaque (1996) at the original burial ground. Plans are underway for the Black Loyalist Heritage Complex, which will include a museum, visitor centre, library,

and heritage garden with crops such as cotton, cocoa, rice and sugarcane.

▶ *Take Rte.3 south to Hwy. 103 and follow it southwest 24km/15mi to Barrington.*

Barrington

The township was founded by several families from Cape Cod, Massachusetts; their two-storey **meeting house** (1765) still graces the town today. The municipality was incorporated in 1879, and today Barrington bills itself as the "Lobster Capital of Canada." Indeed, stacked lobster traps are a common sight. Live lobsters are sold in town and area restaurants serve lobster dinners, especially during the **Lobster Festival** *(Jun)*.

Barrington Woolen Mill Museum

2368 Rte. 3. ◷*Open Jun–Sept Mon–Sat 10am–6pm. Sun 1pm–6pm.* ◷*$3.* ☏*902-637-2185. www.museum.gov.ns.ca.*
In operation from 1882 to 1962, this water turbine-driven mill located on the Barrington River produced much of the yarn and cloth processed from the fleece of Shelburne County's many herds of sheep. Today, a costumed interpreter explains the operation of the spinning mule, skeiner, loom and other equip-

ment used to produce woolen articles at the time.

Excursion

Cape Sable Island★

10km/6mi southwest of Barrington via Hwy. 103. Take Exit 29 to Barrington Passage and follow Rte. 330 over the causeway. www.capesableisland.ca.
The most southerly point in Atlantic Canada, this small, 15sq km/5.8sq mi island consists of two bulbous peninsulas joined in the middle near Centreville. The main town, **Clark's Harbour** (pop. 1,076) was settled by fishermen from Massachusetts c.1760. Used in the lobster-fishing industry, the Cape Island fishing boat was first built here in 1905. Lobster fishing and boat building are the island's main occupations. Sandy beaches at Northeast Point, Stoney Island, South Side and The Hawk are prime **birding-watching** spots for piping plovers, Ruddy Turnstones, Red Knots, Sanderlings, and Dunlin. Hawk Beach provides a view of the tallest lighthouse in the province, 30.7m/101ft **Cape Sable Island Lighthouse** (⊶*not open to the public),* built in 1861 and replaced by a concrete tower in 1923.

SOUTHWEST NOVA SCOTIA

Encompassing Yarmouth County and Argyle and Clare municipalities, Southwest Nova Scotia has long served as the province's front door for visitors arriving by ferry from Maine to Yarmouth (today some 45,000). The port town of Yarmouth functions largely as a service centre for Yarmouth, Digby and Shelburne counties; it is very much a working community, with lobster fishing, seafood processing, and light manufacturing playing key economic roles. The cold North Atlantic waters off Southwest Nova Scotia are ideal for lobster reproduction, and the area is a major supplier of lobsters for Canada, the US and Europe. A large fleet of Cape Island lobster-fishing boats operates out of John's Cove, near Cape Forchu. Cradling Yarmouth are the predominantly French Acadian villages of the Clare municipality, or La Baie Ste-Marie, and to the east, the Acadian communities of the Argyle municipality, or Par-en-Bas. The colourful Acadian culture has melded with the Yankee traditions of Yarmouth's founding New Englanders to make the coast a distinctive one. In many of the villages, the Acadian flag—a tricolour red, white and blue with a yellow star in the blue field—is flown. Traditional dishes such as rappie pie and *fricot* (a stew) are staples in Acadian homes and can be found on the menu in some area restaurants. Every year resident Acadians celebrate their heritage with two- and three-week festivals *(Jul–Aug)* in the Argyle and Clare municipalities. Yarmouth's citizens pay homage to their maritime past with an annual festival of the sea *(Jul)*.

Yarmouth★★

POPULATION 7,162 – MAP P 116

At Nova Scotia's tip, three rocky headlands protrude into the Atlantic Ocean. Yarmouth resides on the middle one, along a narrow, protected harbour. Underpinned by an even-keeled economy, educational and cultural amenities and recreational diversity, Yarmouth is appreciated by its residents, but largely overlooked by visitors. It has preserved the Victorian structures built by the town's captains of industry and gradually overhauled its industrial waterfront. With lakes, rivers and beaches nearby, Yarmouth continues to be a magnet for outdoor activity. In summer Yarmouth residents are preoccupied with cottage life, or "going to the camp," in local parlance; even though their retreat may be a mere 9km/6mi away, it is a change of venue eagerly awaited. Further fortified with an active ex-pat community from the US, Yarmouth's future is looking positive.

- **Information:** Yarmouth and Acadian Shores Visitors' Information Centre, 228 Main St. (across from the CAT Ferry Terminal). Open mid-May to mid-Oct. ☎902-742-5033. www.yarmouthandacadianshores.com.
- **Orient Yourself:** *See Map*. Downtown centres on five blocks of Main Street along Yarmouth Harbour. The CAT ferry terminal for passage to Portland and Bar Harbour, Maine sits at the foot of Forest Street. Starrs Road is home to three shopping malls.
- **Parking:** 1hr free parking is allowed on Main Street and 2hrs' free parking in municipal lots.
- **Don't Miss:** Cape Forchu Light Station.
- **Organizing Your Time:** June can be rainy and foggy, but late July and August are ideal for outdoor activities. Reserve a day for museums and shopping and a day to explore nearby Acadian villages.
- **Especially for Kids:** The Firefighters' Museum.
- **Also See:** ANNAPOLIS VALLEY

A Bit of History

In 1604 Samuel de Champlain named the place Cape Forchu, meaning "forked or cloven cape" in French. In the 1760s settlers from Yarmouth, Massachusetts, named the town they built after their former home, although there is speculation that it was named for the mistress of King George II, Lady Yarmouth. French Acadians arrived in 1767, after their return from 12 years of

Yarmouth's Heritage District

Bruce Bishop/Michelin

Practical Information

GETTING THERE AND GETTING AROUND

BY AIR

Yarmouth Airport (YQI) is reserved for non-commercial aircraft and private jets only. ☎902-742-6484.

BY BOAT

Passenger and car ferry service connects **Bar Harbor,** Maine (3hrs) with **Yarmouth** NS, and **Portland,** Maine (5hrs 30min) with **Yarmouth** NS (departure times May 30–2nd week Oct 8am and 4pm), but service alternates between Bar Harbour and Portland. Check schedules. No service 3rd week Oct–May. Reservations required. US$10 port and security fee each way. USD $69/person Bar Harbor, USD $99/person Portland. USD $115/vehicle Bar Harbor, USD $164/vehicle Portland. Fuel surcharge USD $25/vehicle. ☎877-359-3760 (Canada/US). www.catferry.com.

BY CAR

Major car rental companies can be found at the Yarmouth ferry terminal *(seasonally)* and at Enterprise Rent-a-Car (123 Starr's Rd., ☎902-742-5559); Avis Car & Truck Rental (248 Pleasant St., ☎902-742-3323) and Budget Car & Truck Rental (248 Pleasant St., ☎902-742-9500).

BY TAXI

Taxi pick-ups must be phoned:
Yarmouth Town Taxi ☎902-742-7801 or ☎902-742-7511
Clements Taxi ☎902-748-5526
Newfy's Taxi (Tusket) ☎902-648-4503
Tri County Cab ☎902-742-2323 or ☎902-742-2324
Taxis are often at the ferry terminal when the Cat ferry arrives from Maine, although their presence is not guaranteed.

BY SHUTTLE

Cloud Nine Shuttle
(☎902-742-3992 or 1-888-805-3335. www.thecloudnineshuttle.com) has daily shuttle service from Yarmouth to Halifax and back, and its schedules usually provide for convenient airport, train station or ferry terminal pick ups or drop offs.

Campbell's Shuttle Service
(☎902-742-6101 or 1-800-742-6101. www.campbell-shuttle-service.com) also provides daily service from Yarmouth to Halifax and back.

GENERAL INFORMATION

VISITOR INFORMATION

Yarmouth and Acadian Shores Visitors' Information Centre, 228 Main St. (across from the CAT ferry terminal). Open mid-May–mid-Oct. ☎902-742-5033. www.yarmouthandacadianshores.com. Dept. of Tourism, ☎902-425-5781 or 800-565-0000. www.novascotia.com.

ACCOMMODATIONS

For a listing of suggested hotels, see the Address Book. Hotels, motels, inns and bed & breakfasts can be booked through **Check In Nova Scotia** ☎800-565-0000, *a free reservations service.*

LOCAL MEDIA

Weekly: *The Vanguard (www.novanewsnow.com).*

SPORTS

Spectator

Special events, hockey tournaments and charity drives are held at the **Mariners Centre** (31 Cottage St., off Starr's Rd. or Parade St., ☎902-742-2155, www.mariners-centre.com) throughout the year.

Golf

Even though some summers can be foggier than others, residents in Yarmouth and the Acadian Shores are big golf fans. Three courses within an hour's drive offer reasonable greens fees.

Clare Golf & Country Club – Rte. 1, Comeauville. Open Apr–Oct. ☎902-769-2124. www.claregolf.ca (18-hole, Par 71 course)

West Pubnico Golf & Country Club – Rte. 3, West Pubnico. Open mid-Mar–Nov. ☎902-762-2007. www.nsga.ns.ca/pubnico/wp.htm. Club is wheelchair accessible. (18-hole, Par 72 course)

Yarmouth Links – South End, Yarmouth. Open Apr–Oct. ☎902-742-2161. www.nsga.ns.ca/yarmouth/yl.htm (18-hole, Par 72)

ENTERTAINMENT

Nightlife

During the summer months, **Rudder's Seafood Restaurant & Brew Pub** frequently has live music (96 Water St., ☎902-742-7311, www.ruddersbrewpub.com); **Captain Kelley's Pub & Lounge** has entertainment on Friday and Saturday nights throughout the year (577 Main St., ☎902-742-9191, www.captainkelleys.com); The **Rodd Grand Hotel** offers a summer dinner theatre featuring local actors and musicians (late Jun–Aug., Mon–Sat.; seating begins at 6:30pm; $33; ☎902-742-2446; www.roddhotelsandresorts.com).

Empire Studio 5 has five cinemas showing first-run movies daily (136 Starr's Rd., ☎902-742-7819. www.empiretheatres.com).

Performing Arts

Th'YARC Playhouse and Arts Centre (Office hours Tue–Fri., 10–5, 76 Parade St. ☎902-742-8150. www.yarcplayhouse.com) is an English-speaking community theatre as well as a venue for visiting musicians, choral groups, one-man shows, lectures, etc. Visit the website for schedules.

Université Sainte-Anne (9650 Route 1, Point d'Eglise/Church Point. ☎902-769-2114. www.usainteanne.ca), the province's only French university, often has cultural and musical performances throughout the year, primarily performed in French.

The following theatre groups perform mostly during the area's Acadian festivals, rather than at a permanent venue. **Les Araignées du boui-boui Le Théâtre d'la Piquine**

Summer concerts at churches, community centres and sometimes at the Yarmouth County Museum and Archives will be advertised in the local weekly newspaper, *The Vanguard* (www.novanewsnow.com).

TOURS

Self-Guided Walking Tours Pick up a copy of the free "Yarmouth & Area Community Visitors' Guide" from any tourist outlet and many restaurants; a self-guided walking tour is included. A brochure is also available at tourist bureaus on self-guided Garden Tours of Yarmouth.

Experience Yarmouth Tours by Rodd Rodd Grand Hotel (417 Main St. ☎902-742-2446. www.yarmouthtours.com) offers guided tours of the town and Cape Forchu in small buses. Booking are usually on a first-come, first-served basis and guides will be at the Ferry Terminal and at the hotel throughout the day.

Coastal Excursions

Lower West Pubnico. – ☎902-762-0338. Jun–mid-Oct. www.coastalex-cursions.ca Calvin D'Entremont, an enterprising lobster fisherman, offers guided van tours Jun–mid-October when lobster fishing is not allowed.

Hinterland Adventures & Gear – 54 Gates Lane, Weymouth (Tsee Fundy Coast and Annapolis Valley chapter) ☎902-837-4092 Late Apr–Oct. www.kayakingnovascotia.com This company specializes in self-guided or all-inclusive sea kayaking trips. Canoe and kayak rentals available.

SHOPPING

SHOPPING MALLS

Yarmouth Mall (76 Starrs Rd. ☎902-742-9518)

FARMERS' MARKET

Farmers' Market May–Oct Sat mornings at Canadian Tire Store parking lot, Starr's Rd.

SELECTED SHOPS

Acadian Glass Art (357 Main St., ☎902-742-4308)

RH Davis & Co. Ltd. (361 Main St., ☎902-742-3557)

Lovitt House Treasures (10 Parade St., ☎902-749-0405)

Tooie's Country Store (427 Main St., ☎902-742-6968)

Yarmouth Wool Shoppe Ltd. (352 Main St., ☎902-742-2255)

Sign of the Whale Nova Scotia Crafts & Art Gallery (Rte. 1, Dayton. ☎902-742-8895)

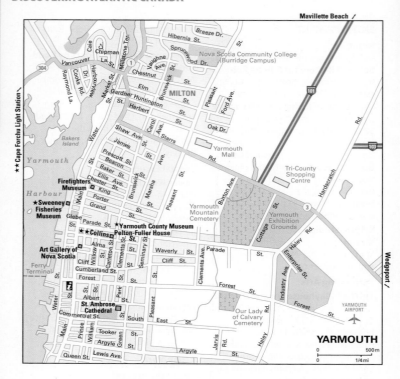

YARMOUTH

banishment at the hands of the British. In 1785 an influx of settlers loyal to the British crown came to the area after the American Revolutionary War. Yarmouth became an important **shipbuilding** town, enjoying its heyday in the 1870s. The Yarmouth Steamship Company was founded, operating until 1900. As an important port, Yarmouth shipped goods to Boston, New York and points beyond. In the 1920s and early 30s, when the US was in the grip of Prohibition, **rum running**—smuggling alcoholic beverages to the US by boat—was a quick way to make money. During the World War II, the town became known for its Royal Canadian Air Force training camp.

The Art Gallery of Nova Scotia deemed Yarmouth a good location for a satellite branch of its Halifax site, and the new gallery opened in 2007. The Yarmouth County Museum possesses the third largest collection of ship portraits in the country. Regional plays, musicals and other crowd-pleasers are performed at the **Y'Arc Playhouse and Arts Centre**

(Parade St.; www.yarcplayhouse.com). Yarmouth's annual celebration of the sea features concerts, a classic car show, a fishfeast, parade and other events, all capped by a fireworks show over the harbour *(Jul; www.seafest.ca).*

Sights

Collins Street Heritage District★★

Bounded primarily by Parade, Carleton, Willow and Cliff Sts., off Main St.
Yarmouth's historic heart boasts 30 heritage properties built for the town's shipbuilding magnates and merchant elite in the 1880s and 1900s in several architectural styles. Of note are the 1887 Italianate **MacKinnon-Cann Inn** *(27 Willow St.),* the 1893 Queen Anne Revival **Charles C. Richards House** *(17 Collins St.)* and the 1862 Georgian **Lovitt House** *(10 Parade St.).* A self-guided walking-tour brochure is available from the Nova Scotia Tourism Centre opposite the ferry terminal.

Bruce Bishop/Michelin

Ship's store in W. Laurence Sweeney Fisheries Museum

Yarmouth County Museum and Archives★

22 Collins St. ⏱*Open mid-May–mid-Oct Mon–Sat 9am–5pm, Jul–Aug 9am–6pm, Sun 1pm–6pm.* ✆*$3.* ☎*902-742-5539. www.yarmouthcountymuseum.ednet. ns.ca.*

This museum has been housed in a granite Gothic church since 1969. Today over 20,000 artifacts exhibiting Yarmouth's seafaring past are on display. The collection of **ship paintings**★, numbering more than 120, is the third largest in Canada. Two unusual items are the original Yarmouth light's 3,300-pound lens (1839); and an engraved runic stone found here in 1812, which some purport to be a message written by Norse explorers around AD 1007.

Next door, the 1895 **Pelton-Fuller House** *(20 Collins St.; guided tours mid-May–mid-Oct, same hrs as museum; ✆$3; ☎902-742-5539)* is remembered for owners Alfred C. Fuller (1885-1973) and his wife, Evelyn Pelton Fuller, who made it their summer residence in the mid-1960s. Born in Nova Scotia, Fuller started the **Fuller Brush Company** in 1906, known for its door-to-door sales. Inside, the interior is appointed with family furnishings and works of art.

Firefighters' Museum of Nova Scotia★

451 Main St. ⏱*Open Jul–Aug Mon–Sat 9am–9pm, Sun 10am–5pm. Jun & Sept Mon–Sat 9am–5pm, Sun 1pm–4pm. May*

& Oct Mon–Fri 9am–4pm, Sun 1pm–4pm. ✆*$3.* ☎*902-742-5525. www.museum. gov.ns.ca/fm.*

Kids This attraction is devoted to antique fire-fighting vehicles and equipment that date back to pre-Confederation days. All are in mint condition. Of special interest are the collections of antique **toy fire engines,** and badges from fire departments around the globe.

Art Gallery of Nova Scotia

341 Main St. ⏱*Open year-round daily 10am–6pm.* ✆*Contribution requested.* ☎*902-749-2248. www.artgalleryof novascotia.ca.*

Housed in 20C bank building, the western branch of the Art Gallery of Nova Scotia (AGNS) exhibits works from the main gallery in Halifax—as many as four visiting collections at any one time. Regularly changing exhibits generally focus on Maritime artists.

W. Laurence Sweeney Fisheries Museum★

112 Water St. ⏱*Open mid-May–late-Oct daily 10am–6pm.* ✆*$3.* ☎*902-742-3457.* **Kids W. Laurence Sweeney** (1905-1983) was the patriarch of a prominent Yarmouth family, whose fortunes derived from fishing and shipping. This museum is housed in former Sweeney-owned structures, now restored and under one roof: the 1905 foundry on Water Street. Visitors can enter Sweeney's office, tour a fish-cutting shed, view a typical ship's

Address Book

⌖For dollar sign categories, see the Legend on the cover flap.

WHERE TO STAY

$$ Guest-Lovitt House – *12 Parade St., Yarmouth.* 📇 ⬜ ☎902-742-0372 or 866-742-0372. *www.guestlovitt.ca. 4 rooms.* This B&B sits within one of Yarmouth's stately houses in the heritage district. Guest rooms are impeccably furnished. The widow's watch on top of the house offers a view of the harbour and can even receive a wireless Internet signal. An outdoor hot tub and complimentary ride in the owners' 1913 Model T car are included in the rate, Nova Scotian weather permitting, of course.

$$ Harbour's Edge B&B – *12 Vancouver St., Yarmouth.* 📇 ⬜ ☎902-742-2387. *www.harboursedge.ns.ca. 4 rooms.* Another of Yarmouth's heritage houses, this one built c.1864, has been converted into a popular lodging looking south over Yarmouth harbour. Guest rooms are appointed with traditional furnishings of the period, three with four-poster beds. Two have en suite bathrooms; two have private bathrooms nearby. Harbour's Edge is a tidy property for leisure or business travellers.

$$ La Maison d'Amitie/House of Friendship B & B – *197 Base Line Rd., Mavillette.* 📇 ⬜ ☎902-645-2601. *www. houseoffriendship.ca. 3 rooms.* Newly built and opened in 2005, this cliffside getaway boasts great views of St. Mary's Bay from the house and grounds. Owned by a semi-retired couple originally from Pennsylvania, House of Friendship offers a quiet oasis by the ocean. Beautiful Mavillette Beach lies down the road *(a 20min walk)*; the village of Meteghan is a 5min drive away.

$$ MacKinnon-Cann Inn – *27 Willow St., Yarmouth.* ✕📇♿⬜☎902-742-9900 or 866-698-3142. *www.mackinnon canninn.com. 7 rooms.* Restored over several years, this former duplex offers modern amenities in a sumptuous setting. The parlour and dining room are lavishly appointed. Each guest room is decorated in the style of a decade of the 20C when the MacKinnons and the Canns actually lived here. The inn is a 2min walk from the Yarmouth County Museum.

$$ Ye Olde Argyler Lodge – *52 Ye Olde Argyler Rd., Lower Argyle.* 📇 ⬜ ☎902-643-2500. *www.argyler.com. 6 rooms. Closed Nov–mid-May.* This lodge has achieved a reputation for excellent dining (the owner's son is a trained chef) and comfortable rooms in a rural setting overlooking Lobster Bay. Appointed with traditional furnishings and flowered fabrics, four rooms have bay views, all have en suite bathrooms. Open to the public, the **dining room ($$)** serves Canadian fare with an emphasis on fresh seafood. The private beach is perfect for bonfires at night. Internet access is available.

$$$ Trout Point Lodge – *189 Trout Point Rd., East Kemptville.* 📇 ⬜ ☎902-761-2142. *www.troutpoint.com. 11 rooms, 2 cottages. Closed Nov–Apr.* Located next to the Tobeatic Wilderness Area, this luxurious forest hideaway has been constructed with hand-cut granite and logs by New Brunswick builders. An Acadian craftsman from Wedgeport made the wildwood head- and base-boards for the beds. Some rooms have fireplaces and patios; bathrooms have air-jet tubs. Wi-fi is available through-out, and breakfast is included. Near the Tusket River, a wood-fired hot tub and sauna are popular with guests. Cooking programs include excursions to seafood companies in Yarmouth. A prix-fixe **dinner ($$$$)** is offered nightly that features Acadian-Creole dishes; alco-holic drinks are extra.

Sue Hutchins/Chebogue Point Productions

Parlour, MacKinnon-Cann Inn

WHERE TO EAT

$ Jo-Anne's Quick & Tasty – *Rte. 1, Dayton.* ♿🅿☎*902-742-6606. Closed late Nov–early Mar.* **Canadian.** A waitress from the original Harris' Quick & Tasty bought the business from Clara Harris who was retiring. Luckily Clara's recipes didn't retire: the fresh seafood dishes, hot lobster sandwich, and clams and chips are as delicious as ever. For an appetizer, try the Solomon Gundy (marinated herring), and for dessert the mile-high lemon meringue pie. Don't expect an extensive wine list (there isn't one), but this unassuming restaurant does have a liquor license.

$ Old World Bakery and Deli – *232 Main St., Yarmouth.* ✕♿☎*902-742-2181.* **Delicatessen.** Yarmouth's only independently-owned bakery, this cafe and deli gained an immediate following after its opening in 2007. Located steps from the ferry terminal, it serves up tasty baked goods, soups, sandwiches and Mediterranean dips and spreads. Old World is a good spot for a nutritious and relatively inexpensive lunch.

$$ Stanley Lobster Pound – *1066 Overton Rd., Cape Forchu. Closed mid-Oct–May.* ☎*902-742-8291. www.yarmouthonline.ca/stanleylobster/commercial.htm.* **Seafood.** Lobster on the beach is a wonderful treat on a sunny day, and the cooked crustaceans can be purchased en route to the Cape Forchu Light Station here at this lobster pound. They can be eaten on the premises, or purchased as take-out. Lunches and dinners on-site come with salad and dessert. The picnic area is nothing fancy, but there's something pleasant about eating freshly steamed lobster outdoors.

$$ Chez Bruno Café/Bistro – *222 Main St., Yarmouth.* ♿🅿☎*902-742-3438. www.chezbrunocafe.com.* **Belgian/Canadian.** Chef Bruno originally hails from Belgium; his wife, Lisette, is a local Acadian. Together they operate a great restaurant with signature dishes. Try the spinach salad with homemade poppyseed dressing as a starter and follow with fresh halibut filet with vanilla sauce. The restaurant sometimes also offers international fare (Japanese, Thai, Indian) on a prix-fixe dinner menu.

$$ Chez Christophe – *2655 Rte. 1, Grosses Coques (Clare region). Closed Sun & Mon. Breakfast, lunch & dinner.* 🅿☎*902-837-5817. www.chezchristophe.ca.* **Acadian.** Named after the grandfather of chef/owner Comeau, and housed in his late grandfather's home, Chez Christophe is known throughout western Nova Scotia as one of the best restaurants for local Acadian cuisine. Try the *fricot*, a hearty soup of meat and potato dumplings, or the *râpure* (rappie pie). Live music by local musicians sets the ambience. A **guest house ($)** with five rooms and shared baths sits across the road.

$$ Rudder's Seafood Restaurant & Brew Pub – *96 Water St., Yarmouth.* ✕♿🅿☎*902-742-7311. www.ruddersbrewpub.com.* **Canadian.** Live music, a great location on the waterfront, a summer patio, microbrewery beer and fresh seafood dishes have made Rudder's a popular restaurant in Yarmouth in recent years. The hot lobster sandwich is a perennial favourite, and the fisherman's platter of clams, scallops and haddock will appease the hardiest of appetites. Brewed on the spot, Rudder's Red and High Street Wee Heavy are a few of the pub's quality ales.

---

store, and stop at a carpentry shop and a machine shop. The floorboards and ropes throughout are originals from Sweeney's own wharves. Children will especially like the miniature coastal freighter.

Saint Ambrose Cathedral

43 Albert St. 🕐*Open year-round daily 8am–4:30pm, except services (Sat 5pm, Sun 9am, 11:15am & 6:30pm).* ☎*902-742-7151. www.dioceseyarmouth.org/pages/stambrose.html.*

Built of brick in 1889, this large edifice is crowned by a square belfry. Squat conical towers flanking the entrance house circular stairwells to the choir loft.

The first Anglophone Catholics in Yarmouth were Irish, arriving between 1825 and 1830. For years masses were given in people's homes, until this "All Saints" church came into being. Later named

Cape Forchu Light Station, near Yarmouth

Bruce Bishop/Michelin

Saint Ambrose, the church was doubled in size in 1910.

The interior holds vaulted ceilings and 12m/40ft stained-glass windows. The glass for the domed window above the altar was shipped from France in molasses to prevent breakage.

Additional Sights

Stanley Lobster Pound

1066 Overton Rd. (Rte. 304). ○*Open Jun early–Oct daily 9am–6pm. Stanley Lobster Co., Ltd.* ☎ *902-742-8291. www.yarmouthonline.ca/stanleylobster/commercial.htm.*

En route to Cape Forchu Light Station, this retail firm does a brisk trade not only in live lobsters, but also in live Jonah crabs, haddock, halibut, cod, pollock, hake and even shark. In this part of the province, lobster season extends from November to May. The harder the shell, the tastier the lobster; here lobsters are caught during winter months, when the water is coldest and shells are toughest. Opened in 1991, the company maintains a walk-in warehouse where patrons can select their own lobsters. There are no formal tours, but the owners will show visitors around upon request.

Seamen's Memorial

Overton Rd. near John's Cove (Rte. 304). Positioned near the water, a monument to those lost at sea has been erected by the Yarmouth County Historical Soci-

ety. Inlaid with large stones from area beaches, the obelisk sits on the site of the county's first launching, in 1764.

Cape Forchu Light Station★★

9km/6mi south of Yarmouth, at end of Rte. 304. From Main St. turn left at horse fountain onto Vancouver St. to access Rte. 304. ○*Grounds open dawn to dusk.* ∾*Contribution requested.* ✕☎*902-742-4522. www.capeforchulight.com.*

Standing sentinel over the entrance to Yarmouth Harbour on Cape Forchu, this 23m/75ft lighthouse with red vertical strips is topped by a red "applecore" lantern room. The free-standing, cylindrical lighthouse is a 1960s replacement of the original 1840 tower. Although the lighthouse is no longer in regular use, its 1,000,000-candlepower beam is still capable of projecting 18km/30mi out to sea. The Cape Forchu property is technically a light station because it is onshore and has outbuildings.

The lighthouse cannot be ascended, but a lookout permits a **view**★ of Yarmouth and the shoreline. The two-storey lightkeeper's house now contains a tea room and a small museum with exhibits on the light station. An outbuilding houses a gift shop, and a grassy picnic area fronts the entrance. On the Atlantic side, an outcropping of volcanic rocks descends into the water, tempting visitors to clamber, but mind the warning signs: ⚠*the rocks can be very slippery, and "rogue" waves are not uncommon during a storm.*

Municipality of Argyle ★

MAP INSIDE FRONT COVER

Abutting Shelburne County to the east, this municipality is essentially a wide-spread Acadian community comprised of small villages. Lying within Yarmouth County, it is an area of rugged, indented coast and large inland lakes, such as Great Pubnico Lake and farther north, Great Barren Lake. Several villages with variations on the name Argyle hug Route 3, the Pubnicos sit along Route 335 on a coastal peninsula, and Wedgeport and its neighbouring cousins, Upper and Lower Wedgeport, reside on a headland bisected by Route 334. Approximately 8,700 residents, mostly Francophone, live in the municipality. Their ancestors have toiled the land and fished the sea here since the early 1600s, a patrimony interrupted from 1755 to 1767 by the Deportation. Tradition and family roots run deep, with centuries-old recipes, music and stories passed down from generation to generation. Certain surnames usually tie identity to place: *d'Entremont,* for example, immediately associates the bearer of the name with the Pubnicos. The municipality benefits from the fishing industry; the fishing fleet anchored at Dennis Point Wharf in Lower West Pubnico alone is worth several million dollars.

Information: Municipality of Argyle Tourism, 27 Court House Rd. ☎902-648-2931; www.munargyle.com.

Driving Tour

Approximately 165km/102mi round-trip

▶ *Leave Yarmouth by Rte. 3 east. Near Arcadia, take the turnoff for Rte. 334.*

Route 334 heads south along the Tusket River, which merges into broad Lobster Bay, dotted with a number of islands. Upper Wedgeport is passed after 12km/7mi. Just 2km/1m beyond,

the larger village of Wedgeport appears. In the centre of the village, twin bell towers identify the huge **St. Michael's Church,** known locally for its striking stained-glass windows as well as its hand-carved altar. The original church was built in 1822 and replaced in 1867; the present church dates to 1913 and has seating for 1,000 parishioners. Mass is given in French on Saturdays and in English on Sundays. Notable in years past for its abundant catches of blue-fin

Pubnico's active harbour

Courtesy of the Municipality of Argyle

Courtesy of the Municipality of Argyle

Sport Tuna Fishing Museum

tuna, the community was a sportfishing capital that attracted US president Franklin Roosevelt and famed author Ernest Hemingway, among others. Today the **Sport Tuna Fishing Museum** *(Tuna Wharf Rd. ◷open mid-Jun–mid-Sept daily 10am–6pm; ☎902-663-4345)* recaptures those glory days with fishing equipment, mementos and artifacts. From the museum, the 5.4km/3.4mi *(round-trip)* **Wedgeport Point Nature Trail** leads through the mix-wood forest and coastal marsh of the Tusket River estuary to Wedgeport Point. Along the way interpretive panels explain the various habitats encountered, such as barrier-beach ponds and eelgrass mud flats. Local residents might be harvesting worms on the mud flats or **rockweed** from the sea. The large bloodworms are sold internationally for sportfishing purposes as bait. Nova Scotia's predominant species of rockweed, or seaweed is knot-ted wrack. Besides being an ingredient in fertilizer and livestock feed, it is an important component of the coastal ecosystem, feeding pollock, herring and flounder.

▶ *Return to Rte. 3 and curve east (right) around the river.*

The village of Tusket was settled in 1785 by Dutch Loyalists from New York and New Jersey. It is home to the **Argyle Township Courthouse and Gaol,** the oldest standing courthouse (1805) in Canada. Once a court of law for the area, it has a bell tower. Now restored, both the courthouse and jail are open to the public (◷open Jul–Aug daily 9:00 am–5:00 pm; May–Jun & Sept–Oct Mon–Fri 9am–noon & 1pm –4pm; ☎902-648-2493). Visitors can peer into two jail cells and see the original courtroom.

Angling for a Prize Catch

The local waters here make great fishing opportunities. Freshwater trophies are smallmouth bass and chain pickerel, often found in record sizes in inland rivers and lakes. Reservoirs created by hydroelectric dams hold pickerel and perch, and area lakes have been stocked with smallmouth bass. In the spring a lot of fishermen fish for speckled trout, also called brook trout. American eels—a catadromous fish that spawns in saltwater, but lives in freshwater—are common in the lakes and rivers; they return to the ocean to spawn in the fall.

Near Tusket's former one-room schoolhouse, an old sawmill used to operate and sawdust has accumulated along the river's edge: locals know it's a good place to find freshwater mussels.

The courthouse stands next to a long-time anglers' hangout, **Carl's Pro Hardware** *(8175 Hwy. 3; ☎ 902-648-2212)*, which stocks everything from hammers to groceries and fishing equipment.

▶ *Continue southeast on Rte. 3. At Pubnico, take Rte. 335 south.*

Route 335 begins at the first of half a dozen villages named Pubnico, and leads south along the harbour of the same name. Established in 1653 by Philippe Mius d'Entremont, Pubnico marks the transition from the New England-Loyalist hewn south shore to the Acadian ethos of the southwest shore. Other Pubnicos stringing the eastern edge of this elongated peninsula are, after 3km/2mi, Upper West Pubnico, West Pubnico, Middle West Pubnico and Lower West Pubnico. In the latter, **Le Village historique acadien de la Nouvelle-Écosse**★ (Historical Acadian Village of Nova Scotia) illustrates Acadian life from the mid-1600s to the late-1800s. Occupying the 7ha/17-acre site are 19C buildings that were moved here, such as the Charles Duon House (1832); an 1856 family dwelling whose roof, with its lack of overhang, typifies Acadian houses of the southwest shore; a blacksmith shop; and a fish-processing shed (1875). Costumed staff perform activities of the period, such as tending kitchen gardens typical of the pre-Deportation period; of note is

a demonstration of **hay harvesting** on the nearby salt marshes in a manner dating back to the 1700s *(Old Church Rd.; ⏱ open Jun—mid-Oct daily 9am—5pm; ☎ $4; ☎ 902-762-2530 or 888-381-8999; www.museum.gov.ns.ca/av).*

▶ *Continue to the end of Rte. 335.*

On the tip of the peninsula, at Pubnico Point, the **Pubnico Point Wind Farm** is a sight that cannot be missed: 17 turbine windmills rise 389ft from the ground, their gigantic blades turning to supply power to 13,000 households in the area.

▶ *Return to Rte 335, turn left at Pubnico onto Rte. 3 and go north past Argyle as Rte. 3 heads west and then north to Ste-Anne-du-Ruisseau, about 7km/4mi farther.*

On the return trip to Yarmouth, stop off in Ste-Anne-du-Ruisseau. On Rocco Point Road, the **Eglise Ste. Anne Church** and **First Chapel Site** *(a half mile from the church)* testify to the prominence of the Roman Catholic Church in the municipality since 1767, when the Acadians returned from exile. The present Ste. Anne's church edifice was built in 1900; the interior features stained-glass windows and vaulted ceilings. Adjoining a replica of the original chapel is a burial ground that dates to the 1700s.

Historical Acadian Village

Courtesy of the Municipality of Argyle

Municipality of Clare★

MAP INSIDE FRONT COVER

This municipality, part of Digby County, is situated about 32km/20mi north and east of Yarmouth, facing the vast Bay of Fundy to its west. It covers some 50km/35mi of shore along **St. Mary's Bay**, which is sheltered by the narrow, 71km/44mi-long peninsula known as Digby Neck. Here, along Route 3, is a coastline blessed with sandy beaches, tidal flats, low-lying cliffs and indented harbours. Small shoreline villages are lined with roads that branch out from north-south Route 1 like the teeth of a comb. Prim, sturdy houses and historic churches, many more than a century old, dot these communities, which are populated primarily by Acadians. Like Argyle, they have a rich and storied past along these shores. Known as the Acadian Shore, or French Shore, the area stretches from the village of Salmon River north to St. Bernard. Hard-working fishermen ply the bay's waters for lobsters, scallops, haddock, herring, clams and mussels. Local shops offer crafts and clothing made by village artisans. Most of the cafes serve traditional dishes such as rappie pie or *pâté à la râpure,* which is a baked pie made of raw grated potatoes, whose juices have been replaced by seasoned hot broth and a meat of choice (most commonly chicken). The ubiquitous lobster is a staple here, as well as seafood chowder; homemade pie with seasonal fruit or berries is the classic dessert. Church Point is home to the Université Sainte-Anne, birthplace of the award-winning theatre group **les Araignées du boui-boui;** in the Meteghan area, **le Théâtre d'la Piquine** has enjoyed a popular following. Local artists' studios and galleries line Route 1. To the east into the interior, lakes, both small and large, dot the landscape.

Information: Municipality of Clare Tourism, 1185 Route 1, Little Brook. ☏ 902-769-3655. www.baiesaintemarie.com.

Driving Tour

*93km/58mi from Yarmouth to
St. Bernard via Route 1.*
*♿Many shops along Route 1 are closed
Sun. Restrooms may be far between.
Signage is sometimes low-key: stay alert.*

A good time to visit is late July to mid-August when the annual **Festival acadien de Clare** is held, featuring grand street and boat parades, live theatre, fireworks displays, bonfires and outdoor concerts (*www.festivalacadiendeclare.ca*).

▶ *Leave Yarmouth via Starrs Rd. and turn right onto Rte. 1, heading north to Wellington, which is in the District Municipality of Yarmouth.*

If you wish to see **Sandford,** which has a tiny drawbridge—reputedly the smallest on the continent—turn left in Wellington and follow Rodney Road to the little community. Other-wise continue north on Route 1 to Port Maitland, where **Port Maitland Beach Provincial Park** (♿*see Beaches sidebar*) features a sand and cobblestone beach a kilometre long.

▶ *Continue north on Rte. 1. Beaver River Rd., which is crossed by Rte. 1, marks the boundary between Yarmouth and Clare municipalities. Continue on Rte. 1 past Beaver River and Bartletts Beach, a popular summer spot.*

The community of **Salmon River** sits on the river of the same name. The river is one of the municipality's four major rivers that empty into marshlands along the bay. Farms of cattle, pigs and sheep sprang up around the rich soil. In Salmon River and nearby Beaver River, potatoes became a commercial crop.

▶ *Continue north 6km/3.7mi on Rte. 1 to Mavillette.*

Mavillette Beach is the highlight of 101ha/250-acre **Mavillette Beach Provincial Park**★ (*see Beaches sidebar*). The 2km/1mi-long sandy beach is edged with dunes topped with marram grass. A boardwalk is provided to protect the fragile dunes. At low tide an expanse of sand flats is exposed. The beach offers views of Cape St. Marys Lighthouse and fishing wharf just north.

▶ *Continue north about 10km/6mi on Rte. 1. Watch for signs to Smugglers Cove.*

Smugglers Cove Provincial Park★ perches along the bluffs at the south end of the village of Meteghan. A large cave measures about 15ft tall and 60ft deep and was the hiding place for contraband alcohol during the 1920s and 30s when Prohibition was in effect in the US. The high cliffs permit sweeping **views**★ of St. Mary's Bay.

▶ *Continue north toward Meteghan.*

Saint-Alphonse is home to **Église Saint-Alphonse du Liguori**. The edifice features a pointed roof and massive twin towers flanking the entrance. Completed in 1922, the church is notable for its murals (1946) that backdrop the altar. Guided tours are offered (*Jul–Aug*).

Meteghan is one of the largest communities on this coast. The region's shipbuilding industry had its start here in the late 1800s; Meteghan's shipyards are still active today. The busy port hosts trawlers, lobster boats, crab boats and other fishing vessels at its docks.

▶ *Continue north about 12km/7mi on Rte. 1, past Lower Saulnierville. Turn right on Eustache Comeau Rd. Drive 3km/2mi, bear right at fork and continue 2km/1.2mi.*

The longest of the municipality's rivers, the Meteghan River originates near Weymouth and flows south through Eel Lake before emptying into the bay at the village of Meteghan River. In operation 100 years, until the 1980s, the **Bangor Sawmill**★ is one of 10 former area mills. Oxen pulled sleds loaded with logs to the river to be floated downstream. In 1890 rail cars carried lumber to Meteghan's station for transport to Yarmouth's wharves, where the lumber was exported. Destroyed by fire, the original mill was driven by a cast-iron water turbine that survived the fire, and now restored, powers the current mill, the third on the site. Note the wooden dam; its gate is closed to fill the lake, the water source for the turbine. *Sawing demonstrations mid-May–early Sept*

Festival Acadien de Clare, Cajun Weekend

Courtesy Municipality of Clare

Area Beaches

Most of Southwest Nova's beaches are open mid-May to mid-Oct. **John's Cove Beach** *(off Rte. 304, 1km/.6mi from Cape Forchu Light Station)* is sheltered, and at high or low tide, kids can play in the very cold water. The nearest lake for swimming is north *(where Main Street turns into Rte. 1)*: **Lake Milo** has safe swimming and boating in the summer months. Located inland, 114ha/280-acre **Ellenwood Lake Provincial Park**★ *(20km/12mi northeast of Yarmouth, off Rte. 340)* sits between two lakes, with a supervised beach. To get to the sandy **Comeau's Hill Beach** via Rte. 3, drive towards Tusket. Take a right onto Rte. 334 and then right again onto Melbourne Road. Continue straight through the communities of Little River Harbour and then Comeau's Hill. The beach is located where the road ends. Along the Acadian Shore (Rte. 1), northeast of Yarmouth, are **Port Maitland Beach Provincial Park, Bartletts Beach** and the **Mavillette Beach Provincial Park**★. Port Maitland has a grassy area and picnic tables. Mavillette Beach, with its fragile dunes has a boardwalk and a bird-watching tower.

Tue–Sun 3pm; $3; ☎877-462-5273; www.cardcity.com/mill.

▶ *Continue north about 12km/7mi on Rte. 1 to Church Point.*

Church Point, or Pointe-de-l'Église in French, dates to 1761. Today it is known for the **Université Sainte-Anne**, Nova Scotia's sole French-language post-secondary educational institution, founded 1891. Church Point serves as the principal campus and administrative centre for the university's six branches. University-hosted cultural events are enjoyed by the community year-round. The largest wooden church in North America domi-

St. Mary's Church (Église Ste-Marie), in Church Point

nates the campus. **Église Ste-Marie**★ or Saint Mary's Church, was completed in 1905 and served the community for many years. It is now a museum *($2)* exhibiting religious artifacts and church vestments. Standing 56m/185ft tall, its narrow exterior is surmounted by a single bell tower topped with a spire. Inside, the columns are actually trees cut from area forests, layered with jute and plaster and painted to resemble marble. Some 40 stained-glass windows, the altar and other adornments were imported from France; the crystal chandelier in the central aisle hung in the original 1829 church.

▶ *Continue north about 10km/6mi on Rte. 1 to St. Bernard.*

Rising 21m/70ft in the village of St. Bernard, **Église Saint-Bernard** (St. Bernard Church) is the largest on the Acadian Shores. Completed in 1942, it was constructed over a 32-year period with 8,000 granite blocks transported from Shelburne. Designed in the Gothic Revival style, the church presents a façade of three pointed-arched windows above three heavy doors, topped by a massive pointed window more than 9m/30ft tall. Symmetrical square towers corner the façade. Interior highlights include the altar made of Italian marble and the 2,000-pipe Casavant organ. Seating 1000, this church hosts classical concerts spring through fall on selected Sundays.

FUNDY COAST AND ANNAPOLIS VALLEY

Northeast of the Municipality of Clare, Digby County includes a string of coastal villages with British-sounding names like Weymouth, Plympton and Brighton, and a sparsely populated interior of lakes as well as the Tobeatic Wilderness Area. Though some villages sit along the protected waters of St. Mary's Bay, a dozen cling to the long finger of land between that bay and the much larger Bay of Fundy. Known as Digby Neck, this elongated peninsula ends with Long Island which, in turn, ends with Brier Island—all connected by ferry service. Surprisingly the peninsula is not a sand spit, but a series of forest-topped, boggy-bottomed ridges of basalt rock carved by the Fundy tides into sea stack formations. Whale-watching tours are popular off the Neck: finback, humpback and even right whales feed in the bay waters, along with porpoises, dolphins and harbour seals. Puffins, petrels, kittiwakes and ospreys can be sighted. Flowing 112km/70mi southwest to the Bay of Fundy, the Annapolis River widens into the Annapolis Basin, a tidal lake connected to the bay by a narrow outlet known as Digby Gut. Extending from Digby, with its large scallop fleet, on the Annapolis Basin in the west, to the college town of Wolfville on the Minas Basin to the east, Annapolis Valley encompasses some 160km/100mi. The valley enjoys warmer summer temperatures than on the Atlantic Coast, and it does not receive as much coastal fog. In recent years, the Annapolis Valley has become known for independent vineyards that produce a wide selection of varietals.

Fundy Coast ★

MAP INSIDE FRONT COVER

Long the land of the Mi'kmaq, the coast was later home to the Acadians, descendants of the early French settlers of the 17C. After the British deported the Acadians in 1755, their farms were offered to British subjects, many of whom moved from the US beginning in the 1760s. British colonists loyal to the Crown known as United Empire Loyalists came here from New England, New York and New Jersey after the American Revolutionary War and founded British settlements along the coast in 1783. This short driving tour begins where the Acadian Shore, or French Shore, ends and heads up the coast, taking in communities along the northeast end of St. Mary's Bay and the port town of Digby, known for its sizable scallops. An excursion to Digby Neck, facing the Bay of Fundy on one side, and St. Mary's Bay on the other, is included to see the famous Balancing Rock. Although this coast is becoming more diverse, a decidedly British influence can still be detected in the architecture, especially of the area churches, and the custom of afternoon tea.

- 🛈 **Information:** Fundy Shore and Annapolis Valley, 237 Shore Rd., Digby. ☎902-245-2201 (early May–early Nov). ☎800-565-0000. www.novascotia.com.
- ▶ **Orient Yourself:** Weymouth anchors the south end of this tour, along coastal Route 1, which merges into Highway 101. At the north end, Digby straddles St. Mary's Bay on its south side and the Annapolis Basin on the north. Route 217 extends from Digby south along Digby Neck to the end of Long Island, where Brier Island begins. Ferries service Long Island and Brier Island.
- 👐 **Don't Miss:** Digby scallops and Balancing Rock on Brier Island.
- 🕐 **Organizing Your Time:** Reserve 2 days: one day for the driving tour, another for Digby Neck, including a cruise and dinner in Digby.

Driving Tour

31km/19mi from Weymouth to Digby via Rtes. 1, 101 and 303.

Weymouth

This small community sits on the banks of the Sissiboo River, a location that helped forge its mid-19C prosperity as a shipbuilding, fishing and trading centre. Weymouth was founded by New Englanders, primarily from Massachusetts, in 1783. In 1896 a pulp mill was built near the village, helping to fuel the village's economy for 50 years. In 1929 the downtown was levelled by fire. Today Weymouth capitalizes on its past. The riverfront sports a **mural** of the village in the early 1900s. On Main Street the **Weymouth Trading Post** has kept its doors open since 1837, claiming the distinction as Eastern Canada's oldest general store in continuous operation. A 457m/1,500ft-long **trestle bridge** recalls the days of steam-powered trains and tall sailing ships, when the bridge would pivot to let ships pass. You can see the bridge from the **Cultural Interpretive Centre** at Sissiboo Landing. Exhibits at this centre offer insight into the five cultures that have called the area home: the Mi'kmaq First Nations, the early French settlers, the Acadians,

Weymouth's Historic Teas

Begun during the town's bicentennial celebration in 1983, these historic teas evoke the gracious custom still practiced in Britain today. Sponsored by the Weymouth Historical Society, the teas are held Jul–Sept every Thursday *(3pm–5pm; $5–$7)* in the former St. Thomas Church, now the home of the historical society, on Main Street. Traditional orange pekoe tea, iced tea and coffee, finger sandwiches, sweets and fruit are served. ☎902-837-4715.

African-Canadians and British Loyalists. On view are period clothing, artifacts, documents and a re-creation of 1890s Weymouth that focuses on a **model ship**. A tradition was initiated 25 years ago when Weymouth celebrated the bicentennial of its founding: **historic teas** sponsored by the Weymouth Historical Society are open to the public every Thursday in the St. Thomas Church in summer *(Jul–Sept)*.

▶ *Take Rte. 1 north about 6km/4mi to Rte. 101. Continue northeast on Rte. 101 toward Gilbert's Cove. Turn left on Lighthouse Rd.*

Weymouth Historical Society

Pamela Delaney/Michelin

Address Book

For dollar sign categories, see the Legend on the cover flap.

WHERE TO STAY

$ Summer Solstice Bed & Breakfast – *325 Overcove Rd., Long Island, Digby Neck. ☎902-839-2170. www. summersolstice.ca. 4 rooms: 1 with private bath, 3 rooms share 2 baths. Closed Nov–May.* Overlooking Northeast Cove, this substantial house features a large screened porch on the ground floor and on the upper storey, a spacious balcony for Bay of Fundy views. The inn is owned by an avid naturalist and self-taught whale expert who writes books and gives lectures about the conservation of the species. Guest rooms are decorated in an airy, summer cottage-style. Hot breakfasts might include homemade bread and waffles.

$$ Falcourt Inn – *8979 Rte 201, Nictaux. Exit 18 or 18A off Hwy 101, or from Rte 1, take Rte. 10. Turn left on Rte 201. ☎902-825-3399. www.falcourtinn. ns.ca. 8 rooms, 3 guest houses.* You're in the heart of Annapolis Valley here, in this refurbished former fishing lodge. Comfortable guest rooms, each with private bath, offer views of the nearby mountains and the Nictaux River. Featuring oak floors, oak ceiling and a stone fireplace, the dining room evokes the inn's past as a haven for the original owner's fishing friends in 1919. A continental breakfast is included in the rate.

$$ Garrison House Inn – *350 Saint George St., Annapolis Royal. ☎902-532-5750 or 866-532-5750. www. garrisonhouse.ca. 7 rooms.* This c.1854 three-storey house was initially built as a hotel. Today it overlooks Fort Anne National Historic Site. Garrison House is popular with travellers looking for a homey accommodations with modern conveniences. Rooms are traditionally furnished with wingback chairs and patterned wallpaper; the original plank floors have been preserved. Folk art pieces from the province adorn some of the rooms. Locals as well as guests frequent the 45-seat **dining room ($$)**, which serves regional specialties; fresh seafood is always on the menu.

$$ Hillsdale House Inn – *519 Saint George St., Annapolis Royal. ☎902-532-2345 or 877-839-2821. www. hillsdalehouseinn.ca. 13 rooms. Closed Dec–May.* This two-storey Victorian house (c.1859) sits on 12 acres in the heart of Annapolis Royal. Large guest rooms with bathrooms are found on the second floor. Smaller rooms with bathrooms occupy the third floor, and may be a little warm in mid-summer. Rooms feature four-poster, canopy or iron beds and period antiques. Amenities include flat-screen TVs and Internet access. There are three parlours for guests to enjoy. Full breakfast included. Note that pets are on-site.

$$ Tattingstone Inn – *620 Main St., Wolfville. ☎800-565-7696. www.tattingstone.ns.ca. 10 rooms.* Tattingstone comprises a grand main house (c. 1874), a cottage and a carriage house set on more than an acre of landscaped grounds. Rooms are elegantly appointed with patterned fabrics, table lamps and dark wood furnishings. All have private baths. An outdoor patio, a bright dining room for complimentary cooked breakfasts, and wireless Internet make this a favourite stop for the business or leisure traveller.

$$ Thistle Down Country Inn – *98 Montague Row, Digby. ☎902-245-4490 or 800-565-808. www. thistledown.ns.ca. 12 rooms.* This property has been resurrected to its former 1904 glory by two San Franciscans who have tastefully redone the interior. Rooms in the main house are lavishly decorated with patterned bedspreads and draperies and dark furnishings. Rooms in the adjoining lodge, built in 1996, are comfortable but more functionally furnished. The **Queen Alexandra Dining Room ($$)** is open to the public for homemade seafood chowders and fresh fish dinners with PEI potatoes. Complimentary breakfasts include made-to-order scallop omelettes and local preserves.

$$ Victoria's Historic Inn and Carriage House – *600 Main St., Wolfville. ☎902-542-5744 or 800-556-5744. www.victoriashistoricinn.com. 15 rooms.*

Once the home of an apple orchard magnate, this stately, three-storey mansion has retained much of its 19C grandeur. Luxuriously decorated rooms on three floors and in an adjoining carriage house envelop guests in traditional comfort and refinement. Some rooms have fireplaces and bathrooms with whirlpool tubs; all have modern amenities, including wireless Internet.

$$ Woodshire Inn – *494 King St., Windsor. Turn right into the driveway immediately past the yellow-clapboard house.* ☎902-472-3300. *www. thewoodshire.com. 8 rooms.* Recently renovated and opened as an inn, this brightly painted, three-storey 19C house sports a traditional exterior, but a clean, contemporary interior. Cedar canopy beds with feather duvets and Egyptian-cotton linens are complemented by flat-screen TVs, remote-controlled ceiling fans, Internet access and other high-tech amenities. Bathrooms are spacious and have soaker tubs and showers. The sleek **Cocoa Pesto Bistro ($$)**, named for the owner's former cat, offers contemporary cuisine for lunch *(Mon-Fri)*, dinner *(nightly)* and weekend brunch. Applewood-smoked pork ribs with honey-glaze barbeque sauce is the house signature dish. Products of several Nova Scotian vintners made the wine list. There's a pleasant deck for al fresco dining under market umbrellas.

$$$ Digby Pines Golf Resort and Spa – *103 Shore Rd., Digby (.5km before the ferry terminal).* 🅿♿⌂✕ Spa ⌂ ☎902-245-2511 or 800-667-4637. *www. digbypines.ca. 85 rooms, 31 cottages. Closed late-Oct–early May.* This immense Norman-style château began as a hostelry in 1929. Now, fully modernized, the destination resort occupies 20ha/50 wooded acres (plus a 101ha/250-acre golf course) along the Annapolis Basin. Despite proximity to downtown Digby, the hotel maintains a sense of seclusion. Rooms and suites, all with private bathrooms, are furnished with floral fabrics, comfortable seating and desks. Two and three-bedroom cottages come with a fireplace and veranda. Breakfast is included in the room rate. A spa, fitness facility, 18-hole golf course, heated pool, hiking trails, tennis courts and lawn croquet complete the recreational offerings. Free wireless Internet. Open to the public, the polished **Annapolis Room ($$)** spotlights fresh seafood and regional produce on its menu.

$$$ Queen Anne Inn – *494 Upper George St., Annapolis Royal.* 🅿⌂ ☎902-532-7850 or 877-536-0403. *www.queen anneinn.ns.ca. 12 rooms.* The grande dame of Annapolis Royal's accommodations, this imposing three-storey mansion was designed in the Second Empire style, complete with a windowed tower and mansard roof. Originally built as a private home, it became an inn in 1926 and was totally restored in 1989. Most rooms have hardwood floors and are richly appointed with four poster or sleigh beds, elaborate wallpapers and period antiques. All have private

Woodshire Inn's Cocoa Pesto Bistro

bathrooms, some with claw-foot or jetted tubs. Guests as well as the public can order Atlantic salmon and other regional dishes in the **dining room $$** *(closed Sun & Mon)* or landscaped garden overlooking the Annapolis Basin.

WHERE TO EAT

$ Evangeline Inn and Motel – *11668 Rte. 1, Grand Pré.* ☎888-542-2703. *www.evangeline.ns.ca/borden.html.* **Canadian.** Located at the turnoff to the Grand-Pré National Historic Site, this unpretentious cafe attached to the Evangeline Inn and Motel is a find for well-prepared, inexpensive soups, salads, burgers and sandwiches served by friendly staff. The seafood chowder and homemade pies are a must-try—they're that good. Locally the cafe is known for its breakfasts. The two-storey wood house that now functions as a five-room **inn ($$)** was the boyhood home of one of Canada's prime ministers, Robert Borden, who served from 1911 to 1920. The adjacent **motel ($)** holds 18 rooms and has an indoor pool.

$ Fundy Dockside Restaurant and Bar – *34 Water St., Digby.* ☎902-245-4950 or 866-445-4950. *www.fundyrestaurant.com.* **Seafood.** Edging the Bay of Fundy, this sizable complex comprises a restaurant, accommodations, a nightclub and bar. A 60-year Digby institution, the capacious restaurant serves three meals a day in its family-friendly interior as well as outside on the two-level waterside deck; an extensive children's menu is offered. Local lobster, mussels and scallops are the featured dishes, but the menu also holds pastas and other foods. At night, Club 98 is a Digby hotspot, with a spacious dance floor. **Dockside Suites ($$)** provide overnight lodgings with mini-kitchens, sitting rooms and balconies.

$ Shoreline Restaurant – *88 Water St., Digby.* ☎902-245-6667. *www. shorelinecomplex.ca. Closed Nov–Apr.* **Seafood.** Exuding an authentic mariner atmosphere, this waterfront restaurant, topped with a miniature lighthouse, offers three meals daily with a view of the harbour. A classic menu of local fare focuses on fresh scallops, clams and lobster (there's a lobster tank on the premises). But Shoreline is also known for its steaks and fresh salads. Locals go there for the homemade desserts like coconut creme pie. There are seven **rooms ($)** on the premises for overnight guests.

$$ Captain's Cabin Restaurant – *2 Birch St., Digby. Birch St is the continuation of Water St., Digby's main downtown street, just past Prince William St.* ☎902-245-4868. *www.captainscabin. ns.ca.* **Seafood.** Recently renovated, this large restaurant serves the classic local seafood fare: Digby scallops are the menu's staple, pan-fried, sautéed or deep-fried. This is the sort of place you don a bib and eat a whole lobster with clarified butter. It is unpretentious with down-east, down-home sensibility to it. Surf and Turf isn't just steak and lobster here; it can mean scallops or clams.

$$ Halls Harbour Lobster Pound Restaurant – *1157 West Halls Harbour Rd., Halls Harbour.* ☎902-679-5299. *www.hallsharbourlobster.ns.ca. Closed Nov–Apr.* **Seafood.** This friendly restaurant invites you to experience "lobster in the rough" dining at its lobster pound on the Bay of Fundy. The staff cook the live lobster you select, which you eat indoors in the restaurant overlooking the bay or outdoors on the sheltered deck. The sound of the gulls, the smell of the lobster and the sight of the Fundy tides all combine to enhance your enjoyment. Meals come with a salad, roll, fries or rice. Haddock, shrimp and clam dinners can also be ordered. Coconut cream pie is the restaurant's specialty, and there's a children's menu.

$$$ Acton's Grill & Café – *406 Main St., Wolfville.* ☎902-542-7525. *www. actons.ca. Closed Jan.* **Interntional.** This restaurant in downtown Wolfville has been an institution for years, and its current owner has continued the tradition of using local meats, fish and produce. The menu may offer salmon, scallops and shrimp but they are paired with Szechwan sautéed vegetables and rice noodles with a soy honey glaze. The ambience is pleasant in summer (an outdoor patio) or in winter (a fireplace).

$$$ Tempest World Cuisine – *117 Front St., Wolfville.* ☎866-542-0588.

www.tempest.ca. Closed Mon in winter.
Contemporary. This is innovative dining at its best in a relaxing room designed with clean lines and bold colours (blood red walls). Creative dishes range from a Finnan Haddie and chorizo chowder (local smoked haddock and Spanish pork sausage) to Nova Scotian lamb shank slow-braised in Chianti with risotto Milanese croquettes. Save this restaurant for a special evening, and try the local wines offered. Tasting menus available.

Gilbert's Cove

From the early 1800s, a steady stream of small schooners called coasters transported wood products to and from Gilbert's Cove and neighbouring Plympton and Barton. Standing guard over St. Mary's Bay, **Gilbert's Cove Lighthouse** is one of three remaining lighthouses in Nova Scotia that combine the keeper's house with the lighthouse itself. Built in 1904 the square house is topped by a lantern with a cat walk. The 12/m40ft-high light remained in active service until 1972, at which time it fell victim to vandalism. Repaired and restored in 2004, it now contains a small museum, gift shop and tea room.

▶ *Continue northeast on Rte. 101 about 5km/3mi.*

Savary Provincial Park

This small park makes a nice rest stop. It features a picnic area that provides a view overlooking St. Mary's Bay. If it's low tide, take a stroll on the beach along the rocky shore.

Interior, Trinity Anglican Church

▶ *Continue northeast on Rte. 101 about 10km/6mi to Marshalltown.*

Marshalltown

This rural hamlet sits slightly inland, at the head of St. Mary's Bay. The father of inventor extraordinaire Thomas Edison was born here. But Marshalltown is associated with Canadian folk artist **Maud Lewis** (1903-1970), who lived here from 1938 until her death. A monument in steel is erected here in her memory. Physically handicapped from her teen years on, she drew Christmas cards and painted on wallboard to eke out an existence with her fisherman husband. They lived in a 10ft by 12ft house without running water or electricity. She painted outdoor scenes of people and animals in primary colours. Today her work is displayed in the National Gallery, the Canadian Museum of Civilization, and the Art Gallery of Nova Scotia in Halifax.

Digby

This waterfront town of 2,300 people is both a bustling port and a business centre. Sitting at the southern edge of Annapolis Basin, Digby is home to a large scallop fleet as well as ferries that cross the Bay of Fundy to Saint John, New Brunswick. Settled by United Empire Loyalists in 1783, the town was named for their leader, Capt. Robert Digby. Budding tourism began with the 1929 construction of a resort on the outskirts of town by the Dominion Atlantic Railway, now renovated and accommodating overnight guests as the **Digby Pines Golf Resort and Spa** (⬤*see Address Book*). Local restaurants, several along Water Street (⬤*see Address Book*), feature **Digby scallops** grilled, fried, stuffed, boiled, broiled or rolled in cornmeal and sautéed in butter. Every year the town celebrates the

Courtesy http://www.unityserve.org/trinity

bounty of the sea with its **Digby Scallop Days Festival** (Aug).

Trinity Anglican Church

109 Queen St. at the corner of Mount. ☎902-245-6744. www.unityserve.org/trinity.
This Gothic Revivial church features a corner bell tower with a steeple, a steeply pitched roof and narrow, pointed windows inset with stained-glass. The original edifice dated to 1788. The present structure was completed in 1878 and was constructed solely by shipwrights. The showpiece of its fine wooden **interior** is the buttressed ceiling, which recalls an inverted hull of a ship. The church was designated a National Historic Site in 1990, for its frame construction typical of late-19C American design. An adjoining cemetery contains the graves of several Loyalists and their descendants.

Admiral Digby Museum

95 Montague Rd. ○Open mid-Jun–Aug Tue–Sat 9am–noon & 1pm–5pm, Sun 1pm–5pm. Rest of the year call for hrs. ☜Donation requested. ☎902-245-6322. www.admuseum.ns.ca.
This museum occupies a mid-19C Georgian-style house with low doorways and walls cemented with lath and horsehair plaster. On two floors, period rooms contain furnishings and artifacts relating to the heritage of Digby and neighbouring communities. Of note in the first-floor parlour are an organ and a vintage phonograph with a large cygnet horn. The **Marine Room** displays charts, ship models, maps and photographs. Upstairs, a gallery devoted to the Loyalists presents uniforms, documents, furniture and household artifacts.

Excursion to Digby Neck

142km/88mi round-trip from Digby via Rte. 217, including ferry (5min; $5; no return fare) to Long Island and ferry (7min; $5; no return fare) to Brier Island.
South of the town of Digby and bisected by Route 217, the narrow peninsula known as Digby Neck extends into the Bay of Fundy. The Neck is the western extension of the North Mountain range

from the Annapolis Valley, and along with **Long Island** and **Brier Island** at its tip, the peninsula forms the northwest shore of St. Mary's Bay. This excursion entails a meandering drive of 71km/44mi, one way, and car ferries to Long Island and Brier Island that leave regularly in summer. **Whale-watching** cruises are popular here, the beaches have been mostly left untouched and bird-watching is a favourite pastime. *For whale-watching cruises, contact Freeport Whale & Seabird Tours (☎902-839-2177), Mariner Cruises (www.novascotiawhale watching.ca) or Pirate's Cove Whale Cruises (www.piratescove.ca).* One unusual rock formation on Long Island is the **Balancing Rock★★**, as it is called. A sea stack, it is a column of basalt that stands straight up and appears to be teetering on its end. *Watch for signs on your left after getting off the ferry.* After a short trail to the coastline, a sharp descent leads to a viewing platform. ⊙*The wooden stairs can be very slippery when wet.*
Turning right after getting off the ferry brings you to **Boar's Head Lighthouse.** See if you can find the head of a boar in the rocks, shaped by the erosion of the power Bay of Fundy Tides. In Tiverton, visit the small Island Museum. Continue south to Freeport at the end of Long Island, which overlooks a harbour with fishing boats. Brier Island boasts two lighthouses: **Grand Passage Lighthouse** at North Point, and **Brier Island Lighthouse** at Lighthouse Cove.

Balancing Rock, Digby Neck

Annapolis Valley★★

MAP INSIDE FRONT COVER

With its farms, orchards and vineyards, the verdant valley of the 112km/70mi-long Annapolis River beautifies the central part of the province on the western side of Nova Scotia. The Cornwallis River winds through the eastern part of the valley, and the North and South mountains, lying 150km/93mi apart, protect it from heavy winds and fog. Ever since French explorer Samuel de Champlain founded Port Royal near present-day Annapolis Royal in 1604, the surrounding valley has been bountiful with crops, thanks in large measure to the know-how of the Acadians. Some of the earliest French colonists settled in this region; their descendants, known as Acadians, built dikes to reclaim vast stretches of marsh-land for agricultural production. This arable land supports about 1,000 small farms. In recent years, vineyards have been established in the valley. Apples and other fruits and crops are grown in the fertile soil, while dairy cattle graze the meadows bordering the river. Some of the villages overlook the broad Bay of Fundy, facing New Brunswick's southern shores, but the majority of communities nestle in the valley's interior. To explore the small towns of the Annapolis Valley, drive along the "old" Route 1, and savour a slower pace of life. The town of Wolfville with its fine restaurants, and the Acadian settlement of Grand Pré are must-sees. Picturesque houses and inns, farmers' markets, specialty shops and estate wineries line the route. In some areas roadside fruit stands and "U-pick" farms are common.

- **Information:** Fundy Shore and Annapolis Valley, 237 Shore Rd., Digby. ☎902-245-2201 (early May–early Nov). ☎800-565-0000. www.novascotia.com.
- ▶ **Orient Yourself:** The valley's principal communities are Digby, at the south end, and Annapolis Royal and Windsor, at the upper end, linked by Highway 101 and in some parts, coastal by Route 1. Windsor connects to Halifax on the Atlantic side via Highway 101. New Minas is the shopping centre for the east end of the valley, with most major chains stores and supermarkets, but many unusual boutiques and galleries can be found in Wolfville and Canning (&see sidebar Annapolis Valley Shopping).
- **Don't Miss:** Annapolis Royal for its history. Hall's Harbour is a photographer's delight.
- **Organizing Your Time:** Allow 2 to 3 days and stay at one of the many lovely inns. Best times to visit: when the apple blossoms appear (late-May early Jun) and in harvest time in autumn.
- **Kids Especially for Kids:** The Oaklawn Farm Zoo in Aylesford.

A Bit of History

The earliest settlement was a French colony at **Port Royal** under the noble-man Pierre du Gua, **Sieur de Monts.** Granted permission by Henry IV of France to develop the fur trade, de Monts began his expedition to the New World in 1604. The first winter in Canada was spent on an island in the St. Croix River in New Brunswick. The next year the company moved to the Annapolis Basin, where a habitation was built. It was destroyed in 1613 by a British force from Virginia. By 1635 the French gov-ernor had built a new Port Royal on the site of Annapolis Royal. Over the next century the French settlement grew, forming the region called Acadia. Port Royal suffered many raids by the New England colonies to the south. The fort constructed by the French fell into the hands of a New England expedition in 1710. The British changed its name to **Annapolis Royal.**

The British were now in charge of Aca-dia, and it was fitting that the new capi-tal be named after **Queen Anne** (1665-

View of Annapolis Valley and Minas Basin from the Look Off

1714). The native Mi'kmaq had coexisted peacefully with the Acadians. But after the expulsion of the Acadians in 1755, an influx of New England planters arrived, followed by black and white Loyalists, as well as Protestants from abroad. Acadian farms were occupied by or sold to the new settlers. Seeking to retain their land and hunting rights, the Mi'kmaq signed several treaties with the Crown over a 50-year period.

Before Deportation, **Grand-Pré** was the most important Acadian settlement in the province, home to some 200 farms lining the Minas Basin. Realizing the richness of the soil covered by the sea at high tide, they constructed **dikes** to keep the sea out, while marsh water was allowed to escape through floodgates. The cultivated land supported crops, livestock and orchards. The Acadians operated water-powered sawmills in the area that were vital in developing the lumber and grain-milling industries.

Driving Tour

272km/168mi from Digby to Windsor via Rte. 1 and Hwy. 101

▶ *From Digby, take Hwy. 101 northeast toward Annapolis Royal.*

Highway 101 follows the shore of the Annapolis Basin with pleasant views.

▶ *Take Exit 24 and follow River Rd. inland along the Bear River 5km/2mi into the village of Bear River.*

Bear River

This village clings to the slopes along its namesake river, a tidal river that fluctuates 6m/20ft with the tide change. Along the main street, several wooden buildings perch on stilts above the water. An enclave of artists and artisans, the village boasts a dozen or so studios, craft shops and galleries. Largely a glacial valley, the area abounds with rolling hills, and the combination of steep slopes, well-drained soil and a climate modulated by the bay are conducive to the growing of grapes. A French settler is credited with creating the first vineyard in the province in 1611—in Bear River. There are several in Annapolis Valley, and recently another winery opened here (*see below*). The village is also home to the Bear River First Nation Reserve, established in 1820, where some 100 Mi'kmaq reside, as their ancestors have in the area for thousands of years.

Bear River First Nation Heritage and Cultural Centre

194 Reservation Rd. The building has a wigwam-shaped entrance. Open Jul–Aug Wed–Sun 9am–8pm. $5. 902-467-0301. www.bearriver culturalcenter.com.

In summer this recreation centre displays traditional Mi'kmaq drums, beadwork

Pamela Delaney/Michelin

Bear River's stilt buildings

and other items. On view is a 4m/14ft-long **birch-bark canoe** crafted in recent years by a local artisan.

Bear River Vineyards

133 Chute Rd. (from main street, go east to the first street on the left, Chute Rd.; winery is 1km/.6mi on left). Guided tours & *tastings Jul–Sept daily 10:30am–4:30pm. Call ahead to confirm.* ☎ *902-467-4156. www.wine.travel.*

Stretching over 4.5ha/11acres, this vineyard sits on a hill affording gorgeous **views**★ of the river and town. A farmhouse, an 1883 barn and a solar-powered guest cottage anchor the property. The barn is a bank barn, built on a slope so that gravity helps transfer the grape juice to the fermenting room. Tours take a look at the equipment used in the harvesting, fermenting and bottling stages, and include a walk in the vineyard, a visit to the cellar and tastings in the barn's wine shop.

▶ *Return to Hwy. 101 and turn right to continue northeast. In less then 3km/1.8mi, take Rte. 1 along the shore, as Hwy. 101 turns inland.*

Route 1 continues along the shore of the Annapolis Basin.

▶ *Along Rte. 1, watch for signs for Upper Clements Park.*

Upper Clements Park

In Upper Clements, off Rte. 1. ◷*Open mid-Jun–Labour Day daily 10am–7pm.* ◉*$8; rides $2.60 or 10/$22.75.* ♿▯ ☎*902-532-7557 or 888-248-4567. www.upperclementsparks.com.*

Kids This theme park features just under 30 rides and attractions geared to children, although adults will enjoy a number of them, like driving an antique car. Bumper cars, bumper boats, pedal boats and pedal karts put kids in the driver's seat. A carousel, roller coaster and water toboggan take them along for a ride. The Evangeline mini-train makes a leisurely loop around the park. A climbing tower, waterslide and mini-golf area keep children engaged.

▶ *Return to Rte. 1 and continue north.*

Annapolis Royal★★

See ANNAPOLIS ROYAL.

Remains of the old French dike system can be seen from the road. Route 1 crosses the river and continues through country that becomes more rural; wide meadows line the riverbanks.

At **Bridgetown**★ elm-shaded streets contain fine houses, many built by Loyalists. Lawrencetown and **Middleton** are similarly graced with trees. Apple orchards line the hills, particularly between Kingston and Waterville, where fruit stands and "U-pick" farms are frequent.

▶ *Continue on Rte. 1 about 16km/10mi from Middleton to Aylesford.*

Oaklawn Farm Zoo

997 Ward Rd., in Aylesford. From Rte. 1 in Aylesford, turn south at the main intersection and follow the blue "zoo" signs. ⏱*Open Easter weekend–mid-Nov daily 10am–dusk.* 💲*$6.50.* ☎*902-847-9790. www.oaklawnfarmzoo.ca.*

Kids Rather than a typical zoo, Oaklawn is an open farm specializing in the breeding and protection of rare and endangered species. Here big cats, exotic birds, reptiles, horses and primates reside in massive pens, some of which can be walked through by visitors. A relaxed animal-fanatic atmosphere prevails in the privately owned facility. The petting zoo's goats and the monkeys' antics entertain kids; adults are drawn to the purring big cats and the geriatric pride of lions, all born and raised on-site. There are still fences to protect the animals and visitors, but the owners' devotion to these creatures is evident in every detail of facility design and animal care.

▶ *Continue about 13km/8mi on Rte. 1 past Kentville. At the junction with Rte. 359, turn left and take Rte. 359 north 16km/10mi.*

Halls Harbour★

16km/10 mi north of Kentville on Rte. 359.

Situated on the Bay of Fundy's Minas Channel, Halls Harbour is a fishing village so picturesque that it looks like a Hollywood set. But this village is the real thing, and worth the short drive to hone one's photography skills or simply dream about owning a seaside cottage here. Twice a day the Bay of Fundy tides fill the harbour's basin, as much as an inch a minute, only to recede in six hours and strand the fishing fleet on the harbour's muddy bed.

Halls Harbour Lobster Pound

1157 West Halls Harbour Rd. Open May–Oct. ⚓*Tours available.* ☎*902-679-5299. www.hallsharbourlobster.ns.ca.*

Some of its buildings may date to the 1820s, but this pound is a state-of-the-art holding facility for lobsters. Indeed, it is one of the largest lobster pounds in the country, having a capacity to store 65,000 pounds of lobsters. The latest technology has been applied to refrigerate the water and floating pools. A restaurant (♿ *see Address Book)* and gift shop are on-site.

▶ *Continue 41km/25mi on Rte. 1 to junction with Rte. 358.*

Pamela Delaney/Michelin

Resplendent resident at Oaklawn Farm Zoo

The library at Prescott House

Pamela Delaney/Michelin

Excursion to Cape Split★★
28km/17mi north by Rte. 358.

Prescott House Museum★
1633 Starr's Point Rd. in Starr's Point, off Rte. 358, about 5km/3mi north of Rte. 1. ⓧOpen Jun–mid-Oct Mon–Sat 9:30am–5:30pm, Sun 1pm–5:30pm. ⌖$3.25. ♿☎902-542-3984. http://museum.gov. ns.ca.

This whitewashed brick house, designed in the Georgian style with a hipped roof, was built in the early 19C by **Charles Ramage Prescott** (1772-1859), legislator, merchant and acclaimed horticulturalist. On this estate Prescott experimented with new strains of wheat; planted nut trees, grapes and pear trees; and introduced varieties of cherries and apples such as Gravenstein and Baldwin. He gave away cuttings to valley farmers and is partly responsible for the development of the apple industry in this area.

In the 1930s Prescott's great-granddaughter transformed the house, neglected since his death. She brought in furnishings, added a **sun room** in the 1950s and restored the grounds. Some 50 varieties of roses once graced the gardens, which are still lovely today.

The interior of the house contains seven fireplaces. On the first floor, the dining room, **library** and **drawing room** are attractively furnished with oriental rugs, family portraits and some original pieces, including Prescott's 1811 silver tankard. The collection of hand-stitched samplers is particularly noteworthy. Bedrooms on the second floor may be visited as well as the basement kitchen and servants quarters.

▸ *Return to Rte. 358 and continue north.*

The Look Off★★
Approximately 14km/9mi north of Starr's Point. Follow the signs on Rte. 358. Watch for paved pull-off with metal guardrail.

Watch for the official markers for this site—one cannot pass by without stopping. The **view**★★ of Annapolis Valley is magnificent: a 180-degree sweep of patterned farmlands reaching toward the vast Minas Basin and interrupted only by the South Mountains in the distance. At least four counties are visible from this popular vantage point, some 200m/600ft above the valley floor.

About 8km/5mi north of the Look Off, as Route 358 descends into the tiny community of Scots Bay, there is a lovely **view**★ of this bay, the Minas Channel and the Parrsboro Shore of Nova Scotia. At Little Cove boats can be seen resting on the channel bottom at low tide.

Cape Split

Rte. 358 ends. Hiking trail 13km/8mi through woods to tip of cape.

This hook of forested land juts into the Bay of Fundy, edged by magnificent cliffs. Since the tides constantly ebb and flow, the bay's waters in the Minas Channel are muddied. From road's end there are **views** of the wide bay, the shoreline of the cape and the Parrsboro Shore. *☺Caution: be forewarned that the tide comes back in with great speed, raising the water 12m/40ft higher than at low tide. Tragically, people have drowned when the waters rapidly returned.*

▶ *Return via Rte. 358. After about 9km/6mi, take the unpaved road on the left (Stewart Mountain Rd.). At the junction, turn left. The road terminates at a provincial park. Follow signs. Hiking trails for Cape Blomidon are shown on the panel in the visitor parking lot.*

Blomidon★

As the road leaves the woods and descends into flatlands, the first **view**★ of the Minas Basin is grand. The patchwork farmlands of this rural coastland stretch to the cliffs of the basin. Bright red barns and two-storey farmhouses dot the landscape, dominated by the red cliffs of Cape Blomidon. From the end of the picnic area, the **views**★★ in both directions of the wide red beach (at low tide), and the stratified pink cliffs, contrasted with the blue waters of the basin, are breathtaking. *☺Caution: be forewarned that the tide returns with great speed. People walking along the bluffs when the tide was out have drowned when the waters rapidly returned.*

▶ *At Blomidon junction, continue south via Pereau and Delhaven to Rte. 221.*

About 2km/1.2mi south of the junction, there is a **view**★ from Pereaux Small Crafts Harbour of the hole in a rock formation known locally as **Paddys Island,** fully visible at low tide.

▶ *At the junction with Rte. 221, turn right to Canning for Rte. 358 back to Rte. 1.*

Wolfville★

This picture-perfect town is home to **Acadia University,** founded in 1838. Several mansions have been converted into wayside inns. Boutiques and restaurants line the main thoroughfare and during college sessions, the community is alive with scurrying students. Given its small size, Wolfville offers a remarkable array of dining options and lodgings. A downtown cinema has been restored; fair-trade coffee and tea is sold in many shops; restaurants ranging from budget to pricey offer fine cuisine. Both newcomers and locals enjoy the laidback atmosphere.

Gwen Cannon/Michelin

Beach at Cape Blomidon

Annapolis Valley Shopping

Here is a selection of some of the many creative and noteworthy shops that can be found in the Annapolis Valley.

• **ArtCan Gallery & Café,** *9850 Main St., Canning.* ☎902-582-7071, *www.artcan. com.* This combined art gallery and café with good food at fair prices, offers Nova Scotian original art for sale. The windows overlook the historical Canning Ship-yards *(no longer in use). Closed Mon; open for lunch and dinner 6 days a week.*

• **Ernest Cadegan Gallery,** *1943 Saxon St., Canning.* ☎902-582-3243. *www.ernest cadegan.com.* Cadegan photographs speak to the singular tone that is Nova Scotia. His studio/gallery is open by chance or appointment, but his work is also available at Harvest Gallery in Wolfville and at Domaine de Grand Pré winery's gift shop in Grand Pré.

• **Hantsport Studio Pottery,** *70 Main St., Hantsport.* ☎902-684-0378. *www.hant sportstudio.com.* Using lead-free glazes and quality porcelain, renowned potter Les Wright creates handcrafted pieces that are beautiful and fully functional *($20 and up). Open year-round Sat–Sun 10am–4pm or by appointment.*

• **Harvest Gallery,** *462 Main St., Wolfville.* ☎902-542-7093. *www.harvestgallery.ca.* Showing the works of 25 local artists, including world-renowned Alex Colville, this gallery is the quintessential valley outlet for photography, original oils, sculpture and pottery. *Open year-round Mon–Sat 10am–6pm (Fri til 8pm), Sun noon–5pm.*

• **Box of Delights,** *466 Main St., Wolfville.* ☎902-542-9511. This bookstore carries an excellent selection of books by local writers about Wolfville, the valley and all of Nova Scotia, plus maps, guidebooks, and puzzle books for summer days on the beach. Top-quality children's books can be foundon the lower level, along with a play area for the kids. *Open Mon–Fri 9am-5:30pm (Fri til 8pm), Sat 9am–5pm, Sun noon–5pm. Jul & Aug weekdays til 8pm.*

Hennigar's Farm Market in Greenwich

Pamela Delaney/Michelin

• **Hennigar's Farm Market,**
10272 Rte. 1, Greenwich. ☎902-542-3503. More than just a farm market, Hennigar's offers a walking trail, kids' petting zoo and a golf course. The market carries home decor, plants, giftware, bakery goods, fudge, ice cream, apple cider and local products. On premises is the **Cook House ($)**, a popular spot for take-away fish and chips or to eat a hot dog on the outdoor deck. *Open daily 8am–9pm. Closed Dec 24 to weekend before Easter.*

• **Tangled Garden,** *Rte. 1, Grand Pré.* ☎902-542-9811. *www.tangledgarden. ns.ca.*
This remarkable garden shop offers garden tours, an art gallery, elegant home decor products made from dried flowers and grasses, and foods and beverages made from fruits and herbs grown on the premises. The liqueurs are sophisticated, the vinegars fragrant, and the jellies tantalizing, with names like "raspberry-thyme" *(samples available).* Peek into the kitchen to watch delectables created. *Open daily 10am–6pm.*

• **Haat En Kül,** *378 Main St., Wolfville.* ☎902-542-4365. Ethically sourced clothing for men and women made mostly from bamboo or recycled cloth. Jewellery made from recycled items, such as antique buttons, is unique and wearable. *Open year-round Mon–Sat 10am–6pm, Sun noon–5pm.*

Pamela Delaney/Michelin

A rustic barn at the Tangled Garden shop in Grand Pré

Even **eagles** have adopted the area and are in view *(Nov–early Mar)* in and around the village of Sheffield Mills, near Canning. A formal watch is held every year; best viewing months are late-January and early February. Map of viewing sites is available at the Sheffield Mills Community Hall *(98 Black Hole Rd., Exit 12 off Hwy 101, and follow the blue eagle signs.* ☎*902-582-3044 or 800-565-0000. www.eaglens.ca).*

Grand-Pré National Historic Site★

4km/2.5mi east of Wolfville. ⏰*Open mid-May–mid-Oct daily 9am–6pm.* 💲*$8.* ♿ 🅿 ☎*902-542-1952 or 866-542-3631. www.grand-pre.com.*
Inhabited between 1680 and 1755, the former Acadian village of Grand-Pré (French for "great meadow") is now a spacious park overlooking the flat dike-lands the early settlers reclaimed. The hedged lawns, flowerbeds and shade trees serve as a permanent memorial to the Acadians.

A precipitating event of **Deportation** occurred here. In 1747 nearly 100 New England soldiers billeted in the village were killed, as they slept, in a surprise attack by a French force from Quebec. The British suspected treachery among the Acadian inhabitants. Fear of future attacks hardened the British toward

them. In 1755 Gov. **Charles Lawrence** delivered an ultimatum: take an unqualified oath of allegiance or be removed from Nova Scotia. Fearing they would be forced to fight French soldiers, the Acadians refused to take the oath, and were expelled by the thousands. Some eluded capture by hiding. But the majority were dispersed, not able to return for 12 years. After Deportation, their farmlands were given to planters from New England, and later to Loyalists.

The American poet **Henry Wadsworth Longfellow** chose Grand-Pré as the setting for his poem *Evangeline*. Published in 1847, the work tells of a young couple's separation during Deportation and Evangeline's subsequent search for her love, Gabriel—only to find him dying. On the site of the first church of Grand-Pré stands a small **chapel**. Completed in 1930, the chapel is constructed of local stone in a style reminiscent of churches in France. A bronze **statue** of Evangeline by **Louis-Philippe Hébert** stands on the grounds. Opened in 2003, a large interpretive centre includes a theatre, a state-of-the-art exhibit hall, and a dramatic mural by Wayne Boucher that incorporates the colours and star of the Acadian flag. Shown frequently, a film *(22min)* with some 3D elements is a good introduction to the site. **Displays** in the exhibit hall are arranged accord-

Chapel at Grand-Pré National Historic Site

Pamela Delaney/Michelin

Haliburton House Museum★

1414 Clifton Ave. Follow signs from cause-way. ○*Open Jun–mid-Oct Mon–Sat 9:30am–5:30pm, Sun 1pm–5:30pm.* ⊚*$3.25.* ☎*902-798-2915. http://museum.gov.ns.ca.*

At the end of a long driveway stands this house, built in 1836 on the tree-covered estate of **Thomas Chandler Haliburton** (1796-1865), judge, legislator and author. After his formal education, he established a law practice in Annapolis Royal and later served as a justice on the provincial Supreme Court. Although he wrote works on history and politics, he was the first Canadian author to achieve international renown with the publication of *The Clockmaker; or, The Sayings and Doings of Samuel Slick of Slickville* (Ⓛsee sidebar).

ing to three themes: the Acadian settlement, the British takeover and the final Deportation.

Windsor

Famous as the home of Thomas Haliburton, one of the most prominent Nova Scotians of his day, the town is set at the confluence of the Avon and St. Croix rivers. The Avon is sealed off from the Bay of Fundy by a causeway. Once the shipping point for lumber and gypsum mined nearby, the town was the site of the 18C Acadian settlement of Piziquid, which was taken over by New Englanders after Deportation and renamed Windsor.

Shand House Museum

389 Avon St. ♿*Street parking prohibited. Upon entrance to Windsor, watch for signs to separate parking area.* ♿*Uphill walk to the house.* ○*Open Jun–mid-Oct Mon–Sat 9:30am–5:30pm, Sun 1pm–5:30pm.* ⊚*$3.25.* ☎*902-798-8213. www.shand.museum.gov.ns.ca.*

The most imposing of the houses atop Ferry Hill overlooking the Avon River, this Victorian dwelling was completed in 1891. The staircase is crafted of cherry, and several rooms feature oak interiors. The furnishings are those of the original and only owners. Visitors can ascend the square tower.

Sam Slick

Thomas Chandler Haliburton became famous as the creator of the character Sam Slick, a fictitious Yankee peddler. His 22 stories about Sam were first published in installments in the newspaper the *Novascotian*. In 1836 the newspaper's owner, Joseph Howe, published them as a book under the title *The Clockmaker; or, The Sayings and Doings of Samuel Slick of Slickville*. It became so popular, a second series followed in 1838. In total an estimated 80 editions were printed during the 19C. Filled with wisecracks and social satire, the book is basically a series of moral essays, made palatable by Haliburton's humour. A caricature of the proverbially dishonest 19C Connecticut salesmen who roamed rural areas, Slick travels all over Nova Scotia, making fun of its unenterprising inhabitants. Many of the epigrams he coined are still in use today: "six of one and half a dozen of the other," "an ounce of prevention is worth a pound of cure," "facts are stranger than fiction," "the early bird gets the worm," "as quick as a wink," and "jack of all trades and master of none" are among the most familiar.

A Sampling of Wineries

Some wine pundits have predicted that Nova Scotia's Annapolis Valley will rival the success of California's Napa Valley—just give it about 20 years to catch up. Wolfville may be command central when it comes to experiencing some of Nova Scotia's up-and-coming wineries. Three lie within a 15min drive of the town. **Domaine de Grand-Pré** in Grand Pré *(11611 Rte. 1, Exit 10 off Hwy. 10, follow the signs;* ○*May–mid-Oct 11am–6pm;* ✗ ⑆ 🅿 ☎*902-542-1753; www.grand prewines.ns.ca)* is the closest, and in addition to tastings and tours, its restaurant, **Le Caveau ($$)** impresses patrons with al fresco dining underneath a canopy of grapevines. This winery is perhaps most well known among Nova Scotians for its L'Acadie Blanc wine, made from a grape that grows especially well in the Annapolis Valley. **Blomidon Estate Winery** in nearby Canning *(10318 Hwy. 221, Exit 11 off Hwy. 101, follow signs through Canning;* ○*call for hours;* 🅿 ⑆ ☎*902-582-7565 or 877-582-7565; www.blomidonwine.com)* is a smaller family-run business that offers tastings, a wine shop and use of well-positioned picnic benches in the vineyards if you choose to bring your own lunch. **Gaspereau Vineyards** in Gaspereau *(2239 White Rock Rd., Exit 11 off Hwy. 101 and follow signs;* ○*mid-May–mid-Oct 9am–6pm;* ⑆ 🅿 ☎*902-542-1455; www.gaspereauwine.com)*, owned by Jost Vineyards in Central Nova, is a boutique operation that has won several awards; it offers tours and samples. With experts on board from France and Ontario, **Benjamin Bridge** vineyards is producing sparkling wines and still varietals to rival Old World wines, including Sauvignon Blanc *(1842 White Rock Rd., Wolfville;* ○ 🅿 *call for hours;* ☎*902-542-4407; www.benjaminbridge.com)*.

Fort Edward National Historic Site

Off King St. near the causeway. ○*Grounds open year-round. Fort open Jul–Aug Tue–Sat 10am–6pm.* 🅿 ☎*902-532-2321. www.pc.gc.ca.*

Possessing the oldest blockhouse in Canada, this fort tops a hillock at the edge of town. Built in 1750 as a British stronghold in Acadian territory, the blockhouse was later a point of departure for Acadians assembled for Deportation.

From the grassy fortification, there are **views** of the tidal river, the causeway and Lake Pesaquid. Made of squared timbers, the wooden **blockhouse** is the fort's only remaining building. The walls of its two storeys—the upper storey overhanging the lower—are pierced by square portholes for cannon and loopholes for musket fire. Inside are displays on the blockhouse defence system and the fort's history.

Fort Edward National Historic Site

Annapolis Royal ★★

POPULATION 444 – MAP INSIDE FRONT COVER

One of Canada's oldest settlements, this gracious town has a pleasant **site** overlooking the great basin of the Annapolis River. Acadians reclaimed the marshland by building a dam across the river with floodgates to control the water level. Twice a day the Bay of Fundy tides rush in, reversing the river's flow. The quiet charm of the town belies its turbulent past as the site of French-English battles and Acadian struggles. The town's full-time population is small, but annually it attracts upwards of 100,000 visitors to its historic sites and elegant inns.

- **Information:** Town Hall, 285 St. George St., ☎902-532-5769 or 877-522-1110. www.annapolisroyal.com
- **Orient Yourself:** The town is small and walkable. Saint George Street is the main thoroughfare. Saturday mornings a seasonal farmers' market gives locals and tourists an opportunity to meet and mingle.
- **Parking:** There are no parking meters. Three municipal lots serve the town. Most inns have their own parking lots.
- **Don't Miss:** The tidal generating station.
- **Organizing Your Time:** If you plan to stay in town, make reservations early as rooms sell out quickly, especially on holiday weekends. *See the Address Book for a selection of lodgings in the area.*
- **Especially for Kids:** Port Royal Habitation is nicely sinister.

A Bit of History

In 1635 the French governor **Charles de Menou d'Aulnay** built a new **Port Royal** on the site of what is now Annapolis Royal. The predecessor of the present Fort Anne was constructed by the French, but funds were insufficient to maintain it. In 1710 the fort fell to a New England expedition under Col. Francis Nicholson.

When the mainland was ceded to the British by the Treaty of Utrecht in 1713, the fortified settlement became the provincial capital, renamed Annapolis Royal after England's **Queen Anne**. Constantly threatened by surrounding Acadian settlements sympathetic to soldiers from Quebec or Louisbourg, it frequently withstood French attack. In 1749 the capital was relocated to Halifax, where British troops were being strengthened.

Officers' quarters, Fort Anne

Pamela Delaney/Michelin

Mathieu Da Costa

Evidence shows that Mathieu Da Costa, reportedly a free black of West African descent, signed a contract in Amsterdam in 1608 to work as an interpreter in the New World for Sieur de Monts beginning in 1609. By that time, reliance on black interpreters was a century-old tradition, having originated with Portuguese voyages off the coast of Africa. The French, Dutch, and Portuguese used interpreters in their trading negotiations with the indigenous inhabitants of Nova Scotia and Newfoundland. It is believed that Da Costa spoke French, Portuguese and Dutch as well as a lingua franca known as pidgin, probably based on the language spoken by Basque fisherman and thought to be the common tongue used in trade with the Mi'kmaq in the early days of the fur trade. Apparently Da Costa's translation services were highly sought among the French and Dutch. It is likely he travelled much of the Atlantic shore during his day.

Annapolis Royal was relegated to an outpost, eventually losing detachments to Halifax. In 1854 the few soldiers remaining were moved to New Brunswick. Much of the area's history is evident today: de Monts' habitation has been reconstructed near Port Royal, Fort Anne has been partially re-created, and the older buildings along **Lower Saint George Street** have been renovated.

Sights

Fort Anne National Historic Site★

Grounds open year-round. Visitor centre open Jul–Aug daily 9am–6pm. Mid-May–Jun & Sept–mid-Oct 9am–5:30pm. $4. ☐ ☎902-532-2397. www.pc.gc.ca.
A peaceful expanse of green in the centre of town, this fort was once the most fought-over place in Canada, suffering 14 sieges during the Anglo-French wars. Under attack for one week, the fort finally fell to British and New England forces in 1710. The French were ousted and a British governor oversaw the garrison and town. In 1713 British sovereignty was sealed with the Treaty of Utrecht, and Annapolis Royal was declared the capital of Nova Scotia. British troops lived in the fort until 1854. In 1917 Fort Anne became the first National Historic Park (now Site) in Canada.
Still visible today, the French-built Vauban-style earthworks were completed in 1708, with later alterations by the British. In one of the bastions stands a stone **powder magazine** of the French

period. From the earthworks there is a **view**★ of the Annapolis Basin.
A distinctive building with high chimneys and dormer windows, the **Officers' Quarters**★ stands in the centre of the fort. Built in 1797 by order of Prince Edward, the quarters, now restored, house a **museum,** which includes a display on the fort's military history.
Outside flies the flag of the Grand Union, a combination of the English cross of St. George and the Scottish cross of St. Andrew. The Union Jack as we know it today did not come into existence until the union with Ireland in 1801, when the cross of St. Patrick was added.

Historic Gardens★

On Upper Saint George St. (Rte. 8) just south of Fort Anne. Open Jul–Aug daily 8am–dusk. May–Jun & Sept–Oct daily 9am–5pm. $8.50. ☎902-532-7018. www.historicgardens.com.
Situated on a 4ha/10-acre site overlooking Allain's River, a tributary of the Annapolis, these theme gardens exemplify the horticultural diversity of the region's past as well as recent gardening technology.
The **Acadian Garden** has a traditional cottage and a replica of the dike system. Formal in style, the **Governor's Garden** is characteristic of landscape architecture in the early 18C, when the English governor was based in Annapolis Royal. The **Victorian Garden** reveals a more natural setting, a trend that became fashionable in the 19C. The **Rose Garden** traces the development of this ever-popular species.

Habitation at Port-Royal National Historic Site

Gwen Cannon/Michelin

Annapolis Tidal Generating Station★

On the Causeway (Rte. 1). Visitor centre ⏰ *open mid-May–mid-Oct daily 10am–6pm.* ♿ 🅿 ☎ *902-532-5454. www.ns power.ca.*

North America's first tidal power project, this station uses a low-head straight-flow turbine to harness the enormous energy of the Bay of Fundy tides to produce electricity. The exhibit area upstairs in the visitor centre explains the project and its construction through models, photographs and a video presentation *(10min)*. A causeway over the dam affords views of tidal activity and of the generating station.

Excursions

North Hills Museum★

5065 Granville Rd. in Granville Ferry. ⏰ *Open Jun–mid-Oct Mon–Sat 9:30am–5:30pm, Sun 1pm–5:30pm.* ⏣ *$3.* ♿ ☎ *902-532-7754. museum.gov.ns.ca.*

This two-storey wood-frame house has retained a pioneer look, despite modifications. The weathered 18C farmhouse contains a Georgian decor and the antique **collection**★ of a Toronto banker. Gifted to the province upon his death in 1974, the paintings, silver, pewter, ceramics and Georgian glass reflects Robert Patterson's refined tastes. Chairs, tables, a desk, dresser and other pieces in walnut, oak and mahogany are among his Chippendale, Hepplewhite and Sheraton furniture collection.

Port-Royal National Historic Site★★

10km/6mi from Annapolis Royal Causeway. ⏰ *Open Jul–Aug daily 9am–6pm. Mid-May–Jun & Sept–mid-Oct 9am–5:30pm.* ⏣ *$4.* 🅿 ☎ *902-532-2898. www. pc.gc.ca.*

This *habitation* (a French word for "dwelling") is a replica of Canada's first European settlement of any permanence. In a style reminiscent of 16C French farms, the weathered, fortified buildings joined around a central courtyard were designed by **Samuel de Champlain** (1567-1635), captain of the expedition of **Sieur de Monts**.

De Monts' company moved to the Annapolis Basin and constructed the habitation in 1605. Boredom and sickness prompted Champlain to form a social club wherein members alternated as grand master and organizers of gourmet feasts. Meat and fowl, including moose, beaver, rabbit, raccoon, goose and partridge, were served. In 1606 member Marc Lescarbot wrote the first play performed in Canada, the **Theatre of Neptune.** The **Order of Good Cheer,** as the club was called, proved successful. Crops were grown, and trade with the Mi'kmaq established. Just as the settlement seemed rooted, de Monts' trading rights were revoked in 1607, and the expedition returned to France.

Destroyed in 1613 by English forces, the buildings were reconstructed in 1939 by the Canadian government, using Champlain's sketch and writings as guides.

Over the gateway entry hangs the **coat of arms** of France and Navarre, ruled by King Henry IV (French kings held the additional title of King of Navarre from 1589 until the French Revolution). A **well** with a shingled roof stands in the middle of the courtyard. Around it are the residences of the governor, priest and artisans. The kitchen, blacksmith's shop, community room where the Order met, and the chapel can be visited, as can the storerooms, wine cellar, and trading room where the Mi'kmaq brought their furs. All furnishings are meticulous reproductions of early 17C styles. Costumed staff demonstrate the activities of fort life.

Each structure has a steeply pitched roof and, except for the storeroom, a fieldstone chimney. A building technique known as **colombage,** the term used in France for log-filled, wood-frame construction, was employed to form the walls. This construction can be appreciated only from the interior, since the exterior of the buildings is covered with lapped boarding. No nails or spikes join the timbers: they are mortised and tenoned and pinned together.

Kejimkujik National Park★

48km/30mi southeast of Annapolis Royal via Rte. 8. Park entrance near Maitland Bridge. ◐Open mid-Jun–Labour Day daily 8:30am–9pm. Rest of the year daily 8:30am–4:30pm. ◐Closed Dec 25. ◉$5.50. Visitor centre same hours (in late fall call for hrs). Canoe & bicycle rental at Jakes Landing. ♿ P ☎ 902-682-2772. www.pc.gc.ca.

Recreation and scenic beauty await visitors at this 404sq km/156sq mi forested park, which became a national park in 1968. Named Kejimkujik [pronounced KEJ-gee-ma-COO-gee], a Mi'kmaq word, it is affectionately called "Keji" by locals. For centuries the park's waterways served the Mi'kmaq as canoe routes and still afford peaceful passage today.

Devoid of mountains, the park sits on a vast, flat plain in the southern interior of the province. Glaciation beginning 100,000 years ago shaped its topography, forming the many rivers and lakes, the largest of which is Kejimkujik Lake. The eskers, drumlins and granite boulders are primarily the result of the last Ice Age some 25,000 years ago. The lakes are shallow and linked by winding rivers, making them attractive to the Mi'kmaq who camped along the rivers to hunt and fish. The park's forests were substantially logged in the early days of area settlement. The waterways provided transport for timber cuttings; logs were floated even to Liverpool via the Mersey River. Limited gold-mining operations of the past, largely unsuccessful, are evident in a few deteriorated cabins and rusted boilers within the park.

The forests are a mix of coniferous and deciduous trees. White pine, eastern

Canoeing at Kejimkujik National Park

Sandra Phinney/Michelin

hemlock, red maple and yellow birch can be found, as can ferns and some orchids. Black bear, white-tailed deer, porcupine, beaver and the rare northern ribbon snake inhabit the park. Some 178 species of birds have been recorded; the most visible are common loon, warblers and woodpeckers; common mergansers and black duck are among the park's waterbirds. Brook trout and yellow and white perch swim in the waters.

The entry road is the park's only road. Stop in at the **visitor centre**, near the Maitland Bridge entrance, for a park map. More than a dozen hiking trails thread the park. The **Mill Falls Trail** leads through fern-filled woods along the amber-coloured **Mersey River** to its foamy rapids. From the fire tower *(on main park road, 10km/6mi from park entrance)*, an elevated **view**★ of Kejimkujik Lake is possible. Guided walks led by park staff are the only way to visit grounds where age-old rock carvings, or **petroglyphs,** have been left by the Mi'kmaq.

CENTRAL NOVA SCOTIA

Central Nova Scotia comprises the mainland extending 306km/190mi, as the crow flies, from Cape Chignecto on the Bay of Fundy in the west to Cape Canso on Chedabucto Bay in the east. From Advocate Harbour, near Cape Chignecto on the north shore of Minas Basin, the Cobequid-Chedabuctou fault zone stretches across the peninsula to Chedabuctou Bay, geologically dividing the province into north and south; exposed faults along the Parrsboro shore remain as evidence of the colliding of ancient continents 400 million years ago. The Cobequid Mountains, part of the Appalachians, rise beyond the shore up to an elevation of 360m/1,181ft; Wentworth Valley is one of Nova Scotia's few ski areas. The Acadian Forest, a mix of northern boreal forest with southern hardwoods, covers much of the interior. There are few large lakes, save Governor Lake, but lakes proliferate nearer the eastern shore. Exploitation of the area's natural resources led to socioeconomic development: vast coal seams in Springhill, timber turned into ships at Maitland, salt marshes that support hay production near Amherst. Geologists and fossil hunters have searched the Joggins Fossil Cliffs, named a UNESCO World Heritage Site in mid-2008, ever since Charles Lyell, considered the founder of modern geology, visited the area in 1842. A marked Scottish influence is seen along the Northumberland Strait, which attracted Highlander Scots in the 18C.

Cows in pasture in autumn, Antigonish

Nova Scotia Tourism, Culture and Heritage

Amherst to Truro ★

MAP INSIDE FRONT COVER

This driving itinerary takes in the landscape of the "arm" of Nova Scotia's peninsula that lies east of the Isthmus of Chignecto. The tour begins in Amherst in the northwestern part of the province and heads south through Cumberland County to the northern shore of the Minas Basin. It follows Highway 2, themed the Glooscap Trail, which is named for the powerful man-god figure in Mi'kmaq legend, the first human, who is said to have birthed the Five Islands and shaped the Bay of Fundy shore. Over the millennia the bay's tides have advanced and receded, carving out caves, keyholes and fingers of rock along the shore. The bay's rich waters attract seals and shorebirds; amethyst and agate can still be found along its isolated beaches. Scenic provincial parks are interspersed with villages named Parrsboro, Economy, Portapique and Masstown, among others. Cumberland County is a major producer of Nova Scotia's blueberries. In the town of Oxford, the **Wild Blueberry & Maple Centre** is open for tours and samples *(10km/6mi east of Springhill; 105 Lower Main St., ☎902-447-2170; www.town.oxford. ns.ca/visit/wbmc.htm).*

- **Information:** Northumberland Shore Visitor Information Centre, Amherst. ☎902-667-8429. www.centralnovascotia.com.
- **Don't Miss:** Cape Chignecto Provincial Park.
- **Organizing Your Time:** This drive is short; include an overnight stay in Parrsboro, Truro or Antigonish.
- **Especially for Kids:** The Fundy Geological Museum in Parrsboro and the Glooscap Heritage Centre near Truro.
- **Also See:** CAPE BRETON ISLAND

Driving Tour

135km/84mi via Hwy. 2

Amherst

Sitting inland from the Cumberland Basin, Nova Scotia's westernmost town lies just 3km/1.8mi from the New Brunswick border. Home to nearly 10,000 residents, Amherst is a manufacturing hub and service centre for Cumberland County. It was founded in 1764 by English immigrants who were later joined by British Loyalists fleeing the US after the American Revolution. Its economy benefited from shipbuilding and later saw an increase in industry and commerce when the Intercolonial Railway's line passed through in the 1870s.

To the east Amherst borders the **Tantramar Marsh**, now a National Wildlife Area that extends inland from the Bay of Fundy some 10km/6mi. Canada geese, sandpipers and other migrating birds visit the area. The Acadians enriched the soils of the marsh by building dikes to prevent the influx of salt water from the tides. Up until the 1930s hay was grown in abundance in the salt marshes, and shipped as far as Europe. Hay barns might still be seen along Highway 2, but few remain.

▶ *From Amherst, follow Hwy. 2 south 19km/12mi south to Springhill.*

Springhill ★

Tourist Information Booth at Community Centre, 6 Main St. ☎902-597-3000. http://town.springhill.ns.ca.

This town is famous as a coal-mining centre that has suffered more disasters than any other place of its size in Canada. In 1891 an enormous blast in one of the mines tore out a vast area. When a subsequent flame swept through the mine workings, 125 men died. Then, in 1916, a subterranean fire filled the galleries. No one was killed, but much damage was done. An explosion and fire in 1956 caused 39 deaths. The next year a fire razed most of the business district of the

Address Book

♿ *For dollar sign categories, see the Legend on the cover flap.*

WHERE TO STAY

$$ Gillespie House Inn – *358 Main St., Parrsboro.* 🅿 ⌂ ☎*902-254-3196. www.gillespiehouseinn.com. 7 rooms. Closed Nov–Apr.* Located in the heart of Parrsboro, this stately inn was restored by the current owners and furnished with antiques and art. The whole home evokes country elegance and gentility. Handsome sleigh beds or four posters crafted of hickory, mahogany or pine dressed with down duvets sit atop hardwood floors with oriental rugs. Some of the bathrooms feature claw-foot tubs. One main-floor guest room is wheelchair accessible. The hosts are avid outdoors people and can recommend much to do in the immediate area, or simply relax on the Victorian veranda in the shade of maple trees. Homemade muffins accompany a cooked breakfast that is included in the rate.

$$ The Maple Inn – *2358 Western Ave., Parrsboro.* 🅿 ⌂ ☎*902-254-3735. www.mapleinn.ca. 8 rooms.* Beautifully restored, this large 1893 Italianate-style house is owned by a young family from Vienna. They have brought a touch of Austrian hospitality to this small Nova Scotian town. Immaculate and well-appointed, the guest rooms are each decorated individually with tradi-tional furnishings, some antique, and flowered wallpaper. The Empire Suite provides an ocean view; the Tower Suite has a whirlpool tub. The dining room, where a complimentary breakfast is served, recalls a country restaurant, and the staff of local high-school students is delightful. The Maple Inn is just a few minutes' walk from the Ship's Company Theatre.

$$ The Regent Bed & Breakfast – *175 East Victoria St., Amherst.* 🅿 ⌂ ☎*902-667-7676. www.theregent.ca. 4 rooms.* Built in 1898, this attractive Georgian house, with a hipped roof and double chimneys, has an equally impressive interior: stained- and leaded-glass windows, intricate wood trim and two fireplaces with carved-wood surrounds. Painted in pleasing historic colours, guest rooms sport four-poster or iron beds, crisp white duvets and hardwood maple floors. With fastidious attention to detail (fine china and Depression glass used for food and beverage service), the owners intuitively cater to the different needs of leisure versus business travellers. Modern conveniences such as high-speed Internet and excellent reading lights have been added. Breakfasts incorporate local products, such as the maple syrup or blueberry sauce that laces French toast with sausage.

$$$ The John Stanfield Inn & Fine Dining – *437 Prince St., Truro (behind the Holiday Inn).* 🅿 ⌂ ☎*877-505-7666. www.johnstandfieldinn.com. 10 rooms.* This imposing Queen Anne mansion, built in 1902, has been converted into an urban inn and meeting facility. Its downtown location in a sea of asphalt and warehouse bays behind a hotel is unfortunate. Inside, however, the fully restored house embraces guests within its highly polished wood interior, complete with hand-carved mantels, tall arches and beamed ceiling. Modern amenities like wireless Internet and jetted bathtubs complement antique furnishings and rich fabrics. Taste-fully appointed guest rooms, all with private bathrooms, feature comfortable furnishings; some have hardwood floors and a fireplace. A complimentary break-fast is included. In the **dining room ($$)** *(Tue–Sun; dinner only)*, appetizers like pan-roasted scallops with lobster pineapple salad preview palate-pleas-ing entrées such as dry-boat halibut, Arctic char, Nova Scotia pork or Ontario veal. The wine list, presided over by the inn's sommelier, is truly international.

WHERE TO EAT

$ Harbour View Restaurant – *145 Pier Rd., Parrsboro.* ☎*902-254-3507.* **Canadian.** True to its name, this totally unpretentious restaurant has not only the aforementioned view of Parrsboro harbour, but also paper placemats, waitresses who appear to be having fun, and a varied menu that focuses on lobster, scallops, clams and other fresh seafood. There isn't much more needed on vacation, except a piece of Harbour View's homemade pies topped with mile-high meringue. The adjacent wharf is a good place to witness how high or low the tide is, since lobster boats may be anchored there—in water, or at the bottom of a muddy bed.

$$ The Lightkeeper's Kitchen – *In the Lighthouse on Cape d'Or, off Rte. 209, 6km/3.7mi east of Advocate Harbour. Closed Nov—Apr.* ☎902-670-0534. *www.capedor.ca.* **Contemporary.** Eating here is like dining at the end of the world. The view from this lighthouse is stunning, and the cuisine does not take a back seat, as is often the case.

The chef changes the menu daily, but one can be assured of seafood, a vegetarian or a meat dish. The dining room seats only about 40 people, so dinner reservations are essential in July and August. Lunch is also served; the chowder is excellent. Note that cash only is accepted and there is a relatively steep hill to walk to the lighthouse from the parking area. The adjacent lightkeeper's house holds four **guest rooms ($$)** for overnight stays.

town. Finally, in 1958, an underground upheaval, or "bump," caused the deaths of 76 men. All the mines closed in 1962, the death knell of an industry already doomed by conversion to oil and gas as heating fuels.

Springhill is the birthplace of one of Canada's beloved singers, Anne Murray (b. 1945), who rocketed to pop stardom in 1970 with a hit called "Snowbird."

Anne Murray Centre

36 Main St. ⏰*Open mid-May–mid-Oct daily 9am–5pm.* ⌾*Contribution requested.* ☎902-597-8614. *www.anne murraycentre.com.*

Opened in 1989, this homage to the hometown girl who made good attracts fans from Canada and the US who have followed Ms. Murray's life and career since 1970. Awards, memorabilia, photographs and videos showcase the singer's accomplishments in the world of contemporary music.

Miners' Museum★

On Black River Rd. Follow signs along Hwy. 2 (Parrsboro direction). ⏰*Open Jun–mid-Oct daily 9am–5pm.* ⌾*$4.50.* ☎902-597-3449. *www.town.springhill.ns.ca.*

This museum commemorates the tragedy of the disasters and the bravery of the rescuers through displays such as newspaper clippings and mining equipment. The **mine tour** is conducted by retired miners. Equipped with hard hats, rubber coats and boots, visitors descend about 270m/900ft into the old Syndicate Mine via a tunnel of regular height, rather than those along which the miners had to crawl. Both old and new mining methods are demonstrated.

▶ *Continue south 46 km/26 mi on Hwy. 2 to Parrsboro.*

Parrsboro

This picturesque town of about 1,600 citizens is noteworthy for its stately residences and quiet pace of life, but rocks

Central Nova Scotia's Rural Routes

Three rural routes can be taken to best see the countryside of this region. Starting from Amherst on the New Brunswick-Nova Scotia border, Highway 2 leads southeast to Springhill, curves west and then south to Parrsboro and along the Minas Basin before crossing the peninsula to Halifax. Also originating in Amherst, Highway 6 heads east along the shore of the Northumberland Strait to terminate at Pictou. Highway 4 begins 41km/25mi southeast of Amherst, sprouting from Highway 104, and travels in an easterly direction to the Canso Causeway, which joins the mainland with Cape Breton Island. From Antigonish Highway 7 goes south to the Atlantic coast, turns west at Liscomb and winds along the eastern shore of the province for most of the way to Dartmouth.

and fossils are bringing in a growing number of visitors today. In 1984 a local resident discovered what is reputedly the smallest **dinosaur print** on earth near Parrsboro's harbour. Two years later scientists uncovered 100,000 pieces of fossilized bones: evidence of primitive sharks, reptiles, and fish as well as dinosaurs. It has been called the most significant find of the Triassic-Jurassic period in North America. The cliffs around the town are known to contain fossils of prehistoric plants and animals.

Today Parrsboro maintains two museums that tout the area's geology and hosts the annual **Nova Scotia Gem and Mineral Show,** which brings in rockhounds and gem dealers from around the country. Eldon George, who discovered the dinosaur print, has put it on display in his mineral shop-museum in town.

The **Ship's Company Theatre** (18 Lower Main St.; ☎902-254-3000; www. shipscompany.com) has been in existence since 1984. Its new building, opened in 2004, was constructed around the *MV Kipawo*. The vessel was once used for ferry service from Parrsboro across the Minas Basin. The venue is dedicated to showcasing mostly Nova Scotian playwrights (Jul–mid-Sept).

Fundy Geological Museum

162 Two Island Rd. ⏱Open mid-May–Oct daily 9:30am–5:30pm. Late Mar–early May Mon–Sat 8:30am–4:30pm. ✆$6.25. ☎902-254-3814 or 866-856-3466 (Canada only). www.museum.gov.ns.ca.

Sea stacks at Cape Chignecto

Sandra Phinney/Michelin

🧒 This museum mines the wealth of fossil finds in the area. Opened in 1993 it seeks to interpret the geological history of the Bay of Fundy and showcase specimens discovered nearby. Some of the bones on view are 200 million years old. A highlight of the exhibit hall is a full-scale replica of a prosauropod skeleton. Minerals, amethysts and fossils that have been found locally round out the displays. A short film *(4min)* explains the Bay of Fundy tides.

In the research laboratory, visitors can watch museum staff analyzing and classifying the dinosaur bones.

Parrsboro Rock and Mineral Shop and Museum

349 Whitehall Rd. ⏱Open mid-May–Oct daily 10am–6pm. ✆Contribution requested. ☎902-254-2981.

This is Eldon George's shop, the man who discovered the small dinosaur print in the area in 1984. It's on exhibit here along with other fossils and minerals. He stocks supplies and equipment for prospecting. A lapidary, silversmith and goldsmith by trade, George displays his creations in the shop and arranges tours to fossil sites nearby.

Excursion

Cape Chignecto Provincial Park★★

100km/62mi round-trip by Rte. 209, west of Parrsboro. Red Rocks Entrance at West Advocate. ⏱Open early May–Nov. ⚠☎902-392-2085. www.capechignecto. net or www.novascotiaparks.ca. ♿All visitors must check in and check out with park staff.

The largest of all of Nova Scotia's provincial parks, this newly minted park (1998) has impressive statistics. Cape Chignecto covers 4,200ha/10,378 acres and extends along 29km/18mi of coastline; cliffs 185m/600ft tall plunge into the Bay of Fundy. It is a geologist's dream: the exposed folds and faults between Red Rocks and McGahey Brook point to a massive collision of continents 400 million years ago. **Spicer's Cove** reveals red rhyolite cliff faces, the work of age-old volcanic activity. Squally Point retains evidence of glacial retreat in its tide-honed terraces and an elevated **beach** that sits 35m/115ft above sea level. Caves, spits, sea stacks, and keyhole rock formations are some of the park's diverse geological treasures. The scenery and views are incomparable, and as no vehicles are allowed, the heavy forest remains emission-free, offering relatively pure air at every step.

Eight well-marked trails originate from the visitor centre near the Red Rocks entrance. The lengthy **Coastal Trail** winds 51km/32mi along the north shore of the Minas Basin, encompassing the cape itself and then heads north along the Chignecto Bay's eastern shore. The much shorter **Fundy Ridge Trail** *(5km/3mi)* offers good views of the bay. From the Eatonville day-use area, which opened in mid-2008, the trail to the sea stacks at Three Sisters is only 2.2km/1.4mi round-trip. Otherwise, **Three Sisters** can be accessed from the lengthy 28km/17mi Eatonville Trail. A cabin and bunkhouse, considered to be in a wilderness area, can be reserved for overnight camping.

▶ *From Parrsboro continue east 32km/20mi on Hwy. 2 to Five Islands.*

Five Islands Provincial Park★

🕐*Open late-Jun–early Sept.* ⛺*Camping reservations* ☎*888-544-3434. www. novascotiaparks.ca.* ☺*Note: hiking trails are temporarily closed due to recent storm damage. Don't get caught on the tidal flats when the swift-moving tides rush in: get a tide schedule in advance of your visit.*

Encompassing 637ha/1,573acres, this park stretches along the Bay of Fundy, preserving sand dunes from the Triassic period, lava flows dating to the Jurassic period, lake deposits from the time dinosaurs roamed the earth and rock formations sculpted by glacial and tidal actions. The park's 90m/300ft red-sandstone cliffs tower over the bay's tides. Beech, yellow birch, sugar maple and other hardwoods top the hills; a mix of trees edge the shore. Mi'kmaq legend says that **Glooscap,** the first human, possessing godlike strength, threw five boulders and clumps of mud at a large beaver who had damaged his medicine

☺ **A Bit of Advice** ☺
A Caution

Given their importance to science, the fossils exposed continuously by the Bay of Fundy tides are protected by the Special Places Protection Act, which applies to all fossils found in the province. The Fundy Geological Museum requests that visitors who spot fossilized bones or tracks in the area report them to the museum before digging them up, so as not to be in violation of the law.

garden, thus creating the five islands lying offshore. Aligned in a row off the point known as The Old Wife, Moose Island, the largest and closest to shore, holds a nesting site for eagles; Diamond, Long, Egg (the smallest) and Pinnacle dot the waters farther off the shore. The park affords opportunities for beachcombing, clam digging, hiking and sea kayaking. Amethyst, jasper and agate can be found along the beaches.

▶ *Continue east 50km/30mi on Hwy. 2 to Truro.*

Truro

🛈*Welcome Centre, Victoria Square.* ☎*902-893-2922 (May–Oct). www.town.truro. ns.ca.*

Set on the Salmon River near its mouth, this town of nearly 12,000 people in

Lighthouse, Five Islands Provincial Park

Nova Scotia Tourism, Culture and Heritage

Colchester County experiences the high tides of the Bay of Fundy and the tidal bore. Site of a thriving Acadian community called Cobequid before the Deportation, Truro was later settled by people from Northern Ireland and New Hampshire. Today this manufacturing centre sits at the intersection of several major highways and is home to the Nova Scotia Agricultural College. The central business district with shops and services lies along Prince Street and intersecting streets.

In 1948 the province's only **Palaeo-Indian site,** dating from the last Ice Age, was discovered in the nearby farming community of Debert, 20km/12mi west of Truro. It is the oldest archaeological site in Nova Scotia (see sidebar below).

Victoria Park

Brunswick St., downtown. Open daily dawn–dusk. *902-893-2922.*
This spacious urban park spreads out near the southern edge of the Salmon River. It was created in 1887 when 10ha/25acres of land were donated locally for a public park. Additional acreage was given the following year and since then, further acquisitions have increased the park to a remarkable 405ha/1,000acres. Natural features of the largely forested expanse include Lepper Brook, a spectacular gorge, Waddell Falls and Joseph Howe Falls. Among the man-made attractions are a large swimming pool, tennis courts, picnic grounds, a playground and a replica of an Acadian well.

Tidal Bore★

For the best viewpoint, take Hwy 2 (Robie St.) west from downtown Truro, pass under Hwy. 102 and turn right on Tidal Bore Rd. to reach the Tidal Bore Observation Deck.

Before you go, obtain a tidal schedule from the welcome centre in Victoria Sq. Arrive at the observation deck 15min prior and stay a full hour, if possible, to see high tide.

Twice a day the tide rushes up the Salmon River from the Bay of Fundy, causing a wave that may vary from a ripple to several feet in height. What is more interesting than this tidal wave is the tremendous inrush of water and the rapid rise in water level immediately following it. In fact, high tide is reached just over an hour after the arrival of the bore. Bore rafting is popular in the area; if you're adventurous, contact the welcome centre for area rafting companies.

Glooscap Heritage Centre★

65 Treaty Trail. Take Exit 13A off Hwy. 102. Open mid–May–late-Oct Mon–Sat 8:30am–7pm, Sun 10am–6pm. Rest of the year Mon–Fri 8:30am–4:30pm. *Closed late Dec–early Jan.* 902-843-3496. *www.glooscapheritagecentre.com.*

The Mi'kmaq legend recounts that the first man on earth was **Glooscap,** born from a lightning bolt. Symbol of hope and wisdom, he used his incredible powers to shape the Fundy Shore. The Millbrook First Nations Reserve just outside Truro initially built a commercial enterprise along the highway. This heritage centre, housed in a spacious, low-lying building, followed in 2006 and includes an exhibit gallery, gift shop, and visitor information centre for the area.

Outside the entrance stands an immense, 12m/40ft bronze statue of Glooscap that can be seen from kilometres away. Inside, baskets in various shapes and patterns, exquisite porcupine quillwork

Unearthing the Past

One day in 1948, when E.S. Eaton was looking for wild blueberries near the old army base at **Debert,** he found some artifacts in the parking lot. By the mid-1950s the site's importance was known, but testing was not undertaken until 1962. Radio-carbon dating revealed that the stone tools he discovered were used more than 10,000 years ago by Palaeo Indians, ancient aboriginal people known to hunt caribou in glaciated parts of North America. Tentative identification of caribou blood on the tools has been made. The 260ha/650-acre archaeological site is now a protected area. *For more information, access http://museum.gov.ns.ca/places/debert/debert.htm.*

and intricate beadwork showcase the skills and artistry of Mi'kmaq artisans. Aboriginal tools, traditional clothing and artifacts are also on display. A multimedia presentation (15min) gives an overview of the history of the Mi'kmaq and an audio exhibit describes the Mi'kmaw language. An on-site gift shop sells books, locally made goods and souvenirs.

Excursions

Shubenacadie Provincial Wildlife Park★

35km/22mi south of Truro. Take Exit 11 from Hwy. 102 to Stewiacke and continue south. ⏰*Open mid-May–mid-Oct daily 9am–7pm, Nov–Apr weekends 9am–3pm.* ⚲*$4.25 summer, $2.50 winter.* ♿☎*902-758-2040. http://wildlifepark.gov.ns.ca.* 🔳This 40ha/99-acre park, owned and managed by the Nova Scotia Department of Natural Resources, has been delighting visitors since 1954. Here, 46 different wildlife exhibits showcase 33 species of mammals and 35 species of birds. The park's most popular animals are the **Sable Island horses,** unique to Shubenacadie. Habitats house everything from ground hogs, raccoons and turtles to arctic wolves, reindeer and black bears. The Creighton Environmental Centre shelters some 30 species of at-risk creatures, such as cougars, Canada's largest cats; lynx, whose paws can function like snowshoes; peregrine falcons, who can fly at speeds up to 290kph/180mph; and piping plovers, shorebirds found along Nova Scotia's coasts. Adjacent to the park is a 10ha/25-acre picnic area with a playground.

Maitland★

About 30km/18mi west of Truro by Rte. 236 and Rte. 215 north.
Overlooking Cobequid Bay in the Minas Basin, the lovely village of Maitland sits at the mouth of the Shubenacadie River. Rolling farmlands lie at the community's backdoor. Maitland was once an important shipbuilding centre best known as the site of the construction of the largest wooden ship ever built in Canada, the **William D. Lawrence.** Each year

Statue of Glooscap, Glooscap Heritage Centre, near Truro

Nova Scotia Tourism, Culture and Heritage

a Launch Day Festival held here commemorates the ship: there's a staged launching of a model of the huge ship as well as a town parade and historical reenactments. Today Maitland's fine houses attest to the wealth created by the former industry. The village boasts a sizable heritage district of some 50 houses dating to the 19C.

Lawrence House Museum★

8660 Rte. 215 ⏰*Open Jun–mid-Oct Mon–Sat 9:30am–5:30pm, Sun 1pm–5:30pm.* ⚲*$3.25* 🅿☎*902-261-2628 or 888-743-7845. www.museum.gov.ns.ca.*
Surrounded by elm trees, this two-and-a-half-storey house, now a National Historic Site, is a splendid example of the grand residences of Nova Scotia's shipbuilders and sea captains. The entrance portico, with its double, curved staircase, is reminiscent of a ship's bridge. William Dawson Lawrence built this house (c.1870) to overlook his shipyard on the Shubenacadie River at the point where it joins Cobequid Bay. Believing he could double a ship's size without doubling its operating costs, Lawrence constructed an 80m/262ft ship that weighed 2,459 tonnes and had three masts, the highest being over 60m/200ft. To complete the vessel took two years, and Lawrence had to

mortgage his house, but the investment proved to be profitable. Some 4,000 onlookers descended upon Maitland to witness the launching in October 1874 of the country's largest ship. The ship eventually sailed all over the world with many varied cargoes.

The house contains most of its original furnishings, including shipbuilding artifacts, pictures of 19C ships and a 2m/7ft model of the *William D. Lawrence*. You can look through binoculars from the housetop to appreciate Lawrence's view of his shipyard. At the museum, there is a permanent outdoor educational display about the area and its shipbuilding past. A lookout across the road from the house affords visitors a good **view**★ of the tidal flats.

Truro to Antigonish★

MAP INSIDE FRONT COVER

Largely accented by Scottish tradition and culture, the area that stretches from Truro to and along the Northumberland Strait eastward to St. George's Bay is known for its warm beaches, lively festivals, historic attractions and working farms. Many a **ceilidh** [pronounced KAY-lee] takes place in this part of Nova Scotia (as well as on Cape Breton Island); filled with Scottish or Irish music, dancing and storytelling, these informal gatherings take place in a community centre, a bar or even someone's kitchen. This driving itinerary starts out from Truro and heads north to the coast before turning east toward St. George's Bay. Inland farms devoted to livestock (cows, sheep) or maple-syrup production or grain crops and coastal villages that were once important shipbuilding ports flank the route. This area is growing, attracting both new residents and new businesses as well as tourists. New Glasgow is one of Nova Scotia's major centres of growth outside Halifax and Sydney. Census figures confirm that its agglomerate population, which includes smaller surrounding communities such as Stellarton, was the fourth largest in the province in 2006. Another hive of economic development is Antigonish, which experienced significant retail growth recently due to a commercial building boom. Don't be surprised by the number of chain stores seen in and around these expanding towns. Despite an abundance of roadside motels—offering the benefits of convenience and cleanliness, but lacking atmosphere—some quaint lodgings can still be found, however isolated they may be.

- **ⓘ** **Information:** Visitor Information Centre, 350 W. River Rd., Pictou. ☎902-485-6213. www.novascotia.com.
- **☺** **Don't Miss:** Pancakes with maple syrup at Sugar Moon Farm. The Museum of Industry near New Glasgow.
- **ⓝ** **Organizing Your Time:** The drive should be taken at leisure over 2 days, with an overnight stop along the way.
- **Kids** **Especially for Kids:** The lambs at Lismore Sheep Farm. Magic Valley amusement park in Green Hill.
- **ⓙ** **Also See:** CAPE BRETON ISLAND

Driving Tour

201km/125mi via Hwy. 4, Rte. 311 and Hwy. 6.

Truro
ⓙ*See TRURO.*

▸ *From Truro, take Rte. 311 north 27km/17mi north to Earlstown.*

Earlstown
Settled by Scots, this tiny rural community sits on the north slope of the Coquebid Mountains. Visitors are wel-

Balmoral Grist Mill Museum

come year-round at the **Sugar Moon Farm,** a working maple farm that began operations in 1973. Guided tours of the sugar camp focus on the history and process of making maple syrup. In the on-site restaurant, enjoy a stack of pancakes with pure maple syrup served all day (◔*Alex MacDonald Rd.; Jul-Aug daily 9am–4:30pm; rest of the year, weekends only 9am–4:30pm; ☎ 902-657-3348; www.sugarmoon.ca).*

▶ *Continue north on Rte. 311 past The Falls and turn right onto Matheson Brook Rd.*

Balmoral Mills★

This tiny community is known for its operating grist mill.

Balmoral Grist Mill Museum★

600 Matheson Brook Rd. ◔*Grounds open year-round. Museum open Jun– mid-Oct Mon–Sat 9:30am–5:30pm, Sun 1pm–5:30pm.* ⊜*$3.25.* ☎*902-657-3016. http://gristmill.museum.gov.ns.ca.* Standing beside a stream in a pleasant valley, this fully operational gristmill was built in 1874. Although commercial use ceased in 1954, the mill has been completely restored. In 2007 the bed stone (the bottom, stationary grindstone) was meticulously replaced and the runner stone (the grindstone on top) was reset.

The red-painted, three-storey structure towers above Matheson Brook in a wooded gorge. When in operation *(a few hours daily)*, the water-driven mill is a hive of activity. Weighing over a tonne, the original millstones grind barley, oats, wheat and buckwheat into flour and meal, which are for sale in the museum shop as well as baked goods. Various milling processes are explained. Below the mill the revolving waterwheel can be seen.

▶ *Return to Rte. 311 and continue north 10km/6mi to Hwy. 6. Take Hwy. 6 northwest to Tatamagouche.*

Tatamagouche

This small community lies along the south shore of Tatamagouche Bay, where the French and Waugh rivers empty into the bay. It was first settled by French-Acadians, but in 1765 the British crown granted 20,000 acres to Col. Joseph F.W. DesBarres [de-BAR], a military cartographer, with the provision that he resettle the area with Protestants. Within 10 years many Highland Scots had moved to the area. The village became a centre of shipbuilding and lumber production. Today it hosts an annual **Oktoberfest** *(last weekend in Sept)*, and is known locally for its railway station that has been converted to an inn.

Train Station Inn★

21 Station Rd. ◔*Open Apr–Oct.* ✕☐⌑ ☎*902-657-3222. www.trainstation.ca.*

Display at Sugar Moon Farm

Sandra Phinney/Michelin

Kids This complex is not just a curio in and of itself (preserved rail cars and a historic train station), it is an operating inn and restaurant. In 1989 the 100-year old Tatamagouche train station was restored and opened as a bed-and-breakfast lodging. Then, over time, seven cabooses from the Canadian National Railway were moved here, refurbished and converted to guest quarters. The first floor of the handsome 1887 station building houses a **railway museum** and gift shop; three guest suites occupy the second floor. The 1928 **dining car** is open to the public at lunch and dinnertime. Kids will love seeing the cabooses all lined up, and browsing among the toys in the gift shop.

▶ *Take Hwy. 6 east 12km/7mi. Turn right onto Rte. 326 and travel 3km/2mi south to Denmark.*

Sutherland Steam Mill Museum

3169 Denmark. ⏱*Open Jun–mid-Oct Mon–Sat 9:30am–5:30pm, Sun 1pm–5:30pm.* 🎟*$3.25.* ☎*902-657-3016. http:// steammill.museum.gov.ns.ca.*
When Alexander Sutherland built this sawmill in 1894, steam was replacing water power as the most efficient means of cutting wood. He and his son made sleighs, carriages and sleds; his brother and partner produced doors and windows for local houses. All machinery is in working order. Tools and equipment

hint at the resourcefulness of the mill workers: a drill press was formed from an old milk separator, one of the planes operates with a car engine, and the copper tub used to soak shingles doubles as a bath tub. The mill "steams up" once a month *(phone ahead for schedule)* and there's an interactive Kids**display** geared to children.

▶ *Return to Hwy.6 and continue east 10km/6mi to River John.*

Lismore Sheep Farm

1389 Louisville Rd. in River John. ⏱*Open mid-Jan–mid-May Thu–Sat 9am-4:30pm or by appointment. Late-May late-Dec daily 9am–5pm.* 🎟*$1.* ☎*902-351-2889. www.lismoresheepfarmwoolshop.com.*
This working farm oversees about 300 sheep, which are primarily crosses of Dorset and Finn sheep. Their soft fleece is conducive to making woollen products. A variety of made-on-the-farm items, such as wool blankets and comforters, are sold in the on-site shop, which also stocks sheepskin products. Nova Scotian wool tartan throws are especially popular. There are displays on the production process, and during the summer the Kids**sheep barn** is opened so visitors can see sheep and lambs up close.

▶ *Return to Hwy.6 and continue east 25km/15mi to Pictou.*

Address Book

☾ *For dollar sign categories, see the Legend on the cover flap.*

WHERE TO STAY

$$ Braeside Country Inn – *126 Front St., Pictou.* ✗🅿️🛏️☎*902-485-5046 or 800-613-7701. www.braesideinn.com. 18 rooms.* On a hillside overlooking Pictou harbour, in the heart of town, this large, three-storey building was built in 1938 as an inn. Over the years, it has been upgraded and equipped with modern conveniences, such as air-conditioning and wireless Internet throughout. Guest rooms are clean and pleasant, albeit modestly decorated; all have private bathrooms. Suites have whirlpool tubs and refrigerators. A continental breakfast is included in the room rate. Braeside's **dining room ($$)**, which specializes in Maritime seafood, is open to the public for dinner seasonally (mid-May–mid-Oct).

$$ Evening Sail B&B – *279 Denoon St., Pictou.* ☎*902-485-5069 or 866-214-2669. www.eveningsail.ca. 3 rooms, 3 suites.* This friendly bed-and-breakfast inn comprises a three-storey main house and a charming guest cottage. The house contains a library for guest use; the dining room, where breakfast is served; and three guest rooms with ensuite bathrooms on the second floor. The cottage holds three suites with private bathrooms, kitchenettes and fireplaces. Beds are topped with individually patterned quilts, and rooms have cable TV. Breakfasts are grand affairs with hot dishes such as quiche, eggs Benedict or French toast with blueberries and lemon sauce. Complimentary passes for a nearby campground's pool. Wireless Internet and a large video library for guest use.

$$ Train Station Inn – *21 Station Rd., Tatamagouche.* ✗🅿️🛏️☎*902-657-3222. www.trainstation.ca. 10 rooms. Closed Nov–Mar.* Guests stay overnight in completely restored cabooses at this train station-turned bed-and-breakfast inn. Each caboose contains a fully-equipped bedroom with private bathroom, TV and air conditioning. These vintage rail cars provide the comforts of a hotel room without the clang-clang

Train Station Inn, Tatamagouche

Sandra Phinney/Michelin

of a moving train. Three additional guest quarters with private bathrooms occupy the upstairs floor of the handsome 1887 train station, but must be booked as one unit. Guests enjoy a complimentary continental breakfast in the 1928 **dining car ($$)**, which is open to the public for home-cooked meals—primarily seafood, chicken and steaks—for lunch and dinner *(Jun–Oct)*.

WHERE TO EAT

$ Gabrieau's Bistro – *350 Main St., Antigonish.* ☎*902-863-1925. Closed Sun. www.gabrieaus.com.* **International.** Known among locals for decadent desserts like Quebec sugar pie or chocolate-pumpkin mousse torte, Gabrieau's also has an extensive lunch menu of soups, salads, pastas, foccacia melts, and wraps, many with an Italian influence. A variety of dinner dishes include seafood vindaloo, braised lamb, and Bromelake duck. Appetizers like seared foie gras and duck confit with poached figs are equally ambitious. If you're just passing through, stop by for a take-away muffin, croissant or cinnamon roll, as these treats are sold from the front counter.

$ Mrs. MacGregor's Tea Room – *59 Water St., Pictou.* ☎*902-382-1878. No dinner. Closed Mon. www.mrsmac gregors.com.* **Canadian and Scottish.** There isn't a real Mrs. MacGregor, but the folks running this charming downtown cafe provide delicious sandwiches, quiches, soups and salads for lunch. This is the place to taste Scottish oatcakes, shortbreads and scones. Desserts are plentiful: the blueberry maple cheesecake and the sticky toffee pudding are standouts. Afternoon tea is elegantly served: typically sweet and savoury tidbits presented on china at tables topped with linen tablecloths. Beer/wine license.

$$ The Alcove Bistro & Lounge – *76 College St., Antigonish.* ☎*902-863-2248. www.alcovebistro.ca. Closed Sun–Mon.* **International.** Exposed brick, a mahogany bar and intimately placed tables help make the Alcove a popular spot for a diverse clientele, especially patrons from the university and couples seeking a romantic venue. Billing itself as "international fusion with a local flavour," the bistro serves dishes like Spanish paella enhanced with local lobster and scallops, or steamed mussels in a Thai dressing. Occasionally a jazz musician performs during dinner.

$$ Piper's Landing – *Hwy. 376, Lyons Brook. From Pictou take Hwy. 376 west about 3km/2mi. Dinner only. Closed Sun.*

&☎*902-485-1200.* **Contemporary.** As many area residents know, it's worth the 5min drive from Pictou for fine-dining at Piper's Landing. Fronting the West Branch of the Pictou River in this small residential community, the restaurant offers an intimate, contemporary setting and creatively prepared cuisine. Try the lobster crepe or the beef tenderloin, but save room for the warm apple rum cake topped with vanilla ice cream. *Reservations recommended.*

$$ Settler's Salt Water Cafe – *67 Caladh Ave., Pictou.* ☎*902-485-2558.* **Seafood.** Located right on the waterfront, next to the Heritage Quay, this popular dining spot hauls in tourists and locals alike for the likes of lobster suppers and blueberry grunt for dessert. Fish and chips, seafood platters (try the fried clams), a variety of hamburgers including fish variations like haddock burgers, plus great chowders and appetizers (order the mussels) continue to make this cafe a bustling one. There's also outdoor dining on the screened deck and a children's menu.

Pictou

A service centre for the area and a growing tourist destination, Pictou sits off the Northumberland Strait, edging a harbour formed by the convergence of three branches of the Pictou River. Originally home to Mi'kmaq, Pictou was settled largely by Highlander Scots

The Hector at Pictou's Heritage Quay

who were brought here on the *Hector* in 1773. The voyage initiated a steady flow of immigrants from Scotland to Pictou during the 100 years following. An annual 5-day **Hector Festival** held here *(mid-Aug)* to recall the arrival, includes a re-enactment of the historic landing. A full-scale reproduction of the ship is moored at the waterfront.

Also at the waterfront in summer and fall is the Pictou County **Weekend Market** held inside the New Caledonia Curling Club *(late-Jun–late-Sept weekends 10am–5pm;* ☎ *902-485-6329 in summer; www. pictouweekendmarket.com).* Crafts made in Nova Scotia and by First Nations Mi'kmaq, seasonal and organic produce and baked goods are among the items for sale.

Two of Nova Scotia's beaches with the warmest water are located nearby: **Caribou Beach,** 11km/7mi northeast, has a mile-long sandy beach, shady spots and a walking trail out to Munroes Island; and 23km/14mi northeast, **Melmerby Beach** at Melmerby Beach Provincial Park also has a sandy beach that stretches over a mile in length.

Jost Vineyards

This large, 18ha/45 acre winery is Nova Scotia's most well-known winery. The wines Jost produce, including ice wines, have won more than 100 international awards. The winery is family-owned and run by Hans Christian, the son of the founder, Hans Wilhelm Jost. He and his family came from the Rhine region of Germany to Nova Scotia in 1970. In addition to visiting one of the vineyards and seeing part of the winery, participants also learn on the wine tour about Jost's famous ice wine, made from grapes harvested at the end of November and early December. Grape varietals are discussed, such as those that are locally grown: Marechal Foch,

Products of Jost Vineyards

DeChaunac, Baco Noir, Leon Millot, Seyval Blanc and the very popular L'Acadie Blanc. *17km/10mi northeast of Tatamagouche off Hwy. 6 at 48 Vintage Lane in Malagash. Complimentary tours mid-Jun–mid-Sept daily noon & 3pm. ☎902-257-2636 or 800-565-4567. www.jostwine.com.*

Hector Heritage Quay★★

29 Cladagh Ave. (on the waterfront) ⏰Open mid-May–mid-Oct daily 9am–5pm. ☜$7. ☎902-485-4371. www.townof pictou.com/the_experience.html.

Completed in 1992, this waterfront complex is devoted to the story of the passage of the ship *Hector* to the New World and the deprivations suffered by its passengers. The facility comprises an interpretive centre staffed by guides in period dress; blacksmith, riggers and carpentry shops; an artist's studio; and a museum store. The centrepiece is a 33m/110ft fully-rigged replica of the *Hector,* which may be boarded.

In the spacious lobby, displays of the tartan banners of the clans who sailed on the *Hector* to Pictou can be seen. Well-done exhibits trace the story of the Highlander Scots and how they got here. In the working shipyard, demonstrations of the trades of the era of sail include iron-forging in the blacksmith's shop, plank-making and caulking in the carpenter shop and knot-making in the riggers shop. Visitors are encouraged to try their skills at these activities.

Aboard the *Hector,* a below-deck galley evokes the hardships endured by the voyagers during the 12-week passage from Scotland to Pictou.

▶ *From Pictou, take Hwy.106 south, then Hwy.104 east to Exit 25 (Rte. 348) for New Glasgow, 22km/14mi away.*

New Glasgow

This former shipbuilding centre is now the largest town in Pictou County, with a population of nearly 10,000, including many descendants of Highlander Scots. Once an active port, it sits on the banks of the East River, a tidal estuary of freshwater and saltwater draining into Northumberland Strait. The town serves as the commercial hub of northeast Nova Scotia.

New Glasgow's annual **Festival of the Tartans** *(mid-Aug)* pays tribute to the town's Scottish roots, as it has for the past 50 years. Festival events include bagpipe competitions, Highland dancing, traditional Highland games and a haggis luncheon.

New Glasgow's black residents constitute the largest community of African Nova Scotians in the northeast part of the province. The **Africentric Heritage Park** *(Vale Rd.)* commemorates all Nova Scotians of African descent. In the middle of the park, a 10m/33ft pyramid-shaped monument tells the story of the migration of the black newcomers to Nova Scotia.

Address Book

For dollar sign categories, see the Legend on the cover flap.

WHERE TO STAY AND EAT

$$$ DesBarres Manor Inn – *90 Church St., Guysborough.* 902-533-2099. *www.desbarresmanor.com. 10 rooms.* Overseeing 2ha/6acre grounds, this stately, two-storey house was completed in 1837 for justice of the Supreme Court W.F. DesBarres. It now is an oasis in the country, offering fine accommodation and attentive service. Antiques and fine furnishings abound throughout the property. Afternoon tea, homemade truffles, and samples of Nova Scotian specialty foods are complimentary. Cocktails and hors d'oeuvres are available each evening. Traditionally furnished guest rooms, each with private bathroom, feature fluffy duvets and luxury linens. The inn's **dining room ($$)** serves Canadian cuisine that incorporates local produce, fish and game prepared by a chef from nearby Cape Breton Island. Also included in the rate, gourmet breakfasts feature Nova Scotian cheeses or maple syrup in creative fare like apple and cheddar crepes. Wireless Internet available.

$$ Seawind Landing Country Inn – *1 Wharf Rd., Charlos Cove. Off Rte. 316, 84km/52mi east of Sherbrooke.* 902-525-2108 or 800-563-4667. *www.seawindlanding.com. 10 rooms. Closed late-Oct–early May.* This former shipbuilder's house sits in seclusion near the tiny Acadian village of Charlos Cove on a remote peninsula that juts into the Atlantic Ocean. The ocean lies steps away, and all guest rooms face the Atlantic; most have a balcony. Rooms are decorated with cottage-style furnishings and quilts on the beds; some have whirlpool baths. The main building houses a music room and a large fireplace, perfect for inclement weather. The inn's **dining room ($$)**, open to the public, is the only place to eat in the area; contemporary fare here focuses on fresh seafood, chicken and meat dishes. In good weather, a **breakfast buffet ($)** is served aboard the inn's 9m/31ft sailing sloop en route to the nearby Barrier Islands; once there, breakfast guests will undoubtedly be observed by a seal colony, bald eagles and various seabirds. Internet available.

The town holds a number of sandstone and brick Victorian buildings and houses, and its riverfront revitalization has been recognized for its excellence.

Museum of Industry★★

147 N. Foord St., in Stellarton, 4km/3mi south of New Glasgow. Take Exit 24 off Hwy. 104. Open May–Oct Mon–Sat 9am–5pm, Sun 10am–5pm (May & Jun Sun 1pm–5pm). Nov–Apr weekdays 9am–5pm. Closed major holidays. $7.50. 902-755-5425. *www.museum. gov.ns.ca.*

The size of seven hockey rinks, Nova Scotia's largest museum boasts some 37,000 artifacts and lots of hands-on exhibits involving the learning of skills and crafts. Built on the site of an Albion Mine pit, the museum explores the mining industry and its effect on the topography and economy of Nova Scotia. Exhibits illustrate changing technology and its impact on local communities. Highlights include the oldest surviving locomotives in the province, a model railway, an operational machine shop with tools dating to 1875, the first Volvo made in Canada, and a fine collection of Trenton glass.

Magic Valley

4488 Highway 4, in Greenhill, 10km/6mi west of New Glasgow. Open Jul Labour-Day daily 11am 6pm. $7 admission, rides extra or $14.95 admission including all rides. 902-396-4467. *www.magicvalley.ca.* **Kids** A great place to be in summer, this large amusement park is geared toward families. Children especially will enjoy the water slides and swimming pool. An old-timey train takes passengers on a half-mile journey through a forest. Pedal boats, bumper boats, mini-cars on a track, a storybook village and a farm with a petting zoo, and even a talking cow, all add up to outdoor fun.

▶ *Take Hwy.104 (the Trans-Canada Hwy.) east 59km/37mi to Antigonish.*

Antigonish

A busy commercial centre, especially in summer when tourists are in town, Antigonish [an-TEE-gon-nish] is known for its **Highland Games** *(mid-Jul)*, which began in 1863.

Today these games attract several thousand visitors to its piping, dancing and caber-tossing competitions, ceilidhs and concerts. The town is home to St. Francis Xavier University, a Catholic-founded school whose campus was moved here in 1855.

In 1959 the university established the Coady International Institute, known worldwide for its work with non-governmental organizations engaged in the community-development process. Today the noted liberal arts institution has 4,000 undergraduates.

Excursion

Sherbrooke★

61km/38mi south of Antigonish by Hwy. 7.

This village occupies a pretty **site** on the St. Mary's River, once the location of a French fort (1655). After capture by the English in 1669, the settlement was abandoned until people were attracted by the rich timberlands in 1800. During the early 19C, sawmills sprang up and wooden ships were built. Gold was discovered in 1861 and for about 20 years, the town flourished. The gold did not last, but Sherbrooke survived as a lumber town. Today is it a peaceful rural community and a centre for sportfishing and tourism.

Sherbrooke Village★★

42 Main St. ◷*Open Jun–mid-Oct daily 9:30am–5:30pm.* ⌫*$10.* ✕ ♿ 🅿 ☏ *902-522-2400 or 888-743-7845. www.museum. gov.ns.ca.*

Kids Restored beginning in 1969, this historic village is actually an extension of the town of Sherbrooke. Streets have been closed to traffic, and only a few houses within the village are private residences. Renovated to reflect the period, the buildings were constructed between 1860 and 1870.

Enter the village through the orientation centre. A church, schoolhouse, post office, blacksmith's shop and several houses can be visited. Built in 1862 with separate downstairs and upstairs cells for men and women, the **jail** occupied half the jailer's house. Of particular interest is the **boatbuilding shop,** where wooden boats are still constructed. Above Cumminger Brothers' general store, visitors can don 19C costumes and be photographed in the ambrotype **photography studio.** The process of producing a

Sherbrooke Village

Wally Hayes/Nova Scotia Tourism, Culture and Heritage

picture from a negative on dark surfaced glass was used until c. 1900. Furnished to the period, **Greenwood Cottage** is an example of a spacious house of the well-to-do, while **McMillan House** reflects the humble status of a village weaver *(spinning demonstrations)*. The hotel serves 1880s fare such as cottage pudding and gingerbread, and the telephone exchange is still operable.

Removed from the village is **McDonald Brothers' Mill** (.4km/.3mi), an operational water-powered sawmill capable of full production. A short walk away through the woodlands, a reconstructed **lumber camp** of the 19C shows the living conditions of loggers.

CAPE BRETON ISLAND

Cape Breton Island is not simply the northeastern end of Nova Scotia, it is a much-loved area where a distinctive kind of Nova Scotian lives. It was with tongue firmly planted in cheek that a book published in 2005 to celebrate the 50th anniversary of the Canso Causeway was titled, *When Canada Joined Cape Breton*. Never mind the fact that the causeway was built to link Cape Breton with the rest of the province, and the country. Largely of Scottish descent, "capers" are a proud and industrious lot, having toiled in the coal mines of Glace Bay and laboured at Sydney's steel plant. Sydney, the only city on Cape Breton Island, is also the port for ferries to Newfoundland. Baddeck, gateway to the vehicular route famous as the Cabot Trail, was the chosen summer residence of Alexander Graham Bell, born in Edinburgh, Scotland, who left his historic mark on the town. On the island's west coast, the Margaree Valley is known for some of Canada's finest salmon fishing. Also on the western side is Chéticamp, the centre of the island's Acadian culture.

At the island's northern end, the cliffs, coastline and headlands of the Cape Breton Highlands have been preserved as a national park, the largest such protected wilderness in the province. Part of the Cabot Trail drive, the park features hiking trails affording views of the coast, and the waters of the Gulf of St. Lawrence. East of Baddeck the salt waters of Bras d'Or Lake [pronounced bra-door] virtually bisect the island. On the east coast, massive Fortress of Louisbourg dominates the small town of Louisbourg. Standing sentinel over the entrance to the St. Lawrence River, the French bastion was once inhabited by the largest garrison in North America. Today restored, this National Historic Site draws visitors from all over to witness life in 18C French society.

A Bit of History

The first inhabitants of this much talked-about island were the ancestors of the present-day Mi'kmaq, the Maritime Archaic Indians. Even today, Cape Breton is home to five Mi'kmaq reserves, more than any other area of the province. In 1521 it is believed that Portuguese venturer **Joao Alvares de Fagundes** attempted to establish a colony on the island, based on a reference to Ingonish in Samuel de Champlain's writings, to harvest the riches of the ocean and trade with the aboriginals. When France controlled much of what is now the Maritime provinces, the island was named **Île Royale,** and a massive fortress was built in the 18C at **Louisbourg** to protect the valuable fishing industry. From 1714 to 1734, some 500 Acadians moved here but were disappointed by the land's limited potential for farming. Nevertheless about 65 families remained at Port Toulouse (later named St. Peter's). More interested in the coastal trade between Acadia and Louisbourg, they fished and received aid from France. By 1726 Port Toulouse had a predominantly Acadian population of nearly 300 residents.

Cabot Trail along Cape Breton Island

In the mid-to late-1700s, the island came under British rule, but it did not join peninsular Nova Scotia until 1820. During the 19C, thousands of Highland Scots emigrated and firmly cemented Cape Breton as the bastion of Gaelic music and culture in eastern Canada. Today the Acadian culture is alive and well along Cape Breton's west coast, and on the island's east coast, there's a strong Scottish influence. Tourism has become a critical part of the island's economy. Extra promotion comes from several well-known Canadian musicians who happen to be Cape Breton natives: the Rankin Family, Rita MacNeil, The Men of the Deeps (a miners' chorus), The Barra MacNeils, and fiddlers Natalie MacMaster and Ashley MacIsaac.

Practical Information

GETTING THERE

BY CAR

The Canso Causeway opened in 1955 over the Strait of Canso between mainland Nova Scotia and Cape Breton Island. Previously, ferries had plied the strait's waters, which are often buffeted by strong winds and currents, as well as ice. Since the 1371m/4,500 ft-long causeway was constructed, the strait has not frozen. The causeway's surface width is 24m/80ft; its depth is 66m/217ft; and the swing bridge *(expect a delay when the bridge is open to let boats through)* measures 94m/308ft in length. There is no fee to cross the causeway.

ROADS

Major highways on the island include the Trans Canada Hwy 105 (Port Hastings to North Sydney); Route 19 (west coast – The Ceilidh Trail – which leads into the Cabot Trail); Route 4 from Port Hastings to Sydney (also called the Bras d'Or Lakes Scenic Drive). Route 22 from Sydney, south-bound, leads to Fortress Louisbourg.

FUEL

Gasoline can be purchased at service centres along Hwy 105, and in towns such as Port Hawkesbury, Port Hood, Inverness, Chéticamp, Baddeck, Glace Bay, Sydney and others.

CAR REPAIR

A & P Transmission, Gardiner Mines, ☎902-849-9058, Transmission repair and general automotive repair

Boardwalk Auto Repair, Sydney, ☎902-539-6222

Doucette's Esso, Ingonish Beach, ☎902-285-2029; For gas, towing and automotive repair. Credit cards accepted.

Fitzgerald's Automotive Repair, Glace Bay, ☎902-842-0832, Licensed mechanic on duty.

BY BUS/LIMOUSINE

Goin' "R" Way Shuttle Service, Glace Bay, ☎902-842-3000 or 800-931-4122, Daily, leaving Glace Bay 6:30am, New Waterford 7am, Sydney 7:15am, North Sydney 7:30am, arrive in Halifax at noon. Depart Halifax 1pm.

MacLeod's Shuttle Service, New Waterford ☎902-539-2700 or ☎800-471-7775, Daily, departs New Waterford at 10am daily for Halifax. Leaves Halifax at 6pm.

Greg Coleman Limousine, Sydney Serving the Island ☎902-567-5744

BY FERRY (SYDNEY)

www.marine-atlantic.ca
☎800-341-7981

Two routes and three ships take passengers to and from North Sydney to Newfoundland and Labrador.

Daily ferry service (year-round) between Port aux Basques, Newfoundland and Labrador and North Sydney.

Tri-weekly ferry service between Argentia, Newfoundland and Labrador and North Sydney. This service operates from mid-June until late September.

VISITOR INFORMATION

PROVINCIAL INFORMATION

These provincial tourism centres offer in-depth local information, travel advice, maps, brochures and reservations.

Nova Scotia Visitor Information Centre (with offices also in Inverness, Margaree Forks and Port Hood) 96 Highway #4, Port Hastings. ☎902-625-4201 Open May–Jan, 8:30am–8:30pm daily

Sydney Visitor Information Centre (municipal) Marine Terminal, 72 Esplanade Open Jun–mid-Oct, 9–5pm daily, ☎902-539-9876

North Sydney Visitor Information Centre (municipal) Ferry Terminal, Entry from Newfoundland, Open mid-June–mid September, 9–5pm daily, ☎902-794-7719

NATIONAL PARK INFORMATION

Cape Breton Highlands National Park, Parks Canada, Chéticamp and Ingonish Beach locations, Open May–mid-Oct, 8am–8pm (hours subject to change) www.pc.gc.ca; ☎902-224-2306

ACCOMMODATIONS

🛏️*For a selection of lodgings, see the Address Books within Cape Breton Island chapters.*

Motel and/or B&B accommodations can be found in the towns of Arichat, Baddeck, Chéticamp, Boularderie Island, Glace Bay, Iona-Grand Narrows, Louisbourg, Mabou, North Sydney, Port Hood, Port Hawkesbury, Pleasant Bay, St. Peter's, Sydney.

USEFUL NUMBERS ☎

⬥ **Police 911 (emergency)**

Non-emergency: The Cape Breton Municipality Regional Police Service provides policing for all communities within the Cape Breton Regional Municipality.

Central : 865 Grand Lake Rd., Sydney. ☎902-563-5100

East : 8 McFadgen St., Glace Bay. ☎902-842-1001

North: 412 Purves St., North Sydney. ☎902-794-1254

⬥ **Canadian Automobile Assn.** 3514 Joseph Howe Dr. ☎902-443-5530

378 Westmorland Rd., Saint John, NB ☎506-634-1400 or 800-561-8807. www.caa.maritimes.ca

⬥ **CAA Emergency Road Service** (24hr). ☎800-222-4357 or *222 on from a mobile phone

⬥ **Shoppers Drug Mart** (24hr pharmacy) *various locations* ☎902-429-2400

⬥ **Post Office (locations in virtually all drug stores)**

⬥ **Road Conditions** Dial 511 or www.gov.ns.ca/Tran/winter/road conditions.asp

⬥ **Weather** www.theweathernetwork.ca.

ENTERTAINMENT

MUSIC AND DANCE
Celtic

Celtic Colours International Festival – www.celtic-colours.com, 850 Grand Lake Rd., Ste. 8, Sydney. ☎902-562-6700 or 877.285.2321. Events which include over 250 musicians, dancers, singers and storytellers are held throughout the island over 9 days in October.

Celtic Music Interpretive Centre – www.celticmusicsite.com, 5471 Rte. 19, Judique (Inverness County), ☎902-787-2708. Weekend pub nights and ceilidhs from mid-Jun–Sept. Cover charge

Glenora Distillery – www.glenora distillery.com, Rte. 19 (Ceilidh Trail), Glenville, Cape Breton, ☎800-839-0491. Free live entertainment n the Glenora Pub daily 1pm–3pm & from 8pm–10pm

Normaway Inn – www.thenormaway inn.com, 691 Egypt Rd., Margaree Valley (off Rte 19), ☎902-248-2987 or 800-565-9463. Live music (&/or regional films) nightly in the main building or in a separate venue,"The Barn."

Red Shoe Pub – www.redshoepub.com, 11573 Route 19, Mabou. ☎902-945-2326. Nightly live music from Jun–Oct.; food and liquor service. Possible cover charge. Owned by the Rankin Family, a Canadian musical institution.

Acadian

Arichat and Chéticamp – Acadian music and cultural performances are held in the towns of Arichat and Chéticamp. Go to www.novascotia.com (click on History & Heritage) for dates and further information (changes annually).

Gaelic

Festival of the Island (Feis an Eilein) – www.feisaneilein.ca, Comunn Féis an Eilein, Christmas Island, Cape Breton. ☎902-622-2627

Johnstown

This Gaelic community on the Bras d'Or Lakes has featured a "milling frolic" and dance as part of its annual festival over the third Friday in August.

Gaelic College – www.gaeliccollege.edu, Englishtown, Cape Breton, ☎902-295-3411. Wed evening ceilidhs throughout the summer; infrequent lobster **dinners & theatre ($$).**

THEATRE

Savoy Theatre – www.savoytheatre.com, 116 Commercial St., Glace Bay. ☎902-842-1577. Restored in the 1970s, this 1920s-era theatre now showcases local musicians, and national and international touring acts.

The Octagon at the Markland Coastal Resort – www.markland resort.com, Dingwall (Cabot Trail), Cape Breton, ☎902-383-2246 or 800-872-6084. Chamber music series, Jun–Sept., Sun. at 4:30pm. Ceilidhs with Island fiddlers on Fri. at 8pm.

Louisbourg Playhouse – 11 Aberdeen St., Louisbourg. ☎902-733-2996 or 888-733-2787. www.louisbourgplayhouse.com. Highlighting local talent: Singers, songwriters, step-dancers, storytellers and comedians. Main floor is wheelchair accessible. This mock Elizabethan-style, open-air theatre is a gift from the set of a 1994 Walt Disney Studios movie filmed in Louisbourg. The Men of the Deeps, a chorus of retired coal miners, sing here regularly.

SHOPPING

Blue Heron Gift Shop, Baddeck, www.blueherongiftshop.com, ☎902-295-3424. The largest selection of Atlantic Canadian books and music (400 + titles) in Nova Scotia, as well as locally made giftware.

Mixed Media Artisans Co-operative, Sydney, www.mixedmediaartisans.com ☎902-576-2380. An artisans-run craft gallery with hand weaving, woodworking, basketry, fused glass, pottery, jewellery and paintings.

Co-operative Artisanale de Chéticamp Ltee, 774 Main St., Chéticamp, ☎902-224-2170. Wide selection of Acadian-made hooked rugs, souvenirs, clothing.

Flora's Gift Shop, www.floras.com, Point Cross, Chéticamp, ☎902-224-3139. Hooked rugs (all sizes to coaster size), pottery, pewter, hand-knit sweaters (95% goods Nova Scotian-made).

Sea Shanty Antique & Craft Shop, RR#1 Englishtown, ☎902-929-2992. Quilts, watercolours by Nova Scotian artist Anne Duggan, hooked items, pottery, pewter, Celtic jewellery, antiques and collectibles.

Cape Breton Clay, www.capebreton clay.com, Off Rte. 19, next to Nile Brook and "The Red Bank" salmon pool on Margaree River, in Margaree Valley. ☎902-235-2467. Handcrafted dishes and bowls by Cape Breton artisan Bell Fraser.

RECREATION

FISHING

OUTFITTERS/GUIDES

All companies listed below also rent equipment.

Big Intervale Fishing Lodge, RR1, Margaree Valley. ☎902-248-2275. Margaree River fishing for Atlantic salmon and brook trout. Local guides, tackle shop, licenses, instruction and equipment.

Cape Breton Fly Fishing Adventures, www.cbflyfishing.com, 25 Kelmere Dr., Coxheath, ☎902-371-4347. Rainbow, brown, and speckled trout, also Atlantic salmon excursions by a licensed guide. Float tubes and equipment available.

Bras d'Or Lakes Outfitters, RR #2, Boisdale, ☎902-871-2549. Special-izing in the Margaree and North rivers: outfitters for Atlantic salmon, rainbow and speckled trout, and saltwater sport fishing for cod, hake and mackerel.

Green Highlander Lodge, 525 Chebucto St. Baddeck, ☎902-295-2303. Atlantic salmon and speckled trout fish-ing on the Baddeck, North, Margaree and Middle rivers. Fully guided and outfitted. Flycasting instruction for all levels.

FISHING LICENSES

Available through local tour operators. Also for sale at general-merchandise retailers and grocery stores displaying sign in their window.

BOATING

TOUR COMPANIES

Amoeba Sailing Tours – www.amoe basailingtours.com, Baddeck Wharf, Baddeck. ☎902-295-7780 or ☎902-295-1426. 43-seat schooner Amoeba 1hr30min sails on the Bras d'Or lakes.

Cape Breton Seacoast Adventures – Ingonish, ☎902-929-2800 or 877-929-2800. Daily 3hr30min sea kayak tours offered, including all equipment.

Elsie Yacht Charters – 368 Shore Rd., Baddeck, ☎902-295-3500 or ☎800-565-5660. An 18m/59ft yacht built for Alexander Graham Bell in 1917 is available for captained charters. Coast Guard-certified ship and captain.

North River Kayak Tours – RR#4, Bad-deck, ☎902-929-2628 or 888-865-2925.

Half day & full day kayak trips, with all equipment and food included. $55–$99

HIKING

Cape Breton Highlands National Park

25 hiking trails. The park's website offers descriptions on all trails that overlook canyons, highlands and coastal areas. www.pc.gc.ca/pn-np/ns/cbreton/activ/activ1_E.asp.

The **MacIntosh Brook Trail** is a shorter trail (1.7km/1.1 mi) near the entrance to the park, 45min to complete. During the hike, there will be some exposed tree roots, but walking alongside a brook through a hardwood forest with a waterfall at the end is a quiet and comfortable walk.

At the base of North Mountain, the **Lone Shieling Trail** (15min hike of 0.6km/0.4mi) leads through a protected old-growth maple forest, which is why access is restricted. Note the Scottish crofter's hut near the beginning of the trail.

One of the longer (albeit relatively easy) hikes is the **Clyburn Valley Walk** at 3 hours and 8.5km/ 5.3 mi. Natural sites to be seen are the sheer rock face of Franey Mountain (425m/1400ft), hardwood trees, huge boulders and apple trees all located along the Clyburn River. Note the remains of an abandoned gold mine.

Inverness County's Mabou Area – 14 trails (total length of over 35 km/22 mi) are maintained by the Cape Mabou Trail Club. There is no fee to walk the trails. ⚠Caution: parts of the trails are at the edge of cliffs and are not recom-mended for children or those with height fears. A map from the Club is available from local businesses.

WHALE-WATCHING CRUISES

Captain Cox's Whale Watch – www.whalewatching-novascotia.com, Bay St. Lawrence Government Wharf, 578 Meat Cove Rd., Capstick. ☎902-383-2981, ☎888-346-5556. ⏱Open mid-Jun–Sept. ☜$25, Jun 15–June 30: 1:30pm and 4:30pm. Jul–Aug: 10:30am, 1:30pm and 4:30pm. Sept. 15–Sept 30: 1:30pm and 4:30pm.

Captain Mark's Whale & Seal Cruise – www.whaleandsealcruise.com,

Pleasant Bay, NS ☎888-754-5112 or ☎902-224-1316, Jun 11:30am, 1:00pm, 3:00pm, Jul–Oct9:30am, 11:30am, 1:00pm, 3:00pm, 5:00pm, ☜$25
Port Hood Island View Tours, Port Hood – ☎902-787-3490

Cabot Trail Whale Watching, Pleasant Bay – ☎866-688-2424, www.cabottrail.com
Sea Visions, Ingonish – ☎902-285-2628, www.ingonish.com/seavisions
Whale Cruisers (Chéticamp) Ltd. – ☎902-224-3376 or 800-813-3376, www.whalecruisers.com

Baddeck★

POPULATION 907 – MAP P 176

Overlooking Baddeck Bay, this village claims a lovely **site**★★ on the northern shore of **Bras d'Or Lake,** a vast body of saltwater within the centre of the island roughly 100km/62mi long and 50km/31mi wide. This immense inland sea cuts Cape Breton Island in two. It is fed in the north by the Atlantic via two channels, the Great Bras d'Or and the Little Bras d'Or on either side of Boularderie Island. The lake is surrounded almost entirely by high hills and low mountains. Bras d'Or Lake's resemblance to a Scottish loch has attracted many settlers of Scottish origin to its shores. Among them was Edinburgh, Scotland native **Alexander Graham Bell** (1847-1922), humanitarian, researcher and prolific inventor. Today the popular resort town is a service centre for the county and the gateway for the famed road route, the Cabot Trail, which gives Baddeck a significant boost to its tourism-based economy. Indeed, provincial tourism officials estimate that, in summer and fall, Baddeck rivals Halifax in the number of tourist visits.

- **Information:** http://baddeck.com. Visitor Information Centre, Port Hastings. ☎902-625-4201 (late-Apr–early Jan).
- **Orient Yourself:** Highway 105, the Trans-Canada Highway, feeds into the village from the north. A short spur from it, designated as Rte. 205—known locally as Bay Road—leads south along Baddeck Bay to become Baddeck's main street, Chebucto Street. A **welcome centre** sits at the intersection of Chebucto St. and Shore Rd. Both the Trans-Can Highway and Chebucto Street run parallel for a short distance until they merge into the road known as the Cabot Trail.
- **Don't Miss:** The Alexander Graham Bell NHS and the Wagmatcook Cultural & Heritage Centre.
- **Organizing Your Time:** Spend at least one day in Baddeck.
- **Especially for Kids:** The Alexander Graham Bell NHS has an area devoted to children.

Sights

Alexander Graham Bell National Historic Site★★

Hwy. 205. ⏱*Open Jul–mid-Oct 8:30am–6pm, Jun 9am–6pm, May & late-Oct 9am–5pm.* ☜*$7.05.* ♿☐ ☎*902-295-2069. www.pc.gc.ca.*
Bell's favourite shape, the tetrahedron, is used extensively in the design of this fascinating museum. Exhibits illustrate the genius of this remarkable man. A number of films and videos are shown during peak season.

In 1885 Bell first visited Baddeck, where he was to conduct much of his aeronautical work. Eventually he chose this location for his summer residence, naming his home *Beinn Bhreagh,* "beautiful mountain" in Gaelic. His work as a teacher of the deaf led to the invention of the telephone, conceived in Brantford,

Nova Scotia Tourism, Culture and Heritage

Alexander Graham Bell National Historic Site

Ontario, in 1874 and tested in Boston the following year. The discovery brought him fame and the capital to continue other research. In Baddeck he built kites and heavier-than-air craft, using combinations of the tetrahedron shape, an almost perfect form because it is lightweight but strong. In 1907, with other pioneer aviators, he founded the Aerial Experiment Association and sponsored the first manned flight in Canada when the **Silver Dart** flew across Baddeck Bay in 1909. Before his death, he witnessed his hydrofoil craft reach the incredible speed (for 1919) of 114kmh/70mph on Bras d'Or Lake.

There are models of the telephone, Bell's original vacuum jacket (a forerunner of the iron lung), a surgical probe (a device used prior to the invention of the X ray) and his kites. His project to prevent stranded sailors from dying of thirst at sea is on view—a model for producing drinking water from breath and saltwater. A highlight is the superb **photograph collection of oversize black-and-white** prints of Bell's life and work. One wing of the museum is devoted to his hydrofoil, the HD-4. Both the original hull and a reconstruction of the entire craft are on exhibit.

From the museum's rooftop garden, there is a **view** of the wooded headland across Baddeck Bay. Beinn Bhreagh *(not open to the public)*, Bell's Canadian estate, can be seen among the trees.

Excursions

Wagmatcook Cultural and Heritage Centre★

10765 Hwy. 105, in Watmatcook, 16km/ 10m southwest of Baddeck. Open year-round Mon–Fri 9am–5pm. *902-295-1487 or 866-295-2999. www.wagmatcook.com.*

Kids This interpretive centre of native Mi'kmaq culture and lore opened in 2001. The centre invites the public to fully experience the traditions of the First Nations people through a multi-media presentation, storytelling, the "smudge" ceremony by an elder (*photography not allowed during this sacred rite*), crafts demonstrations and local cuisine. Watching the skilled Mi'kmaq artisans make traditional beadwork, moccasins and other items is encouraged. There is no admission, but specialized tours (such as drumming) require a nominal fee. Dancers and singers in traditional dress are normally present on-site. The **restaurant ($$)** serves a lunch of native cuisine such as stewed venison or locally caught poached Atlantic salmon, with bannock bread (pan-fried bread dough), but typically Canadian fare is also on the menu. The gift shop contains many handcrafted items made by local artisans.

Highland Village Museum/ An Clachan Gàidhealach★

4119 Rte. 223, in Iona. 25km/15mi on Hwy. 105 south to Exit 6, then take Rte 223 east 30km/19mi through Little Narrows (continuous ferry; $5). ◐*Open Jun–mid-Oct daily 9:30am–5:30pm.* ◕*$9.* ♿☎*902-725-2272 or 866-442-3542. www.museum.gov.ns.ca.*
Situated on 17ha/43 hillside acres on the Iona peninsula overlooking Bras d'Or Lake, this living history museum is devoted to Nova Scotia's Gaelic language and culture. The museum seeks to evoke the life the early Scots settlers experienced here through its re-created village of 10 period buildings, artifacts and tools, and offered activities. Visitors interested in Scottish history will especially enjoy touring the buildings, watching costumed staff demonstrate traditional skills, and seeing livestock. The complex also includes a music research centre, outdoor amphitheatre and genealogy-family history centre for Cape Breton. During the summer, daily activities include Gaelic singing, fiddling and dancing, storytelling workshops, codfish suppers, candlelight tours, oatcake baking and Gaelic feast days.

Cabot Trail★★

MAP P 176

Named for explorer **John Cabot** (Giovanni Caboto), who is reputed to have landed at the northern tip of Cape Breton Island in 1497, this route is one of the most beautiful drives in eastern North America. Opened in 1936, the paved, two-lane highway makes a circle tour of the northern part of the island. Initially traversing tranquil farmland, the trail then hugs the coast and winds up and down, providing scenic views of the immense Atlantic Ocean, craggy mountains, rocky inlets, magnificent headlands and dense forest. Some areas are reminiscent of the Scottish Highlands, ancestral home of many of the island's inhabitants. The east coast is especially rich in Gaelic culture. Derived from the language of the Celts in Ireland and the Scottish Highlands, Gaelic was the third most common European language spoken in Canada in the early 19C, and can still be heard here today. On the west coast, Chéticamp abounds with Acadian tradition and culture. Here you can find hand-hooked rugs and Acadian dishes. This driving tour is 301km/187mi in length, starting from Baddeck. ◉The trail can be driven in either direction, but visitors may prefer clockwise travel for the security of hugging the mountainside during steep, curvy stretches. It is described in three sections. Near the tip of the island, vast **Cape Breton Highlands National Park** stretches from the western to the eastern side of the island. National Park visitor centres are located at each of the southern entrances to the park.

🛈 **Information:** Destination Cape Breton Association. ☎902-563-4636. www.cbisland.com. Cape Breton Highlands National Park visitor centres: Chéticamp and Ingonish Beach locations; open May–mid-Oct daily 8am–8pm *(hours subject to change)*; ☎902-224-2306

▶ **Orient Yourself:** The driving tour begins in Baddeck and heads south to loop north around the peninsula in a counterclockwise fashion. The national park is entered on the west side and along the northwestern portion before the road leaves the park for an excursion to the island's tip. The road heads back south along the eastern shore and enters the national park for 17km/10mi or so before exiting it at Ingonish. One small portion of the park is again re-entered before the road leaves the park entirely and follows the western shore along St. Ann's Bay.

🅿 **Parking:** There are places to pull over along the road; ◉do not stop on the shoulder because of oncoming traffic.

◉ **Don't Miss:** Margaree Valley with its fly-fishing waters. The Gaelic College in St. Ann's.

◕ **Organizing Your Time:** You can make the circuit in a day, but 2 days allows time to enjoy the villages and the national park.

Driving Tour

*Round-trip of 301km/187mi from
Baddeck.*

From Baddeck to Chéticamp★

88km/55mi.

The Cabot Trail follows the valley of the
Middle River, passes the Lakes O'Law
and joins the Margaree River's verdant
valley★ of meadows, farms and woodlands. Its abundant salmon pools are
reputed to offer some of Canada's finest salmon fishing. Originating in the
Cape Breton Highlands, the northeast
branch of the Margaree meets the
southwest branch at Margaree Forks.
From there the 120km/74mi-long river
flows northward to drain into the Gulf
of Saint Lawrence at Margaree Harbour.
Atlantic salmon spawn amid the gravel
bars of the northeast branch. Acadians
chose to settle near the river's mouth.
Scottish Highlanders arrived in the Margaree Valley in the early 19C.

North East Margaree

This tiny rural community has a
museum of note.

Margaree Salmon Museum★

*Open mid-Jun–mid-Oct daily 9am–
5pm. ☜$1. &☏902-248-2848. http://for-
tress.uccb.ns.ca/historic/marg.html.*

This pleasant little museum features
a large collection of colourful fishing
flies and rods—one actually 5.5m/18ft
long, made in Scotland in 1880. Fishing
tackle on display includes a sampling
of illegal spears used by poachers. The
life cycle of the Atlantic salmon is illus-
trated from birth to return trip upriver
to reproduce. Unlike its Pacific cousin,
the Atlantic salmon can make several
such trips.

▶ *Continue west 7km/4mi to Margaree Forks. From there, Rte. 19 leads
south to Glenville, an optional
74km/46mi round-trip excursion.*

Glenora Distillery

*In Glenville, 37km/23mi south of Margaree
Forks via Rte. 19. Open early May–mid-
Oct. Distillery tours (25min) daily
9am–5pm hourly. ☜$7. ✕&P☏800-
839-0491. www.glenoradistillery.com .*
Billed as "North America's only single
malt whisky distillery and inn," Glenora
opened in 1990 on a 741ha/300-acre site
with log cabins for overnight lodging
built on the mountain overlooking the
glen. The seven distillery-associated
buildings were built with traditional
post-and-beam construction, in the
manner of Scotland's distilleries. Glenora
produces 250,000 litres of Glen Breton
Rare Canadian Single Malt Whisky, aged
in oak barrels. The company is not permitted to use the Scotch appellation
because the single malt is not distilled

Angling in the Margaree River

Sandra Phinney/Michelin

Whales Off the Coast

Whale watching has become as popular an activity here as it is on Digby Neck, off mainland Nova Scotia. In fact, Nova Scotia's first and only **Whale Interpretive Centre** opened on the island in 2000, in Pleasant Bay, to promote awareness of these remarkable denizens of the sea. The best whale-watching sites along the Cabot Trail include the waters off Petit Etang, Pleasant Bay, Cape North, White Point and Ingonish. The waters attract migrating finback and minke whales *(May–Jun)*, pilot whales *(Jul–Dec)* humpback whales and dolphins *(Aug–Oct)*, and seals. Many tour companies guarantee sightings, or the fee is returned. In Pleasant Bay alone, seven whale-watching boats vie for customers. *For a list of whale-watching companies, see the Practical Information section.*

in Scotland. This restriction has not hurt the thriving cottage industry in western Cape Breton Island, since Glen Breton is imported to other parts of Canada and select distributors in the USA. Tours take in the distilling process and end with the sampling of the product. Glenora's inn and dining room attract a steady stream of guests (*see Address Book*).

▶ *Return to the Cabot Trail.*

The Cabot Trail parallels the Margaree River northward, affording pastoral **views**★ of the wide river valley and the town of East Margaree on the opposite side. As the road descends, the **view**★ of Margaree Harbour is lovely. The trail crosses the estuary of the Margaree River and heads north along the Acadian coast, with views of the Gulf of St. Lawrence.

Chéticamp

An enclave of Acadian culture, this fishing community sprawls along the coast opposite Chéticamp Island. A protected harbour and a large stone church dedicated to St. Peter distinguish the town. The Acadian tricolour flag can be seen atop flagpoles scattered throughout the town. Locally made hand-hooked rugs are Chéticamp's claim to fame.

Les Trois Pignons Cultural Centre

15584 Cabot Trail. Open Jul–Aug daily 9am–7pm. May–Jun & Sept–Oct daily 9am–5pm. $5. 902-224-2642. www.lestroispignons.com/troispignons/en/welcome.html.
Of particular note at this cultural centre is the **Museum of the Hooked Rug and Home Life,** which exhibits the tools and crafts of Chéticamp's renowned rug-

makers. The remarkable wool-hooking techniques of **Elizabeth LeFort** (b. 1914) are confirmed in her wall-size rug titled "United States Presidential History," which she hooked in 1959. She used seven miles of yarn in 390 colours to complete the rug, which took six months. In uncanny detail, her work depicts 34 presidents and two presidential seals. She also produced a series of wool portraits of Queen Elizabeth II and prime ministers Lester Pearson, John Diefenbaker and Pierre Trudeau, among other famous figures. Her art has been on display in Buckingham Palace, the White House and Vatican City.

Acadian Museum

Cabot Trail. Open May–Oct Mon–Fri 8am–9pm, weekends 9am–5pm. Rest of the year Tue & Fri 1pm–3pm. 902-224-2170. www.co-opartisanale.com.
Operated by a cooperative of Acadian women, the museum and gift shop feature a large array of hooked mats, rugs and other crafted items. There are demonstrations of hooking, spinning, carding and weaving. The on-site **restaurant** specializes in Acadian cooking (*see Address Book*).

From Chéticamp to Cape Smokey

124km/77mi.

Whale Interpretive Centre★

104 Harbour Rd., in Pleasant Bay. Open mid-May–Oct 9am–5pm. $4.50. 902-224-1411. www.novascotiaheritage.ca.
Opened in 2000, this centre is the first of its kind in Atlantic Canada. As there are 16 species of whales that can be

Address Book

For dollar sign categories, see the Legend on the cover flap.

WHERE TO STAY

$$ Broadwater Inn – *Rte. 205 (Bay Rd.), Baddeck (1.6 km/1mi east of Baddeck). 902-295-1101. www.broadwater.baddeck.com. 6 rooms, 7 cottages. (one cottage). Closed Nov–Apr.* Overlooking Bras d'Or Lake, this splendid property served as the original homestead for Alexander Graham Bell`s pilot, J.D. MacCurdy. One room, with cathedral ceilings and a fireplace, was used by Bell himself as an occasional library sanctuary. All guest rooms have ensuite bathrooms, queen beds and flat screen TVs; a complimentary continental breakfast is included. The **Verandah Suite ($$$)** has a kitchenette and private entrance. The log cottages are ideal for longer stays, and vary from open concept to one-and two-bedroom units; all have sundecks and kitchen facilities and bedding. The Gardener's Shed cottage is barrier-free and ideal for wheelchairs.

$$ Glenora Inn and Distillery – *In Glenville, 37km/23mi south of Margaree Forks via Rte. 19. 800-839-0491. www.glenoradistillery.com. 9 rooms, 6 cottages. Closed late-Oct–early May. Pub open early Jun. Dining room late-Jun.* Within this complex are the inn, six cottages, a **pub ($)** with live entertainment nightly, a **dining room ($$)** serving Nova Scotian food that includes traditional Scottish dishes, a gift shop, and of course, the distillery itself where tours are given daily. Guest rooms with en suite baths in the inn have satellite TV and phones (two "executive rooms" have king beds). Of the log chalets on the hillside, one is wheelchair accessible and all have loft bedrooms, kitchens, TV and traditional furnishings (no phones). Internet access is provided in the main foyer or lobby only. Guests can dine al fresco in the summer under patio umbrellas, with MacClelland's River bubbling in the background.

$$ Normaway Inn – *691 Egypt Rd. Margaree Valley. 3km/2mi off Cabot Trail). 902-248-2987 or 800-565-9463. www.normaway.com.* Nestled within 101ha/250 acres of forest and meadows, this sequestered resort lodge appeals to nature lovers with its mountain biking and hiking, and proximity to trout and salmon fishing and canoeing waters. Guest accommodations include handsomely appointed lodge rooms, as well as cabins with Jacuzzis and woodstoves, and swings on the screened porch. Nightly in the **dining room ($$)** *(open to the public)*, typical fare features fresh produce from the inn's own garden, Atlantic salmon, and locally raised lamb from the Margaree Valley. In summer and fall, live music is offered on some evenings.

$$ Haus Treuburg Country Inn and Cottages – *175 Main St., in Port Hood, 64km/40mi south of Margaree Forks via Rte. 19. 902-787-2116. www.haustreuburg.com. 3 rooms, 3 one-bedroom cottages. Closed Jan–Mar.* Nestled in the village of Port Hood, which lies on the western coast of Cape Breton (with reputedly the warmest waters in the Maritimes), this early 20C home and three cottages sit within an apple orchard. The cottages face west, overlooking the Gulf of St. Lawrence. The decor of the rooms is reflective of Germany and Austria (the owners emigrated to Canada in the late 1990s). A hot breakfast in a casual dining room off the kitchen and home-cooked dinners featuring traditional German dishes, served in a formal dining room, are available at an extra charge ($$). All rooms and cottages have cable TV and VCRs. Wi-fi is available in the main house.

$$ The Water's Edge Inn, Café & Gallery – *22 Water St., Baddeck. 902-295-3600 or 866-439-2528. www.thewatersedgeinn.com. 6 rooms.* Purchased by a couple from Connecticut in 2004, this property is truly on the edge of Bras d'Or Lake. Guest rooms are spacious and individually decorated; all have ensuite bathrooms, mini-refrigerators and cable TV. Four rooms have balconies to enjoy views of the lake. The on-site gallery offers high-end art and crafts from local artisans for sale, and the **café ($)** features fresh salads, sandwiches and desserts.

$$$ Keltic Lodge Resort and Spa – *Middle Head Peninsula, Ingonish Beach.* ✕ P ⌐ Spa ☎*902-285-2880 or 800-565-0444. www.kelticlodge.ca. 74 rooms, 9 cottages. Closed late-Oct–mid-May.* This sprawling cliff-side resort commands a grand view of the Atlantic Ocean from an isolated, forested promontory jutting out on Cape Breton Island's east side. Richly appointed guests rooms have matching bedspreads and draperies, well-made furnishings and private baths. Two- and four-bedroom cottages feature a fireplace in the shared living room; some individual rooms also have a fireplace. Amenities at the complex include a heated outdoor pool, tennis courts, putting greens and an 18-hole golf course. The **Purple Thistle Dining Room ($$)** serves creative Canadian dishes with authority and paired with lovely views of the Atlantic; try the Cape North mussels or the Aspy Bay oysters as an appetizer. The less formal **Atlantic Restaurant ($)** offers steaks, seafood and burgers with equally appealing views of the ocean. There's great hiking on the trails along the headland.

WHERE TO EAT

$ Red Shoe Pub – *11573 Rte. 19, Mabou.* ☎*902-945-2996. www.redshoepub.com. Closed late-Oct–May.* **Canadian.** Owned by Cape Breton's much-loved musical family, the Rankins, the Red Shoe has a fun atmosphere and unpretentious menu. Some people say the pub offers the best meat loaf in the province.

Another specialty is the *tortière* (Acadian meat pie). Residents and tourists also make return visits for the daily, live music. Local guest musicians vary in age and capacities but delight guests all the same: dad on the piano and son on the fiddle, for example. Other performers well-known in Atlantic Canada play frequently *(cover charge after dinner).*

$ Restaurant Acadien – *At the Acadian Museum, Chéticamp.* ☎*902-224-3207. www.co-opartisanale.com.* **Acadian.** Prepare to enjoy an authentic Acadian meal served by women in gingham skirts and lace caps at this popular roadside restaurant. Chicken Fricot (chicken and potatoes cooked in chicken stock), meat pie and fish chowder share the menu with more standard fare (fish and chips, pork chops and hamburgers). Dessert pies are hard to resist. Breakfast, lunch and dinner are served seven days a week here, beginning at 7am.

$$ The Mull Café & Deli – *11630 Route 19, Mabou.* ♿☎*902-945-2244. www. auracom.com/mulldci2/mullcafe.htm.* **Canadian.** Here's the place in western Cape Breton where locals go to dine and socialize. In this casual, friendly setting, a wise choice at lunch might be the grilled haddock, with apple crisp for dessert. On the dinner menu are pastas, vegetarian dishes, chicken, seafood and steaks; try the Atlantic scallop stir fry accompanied by a bottle of crisp Nova Scotian white wine. There's also an outdoor deck for dining year-round. Reservations are suggested for dinner in mid-summer.

Responsible Whale Watching

Whales are wild creatures, at home in the water. While you watch, they may feed, mate, nurse calves, rest, and play. The behaviours associated with these activities are natural. What is not natural is changing those behaviours through irresponsible human activities within the whales' habitat. Help eliminate disturbances to whales and other marine wildlife by minding the following:

- Don't be afraid to express concern to your boat crew if you witness actions on their part that seem to disturb the whales.
- Make sure your tour company provides commentary aboard the boat. Your experience will be greatly enhanced by the interpretation.
- Whales are more likely to engage in natural behaviours when not frightened.
- Let your operator know that getting close to a whale is not your objective.

Source: Deborah Tobin, author of *Struggling To Survive: Saving Endangered Marine Species in Atlantic Canada.*

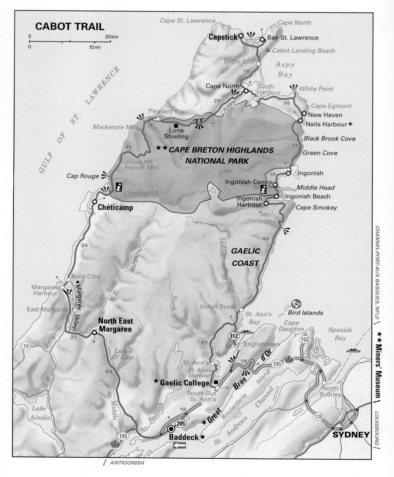

CABOT TRAIL

Cape St. Lawrence · Cape North
Capstick · Bay St. Lawrence
Cabot Landing Beach
Sugar Loaf
Aspy Bay
Cape North · South Harbour · White Point
Pleasant Bay · Cape Egmont
New Haven
Mackenzie Mtn. · Lone Shieling · Neils Harbour ★
Black Brook Cove
★★ **CAPE BRETON HIGHLANDS NATIONAL PARK** · Green Cove
French Mtn. · Ingonish
Cap Rouge · Ingonish Centre · Middle Head
Chéticamp · Ingonish Beach
Ingonish Harbour · Cape Smokey
Chéticamp
GAELIC COAST
Bird Islands
Belle Côte
Margaree Harbour · Indian Brook · St. Ann's Bay · Cape Dauphin · Spanish Bay
East Margaree
North East Margaree · Englishtown
Lake O'Law · St. Ann's Harbour · North Sydney
★ **Gaelic College** · South Gut St. Ann's
Lake Ainslie
SYDNEY
Baddeck ★
ANTIGONISH

CHANNEL-PORT AUX BASQUES, NFLD. | ★★ Miners' Museum | LOUISBOURG

sighted off Nova Scotia's waters, the centre is devoted to the interpretion and preservation of these marine mammals, and sea life in general. On Cape Breton Island, especially along the Cabot Trail, nearly two dozen companies offer whale-watching excursions (👋 *see Cape Breton Island Practical Information*). Displays, exhibits, a video and an aquarium filled with live undersea creatures all help to convince visitors of the importance of continued efforts to save whales from extinction. A life-size **model** of a pilot whale is especially worth seeing. The origin, classification and environments of whales off Cape Breton, as well as current conservation efforts, are explained by on-site guides (in English or French).

Cape Breton Highlands National Park★★

Ingonish Beach. 🕐*Open daily year-round.* 💲*$6 entry fee.* ♿ 🅿 *Information centres at park entrance north of Chéticamp (☎902-224-3814) and at Ingonish Beach (☎902-224-2306)* 🕐*open late-Jun–mid-Aug daily 8am–8pm. Late-Aug–late-Sept 8am–6pm. Early-May–mid-Jun & rest of Sept–mid-Oct daily 9am–5pm. www.pc.gc.ca.*

Spanning coast to coast across northern Cape Breton, this 950sq km/367sq mi wilderness park, established in 1936, combines seashore and mountains. Hills ascend directly from the ocean to form a tableland rising more than 500m/1,700ft, the highest point in the province.

The west coast borders the relatively calm waters of the Gulf of St. Lawrence. On the eastern side the Atlantic Ocean pounds the bare rocks with great force, yet there are several fine beaches throughout this preserve. Whales, and even bald eagles, can be found on either shore. Inland the park is heavily forested and boggy—the realm of moose, lynx and snowshoe hare. Several trails *(obtain a map from the park visitor centre)* reach the interior, but the main attraction is the beautiful coastline.

From the park entrance at the Chéticamp River, Cabot Trail winds up Chéticamp Canyon to emerge on the coast, parallel to the sea. Fine **views**★★ of the ocean and the road weaving up and down in the distance are afforded. From **Cap Rouge** lookout, there is an especially lovely **view**★★. The road gradually climbs French Mountain and heads inland across the plateau, the highest point on the highway.

After crossing several deep, stream-lined valleys, the road descends to Mackenzie Mountain. Then, by a series of switchbacks, it reaches Pleasant Bay with outstanding **views**★★ on the descent. The **Lone Shieling** *(about 6.5km/4mi from Pleasant Bay, then short walk)*, a tiny hut of stone with rounded corners and a thatched roof, is a replica of a Scottish crofter's cottage, common in the Highlands and islands of Scotland. It was built to form a visible link between the adopted home of the Highland Scots who settled Cape Breton and their ancestral land.

Along its course the Cabot Trail climbs North Mountain, descends steeply, affording pretty **views**★, and then enters the valley of the North Aspy River, which it follows to the village of **Cape North**.

▶ *From Cape North, an optional round-trip excursion of 38km/24mi takes in Bay St. Lawrence.*

Bay St. Lawrence★★

This scenic drive rounds Aspy Bay, affording views of its long sandbar, and then heads inland across grassy hills spotted with pink rock to St. Lawrence Bay at the north end of Cape Breton Island. Before

leaving the bay, the road passes Cabot Landing Beach, supposedly the first North American landfall of John Cabot. Whether visited by Cabot or not, it is a refreshing scene of a long beach backed by Sugarloaf Mountain.

At the end of the road is the tiny fishing village of **Bay St. Lawrence,** built around a small lake with a narrow exit to the sea. Near the approach to the village, a large white clapboard church (St. Margaret's) is prominent. From its grounds the **view**★ of the bay community is picturesque. The church's fine wooden interior has a ceiling shaped like the hull of the ship.

▶ *Upon leaving Bay St. Lawrence, turn right and continue 3km/1.8mi to Capstick.*

Capstick

Less populated than Bay St. Lawrence, this hillside settlement consists of a few isolated houses on the grassy slope above the seacliffs. The dramatic **views**★ of the inlets through the scraggy pines are enhanced by the beauty of the water's colour.

▶ *Return to Cabot Trail. After South Harbour, take the coast road.*

Revealing fine **views**★ of Aspy Bay, its sandbar and the long Cape North peninsula, this coastal drive is a pretty one. The road turns south after White Point through the charming fishing villages of **New Haven** and **Neils Harbour**★, the latter with an artificial harbour beside a sandy bay.

▶ *Rejoin Cabot Trail.*

This section of the trail is an especially splendid drive along the coast, particularly after **Black Brook Cove.** Worn pink boulders stretch into the sea, while green forests cover the inlands. There are many little bays and coves, **Green Cove** being one of the loveliest. From Lakie's Head lookout, the narrow peninsula of **Middle Head** and towering Cape Smokey can be identified, sometimes rising from a mist reminiscent of that in the Scottish Highlands.

Capstick houses on the St. Lawrence

The Ingonishs

The relative solitute of the trail is left behind in the resort area of Ingonish Centre, Ingonish Beach, Ingonish Harbour and other Ingonish designations, popular for various forms of recreation like fishing, boating, swimming, golf, tennis and winter skiing. The bay itself is cut into two parts—north and south—by Middle Head, the dramatic setting of the **Keltic Lodge** (*see Address Book*), one of Canada's best-known resort hotels. To the south the promontory known as **Cape Smokey** rises 369m/1,210ft out of the sea. This headland is at times partially obscured by clouds, hence its name.

From Cape Smokey to Baddeck

89km/55mi.

This section of the trail is known as the Gaelic Coast, given the pervasive Scottish tilt. The trail climbs over Cape Smokey and then drops again, permitting several good **views**★. Descending the coast farther inland, the road passes trough several fishing villages.

Offshore are the **Bird Islands,** a sanctuary where vast numbers of seabirds nest in summer. The trail rounds St. Ann's Harbour, offering lovely views after Goose Cove, but especially at South Gut St. Ann's.

Gaelic College★

In St. Ann's.

Founded in 1938 by Rev. A.W.R. MacKenzie, this school is the only one on the continent to teach the Gaelic language and Highland arts and crafts. Attracting youth from all over North America, the college offers such courses as bagpipe music, the Gaelic language, Highland dancing and hand weaving of family and clan tartans. Students can often be seen performing Highland flings and sword dances, as well as step dancing. During July and August, the college hosts a *ceilidh* (KAY-lee) featuring local performers *(Wed evening)*.

Great Hall of the Clans

51779 Cabot Trail Rd., on campus.   *Open early-Jun–Aug daily 9am–5pm. Sept Mon–Fri 9am–5pm.* ◓$5. ☎902-295-3411. www.gaeliccollege.edu.

At the rear of the entrance is a room displaying Highland pioneer crafts and memorabilia. Inside the large meeting hall, wall **exhibits,** some interactive, illustrate clan history and life. A variety of tartans and costumes are also on display. At one end of the hall stands a statue of Angus MacAskill (1825-63), the 236cm/7ft 9in-tall, 193kg/425-pound "Cape Breton giant" who toured the US with Tom Thumb.

Alternative Route★

22km/14mi by Rte. 312 and Trans-Canada Hwy.

This road enters St. Ann's Bay via a narrow spit of land that divides the bay from

St. Ann's Harbour. At the end of the spit, there is a ferry across the outlet (24hrs daily, every 10min. Feb–Apr no crossing if ice. ☎902-861-1911. www.gov.ns.ca).

Excursion

Great Bras d'Or★
18km/11mi northeast along Trans-Canada Hwy from South Gut St. Ann's.

The road ascends Kelly's Mountain with a fine **view**★ from the lookout of the harbour, the spit of land and the ferry. Crossing Cape Dauphin peninsula, it descends to the Great Bras d'Or. There are good **views**★ of this stretch of water, of the bridge that spans it and, in the distance, **Sydney,** Cape Breton's principal city and the site of eastern Canada's richest coalfields, which fostered a sizable steel industry.

Sydney
POPULATION 102,250 – MAP P 176

Nova Scotia's second-largest city, Sydney occupies an inland perch along Cape Breton Island's easternmost peninsula. The city sprawls out on the east side of the South Arm of Sydney Harbour, which empties into the Atlantic Ocean. Since 1995 its municipal population has included the communities of Sydney Mines, North Sydney, New Waterford and Glace Bay, forming what is known as Industrial Cape Breton. North Sydney serves as the departure point for **ferry service** to the province of Newfoundland and Labrador, where ferries dock at Port aux Basques on the island of Newfoundland.

Sydney's marine terminal welcomes cruise ships from June through October, with the majority of them visiting in late summer and fall for autumn foliage tours. The city is also home to Cape Breton University, an undergraduate post-secondary institution, which is known nationally for its Aboriginal Studies programme; the school has the largest Mi'kmaq student population in eastern Canada and turns out the highest number of Mi'kmaq graduates each year. In 2004 one of Cape Breton Island's five Mi'kmaq communities, the Membertou First Nation in Sydney, opened a $7million, 47,000sq ft convention centre with an 850-seat entertainment venue and a 150-seat restaurant in the area. One of Nova Scotia's few casinos is located in Sydney, Casino Nova Scotia (☎902-563-7777; www.casinonovascotia.com/sydney/home.aspx)

- **Information:** Sydney Visitor Information Centre, Marine Terminal, 72 Esplanade. Open Jun–mid-Oct daily 9–5pm. ☎902-539-9876. North Sydney Visitor Information Centre, Ferry Terminal (entry from Newfoundland). Open mid-June–mid September daily 9–5pm. ☎902-794-7719.
- **Orient Yourself:** Sydney's main street is Charlotte Street; King's Road and the Esplanade are other major thoroughfares. Cruise ships from other parts of Canada and the US dock at the marine terminal, which lies along the Esplanade overlooking the harbour. Shops and restaurants are clustered along Charlotte Street, although the Sydney Shopping Centre is found on Prince Street, and the larger Mayflower Mall sits on the outskirts of the city (Grand Lake Road). A small heritage district can be found in and around Charlotte Street.
- **Don't Miss:** The Miners' Museum in nearby Glace Bay.
- **Organizing Your Time:** Sydney requires a day if you plan to go to the Miners' Museum in Glace Bay. Best to see St. Peter's Canal NHS as you leave the island.
- **Especially for Kids:** The model trains and vintage passenger and freight cars at the Sydney and Louisbourg Railway Museum.

A Bit of History

In 1784 Cape Breton Island was under British rule, and not part of Nova Scotia. Sydney was founded in 1785 primarily as a home for Loyalists from New York following the American Revolution. By 1820 Cape Breton was part of Nova Scotia again, and Sydney was reduced from being a colonial capital to a small town. Nothing much happened here throughout the 19C, even though its harbour (known as Spanish Bay to the colonists) was surrounded by the richest coal fields in eastern Canada. By 1904, when the city was incorporated, a steel plant had been built and coal mines were operating, particularly in Glace Bay. After WW II, both industries were on the decline; competition from central Canada eventually killed the steel industry in 2001. Today, with the amalgamation of the five eastern Cape Breton communities, the municipality now relies on tourism and culture, light manufacturing and information technology as its economic base.

Sights

Cossit House Museum★

75 Charlotte St. ◷Open Jun–mid-Oct. Mon–Sat 9:30am–5:30pm, Sun 1pm– 5:30pm. ⊗$2. ☎902-539-7973. www. cossit.museum.gov.ns.ca

Spend awhile in Sydney's oldest house (c.1787) in the city's oldest neighbourhood, where Rev. Ranna Cossit and his wife, Thankful, and their 10 children lived. Today the unadorned, one-and-a-half-storey house with a gable roof has been restored to its late-18C appearance. Several rooms are furnished according to the 1815 inventory list from Sydney's first permanent Anglican minister's estate. Guides in period dress lend authenticity to the site.

Mi'kmaq Resource Centre

On Cape Breton University campus, 1250 Grand Lake Rd., Room CE268. ◷Open year-round Tue–Wed 9am–4:30pm, Thu 9am–noon. ☎902-563-1660. http://mrc. uccb.ns.ca.

Anyone interested in an in-depth knowledge of the Mi'kmaq of the Maritime provinces and Maine will discover a comprehensive font of information at this resource centre. For 10 years, documents and some artifacts pertaining to Mi'kmaq history, culture and language have been collected and stored here on the campus of Cape Breton University. Note that this is not a museum, but primarily a library where assistance is available from on-site staff.

Excursions

Miners' Museum★★

42 Birkley St., in Glace Bay. 19km/12mi northeast of Sydney. Follow museum signs from town to Quarry Point. ◷Open Jun–Aug daily 10am–6pm (Tue 7pm). Sept–Oct Mon–Sun 9am–4pm. Rest of the year Mon–Fri 9am–4pm. Restaurant May–Oct noon–8pm. ⊗$5 (☛guided mine tour an additional $5; protective clothing provided). ✗♿🅿☎902-849-4522. www.minersmuseum.com.

Glace Bay

Home of the Miners' Museum, sprawling Glace Bay has been a mining town since 1720, when French soldiers from Louisbourg found coal in the cliffs at Port Morien to the southeast. The region is underlain with bituminous coal seams that dip seaward under the Atlantic Ocean. By the late 19C numerous coal mines were operating. When iron ore deposits were found in nearby Newfoundland, a steel industry mushroomed in the vicinity of Sydney, using coal as coke in the refining process. Immigrants poured into the area in the 20C for mining jobs. By the early 1950s, use of oil and gas had reduced the demand for coal. Economic depression hit as the mines began to close. The federal government created the Cape Breton Development Corp., which operated the Glace Bay colliery until 1984, when coal mining in the area ceased.

Address Book

For dollar sign categories, see the Legend on the cover flap.

WHERE TO STAY

$$ Cranberry Cove Inn – *12 Wolfe St., Louisbourg.* 📶 🖥 ☎*902-733-2171 or 800-929-0222. www.cranberrycove inn.com. 7 rooms. Closed Nov–Apr. Dining room closed Nov–May.* Built in 1905, this former merchant's home has three storeys connected by a beautifully carved staircase. All but one of the themed guest rooms have Jacuzzi tubs, but each is impeccably appointed with period and modern furnishings. Amenities include wireless Internet and a computer with Internet available to guests *(second floor)*. The **Cranberry Cove Restaurant ($$)** offers Canadian dishes such as halibut Grand Marnier, spinach and berries salad, and desserts like Cape Breton date pudding. The fortress is only a 10min walk away.

$$ Gowrie House Country Inn – *840 Shore Rd., Sydney Mines.* 📶 🖥 ☎*902-544-1050 or 800-372-1115. www. gowriehouse.com. 10 rooms, 1 cottage* **($$$)**. This Georgian house (c. 1830) has been a Cape Breton institution since 1982. Guest rooms are lavishly decorated and have ensuite bathrooms; seven have fireplaces and four have kitchenettes. One of Nova Scotia's top dining spots, the **dining room ($$)** serves four-course meals of contemporary dishes to guests and the public nightly at 7:30pm; the menu changes daily, incorporating fresh market ingredients *(reservations recommended)*. Convenient to the ferry terminal to Newfoundland and Labrador in North Sydney.

$$ Louisbourg Heritage House – *7544 Main St., Louisbourg.* 📶 🖥 ☎*902-733-3222 or 888-888-8466. www. louisbourgheritagehouse.com. 6 rooms. No pets, not suitable for children. Closed late-Oct–mid-Jun.* Dating from 1886 and located in the heart of Louisbourg, this former church rectory looks prim and proper on the outside, set on well-maintained grounds enclosed by a white picket fence. Inside, a friendly welcome and comfortable quarters await. Done in soft pastels, spacious guest rooms feature hardwood floors and beds (some four-poster) dressed with duvets; all have ceiling fans, en suite bathrooms and balconies. Breakfasts might include freshly made scones or crepes. A sister property, the **Louisbourg Harbour Inn Bed and Breakfast ($$)** at 9 Lower Warren Street *(www.louisbourgharbourinn.com)* is located around the corner and has eight guestrooms. Both are within walking distance of restaurants in the village.

WHERE TO EAT

$$ Allegro Grill and Deli – *222 Charlotte St., Sydney.* ☎*902-562-1623. www. allegrogrill.ca.* **International.** Under new ownership, Allegro is housed in a century-old building that has been totally overhauled inside and out. Bold reds and ochres accent the interior's earth tones and natural materials. The chef-owner focuses not only on making his dishes from scratch, but on operating his new venture as a low-impact, "green" business. He describes his menu as "trade winds cuisine": everything from North African to Greek, Argentinian to French. Noontime choices include a cold plate of falafel, tabbouleh (made with gluten-free quinoa), hummus toasted with Greek-style pita and Lebanese-style pickled turnip; the house soup is Egyptian red lentil. The dinner menu features Louisiana-style blackened catfish or lamb chops coated in honey with cracked black pepper. Chops and steaks are grilled Goucho-style.

Overlooking the vast Atlantic Ocean from its 6ha/15-acre site, this low-lying, geometric museum stands as a monument to Cape Breton's coal-mining history.

The museum has well-presented, colourful exhibits on coal formation and mining methods. Coal samples, equipment and transport are also on display. Films *(20-30min)* about Cape Breton's mining industry and labour history are shown in the theatre.

Retired miners conduct **mine tours** *(30min)*, interspersing commentary with tales from personal experience. Visitors walk down a sloping tunnel under the Atlantic Ocean to see the machinery and coal face of the Ocean Deep Colliery. *Note: low mine ceilings may necessitate stooping for periods of time.*

Beside the museum building, a **miners' village** has been reconstructed. The mining company supplied employee housing and owned the village store. Transactions were based on credit secured against a miner's wages. After a week of work, a miner sometimes drew no pay, finding he owed for food, clothing and other necessities. In addition to a store, a miner's house of the period 1850-1900 has been re-created. The restaurant *(hours vary)* serves home-cooked specialties such as "coal dust pie."

Sydney and Louisbourg Railway Museum

7330 Main St., in Louisbourg, 32km/20mi southeast of Sydney. ○*Open Jun Mon–Fri 9am–5pm. Jul–Sept daily 10am–7pm.* ≈*Contribution suggested.* &. P ☎*902-733-2720. www.fortress.uccb.ns.ca/historic/s_l.html.*

Kids Built in 1895, this railway station and freight shed was the office of the S & L (Sydney & Louisbourg) Railway, a busy place in its heyday when coal was delivered directly to ships for export. Louisbourg was a major seaport and shipping terminal for coal from the turn of the 19C through the mid-20C.

The museum exhibits railway artifacts, model trains, and a model of the line as it appeared in the 1940s to 60s. Old passenger and freight cars on the premises date from 1881 to 1914. Memorial hand-made quilts and a Marconi wireless display are on view in the roundhouse.

St. Peters Canal National Historic Site★

88km/55mi southwest of Sydney by Hwy. 4. ○*Open mid-May–mid-Jun daily 8am–4:30pm. Late-Jun–Oct daily 8am–8:30pm.* ☎*902-733-2280. www.pc.gc.ca/lhn-nhs/ns/stpeters/index_e.asp.*

This 800m/2,624ft-long canal was constructed to join Bras d'or Lake with the Atlantic Ocean. In the 1630s French merchants founded a settlement named St-Pierre on a narrow isthmus between the ocean and the expansive lake. Born in Tours, France, **Nicolas Denys** (1598-1688) became an important figure in Acadia's history in the 17C. He was instrumental in developing the settlement as a fishing station and trading post, exchanging European-made goods for furs of the local Mi'kmaq population. A local portage route was used more and more as a "haulover" road for Denys' ships, pulled by oxen from shore to shore. But in 1668 St-Pierre was consumed by a disastrous fire, and no settlement took place for nearly 50 years. The present village of St. Peter's was established in the early 19C,

Sydney and Louisbourg Railway Museum

Nova Scotia Tourism, Culture and Heritage

and the old road was soon put to use hauling ships across the isthmus to the inland waterway. As shipping increased, the idea of replacing the portage road with a navigation channel was seriously considered. In 1854 work on the canal began, but it wasn't until 1869 that the waterway was completed. More than a century later, in 1985, Parks Canada finished the restoration of both the Bras d'Or Lake and the Atlantic Ocean entrances to the canal, and today it maintains the canal as a National Historic Site.

The lockmaster's house from 1876 is still standing, and the canal features Nova Scotia's only operational lock system. Though no longer used for commercial purposes, the canal hosts all kinds of pleasure craft. **Battery Provincial Park** lies adjacent to the canal, and is open for camping and picnicking from mid-May to Labour Day. The **Nicholas Denys Museum** *(46 Denys St.; ☎902-535-2379; http://cbmuseums.tripod.com)* is situated within a short walk of the canal. Established in Denys' honour, the museum exhibits artifacts from the area and a photographic history of the canal.

Fortress of Louisbourg★★★
MAP INSIDE FRONT COVER

Lying 37km/23mi southeast of Sydney by Route 22, the fishing village of **Louis-bourg** occupies the extreme eastern headland of Cape Breton Island. Facing the Atlantic Ocean, the town sits within a horseshoe-shaped harbour of the same name. At the harbour's east entrance rises **Louisbourg Lighthouse**, the third replacement for the oldest lighthouse (1734) in the country. Opposite, the immense 18C fortress of New France dominates the southwest arm of the harbour—positioned to guard the Atlantic approach to Quebec by way of the St. Lawrence River to the north. During the 18C rivalry between France and Britain for control of the New World, Louisbourg was manned by the largest garrison in North America. The $25 million restoration of this National Historic Site is the most expensive preservation project ever undertaken by the Canadian government.

Since 1961 one-quarter of the fortress has been rebuilt according to the original plans and historical records. Furnishings are either original or reproductions. Today, administered by Parks Canada, the fortress plays an integral part in the town's life and culture: many festivals and events are held on fortress grounds throughout the season. In July 2008 the fortress commemorated the 250-year anniversary of the 1758 siege—the second siege—of Louisbourg. Re-enactments of the battle, musical performances, craft displays, demonstrations of military camp life and 18C-type fireworks are just some of the activities that took place during the celebration as well as the unveiling of a new exhibit on General James Wolfe.

- **Information:** Fortress of Louisbourg National Historic Site. ☎902-733-2280. www.pc.gc.ca. Town of Louisbourg Visitor Centre (Main St., next to the post office). ☎902-733-2720. www.louisbourgtourism.com.
- ▶ **Orient Yourself:** The fortress is laid out as a small community. Just past the town of Louisbourg, the **visitor centre** for the fortress is your first stop; the parking is free, and admission tickets are purchased here. Pick up a site map of the fortress at the visitor centre to get oriented and ask for a schedule of the day's events. A 7min **bus ride** takes visitors from the parking lot to the fortress and provides onboard commentary as a preview of your visit. There are gardens and some 50 buildings, most open to the public, including three restaurants and a bakery on the 4.8ha/12-acre site. Costumed interpreters stroll the premises, perform military maneuvers and staff the buildings; they

are also on hand to give directions and answer questions. There are regularly scheduled free guided tours of the site as well.

🅿 **Parking:** Free parking at the visitor centre; 7min bus ride to the fortress.

🍽 **Don't Miss:** An 18C meal in one of the three period restaurants.

🕐 **Organizing Your Time:** Allow a full day for the visit, which must be accomplished on foot. *Be prepared for cool temperatures, rain and fog. Comfortable walking shoes and a light jacket are recommended.* Bring what you'll need from the car: returning to your car is time-consuming.

Kids **Especially for Kids:** There is a Children's Interpretive Centre at the Rodrigue House *(Jul–Aug)*.

A Bit of History

The French had long planned a fortress in Nova Scotia, even considering Halifax as a possible site. When they lost the mainland in 1713, they chose the eastern peninsula of Île Royale (now Cape Breton) and commenced construction of a fortified town in 1719. Following fortification designs elaborated by French military engineers, the plan called for a citadel, six bastions and detached batteries. The considerable expense was still less than the cost of a French warship's six-month patrol of the Atlantic waters to guard the lucrative French fishery. Nonetheless the massive undertaking was riddled with problems: a harsh climate, a boggy site where the mortar sometimes crumbled, scarce building materials and a few corrupt French officials who lined their pockets at royal expense. Difficult living conditions and lack of discipline among the common soldiers contributed to a mutiny in 1744.

In 1745, prior to completion, 4,000 New Englanders attacked the "impregnable" fortress. Less than two months later the French surrendered. In 1748 the British agreed to return the fort to the island colony of King **Louis XV**. The following year the French reoccupied the stronghold, while the British founded Halifax as a counter-fortress.

Ten years later Louisbourg was under siege again, this time by British regulars. **James Wolfe,** the second in command, managed to land his forces, and the "impregnable" fortress had to be surrendered a second time.

Wolfe went on to capture Quebec City in 1759. To prevent further threat to British interests, Louisbourg was destroyed in 1760.

One of Fortress of Louisbourg's gardens

Sandra Phinney/Michelin

Fortress drum corps in uniform

Sandra Phinney/Michelin

Visit

37km/23mi south of Sydney by Rte. 22, southwest of town of Louisbourg. ◷*Open Jul–Aug daily 9am–5pm. May–Jun & Sept–Oct daily 9:30am–5pm. May & second half of Oct, no costumed interpreters or services;* ☛*tours led by Parks Canada guide.* ⌨*$16.20 Jun–Sept ($5.50 May & Oct).* ✕&🅿 ☎ *902-733-2280. www. pc.gc.ca.*

Models of the fortress and displays on the history of Louisbourg provide orientation in the **visitor centre** *(departure point for bus to the fortress)*. Visitors cross a drawbridge to enter the walled town through the elaborate **Dauphine Gate,** manned by a sentry.

The more than 50 buildings *(most open to the public)* on the 4.8ha/12-acre site are constructed of wood or roughcast masonry, some furnished to their 1740s appearance, others containing themed exhibits. In the summer season, costumed staff portray 18C French society's leisure, propertied and working classes. Popular attractions include a **bakery,** where bread similar to the kind King Louis' troops lined up for in 1744 can be purchased.

Visitors can partake of 18C meals served on earthenware and pewter by costumed staff in three **period restaurants.**

Along the quay stands the high wooden **Frédéric Gate,** the entrance through which important visitors to this once-bustling port were ushered from the harbour. The rich furnishings on the ground floor of the **ordonnateur's residence** include a harpsichord of the period. Archaeological artifacts recovered during reconstruction are on display at various locations.

Once one of the largest military strongholds in North America, the **King's Bastion**★★ has become the symbol of reconstructed Louisbourg. Quarters for the garrison provide insight into the lives of the privileged and impoverished in Old World society. The **governor's apartments** consist of 10 elegant rooms, lavishly furnished. Not as comfortable but well accommodated are the **officers' quarters.**

Drafty and spartan, the **soldiers' barracks** are not at all conducive to a long stay. The **prison,** and a **chapel** that once served as the town's parish church, can also be visited.

PRINCE EDWARD ISLAND

POPULATION 139,103 – MAP P 189

The birthplace of Canadian Confederation, and Canada's smallest province, this crescent-shaped island is only 225km/140mi long and covers 5,683sqkm/2,194sq mi. Its deeply indented coastline is no wider than 64km/40mi. Separated from Newfoundland by the Gulf of St. Lawrence, the island lies just 14km/9mi from New Brunswick and 22km/14mi from Nova Scotia across the Northumberland Strait. Iron oxides give the soil its characteristic brick-red colour; and on fine summer days the rolling landscape presents a stunning kaleidoscope of green fields, blue sea and sky, red soil and puffy white clouds. Named after Prince Edward Augustus, Duke of Kent (1767-1820), the father of Queen Victoria, it is made up of three counties: Prince (west), Queens (central) and Kings (east).

With only two urban centres, Charlottetown and Summerside, the island has retained a relaxed pace and pastoral landscape. Billboards and portable signs have been outlawed, and in the outlying farm communities, businesses tend to be shuttered off-season. The harbingers of urban sprawl have arrived, however, and commercial-residential development is threatening parts of the province, especially the Charlottetown-Cavendish corridor. Agriculture continues to be the number one industry. PEI potatoes are famous in Canada. Tourism plays an increasingly important role, seen in the large number of visitors, particularly Japanese, who come for the red-sand beaches, scenic golf courses, famed lobster suppers, lively cultural events and locally made products. All PEI's efforts have paid off: this small province generates an annual gross domestic product of more than $4 billion.

- **Information:** Tourist Office, 6 Prince St., Charlottetown. ☎902-368-4444 or 888-734-7529 or www.gentleisland.com.
- ▶ **Orient Yourself:** *See the map of the island.* In this guide, the province is described in three regions, corresponding primarily to PEI's three counties, although the boundaries of these counties do not neatly follow the natural topographical division into three parts by Malpeque Bay in the west and the Hillsborough River farther east. The **Central PEI** section of this guide focuses on the capital city of Charlottetown and the attractions of Queens County, including PEI National Park and Cavendish; **Eastern PEI** tours the coast of Kings County, where lighthouses seem to appear at every inlet; and **Western PEI** covers the shoreline sights of Prince County, including Summerside. For tourism and marketing purposes, provincial tourism officials have divided the island into four main regions that are marked on provincial maps and roads. The North Cape Coastal Drive (300km/186mi); Anne's Land on the Central North Shore; the former Blue Heron Coastal Drive (198 km/123mi) taking in Central PEI, and the Points East Coastal Drive (412 km/256mi).
- **Don't Miss:** The beaches of the Prince Edward Island National Park. A lobster supper in Hope River or New Glasgow.
- **Organizing Your Time:** Allow at least a week to leisurely tour the island. Basing yourself in Charlottetown is recommended if you visit in the off season (peak season is July through August), since restaurants and attractions may be closed in areas outside the capital city.
- **Especially for Kids:** Avonlea Village; the miniatures of famous buildings at Woodleigh.
- **Also See:** NEWFOUNDLAND AND LABRADOR

PRACTICAL INFORMATION

GETTING THERE

BY AIR

Air Canada and **Air Canada Jazz** provide direct flights from Toronto, Montreal and Halifax (☎902-429-7111 or 888-247-2262). www.aircanada.ca. **WestJet** (☎800-538-5696; www.westjet.com) and **Sunwing Airlines** (☎800-761-1711; www.sunwing.ca) offer flights from Toronto and Montreal, **Northwest Airlines** (☎800-225-2525; www.nwa.com) from Detroit and **Delta** (☎888-750-3284; www.delta.com) from Boston. **Charlottetown Airport (YYG)** is less than 5km/3mi north of downtown. ☎902-566-7997; www.flypei.com. Taxis and major car rental agencies are located at the airport.

BY CAR

Open 24hrs a day, every day, the drive over the 13km/8mi, two-lane **Confederation Bridge** to Borden-Carleton, Prince Edward Island from Cape Jourimain, NB, takes about 12min. A toll is collected at Borden-Carleton upon exiting the island: ☞$40.75/vehicle; cash, debit card and major credit cards accepted; ☎888-437-6565; www.confederationbridge.com.

BY SHUTTLE

PEI Express Shuttle between Halifax, NS and Charlottetown, PEI. Daily departures year-round from Halifax 6:30am–7:30am; arrival at 11:30am. Departures daily from Charlottetown 11:30am; arrival to address in Halifax/Dartmouth 4pm–5pm. ☎877-877-1771. www.peishuttle.com.
Advanced Shuttle Service operates between Halifax, NS and Charlottetown ☎902-886-3322 or 877-886-3322. Daily departures year-round from Halifax 2:50pm; arrival 6:15pm. Departures daily from Charlottetown at 7:45am; arrival 12:30pm. $65 one-way; $125 return.

BY BOAT

Northumberland Ferries connects the eastern part of the island at Wood Islands with Caribou, NS. Departs PEI May–mid-Nov daily 6:30am–7:30pm. Late-Nov–late Dec hours vary. Departs NS May–mid-Nov daily 8am–9pm. Late Nov–lat Dec hours vary. No service late Dec–Apr. One way 1hr 15min. ☞$14/adult passenger, $59/car round-trip. ✕🚻☎902-566-3838 or 888-249-7245. www.nfl-bay.com. From Souris a ferry crosses to the Magdalen Islands, Quebec (☎888-986-3278. www.ctma.com).

GENERAL INFORMATION

VISITOR INFORMATION

The official tourist office publishes an annual **Visitors Guide** and highway map that can be downloaded from the website. Tourism Prince Edward Island, (PO Box 2000, Charlottetown PE, C1A 7N8; ☎800-463-4734, Canada/US; www.gov.pe.ca/visitorsguide).
Gateway Village – *101 Abegweit Dr., Borden-Carleton, 56km/35 mi west of Charlottetown.* 🚻☎902-437-8570 or 800-463-4734. This is the principal **Visitor Centre** for visitors arriving by the Confederation Bridge. Maps, brochures, schedules of events and other information on the island are available. Staff is on hand to answer questions and help with trip planning. The village includes a shopping centre with restaurants and PEI product retail outlets.

ACCOMMODATIONS

🛏*For a selection of lodgings, see the Address Books throughout this section of the guide.*

PEI Bed & Breakfast and Country Inns Assoc. www.bandbpei.com.
PEI Inns of Distinction. www.innsofpei.com.

RESERVATIONS

Tourism PEI's online reservation system. Searches can be made by type, date, location, features, rating, cost and keyword. www.gentleisland.com

ROAD REGULATIONS

Main roads are paved, particularly along the coasts; some roads have either dirt or gravel surface. Speed limits, unless otherwise posted, are 90km/h (55mph) or 80km/h (50mph) on highways and 50km/h (30mph) in urban districts.
Seat belt use is mandatory. **Canadian**

Automobile Assn. (CAA), Charlottetown ☎902-892-1612.

TIME ZONE
PEI is on Atlantic Standard Time. Daylight Saving Time is observed from the 2nd Sunday in March to the 1st Sunday in November.

TAXES
The national GST of 5% and a provincial sales tax of 10% are levied. There is no provincial sales tax on clothing or footwear purchases.

LIQUOR LAWS
The legal drinking age is 19. Liquor is sold in government stores.

RECREATION
Prince Edward Island National Park has **walking trails.** Seaside trails can be found in other parts of the island, but the one in Tignish at the northern end is especially noteworthy for its views. Beaches in the national park are supervised and the water is generally warm enough for swimming. **Biking** is ideal for PEI's gentle terrain; cyclists can go from one end of the island to the other on the 350km/214mi–long Confederation Trail, a rolled stone dust surface suitable for biking or hiking. **Seal-watching** tours are offered from the eastern town of Montague. In the fall, thousands of migrating ducks and Canada Geese make the island popular with small-game hunters. Deep-sea **fishing** charters (usually for mackerel) are offered from several villages around the island, and some outfitters offer ocean excursions where the catch is tuna or shark. Located within a 45min drive of each other, PEI's 33 **golf** courses (both 9- and 18-hole) are known to avid golfers across Canada, reputed to be among the best 100 courses in the country. They are interspersed throughout the island, but 9 lie along the north shore, along the Gulf of St. Lawrence. Twelve academies or clubs offer instruction. For more information, access www.golfpei.ca.

PRINCIPAL FESTIVALS
May-Nov **Charlottetown Festival:** *Charlottetown*

late Jun **Festival of Lights:** *Charlottetown*

Highland Gathering and Military Tattoo: *Summerside* (at College of Piping and Celtic Performing Arts of Canada)

late Jun to mid-Oct **Sandland (sand sculptures):** *Charlottetown*

early Jul **Bluegrass and Old-Time Music Festival:** *Rollo Bay*

Lobster Carnival: *Summerside*

mid-Jul **PEI Jazz & Blues Festival:** *Charlottetown*

mid-Aug **Old Home Week Provincial Exhibition:** *Charlottetown*, www.oldghomeweekpei.com

Sept **Storytelling Festival:** *province-wide*

Late Sept **International Shellfish Festival:** *Charlottetown*, www.peishellfish.com/sf

Cycling in Bothwell

John Sylvester/Tourism PEI/Tourism Charlottetown and

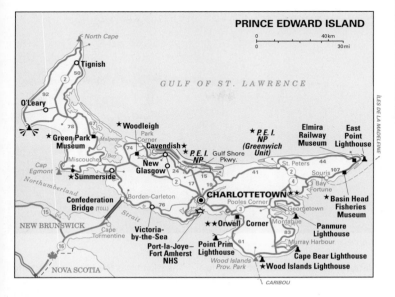

A Bit of Geography

The island's topography, especially in the central and eastern portions, is largely one of low, rolling hills with no mountainous terrain. PEI sits less than 152m/500ft above sea level; the **Bonshaw Hills** in the central interior mark its highest point. The western extremity is relatively flat. Warm-water sandy beaches, sand dunes, saltwater marshes, inlets and bays characterize the shore. The Acadian Forest dominates all of the Maritime provinces. Characteristic species include red spruce, red oak, yellow birch, sugar maple, white pine and eastern hemlock. In low-lying areas black spruce, larch and red maple are common. Pockets of provincial forestland are found in western PEI, and Kings County in the eastern third of the island is abundantly forested. Abundant in season on PEI are deep-purple lupines, wild roses, and orchids like the pink lady's slipper. Fauna on the island is a mix of a few original species with several that have been introduced. The red fox is common, along with snowshoe hares, partridges and pheasants, ducks, raccoons, weasels, red squirrels and coyotes. Some 330 species of birds frequent the province, in particular the great blue heron, piping plover and bald eagles.

The island's climate is varied: often lasting until October, summer weather brings mild temperatures of 20°C/68°F to 30°C/86°F; July is somewhat humid, August less so. Temperatures drop precipitously in the fall, before winter temperatures arrive of 5°C to −5°C in November. Because the Gulf of St. Lawrence and the Northumberland Strait's freeze in winter, PEI experiences heavier snowfall than New Brunswick and Nova Scotia. December through April is typically a period of severe blizzards and storms. Temperatures can climb to 25°C/72°F in May, which sees a steady, light rainfall; but spring temperatures in general are mercurial.

A Bit of History

The Mi'kmaq were the island's first inhabitants. Their legend says that the man-god **Glooscap** created the island of red clay, shaping it as a crescent within the blue waters. *Abegweit* was the name given to the island by these first residents, meaning "cradled on the waves." Today the Mi'kmaq community (or Abegweit First Nation) numbers about 300 people, mostly living on three reserves: Morell, Rocky Point, and Scotchfort.

Confederation Bridge

©Verena Matthew/iStockphoto.com

Jacques Cartier claimed the island for France in 1534, naming it **Île-St.-Jean.** Concerted efforts at colonization did not occur until the early 18C when French settlers founded **Port la Joye** as a dependency of Île Royale (today Cape Breton Island in Nova Scotia). France's plan to strengthen its claims in the New World brought Acadian farmers to Île-St.-Jean in 1720. In 1755 the British demanded an oath of fealty from Acadians on British territory. Several thousand Acadians chose instead to resettle on Île-St.-Jean. In 1758 England captured Île-St.-Jean, removing the Acadians under the Deportation Order. About 30 families went into hiding—the ancestors of the island's present-day Acadians. The Francophone population numbers about 5,600 today.

Renamed St. John's Island under British rule, the island was annexed to Nova Scotia. The land was granted to wealthy Englishmen and military officers, who petitioned the British government to recognize the territory as a separate colony. In 1769 efforts were made, somewhat successfully, to attract Loyalists fleeing the American Revolutionary War, which ended in 1783. In 1799 the colony was renamed Prince Edward Island in honour of the fourth son of King George III of England. By the Victorian era, PEI was becoming a magnet for British aristocratic families seeking fashionable seaside resort life.

The island was the site of the historic **Charlottetown Conference** in 1864, the first of several meetings that led to Canadian Confederation in 1867. PEI ultimately spurned the terms of union and held off joining. In 1873 Prime Minister MacDonald negotiated with island officials, granting concessions and assuming the island's indebtedness from railway construction so that in July 1873, PEI entered Confederation.

Although shipbuilding was the island's principal economic activity during the 19C, PEI's principal industries today are agriculture, tourism and fishing. Agriculture and aquacultural processing form the backbone of manufacturing on the island, renowned for its dairy products, lobsters and shellfish, and more than 50 varieties of **potatoes.** Annually over 700,000 visitors are drawn to the unhurried pace of life here; **farm vacations** are popular. Completed in 1997, the 13km/8mi-long Confederation Bridge over Northumberland Strait links Borden-Carleton, PEI, with Jourimain Island, New Brunswick; it replaced a lengthy and, at times, rough ferry crossing. The heroine of the children's book **Anne of Green Gables** by island-born Lucy Maud Montgomery, celebrated her 100th anniversary in 2008. Entertainment and venues built around Anne have become a cottage tourism industry.

CENTRAL PEI

Central PEI comprises much of Queens County, although the county intrudes into Eastern PEI, claiming all of Hillsborough Bay, as well as Wood Islands in the south. The provincial capital of Charlottetown dominates Central PEI, still gracious but more and more the epicentre of inevitable urban sprawl. PEI National Park and Cavendish, with its multitude of Anne of Green Gables attractions, monopolize the northern shore. Most people arrive on the southern shore, either at the Charlottetown airport or via Confederation Bridge from New Brunswick. If arriving by way of the bridge, one of the first sights visitors see—besides noticing the reddish-orange soil—is Gateway Village in Borden-Carleton (which is in Prince County). This shopping and business complex is anchored by a visitor centre, where information about the island is available; an interpretive centre has exhibits on the bridge's construction, PEI activities and history. Before leaving, take a moment to view (or photograph) Confederation Bridge from St. Peter's Roman Catholic Church on Seven Mile Bay Road in North Carleton: it is a memorable **image** *(from the bridge, take Dickie Rd. east; turn north onto Rte. 10 and continue to North Carleton Rd.; ☎902-887-2020).* The Trans-Canada Highway (Highway 1) leads 56km/35mi east to Charlottetown. Many visitors make their base in Charlottetown, the city with the most services, especially for travellers.

Charlottetown★★

POPULATION 32,245 – MAP P 197

The provincial capital is heralded as the site of the pivotal 1864 Charlottetown Conference, which ultimately led to the birth of Canada as a nation. Located near the confluence of the Hillsborough, West and North rivers, Charlottetown is ideally situated for a capital city. The rivers form a protected harbour, which widens into U-shaped Hillsborough Bay. The bay opens into Northumberland Strait, providing the outlet to the world so vital for commerce. Today the capital city is, indeed, a thriving commercial centre, its port serving as a funnel for the region's agricultural bounty and as a port-of-call: 69,000 cruise-ship passengers came ashore in 2008. The city lies an hour's drive from the island's two major access points: Confederation Bridge from New Brunswick (56km/35mi west), and Wood Islands terminal for ferries from Nova Scotia (61km/40mi southwest). It is the hub of retail services for the island. Shopping varies from boutiques to malls.

Although the city has accommodated big-box chains and other modern additions to the traditional streetscape, it has imposed height restrictions to preserve its historic heart. Many restored buildings, churches and houses designed in 19C architectural styles can be seen on a walk around the core, or a ride on one of the city trolleys, reproductions of those of the 1900s. In summer the weather is usually agreeable: daytime temperatures range from 20°C/68°F to 30°C/86°F. A lively arts and dining scene hums pretty much year-round.

🛈 **Information:** Visitor Information Centre, 6 Prince St. ☎902-368-4444 or 800-463-4734. www.walkandseacharlottetown.ca.

▸ **Orient Yourself:** *See map of downtown.* Easily walkable, downtown is bounded by Water St. to the south, Haviland St. (that turns into Rochford St.) to the west, Fitzroy St. to the north, and Hillsborough St. to the east. The main arteries within this area are the north-south running University Ave. and Great George St. (Province House sits at the end of University Ave. and the beginning of Great George St. Province House faces Victoria Row, a pedestrian-only street.) Other north-south main streets are Prince St. (east of Great George) and Queen St. (west of Great George). Primary east-west streets are Grafton, Richmond, Sydney and Dorchester Sts. Major shopping centres are Confederation Court Mall and Charlottetown Mall (University Ave.)

P **Parking:** Parking is metered, and usually hard to find downtown; spaces are often the "nose-in" variety. Meters cost $0.50/an hour, and are rigorously enforced.

🕭 **Don't Miss:** Province House, and harness racing at Driving Park.

🕐 **Organizing Your Time:** Allow at least 2 days to enjoy Charlottetown.

Kids **Especially for Kids:** The playground at Victoria Park.

A Bit of History

The Island of St. John (Prince Edward Island) came under British rule in 1763, and the following year the surveyor-general, Capt. **Samuel Holland**, was asked to pick a location for a government seat. Named after Queen Charlotte, the wife of George III, the city was founded in 1768, laid out in British grid fashion in 500 lots with four "green squares." In 1835 a residence was built for the governor and a new legislative building, Province House, which is still in use, soon followed. The city prospered as a centre of shipbuilding, fisheries and lumbering as well as an important port. Another driver of industrial development was the arrival of the PEI Railway, which inaugurated a line between the capital and Summerside in 1874. Charlottetown was incorporated in 1855, and reincorporated in 1995 when it was amalgamated with several surrounding villages. Today this small city of close to 35,000 residents covers 42sqkm/16sq mi yet maintains largely the same layout as when it was founded; it has managed to preserve four of the historic squares (Connaught, Kings, Hillsborough and Rochford). The new millennium has brought substantial retail and commercial development. In 2007 the city doubled its waterfront capacity, at a cost of $18 million, to accommodate larger cruise ships, adding a welcome centre just for arriving cruise passengers. The port also receives fertilizer, petroleum products and other important commodities and ships PEI potatoes and other crops to export markets. The largest employers in the city are the government services sector, retail trade, the hospitality industry, and health and social services. Charlottetown holds the island's only university, the University of PEI, a public liberal-arts institution created in1969, as well as Holland College, a community college that includes a culinary school. The more than 4,000 students of these

James Ingram/Tourism Charlottetown

Victoria Row

Practical Information

GETTING THERE AND GETTING AROUND

BY AIR

Charlottetown Airport (YYG) is the arrival and departure airport for several carriers:

Air Canada and **Air Canada Jazz**. www.aircanada.ca, www.flyjazz.ca Local Office ☎902-894-7174. **WestJet.** www.westjet.com. Reservations ☎888-937-8538. Sunwing (seasonal charter) www.sunwing.ca Information ☎877-786-9464. **Prince Edward Air** (business charter; max. 15 ppl. per aircraft) www.peair.com Reservations - ☎902-566-4488 ☎800-565-5359.

BY BOAT

Operated by NFL Ferries, passenger and car ferry service connects **Caribou, NS** with **Woods Island, PEI** (75 mins). Daily departures May–Dec; departure times vary depending on the month. Check schedules. Reservations strongly recommended. $15/person. $61/vehicle. Fuel surcharge $7/vehicle. ☎877-635-7245 (Canada/US) or local ☎902-566-3838. www.peiferry.com

There is also daily car ferry service **(CTMA Traversier/Ferry)** between PEI and Îles de la Madeleine (Magdalen Islands, Quebec), which takes 5 hours. Follow Rte. 2 east from Charlottetown to Souris (82 km/51mi). ☎888-986-3278. www.ctma.ca.

BY CAR

Major car rental companies can be found at the Charlottetown Airport and locations in the city. Avis Rent-A-Car (☎800-879-2847, local ☎902-892-3706; www.avis.ca); Budget Rent-a-Car (☎800-268-8900, local ☎902-566-5525; www.budget.com); National Car Rental (☎800-227-7368, local ☎902-628-6990; www.nationalcar.com); Hertz (☎800-263-0600, local ☎902-566-5566; www.hertz.com).

BY TAXI

Co-Op Taxi Line Ltd. (305 Allen St., Charlottetown) offers customized tours at $40/hr or $45/hr per van. ☎902-892-1111 or ☎902-894-1111.

City Taxi (Charlottetown, ☎902-892-6567) includes airport service.

Yellow Cab PEI (Charlottetown, ☎902-566-6666)
grabbaCab (Charlottetown, ☎902-892-6000)
Old Town Taxi (Summerside, ☎902-436-4947)
Dixon's Taxi (Montague, ☎902-838-2491)

PUBLIC TRANSPORTATION

Charlottetown's public-transit **trolleys** *($2)* are replicas of those from the 1900s. ☎902-566-9962.

BY SHUTTLE

PEI Express Shuttle between Halifax, NS and Charlottetown, PEI. Daily departures year-round from Halifax at 6:30am–7:30am; arrival at 11:30am. Departures daily from Charlottetown at 11:30am; arrival to address in Halifax/Dartmouth between 4pm–5pm. ☎877-877-1771. www.peishuttle.com.

Advanced Shuttle Service operates between Halifax, NS and Charlottetown, PEI. ☎902-886-3322 or 877-886-3322.

Daily departures year-round from Halifax at 2:50pm; arrival at 6:15pm. Departures daily from Charlottetown at 7:45am; arrival at 12:30pm. $65 one-way; $125 return.

GENERAL INFORMATION

VISITOR INFORMATION

Tourism Charlottetown (6 Prince St. ☎800-955-1864) www.walkand seacharlottetown.com

Open Jun daily 9am–7pm. Jul–mid-Aug daily 8:30am–9pm. Late-Aug–Labour Day daily 8:30am–6pm. Rest of Sept–early Oct daily 8:30am–5pm. Rest of Oct–Dec 23 daily 9am–3pm. Rest of the year call for hours.

ACCOMMODATIONS

For a listing of suggested hotels, ⓒ see the Address Book.

Hotels, motels, inns and bed & breakfasts can be booked through Tourism PEI's online **reservation system.** Searches can be made by type, date, location, features, rating, cost and keyword. www.gentleisland.com

LOCAL MEDIA

Daily: *The Guardian* (Charlottetown, www.theguardian.pe.ca), *The Journal*

Pioneer (Summerside, www.journalpio-neer.com). **Monthly:** *The Buzz* is a free local monthly arts and entertainment newspaper.

ENTERTAINMENT

LIVE MUSIC

Victoria Row on Richmond Street in the Historic District or one of the waterfront bar patios are good places to enjoy live (outdoor) entertainment. Sydney and Kent Streets are the scene of impromptu or scheduled live music; some restaurants turn into nightclubs after dark.

42nd Street Lounge – *125 Sydney St.* ☎*902-566-4620. http://murphygroupof-restaurants.com/off_broadway.php.* ⊘*Closed Sun.* This cozy lounge above Off Broadway Restaurant is a place to relax. Soft lighting, comfortable wing chairs and lived-in sofas, plank floors and antique tables make up an eclectic mix that is inviting. In addition to wines and spirits, the lounge offers appetizers and desserts. It's a great place for after-dinner drinks or post-theatre snacking.

The Olde Dublin Pub – *131 Sydney St.,*☎*902-892-6992. www.oldedublin-pub.com.* It's been around for more than 30 years. This Irish-style pub still offers live Celtic music several nights a week and inexpensive pub grub specials.

Peake's Quay Restaurant & Bar – *11C Great George St.* ⊘*Closed Nov–Apr.* ☎*902-368-1330. www.peakesquay.com.* A younger crowd frequents this bar, thanks to its DJ and live-band music four times a week. This restaurant has the largest al fresco dining in the city, with more than 200 seats overlooking the Quartermaster Marina.

PERFORMING ARTS
Charlottetown
Confederation Centre of the Arts – 145 Richmond St., Charlottetown. ☎902-628-1864 or ☎800-565-0278. www.confederationcentre.com

Feast Dinner Theatre – 615 Water St. East, Summerside and Rodd Hotel Charlottetown, Kent & Pownal Sts. ☎902-436-7674 or ☎888-748-1010. www.feastdinnertheatres.ca

Outlying Areas
As driving distances on the island are not great, one can drive to many outly-ing communities from Charlottetown and return to your lodging the same night. The following offer live musical or theatrical performances:

Centre for Performing ARTS – 20 School St., Montague. ☎902-838-2787.

Eddie May Murder Mystery Dinner Theatre – 26 Upper Tea Hill Crescent, Stratford. ☎902-569-1999 or ☎888-747-4050). www.eddiemay.com

Kings Playhouse, Georgetown

Town of Georgetown

Harbourfront Jubilee Theatre – 124 Harbour Dr., Summerside. ☎902-888-2500 or 800-708-6505. www.jubileetheatre.com

Kings Playhouse – 65 Grafton St., Georgetown. ☎888-346-5666. www.kingsplayhouse.com. This handsome barnlike structure is a popular regional venue for plays and theatrical productions. The original building was designed by William Critchlow Harris, architect of St. Paul's Church in Charlottetown, and built in 1897 as a town hall/community centre; it survived a train crash that left a gaping hole, but in 1983 was destroyed by fire.

La Cuisine À Mémé. – Acadian dinner theatre in French and English. Le Village de l'Acadie, Mont-Carmel. ☎902-854-2227 or ☎800-567-3228.

V'nez Chou Nous Acadian Dinner Theatre Productions – Acadian dinner theatre. Reservations only. Rte. 2, Tignish. ☎902-882-0475.

Victoria Playhouse – Main & Howard Sts., Community Hall, Victoria-by-the-Sea. ☎902-658-2025 or ☎800-925-2025. www.victoriaplayhouse.com

TOURS

Walking Tours – Historic Great George Street Tour explores Charlottetown's famous thoroughfare and surroundings; departs 11am daily. Ghostly Realm Tour takes in the darker side of historic downtown: departs 7:30pm. Both tours 1hr in duration: $10 each; leave from Founders' Hall, 6 Prince St. ☎902-566-5466 or ☎877-286-6536. www.princeedwardtours.com.

Prince Edward Tours – Day and custom tours. ☎902-566-5466 or ☎877-286-6532. www.princeedwardtours.com.

PinnacleTours – Personal guides for individuals and groups. ☎902-367-7789. www.pinnacletourseast.com.

SHOPPING

MALLS

Charlottetown Mall (670 University Ave., Charlottetown. ☎902-368-8854). The Shops of Confederation Court Mall (119 Kent St, Charlottetown. ☎902-894-9505. www.confedcourtmall.com). Cavendish Boardwalk (Cavendish, Rusticoville. ☎902-963-3111). For information on individual shops, access www.walkandseacharlottetown.com/what-to-see-and-do/shopping.

SPORTS (SPECTATOR)

Charlottetown Yacht Club hosts Charlottetown Race Week in mid-July annually. ☎902-892-9065.

Charlottetown Driving Park hosts the well-known Gold Cup and Saucer Race for harness racing, annually in mid-August since 1959. ☎902-892-6844.

The **University of PEI Panthers** are college varsity teams in basketball, volleyball, hockey, soccer, swimming, field hockey, and rugby. Call ☎902-566-0627 for schedules.

---

campuses lend a lively element to the capital's population mix.

Sights

Waterfront

The waterfront stretches along Charlottetown Harbour from Victoria Park, at the western end, to Founders' Hall and the adjacent cruise-ship terminal. Situated along the water, 16ha/40-acre **Victoria Park** is a spacious swath of grass and woods with picnic areas, tennis courts, a swimming pool, baseball fields and a playground. From the park expansive **views**★ extend across the harbour to the site of Fort Amherst. A boardwalk lines the western and southern edge of the park; it's a great vantage point for sunsets.

The park is also home to the Neoclassical Government House, the lieutenant-governor's home. The harbour hosts busy Quartermaster Marina and an active yacht club, founded in 1938, which sponsors **Race Week** in June of each year. The southern end of Great George Street is a hive of retail shops, restaurants and services, especially Peake's Wharf, where boat tours may be booked.

Government House

Generally not open to the public, except Jul–Aug by ☞guided tour only, Mon–Fri 10am–4pm.

A large, Georgian-style wooden structure with a colonaded entry way, the official residence of the lieutenant-governor, was designed by Isaac Smith and built in 1834. It is known as Fanningbank, after Governor Edmund Fanning who designated the land for the house in 1789. Today it functions ceremonially as a centre of hospitality and official welcome for visiting dignitaries. On the grounds are an artillery shed and half a dozen cannon pointed toward the harbour.

Southwest of Government House stands the former residence of a wealthy shipping entrepreneur, Beaconsfield Historic House, an 1877 confection with 25 rooms by architect William Critchlow Harris. Open for tours, it houses period furnishings and a contemporary bookstore and serves as headquarters for the Prince Edward Island Museum and Heritage Foundation.

City Hall

Corner Kent and Queen Sts. ⏲Open Mon–Fri 8:30am–4:30pm (til 4pm in summer). ☎902-566-5548. www.city. charlottetown.pe.ca.

This Romanesque Revival-style edifice was built of brick in 1888. It is the island's oldest civic hall. The stalwart, two-storey structure, with arched bays and a bell tower, holds the offices of the city mayor, city council and city departments.

Confederation Centre of the Arts★

145 Richmond St. ⏲Open Jun–Sept Mon –Sat 9am–9pm. Rest of the year Mon–Sat noon–5pm. ✕&☎902-628-1864 or 800-565-0278. www.confederationcentre.com.

Occupying an entire city block, this national memorial to the Fathers of Confederation (1964) commemorates the centennial of the 1864 Charlottetown Conference. Centrally located, it was built on the site of Charlottetown's former marketplace. A gift from the people of Canada, the centre houses theatres, the provincial archives, display areas and a restaurant.

The **art gallery**★★ features selections from its large collection of 15,000 works by Canadian artists, most notably **Robert Harris** (1848-1919). In the late 19C and early 20C, he was Canada's renowned portrait painter, completing some 300 works during his lifetime. His most famous work, commissioned in 1883, was *Meeting of the Delegates of British North America,* more commonly known as *The Fathers of Confederation.* Sadly, the original painting, which hu ng in Ottawa's Parliament Buildings, was destroyed by a fire there in 1916.

The main theatre hosts the annual **Charlottetown Festival** musical production *Anne of Green Gables.* Free outdoor musical and dance performances

Peake's Quay Marina

Art Gallery, Confederation Centre of the Arts

are often staged in summer at noon in the courtyard with concrete, bleacher-style seating.

St. Dunstan's Basilica

45 Great George St. ⏰Open year-round Mon–Fri 8:30am–4pm. ♿☎902-894-3486. www.stdunstans.pe.ca.

The twin 61m/200ft spires of this Gothic church, erected in 1917, punctuate Charlottetown's skyline. Interior features include fan vaulting, streaked marble and a stunning **rose window** from Munich, Germany. The contemporary stained-glass windows were designed by island native Henry Purdy.

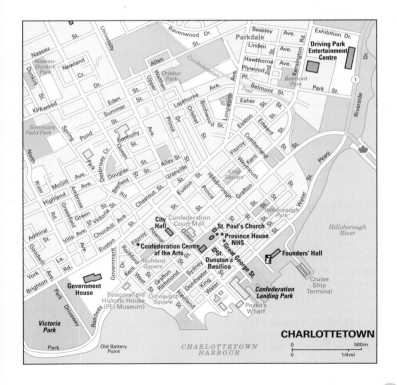

Province House National Historic Site★★

2 Palmer's Lane, adjacent to Confed-eration Centre of the Arts, at the top of Great George St. Open Jul–Aug daily 8:30am–6pm. Jun & Sept–mid-Oct daily 8:30am–5pm. Rest of the year daily 9am–5pm. *902-566-7626. www.pc.gc.ca.*

A native of Yorkshire, England, Isaac Smith designed this three-storey sand-stone building, which was completed in 1847 in the Georgian style with Neoclas-sical details. Before an 1837 vote to set aside £5,000 British pounds for the con-struction of a building, members of PEI's legislative body met in private homes and even taverns. All construction and interior finishing work was executed by island craftsmen using native materials, save for stone, which was imported from Nova Scotia. The colonial building incor-porates the Classic features of a central portico, double chimneys and symmetri-cal wings; the second-story facade has columns and a massive tympanum. From 1979 to 1983 the building underwent a thorough $3.5million restoration. Des-ignated a National Historic Site in 1983, Province House is administered jointly by Parks Canada and the province.

The **Confederation Chamber,** site of the famous Charlottetown Conference of September 1–8, 1864, is restored to its 19C appearance, with many of the original furnishings. Take time to watch the **audio-visual presentation** *(17min)* about the Charlottetown Conference and to look for evidence of a tax record in the stones of the main floor. The pro-vincial legislature still meets in the leg-islative chamber, where the ruling party sits to the left of the Speaker.

St. Paul's Anglican Church

101 Prince St. Guided tours Jul & Aug; call for details. *902-892-1691. www. stpaulschurch.ca.*

Completed in 1896 this ponderous red-sandstone edifice with stringcourses of grey freestone is the second iteration of the original church, built in 1769. One of the Maritime provinces' prolific archi-tects, **William Critchlow Harris** (1854-1913), designed the present church in traditional cruciform shape. The inside showcases a rib-vaulted ceiling, his

trademark, which gives the illusion of more space than the interior actually has. Stained-glass windows feature prominently in the design, as does the handsome wooden door. Known for his church architecture, Harris, the brother of noted portrait painter Robert Harris, was a dedicated violinist and recognized the importance of acoustics. St. Paul's superb acoustics so impressed the clergy of the day that more than 20 churches in PEI and Nova Scotia were subsequently built according to Harris' plans.

Great George Street★

From Sydney St. to Water St.

This historic street leads down to the waterfront from Province House. Bor-dered by Georgian row houses and shaded by trees, it makes a pleasant stroll to Confederation Landing Park. You'll cross over pedestrian-only Vic-toria Row, site of a lively night scene; and pass St. Dunstan's as well as The Great George inn (*see Address Book*), an elegant 55-room lodging that occu-pies 13 heritage buildings, including a former stables.

Confederation Landing Park

Water Street

Stretching out over one of the quays, this waterfront park, complete with lawn, trees, benches and seasonal plantings, makes a pleasant spot to sit and enjoy the boats in the marina and the views across the harbour. The park memorial-izes the site of the historic landing of the Fathers of Confederation on the HMS *Queen Victoria.* The 23 delegates met in Charlottetown for one week in 1864 to thrash out the creation of the Canadian nation. You can find out the details at nearby Founders' Hall.

Founders' Hall

6 Prince St. Open mid-May–early Oct daily generally 9am–4pm. Mid-Oct–Nov Tue–Sat 9am–3pm. Rest of the year, call for hrs. Closed Jan & Dec. *$7. *902-368-1864. www.foundershall.ca.*

Managed by Tourism Charlottetown, this interpretive pavilion and retail com-plex opened in 2001. It is housed within a restored 1906 waterfront building that functioned as a railway maintenance

Address Book

For dollar sign categories, see the Legend on the cover flap.

WHERE TO STAY

$ Heart's Content Bed and Breakfast – *236 Sydney St. at Weymouth. ☎902-566-1799. www.stayincharlottetown. com. 4 rooms.* A downtown location within walking distance of waterfront makes this B&B a good value for the money. Brimming with bric-a-brac and antiques, the 1860 heritage house sits adjacent to Hillsborough Square park. The tidy bedrooms share two bathrooms. Street parking, storage for bicycles and a continental breakfast included in the rate are sure to please any heart seeking easy-on-the-wallet accommodations and proximity to Charlottetown's sights.

$$ Dundee Arms Inn – *200 Pownal St. ☎902-892-2496 or 877-638-6333. www. dundeearms.com. 22 rooms.* Built in 1903, this imposing Queen-Anne mansion has a tower, and a gazebo out front. The home was a private residence until 1956. Fully restored, it holds an inn with a reputation as one of Charlottetown's finest accommodations. Rooms are furnished with poster, iron or sleigh beds topped with flower-patterned bedspreads; all have private bathrooms. Modern amenities, such as wireless Internet, are found throughout the house and an annex (rooms are less expensive in the latter, located adjacent to the inn). There's an on-site pub, popular with local residents. Open to the public, the **Griffon Room ($$)** serves Canadian dishes, with an emphasis on island seafood. Inn guests receive a 10 percent discount at both restaurant and pub. A continental breakfast is complimentary off-season *(Oct– May)*. Dundee Arms sits on a residential street two blocks from the Confederation Centre of the Arts.

$$$ The Elmwood Heritage Inn – *121 North River Rd. ☎902-368-3310 or 877-933-3310. www.elmwoodinn. pe.ca. 7 rooms.* Situated near Victoria Park, this lovely inn is owned and operated by the MacDonald family who have been in the accommodation business on PEI for 26 years. The three-storey, 1889 Victorian house has 28 rooms and 8 working fireplaces and is located away from the downtown core in a parklike setting. Guest rooms are sumptuously appointed, and baths have either clawfoot soaking tubs or double-size whirlpools. Third-floor rooms are less expensive ($$), as are rates in the off-season *(Oct–May)*. One first-floor room is wheelchair accessible. A full breakfast featuring lemon-ricotta pancakes or other hot dish is included.

$$$ The Great George – *58 Great George St. ☎902-892-0606 or 800-361-1118. www.innsongreatgeorge.com. 55 rooms.* Located near Province House in the heart of downtown, this long-favoured inn is the address of choice for those in the know. The George comprises 13 heritage buildings that include a carriage house and former stables, all fully refurbished. Guests can choose from loft bedrooms and efficiency units, two-storey suites, and two-bedroom flats equipped with laundry facilities and kitchen. All of the elegantly appointed guest rooms are furnished with antiques and European duvets; some have canopy beds, Jacuzzis and fireplaces. An exercise room and made-from-scratch breakfast served in the cozy Pavilion lobby round out the amenities.

$$$$ Fairholm Inn – *230 Prince St. at corner of Fitzroy. ☎902-892-5022 or 888-573-5022. www.fairholm.pe.ca. 7 rooms.* This stately two-storey mansion (1839), with its double-bay façade, houses one of Charlottetown's finest inns. Richly appointed with antiques, spacious high-ceilinged rooms are equipped with marble fireplaces and terrycloth robes while adjoining bathrooms feature clawfoot tubs and Jacuzzis. Catch up on your reading in the ornate sitting room with plush oversize sofas, or relax in the cheerful sun room and enjoy garden views. Complimentary breakfast is served in the formal dining room. The downtown core is only a short walk away.

WHERE TO EAT

$$ Claddagh Oyster House – *131 Sydney St. ☎902-892-9661. www.claddagh*

oysterhouse.com. **Seafood.** Islanders love their oysters, and it's apparent that visitors do too. This restaurant/bar completed renovations in 2006, and patrons approve of the contemporary update to its historic, downtown building. Bold red walls and banquettes make the black lacquered chairs pop. While oysters are the specialty, main courses of lobster, island lamb and "omega 3" pork also satisfy hungry diners with generous portions.

$$ Lobster on the Wharf – *Prince St. Wharf.* ☎*902-894-9311 or 877-919-9311. www.lobsteronthewharf.com.* **Seafood.** ♿ For a wide array of fresh seafood, head to this casual waterside eatery where families can dine indoors or out at tables covered with checkered cloths. Lobster, snow crab, clams, scallops, shrimp, oysters, haddock and salmon are all on the menu, along with island lobster roll and fish-and-chips. Most plates include potato or rice and vegetables. And there's a children's menu.

$$ Lot 30 – *151 Kent St.* ☎*902-629-3030. www.lot30restaurant.ca.* **Contemporary.** Opened in 2008, this new eatery is owned and operated by noted PEI chef Gordon Bailey. Fresh market produce and seafood rule here (there isn't a freezer in the place), so menus change nightly. On a typical evening, seven appetizers, seven entrées and three desserts are offered; reservations are definitely recommended. "Lot 30" refers to the 1764 survey of the city when it was sectioned off into 500 lots: Chef Bailey's newest venture is #30 on today's Kent Street.

$$ Off Broadway Restaurant – *125 Sydney St.* ☎*902-566-4620. www.offbroadwayrestaurant.ca.* **Contemporary.** Low ceilings, exposed brick walls, intimate booths and dim lighting set the stage for a relaxing dining experience. Try the seafood bouillabaisse or the seafood coconut curry, in which mussels, lobster and scallops play starring roles. Or a seafood choice may be added to the grilled filet mignon. The house sommelier is on hand to offer wine pairings for your meal. Desserts here mean good things like strawberry-rhubarb tartlets.

$$ The Pilot House – *70 Grafton St.* ♿☎*902-894-4800. www.thepilothouse. ca.* **Canadian.** *Closed Sun.* Serious foodies have called the dining here "excellent" and the service "impeccable." Opened in 2002, the restaurant is housed in a former hardware building, built in 1896, that has been totally refurbished with ochre walls contrasted with black-and-red patterned banquettes. One of the popular main course selections in the dining room is the breast of chicken stuffed with lobster and carmelized onion, but steaks and prime rib are on the menu as well. Seating 50 and offering lower prices, the pub serves such tasty dishes as a seafood torte or a Thai peanut pizza.

$$ Sirenella Ristorante – *83 Water St.* ♿☎*902-628-2271. www.sirenella. ca. Dinner only Sat. Closed Sun.* **Italian.** Owned since 1992 by Italo Marzari, a former maitre d' at the Fairmont Royal York in Toronto, and later an instructor at PEI's culinary institute, this Italian restaurant has dishes that sing the praises of northern Italy. When one is unsure whether to order the veal, seafood or homemade pasta, allow Marzari to send over a platter of some delicacy, most likely an assortment of carpaccio, prosciutto, antipasti and other delights that go well with a glass of red wine. A secondi of the *capesante delizia* (scallops with garlic, pesto and tomato sauce) might just turn into your new favourite food. Outdoor patio dining is available.

Off Broadway Restaurant

Bruce Bishop/Michelin

Tourism Charlottetown & The Prince Edward Island Convention Partnership

Harness Racing, Charlottetown Driving Park

shop. Founders' Hall interprets and pays homage to the founding of Canada between 1864 and 1867 by the Fathers of Confederation. Interactive displays depict in sequence the major events of Canadian history, including the Confederation Conference up to the creation of the country's latest territory, Nunavut, in 1999. Walking tours of the historic areas of Charlottetown leave from here, led by costumed (and bilingual) actors. An on-site gift shop sells souvenir and island-made products.

Charlottetown Driving Park

21 Exhibition Dr. ○*Open Mon–Thu 11am–midnight, Fri–Sat 11am–2am.* ○*Closed Good Friday & Dec 25.* ✕&🅿️☎*902-620-4222 or 877-620-4222. www.cdpec.ca.*

This sporting/entertainment facility (2005) has its roots in harness racing here as far back as 1889 when a track in the east end first opened. The island is known for this spectator sport. Racing on community tracks and even on ice has been practiced for decades. Islanders love horses and PEI boasts one of the largest horse populations in Canada. Visitors from Atlantic Canada and beyond have made an annual summer pilgrimage to watch the live races. The centre also has simulcast racing, slot machines, and a gaming area (⊘*restricted to those 19 years of age and older*).

The **Top of the Park** dining room overlooks the racetrack and has flat screen TVs at many of the tables.

Additional Sights

Charlottetown Farmers' Market

100 Belvedere Ave. ○*Open Jul–Aug Wed & Sat 9am–2pm. Rest of the year Sat 9am–2pm.* ☎*902-626-3373.*

This market has fresh island fruits and vegetables in season, deli items, bakery goods, meats, sausage and seafood as well as prepared international foods (Italian, African, Indian, Chinese, French and other dishes). Kim Dormaar & Sons' PEI-smoked salmon, organic produce from the Doctor's Inn, and other island-produced delights are on hand. Arts and crafts are for sale.

Ardgowan National Historic Site

Mount Edward Rd. & Palmer's Lane. Grounds open dawn–dusk. ⊶ *House not open to the public.* ☎*902-566-7626. www.pc.gc.ca/pei*

These spacious grounds hold Victorian gardens, shade trees and the former home of a Father of Confederation, William Henry Pope. An example of a 19C *cottage ornée*, or picturesque cottage, Ardgowan has been restored to the period and serves as Parks Canada's PEI administrative offices.

The grounds are open for strolling and picnicking. Panels interpret the history of the site. Orchards, ornamental hedges, perennials and a croquet lawn are maintained by Parks Canada staff. The gardens are at their best from June to September.

Charlottetown Circuit★★

MAP P 189

If there could be such a thing on Prince Edward Island, then the Central North Shore of Queens County contains a less raucous, more polite version of New York's Coney Island. Old timers may decry the area as far too commercial, but if commercial can be tastefully done, then the Islanders on the north shore have succeeded, although the kitsch is gradually sneaking in. There are good restaurants, campgrounds, four golf courses, cottages for rent, an amusement park and a virtual mini-industry built around that little red-headed orphan, Anne Shirley. Although a fictitious children's book heroine, Anne had all her adventures in the Cavendish area, thanks to native author Lucy Maud Montgomery, who lived here and wrote here. Her novel *Anne of Green Gables* is a Canadian classic. The other big attraction is Prince Edward Island National Park.

- ▯ **Information:** Cavendish Visitors' Information Centre, Rte. 6 at Rte.13, before the entrance to the national park. ☎902-963-7830. www.gentleisland.com.
- ▸ **Orient Yourself:** This drive circles most of Queens County.
- ▨ **Don't Miss:** The miniatures of famous buildings at Woodleigh; charming Victoria-by-the-Sea.
- ◕ **Organizing Your Time:** The tour takes a full day to drive and take in the attractions along the way.
- Kids **Especially for Kids:** Avonlea Village; Shining Waters Family Fun Park.

Driving Tour

190km/118mi circuit from Charlottetown.

Charlottetown★★
♿*See CHARLOTTETOWN.*

Prince Edward Island National Park★

In Cavendish, 24km/15mi northwest of Charlottetown. ◕*Open year-round.* ⌾*$6 entry fee. Cavendish visitor centre open mid-Jun–mid-Aug 8am–9pm, late–Aug–mid-Oct 9am–various closing times.* ♿ ▯ ☎*902-672-6350. www.pc.gc. ca.* ▨*To preserve the dunes, please use boardwalks and designated footpaths.*

Fringing the Gulf of St. Lawrence, one of Canada's smallest but most popular national parks stretches about 40km/25mi from Cavendish to Dalvay along the north shore of the island. Interspersed with boardwalks and paths to the water's edge, the **Gulf Shore Parkway** offers displays on shoreline ecology and views of eastern Canada's **beaches,** sand dunes, sandstone cliffs, barrier islands, salt marshes and freshwater ponds. Home to the red fox, the fragile dunes are naturally netted with hardy marram grass, which helps to hold the dunes in place.

Sandy beaches offer some of the island's warmest waters; seven are supervised by lifeguards *(late-Jun–late-Aug)*, including less crowded Brackley and Cavendish beaches; some have changing rooms and food concessions. Several trails, the majority easy and short *(under 3km/2mi)*, take in coastal and forested landscapes. The 364ha/900-acre park attracts some 300 bird species.

Near the park's east entrance, a glance south reveals **Dalvay-by-the-Sea**, a Queen Anne-style structure (1896), formerly the summer home of Standard Oil magnate Alexander MacDonald and now and a hotel (♿*see Address Book).*

The **Greenwich** unit, designated as part of the park in 1999, is located about 20km/12mi farther east.

Cavendish★

This rural village of fewer than 400 people sits within a patchwork of buff-and-green coloured fields at the western end of Prince Edward Island National Park. Lying at the intersection of Routes 6 and 13, it serves as the main visitor centre for

Green Gables House

Parks Canada PEI/John Sylvester

the park, but it is primarily associated with the *Anne of Green Gables* saga and the many attractions it has spawned. Home of Anne's originator, author Lucy Maud Montgomery, the small farming community has evolved into a bustling tourist destination in summer, when thousands of Anne fans descend upon the area. Cavendish witnessed an explosion of development in the second half of the 20C and now anchors a sea of motels, restaurants, shopping centres, amusement parks and campgrounds.

Green Gables House★

Rte. 6, in Cavendish west of Rte. 13. ◔*Open late-Jun–mid-Aug daily 9am–6pm. May–mid- Jun & late Aug–Oct 9am–5pm. Nov–Dec & Apr Sun–Thu 10am–4pm, Jan 7–Mar Thu–Sun noon–4pm.* ◔*Closed Dec 24–26 & 31, Jan 1–6.* ⊜*$7.05.* ✕&P☎*902-963-7874. www. pc.gc.ca.*

Kids This green and white farmhouse belonged to relatives of **Lucy Maud Montgomery,** author of *Anne of Green Gables* (1908). During her childhood in Cavendish, Montgomery visited here frequently. She used the house as a setting for her novel, which tells the story of an irrepressible orphan girl, Anne Shirley, adopted by a strict but kindly brother and sister living at Green Gables farm. Once described by Mark Twain as the

"sweetest creation of child life ever written," this story has become popular in 20 languages and draws summer visitors from as far as Japan.

Today the refurbished house (damaged by fire in 1997) re-creates scenes from the book, including Anne's gabled bedroom. In the downstairs hall, Montgomery's typewriter and several family photographs are displayed.

Avonlea★

8779 Rte. 6, in Cavendish. ◔*Open Jun daily 10am–5pm. Jul–Aug daily 10am–6pm. Sept daily 10am–4pm.* ⊜*$19.* ✕& P☎*902-963-3050. www.avonlea.ca.*

Kids Geared toward children, this wholly interactive re-created village takes everyone back to 1908 when Anne of Green Gables was a precocious young teenager. A dozen structures, including a church, school, general store and train station replicate the "Avonlea" community. Activities for kids like potato-sack races, group dances, wagon rides and pony rides abound. Actors and musicians are in period dress, and bring to life some of Anne's adventures and mishaps in the book. Visitors can take advantage of a picnic area, as well as a Victorian tea service *(Tue–Thu afternoons by reservation)*. In 2008 the new 200-seat **Montgomery Theatre** was added to the village, within the Long River Church;

its LED lighting is reputedly the first of its kind anywhere for a theatre. Annually, plays from the period in which Lucy Maud Montgomery lived are performed here *(village hours extended for theatre productions)*.

Shining Waters Family Fun Park

Rte. 6, in Cavendish, off Avonlea Blvd. ○*Open mid-Jun–Sept daily 10am–6pm (Jul–Aug to 7pm).* ○*$18.* ✕ 🅿 ☎*877-963-3939. www.shiningwaterspei.com.*

Kids This theme park is a great spot for the kids indoors and out in more than 30 attractions involving water or dry land.

Discovery Woods features 305m/1,000ft of trails through forested areas with a suspension bridge and a tree house. Waterslides, a mini-zoo, paddleboats, rowboats, a haunted house and food stations add to the enjoyment. This is a modern amusement park, but without the big, mechanical rides.

New Glasgow

11km/7mi southwest of Cavendish by Rte. 13.

Another of Queens County's wee villages, charming New Glasgow is situated along the Hunter River: just a church and a few buildings at the junction of two rural routes.

It is known for its summertime **lobster suppers** *(mid-Jun–late-Sept;* ☎*902-964-2870; www.peilobstersuppers.com)* served in a gigantic hall seating 500 diners.

PEI Preserve Company

2841 New Glasgow Rd. ○*Open Jul–Labour Day 8am–9:30pm. Reduced hours mid-Apr–late Oct.* 🅿✕⬥ ☎*902-367-1888 or 800-565-5267. www.preserve company.com.*

Jams, salsas, chutneys, jellies and honeys are all made here in a restored 1913 butter factory. Visitors can sample dozens of preserves and several mustards and chutneys, and a tea of the day. The 12-acre **New Glasgow Country Gardens** *(*☎*902-964-4300)* includes a **Butterfly House.** Short walking trails are marked, and Sunday concerts take place in the summer. The cheery, on-site **Café on the Clyde ($$)** *(*☎*902-964-4301)* serves breakfast, lunch and casual evening fare, complemented by views of the river. On the grounds River Theatre offers late-morning Gaelic music and in the evening, country music *(Jul & Aug; for information* ☎*800-424-9155)*.

Anne of Green Gables Museum at Silverbush

In Park Corner on Rte. 20. ○*Open Jun–Sept daily 9am–4pm (Jul–Aug til 5pm). May & Oct daily 11am–4pm.* ○*$2.75.* ⬥🅿 ☎*902-886-2884 or 800-665-2663. www.annesociety.org.*

Throughout her life, author Lucy Maud Montgomery visited relatives at this spacious house built by her uncle and aunt in 1872. Her 1911 wedding was held in the drawing room. The dwelling and its 45ha/110-acre surroundings appear in

The village of New Glasgow

Bruce Bishop/Michelin

Address Book

For dollar sign categories, see the Legend on the cover flap.

WHERE TO STAY

$$ The Orient Hotel – *Victoria-by-the-Sea.* 📇 🛏 ☎902-658-2503 or 800-565-6743. www.theorienthotel.com. *7 rooms.* This brightly painted, three-storey hotel has welcomed overnight guests since 1900. Now a B&B inn operating year-round, the Orient offers individually decorated guest rooms, all of which have a private bathroom and cable TV. Included in the rate is a hot breakfast that comes with homemade preserves. The cozy **Mrs. Proffit's Tea Room ($)** on the premises prepares full-service teas in the English manner.

$$ Sundance Cottages – *34 MacCoubrey Lane, Cavendish Beach. 23 cottages.* 📇 🛏 ☎902-963-2149 or 800-565-2149. *Closed Nov–Apr.* www.sundancecottages.com. Set on 3.6ha/9acres, Sundance is a quiet, family-owned resort. Facing the Gulf of Saint Lawrence, the homey cottages come with extra amenities, such as garlic presses in the kitchens and complimentary mountain bike rentals and barbecues. A heated outdoor pool, children's pool and play area are bonuses. The central location makes it one of the best accommodations within proximity to supervised Cavendish Beach, just minutes away.

$$$ Barachois Inn – *2193 Church Rd., Rte. 243, Rustico.* ☎902-963-2194 or 800-963-2194. 🛏*8 rooms.* www.barachoisinn.com. Topping a hill in the tiny hamlet of Rustico, PEI's oldest Acadian community, this inn sits opposite a picturesque church surrounded by green fields. The lodging comprises two three-story houses with mansard roofs, the one a historic dwelling built in 1880 as a country home. The newer structure contains large, modern suites with a fireplace, microwave, coffee maker and therapeutic bathtub. All rooms have a private bathroom; amenities include bathrobes, in-room telephones and wireless Internet. A hot breakfast, included with the rate, is served in the well-appointed dining room.

$$$$ Dalvay-by-the-Sea – *North Shore, near the east entrance to PEI National Park.* 📇✕🛏☎902-672-2048. www.dalvaybythesea.com. *26 rooms, 8 cottages. Rates include dinner and breakfast for 2 people. Closed late-Sept–mid-Jun.* Former residence of oil magnate Alexander MacDonald, this gabled Queen-Anne style mansion now houses a prestigious resort. The lobby features beautiful woodwork and an enormous fireplace with a hearth of local sandstone. In addition to individually decorated guest rooms, Dalvay offers three-bedroom cottages, all equipped with a small refrigerator and a gas fireplace. Full meal service, including afternoon tea, is available in the pine-panelled **dining room ($$$)**, where exceptional Canadian cuisine awaits. The signature warm date pudding is topped with toffee sauce and ice cream. Tennis, croquet and lake boating are some of the many activities available.

$$$-$$$$ Shaw's Hotel – *99 Apple Tree Rd., Brackley Beach.*☎902-672-2022. www.shawshotel.ca. *15 rooms, 25 cottages.* 🛏 *Closed late-Sept–May.* Billed as Canada's oldest family-operated inn, this seaside hotel, established in 1860, sits in relative isolation by the beach. The focal point of the compound, complete with two barns, is a two-storey farmhouse with a bright-red mansard roof and striped awnings. More expensive than the rooms, the cottages have varying numbers of bedrooms; some have a fireplace and cable TV. Rooms in the main house are snug, but nicely done. In the **dining room ($$$)**, the emphasis is on seafood (lobster is served twice a week), but prime rib, beef, chicken, duck and Italian pastas are on the menu. Shaw's is especially attentive to children: a playground, art program and hay rides keep them occupied.

WHERE TO EAT

$$ Fisherman's Wharf Lobster Suppers – *7230 Rustico Rd., North Rustico on Rte 6.* ☎877-289-1010. www.fishermanswharf.ca. *Closed Nov–Apr.* **Seafood.** This huge restaurant has an 18m/60ft-long

Bruce Bishop/Michelin

The Dunes Gallery, Brackley Beach

salad bar with steaming hot PEI mussels and every salad item imaginable. Lobsters arrive steamed in the shell, with a bib and utensils. The restaurant's record was 2,200 people served in one day. Since 1980 the place has served between 70,000 and 100,000 hungry seafood lovers. While in North Rustico, visit the **Rustico Harbour Fishery Museum** *(318 Harbourview Dr.; open mid-Jun–Sept, call for hrs; ☎902-963-3799)* on the boardwalk.

$$ The Dunes Gallery – *In Brackley Beach. ☎902-672-1883. www.dunes gallery.com.* **Contemporary.** This dramatic cedar and glass structure houses an art studio, an art gallery, a furniture store featuring Thai and Indonesian goods, a gift shop, and a cafe. The **cafe** *(closed Oct–May)* serves creative cuisine on the gallery's attractive pottery. At lunchtime, try the Lebanese chicken sandwich on pita. For dinner, try the Dunes Duet (seared scallops and jumbo shrimp in a red pepper cream sauce and topped with peach salsa). Be sure to stroll the tranquil gardens bursting with colourful flowers, the deckside lily pond *(3rd floor)* and the top-floor lookout.

$$$ dayboat pei – *5033 Rustico Rd., Hunter River. ☎902-963-3833. www. dayboat.ca. Lunch Jul & Aug only. Closed Nov–late May.* ♿ **Contemporary.** Dayboat and its innovative dishes have remained consistently fine since its opening in 2005. Wood floors, chairs

and unadorned tables set the stage for concentration on the food. Trained in Paris, chef François de Mélogue is a slow-food adherent and owns 1,900 cookbooks. Freshly shucked oysters as a starter may be prepared breaded with an avocado mousse, or au gratin with fennel and Gouda. The haddock, scallops, lobster, cod, halibut and salmon are always fresh and perhaps paired with an orange vanilla seed vinaigrette or a smoked bacon lobster salsa. Meat lovers have menu choices of island back ribs, Atlantic steak and other dishes.

$$ Olde Mill Restaurant – *Rte. 13, New Glasgow. ☎902-964-3313. www.oldeglasgowmill.ca. Closed mid-Oct–May.* Built in 1896 as a community hall, and housing a restaurant since 1997, the Olde Mill fits a comfortable niche in the pretty community of New Glasgow, at least during the summer and fall. The restaurant is a busy spot, seating 100 within three dining rooms. The main dining room's windows overlook the River Clyde. A well-stocked wine wall lets patrons choose a bottle by comparing labels. In 2008 the restaurant revised its menu to incorporate such customer-pleasing dishes as breast of chicken stuffed with brie with a maple syrup glaze; scallops sautéed in vermouth and shittake mushrooms; and lobster Thermidore (lobster baked in a sherry and cheese sauce). *Reservations recommended for dinner.*

the *Anne of Green Gables* series, including the Lake of Shining Waters, as Ms. Montgomery called it. First editions of the author's books, personal correspondence and family heirlooms are displayed throughout the house.

Enjoy a ride in a horse-drawn surrey (👜$4; 1hr) over gentle hills to the lake.

Woodleigh★

In Burlington on Rte. 234 northeast of Kensington. ⏰Open Jul–Aug daily 9am–7pm. Jun & Sept daily 9am–5pm. 👜$8.65. ✕☎ 902-836-3401. www.woodleigh replicas.com.

Scattered about a pleasant, tree-shaded 16ha/40-acre site are some 30 large-scale replicas of historic British structures. Highlights include an 8m/26ft replica of York Minster Cathedral, complete with 145 glass windows; St. Paul's Cathedral in London and Scotland's Duvnegan Castle.

Ernest Johnstone, a native of PEI serving in Britain during WWI, fell in love with England and Scotland. After the war he bought a farm in Burlington, naming it Woodleigh for his ancestral Scottish home. For some 50 years he worked to shape the land to resemble a well-manicured English garden.

After service in WWII, he and his son started constructing re-creations of celebrated buildings in the British Isles. They first built Glamis Castle; Anne Hathaway's Cottage soon followed. Curious onlookers arrived in such droves that the grounds were opened to the public in 1957.

Victoria-by-the-Sea

www.victoriabythesea.ca.
Located on the south shore overlooking Northumberland Strait, this tiny seaside community of fewer than 200 residents is undoubtedly the island's most picturesque hamlet, complete with an active wharf and a provincial park. In 1819 a wealthy immigrant laid out a grid pattern of streets on the land of his estate. The village that sprang up eventually became a thriving seaport, carrying on trade with the East Coast, Europe and the West Indies. Exhibits at the **Seaport Museum** within the operating lighthouse highlight Victoria's history.

Dominating the end of Main Street, the colourful **Orient Hotel** (👜*see Address Book*) welcomes overnight guests and patrons to its tea room. In addition to other lodgings, a Belgian-chocolate shop, a candle shop, art gallery, glass studio, antiques store and cafe, the village boasts a playhouse, museum, lighthouse and nearby beaches. Every summer since 1981, contemporary Canadian plays and musicals have been performed by the **Victoria Playhouse** (☎ 902-658-2025; www.victoriaplayhouse.com), located at Victoria Hall.

From Victoria's beach, the 32km/20mi **Bonshaw Hills Trail** climbs to the top of the island's only hills and weaves past farmland and fields and into a hemlock forest near Appin Road before ending at West River Bridge near St. Catherines.

Port-la-Joye–Fort Amherst National Historic Site

In Rocky Point, on Blockhouse Point Rd., off Rte. 19. ⏰Grounds open daily mid–Jun–late Aug. ✕☎902-566-7626. www. pc.gc.ca.

Port-la-Joye, the first permanent European settlement on the island, was established here by the French in 1720 to supply food to Fortress Louisbourg in Nova Scotia. It was inhabited by Acadian families who worked the land until the Deportation of 1755. Struggles for control of the settlement were ongoing between the French and British until 1758, when the French surrendered to the British following the Crown's victory over Louisbourg.

Britain's first military fortification on the island, Fort Amherst, was erected as a series of defences on the site of the original French garrison. The British occupied the post until 1768. Designated a National Historic Site in 1967, the site was opened to the public in 1973.

Today only the earthworks remain—rolling, grass-covered mounds from which sweeping **views**★★ of Charlottetown harbour extend. Interpretive panels convey the history of settlement and the Franco-British conflict.

In the **visitor centre,** displays and a video presentation *(15min)* offer an introduction.

EASTERN PEI

Eastern PEI encompasses the patchwork fields, forests, coastal hamlets and long stretches of beaches that make up Kings County. More peaceful than tourist-laden Cavendish and bustling Charlottetown, the county has the fewest residents and is more rural than the rest of the island. Rather than farming, lumber and fishing are the economic mainstays here. Astride the Brudenell River, which empties into Cadigan Bay, Georgetown is the county seat, or shiretown in official parlance, where PEI's only remaining shipyard is located. The largest town in Kings County is Montague, where the majority of services for the area are found. From Wood Islands, a ferry crosses Northumberland Strait to Nova Scotia, and from Souris a ferry goes to Quebec's Îles de la Magdeleine, a five-hour passage. Side roads lead through lush forests past small communities with names like Cardigan, Greenfield and Glenmartin that hearken back to the province's British heritage. Some 30 beaches wait to be combed, nearly a dozen golf courses are here (including the highly ranked Links at Crowbush Cove), more than 300 bird species can be sighted, and the province's only winery offers tours and tastings.

Eastern Shores ★

MAP P 189

Wandering along the deeply indented bays and harbours of the island's eastern shoreline, this driving itinerary takes in the major attractions of Eastern PEI and offers a closer look at Kings County's vibrant fishing industry. From Charlottetown, the drive follows the Trans-Canada Highway (Highway 1) south along the coast of Queens County through Stratford, Cherry Valley and over Orwell Bay to Orwell. The route winds south through Eldon, passing Point Prim to curve east at Wood Islands, where ferries cross to Nova Scotia. Entering Kings County, the drive leaves the Trans-Canada Highway and continues on Route 4 along the southern edge. Following rural routes, the drive turns north at Murray Harbour and zig zags around inlets and bays before reaching Pooles Corner. It veers east to Georgetown, which sits on a peninsula jutting out into Cardigan Bay. Traversing the extreme northeast headland, the route then passes Souris, departure point for ferries to Quebec's Magdalen Islands, and explores the Basin Head area before taking in Elmira. The route then traces the edge of the northern shore west to St. Peters before returning to Charlottetown.

- 🛈 **Information:** Visitors' Information Centre (VIC), 1915 Greenwich Rd. (Rte. 2), St. Peters Bay. ☎902-961-3540. For visitors arriving by ferry from Nova Scotia at Wood Islands, the visitor centre is just beyond the ferry terminal in the Plough the Waves Centre (☎902-462-7211).
- ▸ **Orient Yourself:** Departing from Charlottetown, the circular route follows the coastline counter-clockwise, from south to north.
- ☺ **Don't Miss:** Orwell Corner Historic Village.
- 🕓 **Organizing Your Time:** Allow a full day for visits to the attractions.
- 🄺 **Especially for Kids:** The farmyard and wagon rides at Orwell Corner Historic Village.

Driving Tour

325km/233mi circuit indicated by signs showing the white starfish on a blue and orange background of the island's designated **Points East Coastal Drive** *(www.pointseastcoastaldrive.com).*

Experience PEI

Ever wanted to go clamming and cook up your haul on the spot? Make a seaweed pie? Take the reins for a spin around a harness-racing track? How about the ancient art of smelt spearing? A program run by island innkeepers Mary and Bill Kendrick, allows visitors and even other islanders to meet people in PEI with interesting professions or hobbies. **Experience PEI** puts novices in touch with island experts for creative workshops. In addition to learning a skill, you'll meet other people and most likely be regaled by the jokes and stories of the instructor. Workshops range from an evening to a week and cost from $45 to $150. ☎866-877-3238 or www.experiencepei.ca.

Orwell

Known for its historic attractions, this small village lies within Queens County. It is also home to Macphail Woods, a prized birding spot and focus of extensive ecological management.

Orwell Corner Historic Village★★

In Orwell, 30km/19mi east of Charlottetown on the Trans-Can Hwy (Hwy.1). ◐*Open Jul–Labour Day daily 9:30am–5:30pm. Jun Mon–Fri 9am–5pm. Labour Day–mid-Oct Sun–Thu 9am–5pm.* ☜*$7.50.* ✕ 🅿 ☎*902-651-8510. www.orwellcorner.isn.net.*

Kids This superbly restored crossroads village, settled in the early 19C by pioneers from Scotland and Ireland, retains the flavour of the island's agricultural origins. Visitors can tour the 1864 **farmhouse,** which served as post office, general store and dressmaker's shop, along with a church, school, community hall, blacksmith shop, shingle mill and animal barns. Chickens, goats, pigs and sheep run about the **farmyard,** and rides are available in wagons pulled by Belgian and Canadian draft horses. A tea room serves baked goods and sandwiches. Fiddle music and step dancing are features of the traditional *ceilidh* [pronounced KAY-lee] *(Jun–Sept Wed 8pm).* Enjoy the view from **Orwell Bay Scenic Look Off** just off the historic village's parking lot *(signs indicate access).* Picnic tables are on-site and packed lunches are available from the tea room.

Sir Andrew MacPhail Homestead

Off the Fletcher Rd. just east of Orwell Corner Historic Village. ◐*Open year-round Wed & Sun 11am–7:30pm, Thu, Fri & Sat 11am–4:30 pm.* ✕ 🅿 ☎*902-651-2789. www.islandregister.com/macphail foundation.html.*

Slightly off the beaten track, this house was the home of accomplished scholar and doctor, **Sir Andrew MacPhail**

Orwell Corner Historic Village

Orwell Corner Historic Village

Seals and Their Admirers

From Montague *(www.townofmontaguepei.com)*, seal-watching tours are offered by several companies. **Cruise Manada Seal-Watching Boat Tours** *(departs from Montague Marina on Rte. 4; ☎902-838-3444; www.cruisemanada.com)* has been around for 23 years. Cruises depart three times a day in an all-weather boat, so don't be concerned if it's a rainy day. Seeing seals and seabirds is virtually guaranteed, but one can also learn local history from the commentary. Afterwards, have what some locals call the best bread pudding on the island at **Windows on the Water Café** *(see Address Book).*

(1864-1938). Following 20 months in the ambulance corps of World War I, he was knighted in 1918. He wrote a semi-autobiographical book that is considered an important account of life in 19C PEI. The 57ha/140-acre homestead retains much from his life here. Home-cooked lunches and dinners (and afternoon tea) are served at the house.

Also on the property, in the homestead's restored barn, the **Macphail Woods Nature Centre**★ *(& ☎902-651-2575; http://macphailwoods.org)* features displays on the natural history and biodiversity of PEI; a number of preserved birds and animals are on view. From the centre four walking trails lead into the woods along the Orwell River; the **Rhododendron Trail** is less than a kilometre and Wildflower Trail is the 5km/3mi. The centre sponsors free **birding tours**, including an Owl Prowl walk *(check the website for schedule).*

Point Prim Lighthouse

On Rte. 209, off Trans-Canada Hwy., between Belfast and Pinette. ◐*Open Jul–Aug.* ☎902-659-2412.

South of Eldon, Route 209 leaves the Trans-Canada Highway and traverses a peninsula that juts into the Northumberland Strait. Near the end, a dirt road leads to a green expanse that holds the Island's oldest lighthouse, built in 1845. Oddly, its design was conceived by an architect, Isaac Smith, who designed Province House in Charlottetown. It is the only round brick lighthouse in the country. Tiny windows punctuate the 21m/68ft tower, topped with a red lantern room. Climb the lighthouse for a sweeping view of the Northumberland Strait and surroundings.

Wood Islands Lighthouse and Museum★

Off Rte. 1, Lighthouse Rd. by the ferry terminal. ◐*Open mid-Jun–mid-Sept.* ☎902-962-3110 or off-season 902-962-2022. *www.woodislands.ca/lighthouse.html.*

Trimmed in bright red, this white wooden lighthouse, dating to 1876, adjoins the lightkeeper's house. The kitchen, lightkeeper's room, small bedroom and seven other rooms over three floors have been restored; each houses displays on such topics as island ferry service, fisheries and rum running. Climb the 54 steps to the tower for a **panoramic** view of the coast.

Rossignol Estate Winery

Rte. 4, Little Sands, Murray River. ◐ *Open May–Oct Mon–Sat 10am–5pm, Sun 1pm–5pm.* ☐ ☎ 902-962-4193. *www. rossignolwinery.com.*

Surrounded by flat, green fields, this unpretentious 3.6ha/9-acre vineyard, opened since 1994, somehow manages to produce approximately 50,000 bottles a year; the winery sells all but ten percent on the island. In addition to grape wines, it also produces blueberry, maple and rhubarb wines, as well as apple cider. No pesticides are used on the crops, and only barrels made of 100-percent oak are used for fermentation. Tastings are on a drop-in basis and informal.

Kings Castle Provincial Park

In Gladstone, off Rte. 348, 3km/2mi east of Murray River. ◐*Open early Jun–mid-Sept.* ✕ ☐ ☎902-962-7422. *www.gov. pe.ca/visitorsguide.*

Kids Geared to children, the park is dotted with life-size concrete statues of a number of storybook characters like the

Point Prim Lighthouse

Big Bad Wolf, the Three Bears and the Three Little Pigs. There's a playground and a beach along the Murray River. Picnic sites and a barbecue area plus walking trails make this a great spot for families.

Souris

6km/4mi east of Rollo Bay. ☎902-687-2157. www.sourispei.com.
A fishing port of 1,300 residents, Souris [pronounced Soo-REE] is one of the larger towns in Kings County. It was founded by Acadians in the early 1700s. In French, *souris* means mouse, and it is thought that the community was named for a spate of field mice that pestered

the early settlers. The port has been the departure point, since the 1960s, for the car ferry to Quebec's Magdalen Islands, some five hours away in the Gulf of St. Lawrence.

New Harmony Road

Rte. 303, a 1.2km stretch of unpaved road from Greenvale Rd. to Taratum Rd. (Rte. 304). From Souris, take Rte. 335 east to New Harmony Rd. (Rte. 303) and go left for just over a kilometre.
Officially described as one of the finest scenic heritage roads in the province, this brief stretch of red-clay road, less than a kilometre long, is lined with a

Beacons of Light

Lighthouses recall a time when men risked life and limb to provide for their families, and when navigational equipment and weather forecasts were infinitely inferior to what is used on ships today. In eastern PEI, five lighthouses, including **Point Prim** above, remain open to visitors in the summer. The **East Point Lighthouse** (☎902-357-2106: www.eastpointlighthouse.com) is located at the northeast end of the province and was built in 1867 at a height of 19.5m/64ft. In 1882 a British warship shipwrecked off East Point, partly due to a mistake in the lighthouse's coordinates on navigational charts. In 1883 the lighthouse was moved to its present location to be in accord with the charts. **Cape Bear Lighthouse & Marconi Museum** (☜$3.50; ☎902-962-2917), off Route 18 in the southeast, was the first Marconi station to receive the SOS distress call from the *Titanic* in 1912. Although the station is gone, the c.1881, four-storey lighthouse still stands and houses the museum dedicated to the founder of the radio. The **Wood Islands Lighthouse** (☎902-362-3110) is the first one to be seen on PEI when arriving by ferry from Nova Scotia; it dates to 1876. Tours, some guided, are conducted daily, and a Fishery and Coast Guard museum is on-site. There's a scenic beach near the **Panmure Lighthouse** (15km/9mi east of Montague on Rte 347; Panmure Island; ☎902-838-3568; www.peisland.com/visit/panmure/island/htm).

Address Book

For dollar sign categories, see the Legend on the cover flap.

WHERE TO STAY

$$ Maplehurst Properties – *Rte. 310 Panmure Island.* ☎*902-838-3959. Offseason: 386-677-3840. www.maple hurstproperties.com. 4 rooms, 2 cottages (minimum one-week stay required). Closed mid-Oct–mid-May.* Spread over 25 beachfront acres on an island in Cardigan Bay, this estate includes a three-storey, 13-room Georgian manor and a spacious two-bedroom, two-bath cottage, complete with kitchen. Rooms in the house are appointed with antiques and have en suite bathrooms. Two rooms have a private veranda. A living room, sunroom and library are available for guest use. Full breakfast included in the rate and complimentary cookies and sodas in the butler's pantry. Wireless Internet.

$$$ Inn at Bay Fortune – *Rte. 310, just off Rte. 2, Bay Fortune.* ☎*902-687-3745 or 888-687-3745. www.innatbay fortune.com. 18 rooms, 2 cottages.* ✕🚶♿🅿 *Closed late May–mid-Oct.* This upscale inn has a reputation for its Maritime cuisine and secluded setting. Spacious suites in the north tower and main house come with comfortable furnishings and private bathrooms; some have whirlpool baths, balconies, fireplaces. Served on a glass-enclosed **veranda ($$$)**, creatively prepared Canadian dishes incorporate the bounty of the island (venison, wild mushrooms, blue mussels, Colville Bay oysters) as well as produce from the inn's extensive gardens, which are definitely worth touring. The menu changes daily.

$$$$ Inn at Spry Point – *On Rte. 310 (Spry Point Rd.), just off Rte. 2, Souris.* ☎*902-583-2400 or 888-687-3745. www.innatsprypoint.com. 15 rooms.* ✕♿🅿*. Closed Oct–mid-Jun.* A remote promontory above Northumberland Strait provides the setting for this large, airy inn, a sister property of Inn at Bay Fortune. Trails cross the forests near the inn's grounds, and waves crash on the nearby sandy beach. All of the large guest rooms have private balconies or terraces that afford lovely views.

Most of the beds are four-posters. Overlooking the ocean, the **dining room ($$$)** offers local produce, fresh fish and Island meats; the table d'hôte menu changes daily.

$$$$$ Inn at St. Peters – *1668 Greenwich Rd., St. Peters Bay.* ☎*902-961-2135 or 800-818-0925. www.innatstpeters. com. Rates include breakfast & dinner. 16 rooms. Closed mid-Oct–late-May.* This spacious, two-storey inn with a long veranda sits on a 5ha/13-acre expanse above St. Peters Bay. Each guest room has either a four-poster or a sleigh bed, plus a fireplace, sofa, mini-refrigerator, private bathroom and a deck overlooking the bay. Gardens filled with colourful flowers, herbs and vegetables line the back lawns. With windows facing the bay, and a large fireplace, the 55-seat **dining room ($$$)** *(reservations recommended)* offers inspired contemporary dishes with an emphasis on fresh seafood and produce picked from the gardens.

WHERE TO EAT

$$ Trailside Inn and Café – *109 North Main St., Mount Stewart. Rte 22 off Rte. 2.* ♿*(cafe)* ☎*902-676-3130. www. trailside.ca.* **Seafood.** Don't let the exterior of this renovated country store turn you away. Trailside's varied menu concentrates on seafood. Be sure to try the signature tarragon-scented seafood stew or the salmon pie, and enjoy an ambitious program of live music throughout the summer. On Sundays regulars frequent the gospel brunch. The inn offers four **rooms ($)** for overnight stays, each with private bathrooms, and Trailside Adventures rents bicycles and canoes.

$$ Windows on the Water Café – *106 Sackville St., Montague.* ☎*902-838-2080. Closed Oct–Mid-May.* **Canadian.** This Montague restaurant is popular with locals for its delicious lunchtime or dinnertime meals at wallet-pleasing prices. The seafood chowder is a good choice for a starter. Then try a seafood entrée, since most any catch is fresh, and save room for the cafe's desserts, especially the bread pudding. There's a deck to enjoy refreshing water views.

Lobster Suppers

An island tradition, lobster suppers began more than 40 years ago as a fund-raiser for the Junior Farmers Organization; the first meal cost $1.50. It is said that PEI churches also used them to pay off their mortgages. The summertime *(mid-Jun–late Sept)* suppers became so popular they were soon commercialized to cater to huge crowds. **St. Ann's Church** *(☎902-621-0635. www.lobstersuppers.com)* in Hope River offers daily afternoon and evening sittings *(except Sunday)* in its large basement. **St. Margarets Lobster Suppers** *(☎902-687-3105)* serves lobster and ham dinners in its licensed dining room, and **New Glasgow Lobster Suppers** *(☎902-964-2870. www.peilobstersuppers.com)* operates in a two-level, 500-capacity hall, with lobster pounds on-site. Here's how it works. Paying a set price as they enter, patrons are seated at long wooden tables, family style, and offered bibs and moist towelettes in preparation for the all-you-can-eat feast. Homemade chowder served with freshly baked rolls is the traditional opener, followed by several salads (potato, coleslaw and green). Then a tall bucket of freshly steamed mussels is brought to table. Next comes the lobster itself (one, one-and-a-half or two pounds, based on what you paid), served in the shell, with vegetables on the side. Cake or pie with ice cream is often served as dessert. The price includes your choice of beverage (beer and wine are usually available at an extra cost). Ham or fish are often offered for those who don't like lobster. Whatever you choose, you won't walk away hungry.

thick canopy of trees that form a tunnel of foliage denser than a typical allée. It is said that, during Prohibition, the covered road was a hideout for illegal goods unloaded from rumrunners' boats offshore. Driving it is permissible, although hiking and biking are encouraged.

Just east of the road, the provincial government maintains the 107ha/265-acre **New Harmony Demonstration Woodlot** *(marked with sign)*, where a self-guided interpretive trail *(1hr; brochure available at trailhead)* enters stands of white-spruce. Descriptive trailside panels explain forest ecology.

Basin Head Fisheries Museum★

In Basin Head, 10km/6mi east of Souris on Rte. 16. 🕐*Open mid-Jun–Labour Day daily 10am–6pm, Sept 9am–5pm.* 💲*$4.* ✕🅿☎*902-357-7233. www.gentle island.com.*

This museum occupies a fine site overlooking the mouth of Northumberland Strait. Boats, nets, hooks, photographs and dioramas illustrate the life and work of an inshore fisherman.

Outside, wooden buildings house a small boats exhibit.

Elmira Railway Museum

Elmira Railway Museum

Elmira Railway Museum

In Elmira, 16km/10mi east of Souris on Rte. 16A. ○*Open Jun–Sept daily 10am–6pm.* ◎*$3.* 🚻 📷 ☏*902-357-7234. www.elmira station.com.*

Formerly the eastern terminus of a railway system linking the island with the continent, this station, which began operations in 1912, has been transformed into a museum that recounts the railway's 19C-early 20C development. The rail yard holds an engine house, coal shed, bunkhouse, barn and housing for the engineers and conductors. Displays include photographs, a 1911 station log and still-operational telegraph equipment. A miniature train takes visitors around the grounds.

Greenwich Unit, Prince Edward Island National Park★

Rte. 313, near St. Peters. ○*Open mid-May–early Oct.* ◎*$7.80.* ☏*902-961-2514. www.pc.gc.ca.*

This separate section of the national park is all about the **Greenwich Dunes**, which support a number of bird species and rare flora. These parabolic dunes are unusually large and shifting. In 1998 Parks Canada took over land equivalent to 6km/3.7mi of the peninsula. Aboriginal artifacts, some dating back 10,000 years, as well as early 18C Acadian artifacts have been unearthed on-site.

In the **interpretive centre** 🦽, a multimedia show *(12min)* recounts the Greenwich story, and a three-dimensional model shows the Greenwich peninsula. Accessible by a wooden boardwalk, a supervised **beach** *(late-Jun–Aug)* offers swimming and an observation tower affords fine views. The **Greenwich Dunes Trail** *(4.5km/2.5mi)* and the **Tlaqatik Trail** *(4.5km/2.8mi)* offer views of the dunes, St. Peters Bay and Bowley Pond.

WESTERN PEI

Stretching from the tip of North Cape in the Gulf of St. Lawrence south to West Point and just east of Kensington, the western part of the province is the domain of Prince County, named by surveyor Samuel Holland in 1765 for Britain's Prince of Wales. Famed for its oysters, Malpeque Bay, at the northeast extremity, is the county's dominant natural feature. The county is largely rural, the land devoted primarily to potato farming and the coast to a fishing industry based on lobsters, oysters and crabs. Manufacturing and processing facilities are concentrated in the eastern part of the county at Summerside and farther east at Borden-Car-

The island's major crop: potatoes

Bruce Bishop/Michelin

leton. On the North Cape, at the tip of the province, windmill technology has been introduced. Western PEI is home to the island's largest number of Mi'kmaq, residing primarily on Lennox Island in northern Malpeque Bay. An active Acadian community centres in the area known as the Evangeline region, extending from West Point to Summerside. The names of other communities such as O'Leary, Wellington and Inverness, reflect the county's significant number of residents of Irish, English and Scottish descent. In addition to its vibrant people, the overarching attraction of Western PEI is its rural scenery and traditional working life that somehow have escaped modern encroachment.

Summerside ★

POPULATION 15,000 – MAP P 189

Overlooking Bedeque Bay, Summerside sits on the southern side of an isthmus that links Prince County to the rest of the island. Vast Malpeque Bay lies to the town's north. The province's second-largest city, this town was a draw to tourists as early as 1825, when Joseph Green built an inn called Summerside on a parcel of land here. With the arrival of the railway in the 1870s, the community evolved into a bustling seaport, shipping the abundant crops that were grown in the region. A shipbuilding industry blossomed from 1850 to 1880, and the shipyards attracted a merchant class. By the turn-of-the-19C, Summerside was thriving, and the stately homes of the shipbuilders had been built to be noticeably grand. Many fine 19C and early 20C houses still stand along tree-shaded streets downtown. The large concentration of fox farms in the area from 1890 to 1939 also brought prosperity to the city. In the 1940s a Royal Canadian Air Force Station was established on the outskirts of town, generating more city growth.

Summerside celebrates its past with colourful **murals** painted on some of the downtown buildings. Summerside is the home of the country's only bagpiping college. Lively summer entertainment (piping, drumming, dancing) is presented by the college students annually, and several festivals are held throughout the year in Summerside.

- **Information:** Tourism Summerside, 98 Water St., Summerside. ☎902-436-7784, www.visitsummerside.com.
- ▶ **Orient Yourself:** The city is bordered by Water St. (Rte. 11) to the south, South Dr. (west), Pope Rd. (north) and MacEwan Rd. (east). The main artery that runs north-south within this area is Central St. (Rte. 21). Several accommodations, restaurants and shops are found on or around Water St. Harbour Drive, where several key attractions are located, lies directly south of Water St. The city's 4km/2.5mi-long boardwalk makes a nice place for an evening stroll.
- **Parking:** There are more than 1,400 parking spaces downtown, most of which are metered by coin in 15- and 30-min, 2-hour or 24-hour periods.
- **Don't Miss:** The murals depicting Summerside's history painted on downtown city buildings.
- **Organizing Your Time:** Allow 2 days to explore Summerside. A self-guided **walking tour** map is available at the MacNaught History Centre and Archives *(75 Spring St.; open year-round Tue–Sat 10am–5pm; ☎902-432-1296; www.wyattheritage.com).* Information about guided tours of Summerside's Historic House District and Water Street Commercial District can also be obtained from the centre.
- **Especially for Kids:** A supervised beach at the Shipyard Market.

Sights

Shipyard Market

370 Water St. Open year-round daily. ☎ *902-436-8439. www.visitsummerside.com.*
Opened in 2004, this entertainment and events complex has an 1800s feel, comes with its own woodcarver and has its own supervised beach. With a craft co-operative to a Saturday farmers' market, the market is always bustling with activities. The 418sq m/4,500sq ft open space is frequently used for concerts, festivals and large banquets.

Eptek Art & Cultural Centre

Wyatt Centre, 124 Harbour Dr. Open year-round Tue–Fri 10am–4pm, Sun noon–4pm (also open Mon in Sept). $4. ☎ *902-888-8373. www.pei museum.com*

Tourism Summerside

Bagpipe band, College of Piping and Celtic Performing Arts of Canada

A fixture in Summerside for over 20 years, this art gallery and museum often showcases the work of PEI craftspeople. It is part of the provincial government-run Museum and Heritage Prince Edward Island Sites. The Prince Edward Island **Sports Hall of Fame & Museum** is also housed in the building (⏱*open Jun–Aug Mon–Fri 10am–5:30pm, Sat noon–5:30pm;* ⬤*$2;* ☎ *902-436-0423; www.peisportshalloffame.ca).* Opened in 1998, this complex honours more than 120 of the province's outstanding athletes, sports journalists and "builders" of a sport in many sporting fields, including hockey, rugby, baseball, golf, a variety of winter sports, harness racing, auto racing and even badminton. In addition to visiting the inductee shrine, be sure to see the gallery devoted to the history of the island's sports, brought to life through photographs, artifacts and memorabilia.

Harbourfront Jubilee Theatre

Wyatt Centre, 124 Harbour Dr. ⏱*Open year-round for performances.* ♿☎*902-888-2500 or 800-708-6505. www.jubilee theatre.com.*
Run largely by volunteers, this nonprofit theatre opened in 1996. Every summer since 2005, the musical **Anne and Gilbert** has been staged here *(Jul, Aug & Sept)*, delighting audiences with further tales of Anne of Green Gables and her young-adult romance with Gilbert Blythe. Despite 527 seats, the theatre has an intimate feeling to it. Rock concerts, stand-up comedians, and professional choirs are hosted here throughout the year.

Spinnaker's Landing

150 Harbour Dr. ⏱*Open early–mid-Jun 9am–6pm. Late-Jun–Labour Day 9am–9pm. Rest of Sept 9am–5pm.* ☎*902-888-8364. www.spinnakerslanding.com.*
This quaint collection of weathered buildings perches on stilts at the edge of the harbour. Complete with a boardwalk, the landing is the place to pick up souvenirs from the island: the 14 shops are highly individual in their wares. Goods range from Celtic jewellery to antiques and pottery.

College of Piping and Celtic Performing Arts of Canada

69 Water St. E. ⏱*Opening hours, events and prices vary.* ♿☎*902-436-5377 or 877-224-7473. www.collegeofpiping.com.*
If one ever has a calling to play the bagpipes or snare drums or learn the step dance or Highland fling, this college has a stellar reputation for instruction. Unique to North America, it is affiliated with the College of Piping in Glasgow, Scotland. Visitors to Summerside who prefer to be spectators, however, can enjoy summer evening concerts of piping, drumming

and dancing in the college's amphitheatre. Annually in late June, the **Summer Highland Gathering** takes place on the college's 4.8ha/12acres, at times with country music acts interspersed among the Scottish music and dancing.

Summerside Circuit★

MAP P 189

This drive along the coast of the western part of province, known on the island as the North Cape Coastal Drive, is shown by road signs depicting a lighthouse with the sun setting on the horizon. The scenic circuit introduces visitors to shipbuilding at Green Park; Malpeque Bay, famed for its fine oysters; and moss harvesting at Miminegash. Potato farming and fishing are chief occupations; you may see tractors in the potato fields and lobster boats heading out or in with their traps piled high. Stretching from Summerside to West Point, the Evangeline area is home to a colourful Acadian community, centred in Miscouche. The North Cape, at the tip of the province, is the site of windmill technology and stunning sunsets. In between are Mi'kmaq, Scottish, Irish and Acadian communities that continue age-old trades and traditions and celebrate life with good food, music and lively festivals.

- ▣ **Information:** West Prince Visitor Information Centre, Rte. 2 west in Mount Pleasant. ☎902-831-7930. www.gentleisland.com.
- ▶ **Orient Yourself:** This drive avoids inland Route 2 and traverses the rural routes along the coast's capes and beaches in a counterclockwise direction, heading north from Summerside.
- ⊙ **Don't Miss:** Green Park Shipbuilding Museum.
- ◷ **Organizing Your Time:** Allow a full day to enjoy this drive.
- Kids **Especially for Kids:** The Potato Museum.

Driving Tour

288km/179mi circuit along coastal routes indicated by signs showing a lighthouse with a setting sun for the **North Cape Coastal Drive.**

Miscouche
8km/5mi west of Summerside, on Rte. 2.
This hub of Acadian culture was the site of the 1884 Second Acadian National Convention, which drew some 5,000 delegates from around the Maritimes; the tricolour flag was adopted as an Acadian national symbol at this gathering. It is home to two important Acadian sights.

Acadian Museum of Prince Edward Island
◷*Open late Jun–Labour Day daily 9:30am–5pm (Jul–Aug 7pm). Rest of the year Mon–Fri 9:30am–5pm, Sun 1pm–*

4pm. ▣*$3.* ♿☎ *902-432-2880. www. teleco.org/museeacadien.*
Erected in 1991, this modern facility for the preservation of Acadian heritage combines a historical museum with a documentation centre for genealogical research. Main gallery dioramas and texts present Acadian history after 1720, incorporating objects from an extensive collection of artifacts, photographs, textiles and journals donated by area families. Audiovisual presentations in the theatre introduce such topics as religion, education and economy. An adjacent gallery presents temporary thematic exhibits on Acadian culture and heritage.

St. John the Baptist Church
This Roman Catholic Church is one of the island's oldest wooden churches, dating to 1892. The ornate, cream-coloured façade with white trim is flanked by twin corner towers topped by enor-

Lobster traps at Tignish Harbour

mous spires. Inside is a vintage Casavant organ.

Green Park
Shipbuilding Museum★

In Port Hill, 34km/21mi northwest of Summerside on Rte. 12. ◷Open Jun–late Sept daily 10am–5:30pm. ◉$5. ☎902-831-7947. www.peimuseum.com.

Formerly the grounds of an active shipyard, Green Park is today a provincial heritage site commemorating the shipbuilding industry, the island's principal economic activity during the 19C. Erected by the shipyard's owner, **Yeo**

St. John the Baptist Church

House (1865) is a large, steeply gabled Victorian structure restored to reflect the lifestyle of a prominent family of the period. Maps, photographs and tools on display in the **visitor centre** present the art and science of shipbuilding during the industry's 19C heyday.

Tignish

A small, proud community near the North Cape, Tignish has its own **cultural centre** (☎902-882-2230) that depicts the history of the village's Irish and Acadian settlers. Built in 1860 the brick **St. Simon and St. Jude Catholic Church** is still an active parish, and contains one of four original Tracker Pipe Organs, installed in 1882. The **Tignish Heritage Inn and Gardens** (☎902-882-2491. www.tignish.com/inn/index.htm), formerly the church's convent, sits next door and has been open for overnight guests since 1995. Once settled for a day in the town, make a stop at the **Atlantic Wind Test Site** (21741 Rte. 12; ☎902-882-2746; www.weican.ca) a few kilometres north and visit its interpretive centre. A co-venture between the provincial and federal governments, this project harnesses wind power to generate electricity and has been in operation about 25 years.

Black Marsh Nature Trail

Trailhead at the end of Rte. 12 on North Cape.

Walking this 2.7km/1.6mi trail along red sandstone cliffs at the northern end of Prince Edward Island is almost like walking to the end of the world. This is where the Gulf of St. Lawrence meets the Northumberland Strait. There are 10 interpretive stops, including a fragile sub-arctic bog. Signage and information along the trail is fully bilingual.

Irish Moss Interpretive Centre

In Miminegash, off Rte. 14.
☎902-882-4313.

On the northwest side of the North Cape peninsula, this interpretive centre has an interesting story to tell. Here visitors learn about the generations-old harvesting of Irish moss, a dark-coloured seaweed that grows on rocks along low-tide marks. Found along the Atlantic coasts of North America and Europe, it is widely used in modern dairy and some cosmetic products. A short video explains the process. Tools and equipment are on display, as well as samples of the mosses. In the on-site **Seaweed Pie Café**, order the namesake pie—actually a light, whipped-cream-topped sponge cake made with the moisture-binding substance carageenan, an extract from the moss. Seafood chowder, fish cakes and mussels are other menu items.

O'Leary

Sitting in the midst of potato-farm country, this rural community has several attractions worth seeing.

West Point Lighthouse

In Cedar Dunes Provincial Park on Rte. 14. ⏱*Open mid-May–Sept daily 9am–9pm.* ⬤*$2.50.* ✕♿🅿☎*902-859-3605 or 800-764-6854. www.westpointlighthouse.com.*

The tallest on the island, this distinctive 20m/68ft black-and-white-striped, square lighthouse was constructed in 1875. It was manned until 1963, at which time its lantern was automated by electricity. In 1982 restoration of the complex began, and today the lighthouse contains an **inn ($$)** and **restaurant ($$)** (ℰ*see Address Book*) open to the public as well as paying guests. In the museum, photos show the history of lighthouses in PEI, and West Point's past is documented. A narrow stairway rises to the tower, where examples of lighthouse lenses and lanterns are on

view. From the observation platform at the summit, **views** stretch across the shoreline's dark red dunes.

Potato Museum

Off Rte. 142 at 1 Dewar Lane. ⏱*Open Jun–mid-Oct Mon–Sat 9am–5pm, Sun 1pm–5pm.* ⬤*$6.* ✕♿🅿☎*902-859-2039 off-season 902-853-2312 or 902-859-2606. www.peipotatomuseum.com.*

Given PEI's reputation as a leading potato grower, this museum, fronted by a jumbo-size spud, should come as no surprise. Here, visitors can learn how Sir Walter Raleigh, Sir Francis Drake and even Thomas Jefferson, among others, promoted the popularity of the versatile tuber, first cultivated in Peru perhaps as early as 10,000 years ago. An array of harvesting tools and equipment are on display, plus an interactive Potato Hall of Fame, which introduces visitors to the characteristics of one of the world's largest commercial crops. At the canteen, you can sample potato maple-butter tarts, potato fudge or a potato dog.

The Bottle Houses★★

Rte. 11, Cap-Egmont. ⏱*Open mid-May–mid-Oct as follows: Jul & Aug daily 9am–8 pm. June & Sept 10am–6pm (until 4pm*

PEI Quilts

Quilting is an art form in Atlantic Canada, and in O'Leary, at the **Quilt Gallery**, in business since 1995, some of the best locally made examples are found. All quilts are handmade. Fewer younger women in PEI are getting involved with quilting, so guilds, or clubs, have sprung up on the island to teach the skill and encourage new members. O'Leary's club is called the Northern Lights Quilting Guild, and its members sell their products to this gallery, which, in turn, sells the one-of-a-kind works of art around the world. Heirloom quality quilts range in price from $300 to $3,000. *Rte. 142, lower level of Guardian Drug Complex, 536 Main St., O'Leary. Open year-round Mon–Fri 9am–8pm, Sat 9am–5pm, Sun & holidays 1pm–4pm.* ☎*800-889-2606. www.quiltgallerypei.com.*

Address Book

For dollar sign categories, see the Legend on the cover flap.

WHERE TO STAY

$ Briarwood Inn – *253 Matthew's Lane, Alberton. Closed late-Sept–early Jun.* ☎902-853-2518 or 888-272-2246. *www.briarwood.pe.ca. 6 rooms.* 🔲📶 On the Dock River near Cascumpec Bay, this compound of cottages, one-bedroom lodge and three-storey inn is good for longer stays. Guests can explore the expansive grounds and riverfront or laze away in a lawn chair. The two-level cottage has a screened porch; some inn rooms have Jacuzzi tubs. A continental breakfast is included. Wireless Internet. Briarwood's river cruise is a highlight.

$ The Doctor's Inn – *Rte. 167, Tyne Valley.* ☎902-831-3057. *www.peisland.com/doctorsinn. 3 rooms.* 🔲📶 This country home was built in the 1860s. Two-acre gardens brim with flowers, herbs and vegetables. Ask for a tour and marvel at the varieties of lettuce grown. The house has two guest rooms and one single accommodation. The bathroom is shared. Open year-round, the **dining room ($$)** is open to guests, and by 24hr-advance reservation to the public. Cooked on a woodstove, dinners feature the garden's fresh vegetables.

$$ Briarcliffe Inn B&B – *274 Salutation Cove Rd., Rte. 1, Bedeque.* ☎902-887-2333 or 866-887-3238. *6 rooms.* 🔲📶 This welcoming inn is housed in a three-story 1914 house on spacious grounds. Painted in a soft pastel, each room is individually decorated with patterned duvets and comfortable furnishings. A sumptuous hot breakfast is served on Royal Doulton china with crystal stemware. Themed **dinners ($$$)** are available to guests and the public by 48hr advance reservation only.

$$ Silver Fox Inn – *61 Granville St., Summerside.* ☎902-436-1664 or 800-565-4033. *www.silverfoxinn.net. 6 rooms.* 🔲📶 *Minimum 2-night stay Jun–Sept.* This Queen-Anne house, built in 1890 by noted PEI architect William Critchlow Harris, has been a bed and breakfast inn for 28 years. Situated in Summerside's heritage district, it is within walking distance of the waterfront. Each of the tastefully furnished guest rooms is named after a colouration of a fox pelt as homage to a once-thriving industry on the island. All have en suite bathrooms. A back garden with a two-level deck features koi ponds. A full breakfast is included in the rate. Lunch and afternoon tea are available for purchase daily noon-4pm. An optional **dinner ($$)** is served for guests with 24hr notice. Wireless Internet is available.

WHERE TO EAT

$$ Brothers Two Restaurant – *618 Water St., Summerside.* ☎902-436-9654. *www.peisland.com/brotherstwo/index.html.* **Canadian.** For a generation, Brothers Two has been a Summerside institution, mostly because of its steak and seafood offerings, but in recent years, as the host of the summer **Feast Dinner Theatre ($$)** . There's a bit of everything here (including a children's menu): seafood, steaks, chicken and BBQ ribs. Stand-alone seafood dishes, such as poached scallops, charbroiled Atlantic salmon and coconut-battered shrimp, are on the comprehensive menu, as well as gourmet pizza, burgers and sandwiches. For a low-calorie side dish, try the smashed cauliflower. The loaves of house-made bread, especially the Tuscan rosemary, are an extra treat.

$$ West Point Lighthouse – *Rte. 14 and Cedar Dunes Park Rd., O'Leary.* ☎902-859-3605 or 800-764-6854 (North America only). *www.westpointlighthouse.com/rest.htm. Closed Nov–mid-May.* **Seafood.** It's one-stop shopping at the West Point Lighthouse on the southwestern tip of the island. There's a restaurant open for breakfast, lunch and dinner, where the seafood chowder is delicious, as are the cold lobster sandwich and PEI blue mussels. Yet some customers come to eat here simply for the view of the Northumberland Strait and the expansive beach below. There's also a popular patio deck for dining. Vegetarian dishes are available. The complex includes a 9-room **inn ($$)**, with one guestroom located in the lighthouse, itself; all guest rooms have private baths. A museum and gift shop are also on the premises.

Courtesy of The Bottle Houses

Six-gabled house and gardens at The Bottle Houses, Cap-Egmont

May & Oct). $5. ☎902-854-2987. *www.bottlehouses.com.*

At this remarkable site, some 30,000 coloured bottles have been recycled to form several buildings. Begun in 1974 the surroundings gardens, complete with roses, are almost as impressive as the bottle structures. Three structures— a **house** with six gables, a **tavern** and a **chapel**—were built from 1980 to 1983 by the late Édouard Arsenault, a gifted Acadian craftsman. The complex is now run by his daughter, and the attraction has been featured on TV shows and on the Internet. The landscaping includes butterfly, rock, perennial and fragrance gardens.

Our Lady of Mont-Carmel Acadian Church

In Mont-Carmel, on Rte. 11, east of Rte. 124. ◷*Open Jun–Sept daily 8am–8pm. Rest of the year Sun 9am–5pm.* ☎902-854-2789.

Overlooking Northumberland Strait just east of Cap-Egmont, this twin-steepled brick church (1896) replaces two earlier wooden structures, the first of which was built in 1820 as a mission church for the Acadian community of Mont-Carmel. The church's symmetrical façade and rounded interior vaults are reminiscent of religious architecture in France's Poitou region, original home of most of the island's first Acadian settlers.

PEI Products

Industrious islanders offer the public a free glimpse into the manufacturing process as well as free samples at several local businesses. Stop in at **Island Farmhouse Gouda** *(off Rte. 223 in Winsloe North;* ☎902-368-1506)*,* locally known as the Cheeselady's, to view a short video on the Dutch way of making cheese and visit the processing room. Then sample Gouda variations such as pepper and mustard, red chili pepper, herb or garlic.

For some wonderful smoked salmon, visit **Kim Dormaar & Sons'** smokehouse in Ebenezar *(off Rte 10;* ☎902-964-3001; *http://smokedsalmon.isn.net).* Here, a fascinating explanation of the smoking process, a view of the smoking chambers and a generous sampling of products await visitors. Kim will treat you to tidbits of smoked eel, Atlantic salmon, salmon caviar, scallops, mussels, mackerel and trout (try the steelhead with pepper and maple syrup).

NEWFOUNDLAND AND LABRADOR

POPULATION 507,475 – MAP INSIDE BACK COVER

The largest of the Atlantic provinces, Newfoundland [pronounced New-fun-LAND] and Labrador consists of the rocky island named Newfoundland and the mountainous mainland of Labrador, with a combined landmass of 405,720sq km/156,648sq mi. The island lies at the eastern end of the Gulf of St. Lawrence, and is separated from Quebec and Labrador by the Strait of Belle Isle, and from Nova Scotia by the Cabot Strait. Newfoundland boasts a number of superlatives: the easternmost point in North America (Cape Spear), the oldest European settlement in North America (L' Anse aux Meadows) and the oldest English-founded city in North America (St. John's), among them.

The island comprises the Avalon Peninsula, the easternmost landmass, where most people arrive by air carriers to the capital city of St. John's; the Bonavista Peninsula to the north, with its charming village of Trinity; the Burin Peninsula to the south, departure point for the French footholds of islands Saint-Pierre and Miquelon; central Newfoundland, which is relatively undeveloped, except for the towns of Gander and Grand Falls-Windsor; the west coast, which holds Channel-Port aux Basques, departure point for ferries to Nova Scotia; and the Great Northern Peninsula, home to Gros Morne National Park, Port au Choix National Historic Site and L'Anse aux Meadows. Across the Strait of Belle Isle, the tilted, triangular-shaped landmass that is Labrador abuts Quebec and reaches north nearly to the Arctic. Its barren, largely treeless interior gives way to settlements along the deeply indented coast. As well as an array of remarkable people whose ancestry dates back thousands of years—about one-third of Labrador's population is aboriginal—this vast frontier holds a wealth of natural resources that, combined with offshore oil, are bringing prosperity to the province. Thanks to a lack of commercialism, the great outdoors is waiting to be explored. In Newfoundland and Labrador, much of the sea and landscape have been preserved, so far, for mankind's enjoyment.

Newfoundland and Labrador Tourism

Cape Spear, Avalon Peninsula, Newfoundland

Practical Information

GETTING THERE

BY AIR

St. John's International Airport (YYT) (☎709-758-8500. www.stjohns airport.com): **Air Canada** provides direct flights from Calgary, Toronto, Montreal and Halifax (☎888-247-2262. www.aircanada.com); **WestJet** (☎800-538-5696. www.westjet.com) flies directly from Calgary, Toronto and Halifax; **Continental** (☎800-231-0856. www. continental.com) flies from Newark, NJ; and **Lufthansa** (☎800-563-5954. www.lufthansa.com.) from Toronto and Halifax. **Air Canada Jazz** (☎888-247-2262. www.aircanada.com) flies into Gander International Airport (YQX) (☎709-256-6668. www.ganderairport. com) and the **Happy Valley-Goose Bay Airport (YYR)** (☎709-896-5445. www.goosebayairport.com) in Labrador. **Air Labrador** (☎709-753-5593 or 800-563-0342. www.airlabrador.com) and **Provincial Airlines** (☎709-576-1666 or 800-563-2800. www.provincial airlines.ca), which includes **Innu Mikun** Airlines, provide regular connections within the province.

BY BOAT

Passenger and car ferry service is available from North Sydney, NS, to Channel-Port aux Basques (departs year-round daily; 6hrs 30min, 5hrs in summer and to Argentia (mid-Jun–1st week Sept Mon, Wed 7:30am, Fri 3:30pm; rest of Sept Mon 6am; 14hrs). For schedules and reservations, contact **Marine Atlantic,** North Sydney, NS (☎800-341-7981, Canada/US; www.marine-atlantic.ca).). Connecting bus service to inland destinations from Channel-Port aux Basques: **DRL Coachlines** (☎709-263-2171 or 888-263-1854; www.drlgroup.com). **Provincial Ferry Services** (☎709-729-2300. www.tw.gov.nl.ca) serves seacoast towns in Newfoundland and eastern Laborador. **Relais Nordic** (☎800-463-0680. www.relaisnordic.com) links Quebec's lower north shore with Labrador. **Note:** Advance reservations are recommended for all ferry services.

Fuel tanks must be no more than three-quarters full. *For ferry service to* **Saint-Pierre** *and* **Miquelon,** *see SAINT-PIERRE AND MIQUELON.*

GETTING AROUND

BY BUS

DRL Coachlines – Scheduled service and charter tours. ☎709-263-2171 or 888-263-1854; www.drlgroup.com.

BY CAR

See St. John's Practical Information for rental car listings.

ROAD REGULATIONS

The 910km/565mi Trans-Canada Highway (Rte. 1) traverses Newfoundland from Channel-Port aux Basques east to St. John's; most secondary highways are paved. The condition of gravel roads varies according to traffic and weather. Main roads are passable during winter, but it is advisable to check with local authorities before departure (☎709-729-2381, Dec–Mar or access www.roads.gov.nl.ca). **Seat belt** use is compulsory. **Cell phone** use is prohibited, unless it is a hands-free apparatus. Radar detectors are illegal. A person's blood alcohol content must not exceed .05 mg of alcohol per litre of blood. Speed limits, unless otherwise posted, are 100km/h(60mph) on four-lane divided highways, 80km/h (50mph) on secondary highways and 50km/h (30mph) on gravel roads. There are some 125,000 **moose** on the island, and they frequently wander onto highways. Use extreme caution; slow down and do not increase speed until any sighted moose has returned to the forest. Be particularly careful when driving at night and pay attention to signage on roads identifying places where moose often cross.

GENERAL INFORMATION

VISITOR INFORMATION

Travel guides, hunting and fishing guides and road maps are available free of charge from **Newfoundland and Labrador Tourism,** PO Box 8700, St.

John'sNL, A1B 4J6. ☏709-729-2830 or 800-563-6353. www.newfoundlandlabrador.com.

ACCOMMODATIONS

For a listing of suggested lodgings, ⓒ*see the Address Books throughout the chapter.* Hotels, motels, inns and bed & breakfasts cannot be booked through a central number or website. The province has adopted the national Canada Select Accommodations Rating Program. To search for accommodations by category, go online to www.newfoundlandlabrador.com/PlanATrip/PlacesToStay.

For a complete list of St. John's accommodations, go online to www.stjohns.ca/visitors/accommodation/index.jsp. ⓒNote that some lodgings in Labrador do not accept credit cards.

TIME ZONES

Most of Labrador observes Atlantic Standard Time; however, the extreme eastern portion—the area from L'Anse-au-Claire to Black Tickle—operates on Newfoundland Standard Time. Newfoundland Standard Time is 30min ahead of Atlantic Standard Time and 1hr 30min ahead of Eastern Standard Time. Daylight Saving Time is observed from the second Sunday in March to the first Sunday in November.

TAXES

In Newfoundland and Labrador a Harmonized Sales Tax (HST) is levied at a single rate of 14%. ⓒNote HST tax refunds are not available anymore to non-Canadian visitors.

LIQUOR LAWS

Liquor and wine are available only from government stores except in remote areas where local stores are licensed. Beer is available in most convenience stores. The legal drinking age is 19.

RECREATION

Newfoundland and Labrador offers a variety of recreational places and activities. A coastal expanse along Bonavista Bay, Terra Nova National Park offers **canoeing and kayaking,** hiking, biking, fishing, camping—and even swimming at Sandy Pond.

At the other end of the province, Gros Morne National Park is known for its spectacular fjords and scenery. Camping, boating and fishing are major activities; for serious outdoor enthusiasts, **hiking** its many wilderness trails is a must. Some 14 provincial parks permit overnight camping as well as six scenic day-use provincial parks that have picnic facilities and basic amenities; for details www.env.gov.nl.ca/parks. Ocean swimming is not popular in Newfoundland, due to the cool water temperature, but some beaches lend themselves to beachcombing. Scenic coastal trails like the East Coast Trail out of St. John's offer exercise and beautiful views. The province is blessed with a multitude of lakes and rivers, popular with **anglers** (permit required for non-residents). National parks have specific fishing requirements and regulations; visit online www.pc.gc.ca. **Eureka Outdoors** (Corner Brook; ☏709-489-8354; www.eurekaoutdoors.nf.ca) and **Deep Blue Fishing** (Pasadena; ☏709-686-5793; www.deepbluefishing.ca) are two popular angling companies. **Birding** is big on Witless Bay, where puffin tours depart, as well as at Cape St. Mary's Ecological Reserve, home to gannets, on the Avalon Peninsula. (ⓒ*Also see Practical Information for Labrador p266.*)

PROVINCIAL HOLIDAY
The Queen's Birthday (Victoria Day): Monday nearest May 24

PRINCIPAL FESTIVALS

mid-Feb **Corner Brook Winter Carnival:** *Corner Brook*

Jul **Exploits Valley Salmon Festival:** *Grand Falls-Windsor*

    Summer Lobster Festival: *Cowhead, Gros Morne National Park*

    Festival of Folk Song and Dance: *Burin*

    Point Leamington Day Festival: *Point Lemington*

Jul–early Aug **Stephenville Festival:** *Stephenville*

mid–Jul **Bird Island Festival:** *Ellison*

Jul 14 **Bastille Day:** *St. Pierre*

Aug **Royal St. John's Regatta:** *St. John's*

    Annual Newfoundland and Labrador Folk Festival: *St. John's*

mid-Aug **Labrador Straits Bakeapple Folk Festival:** *Point Amour*

- **Information:** Newfoundland and Labrador Tourism. ☎709-729-2830 or 800-563-6353. www.newfoundlandlabrador.com. Also the government's tourism, culture and recreation website: www.tcr.gov.nl.ca. ☎709-729-0862 (in St. John's).
- ▶ **Orient Yourself:** In this guide, the province is divided into six sections, beginning with Newfoundland: the Avalon Peninsula, and the provincial capital of St. John's. From St. John's and environs, the Bonavista Peninsula to the north is explored, and then to the southwest, the Burin Peninsula, including the islands of Saint-Pierre and Miquelon, both part of France. The vastness of the interior of the island, Central Newfoundland, follows. Next comes the Great Northern Peninsula and lastly, across the Strait of Belle Isle, Labrador.
- ⊛ **Don't Miss:** L'Anse aux Meadow, especially if you are a history buff; Gros Morne if you love nature; Saint-Pierre if you've never been to France; and Trinity if you seek tranquillity.
- ⊙ **Organizing Your Time:** Because of the mild weather this time of year, July through September is the best time to visit. To see most of the attractions, two weeks are needed, since sights are clustered at each (east-west) end of Newfoundland and distances are great, especially in Labrador. One week is sufficient if you plan to see just Labrador, or only Newfoundland's St. John's area, Avalon and Bonavista peninsulas. But once you discover Trinity, you may want to linger longer, and Labrador's stark, rugged landscape often compels outdoor enthusiasts to keep on exploring, or at least to return.
- **Kids** **Especially for Kids:** Johnson GEO Centre in St. John's.

A Bit of Geology

Beginnings – The province lies at the northeastern end of the Appalachian mountain system. About 400 million years ago it was formed by the continental drift. Central Newfoundland is actually the remains of an ocean floor from 500 million years ago, and the west coast is part of ancient North America. The east coast was once attached to southwestern Europe or possibly North Africa. For the past 200 million years, erosion has been at work in the province, in the form of glaciation and rivers. About 18,000 years ago, the Laurentide Ice Sheet covered most of Canada, including Labrador. Glaciers retreated 6,000 years later, and deep fjords, like those of Gros Morne National Park's were created and flooded by the sea.

The Island – Called "The Rock" for its craggy profile, the island of the province has a beautiful, deeply indented 9,650km/6,000mi-long coastline, studded with bays, coves and islands. In the north and west, the coast is grandiose with towering cliffs and deep fjords. From the heights of the **Long Range Mountains** in the west, a continuation of the Appalachians, the land slopes east

and northeast. Parts of the interior are heavily forested; others are expanses of rocky barrens and boggy peat lands, a legacy of glaciers, as are the multitude of lakes and rivers. Central Newfoundland is largely flat terrain but with occasional **tolts**—solitary knobs of rock (known as monadnocks in New England), some as high as 100m/62ft, that are the result of erosion by rivers and glaciers.

The most common fish found offshore and inshore in Newfoundland and Labrador's waters are Arctic char, Atlantic salmon, herring, mackerel, rainbow trout, Atlantic catfish, cod (in smaller numbers), turbot, haddock, halibut, ocean perch and flounder. Some shellfish, including lobster and blue mussels, are also found.

Conifers such as balsam fir, white spruce, larch and tamarack are quite common; white birch, the speckled alder, and the pin cherry also may be seen. Newfoundland's wild flowers include lady slippers, pitcher plants, violets, rhododendrons, star flowers, labrador tea as well as wild plants such as sarsaparilla, cranberry and bog rosemary.

Labrador – A rugged land of high mountains (Cirque Mountain, in the **Torngats** of the north, reaches 1,676m/5,500ft),

Labrador also possesses coastal settlements nestling under high cliffs; a barren, largely treeless terrain lies inland. Unlike the island, Labrador forms part of the Canadian Shield. Its 29,000 people reside primarily along the coast and around the mines in Labrador's rich iron-ore belt. As to its wild denizens, Labrador shelters a variety of animal life such as snowshoe hares, wolves and the world's largest caribou herd, numbering some 600,000.

The Banks – In Newfoundland "banks" are not money-lending institutions but vast areas of shallow water in the Atlantic to the south and east of the province—usually less than 100m/328ft-deep extensions of the continental shelf. For 500 years these waters have attracted fishermen to the fish-breeding grounds. The largest and richest of the grounds is the **Grand Banks,** an area of approximately 282,500sq km/109,073sq mi where the cold Labrador Current meets the warmer Gulf Stream. Sinking below the warmer one, the cold current stirs up plankton on the seabed. The plankton rises to the surface, attracting great schools of fish.

Climate – Newfoundland has a temperate marine climate, with winters averaging a normal 0°C/32°F, and summers 16°C/60.8°F or slightly higher. Normal annual rainfall is 1050mm/41in, and snowfall is 300mm/12in on average. Labrador's winters are much colder than the island's, but summer temperatures can be surprisingly higher.

A Bit of History

Earliest Peoples – Prior to European contact, Newfoundland was the ancestral land of the **Beothuk** Indians, most probably the descendants of the Maritime Archaic people of Newfoundland and Labrador. Primarily through stone tools unearthed on the island, ancestors of the Beothuks have been traced to about 1000 years ago. The Maritime Archaic Indians appear to have died out in Newfoundland about 3200 years ago. The language of the Beothuks is

believed to be of the Algonquian family, similar to that spoken by today's Innu in Quebec and Labrador. Unlike Labrador, where moose were present, Newfoundland had only caribou and beaver for the Beothuks to hunt; thus the Beothuks derived their sustenance largely from the sea (some 125,000 moose inhabit Newfoundland today, however, progeny of two males and two females from New Brunswick released in 1904). From the Arctic, Paleoeskimos arrived in Labrador, but they withdrew about 1,500 years ago, leaving the area to be re-occupied by the descendants of the Montagnais-Naskapi (or Innu) and Inui. Today Labrador's aboriginal peoples comprise the **Inuit** (formerly the Thule people who migrated to Labrador from the Arctic about 1300), the **Innu** (descendants of the Algonquian-speaking tribes at the time of European arrival), the **Mi'kmaq** (Algonquian hunter-gatherers) and the **Métis** (descendants of intermarriages between Europeans and Labrador's native people).

European Exploration – An Icelandic trader, Bjarni Herjolfsson, was likely the first European to see North America in mid-985 or 986, and his first sighting would have been Newfoundland. Leif Ericsson, eldest son of Eric the Red, later explored parts of the island at around 1000. **John Cabot** is believed to have entered St. John's harbour on Saint John's day in 1497. By the turn of the 15C, ships from several European countries were using the harbour as a fishing base. Portuguese explorer **João Fernandes Lavrador** was the next European explorer after the Vikings to see Labrador, in 1498. He was a *lavardor* or landholder, in the Azores, the likely source of the name Labrador. (Newfoundland, or new found land is the translation of the Latin *terra nova*.) The subsequent occupation by Basque fishermen, as well as the British and French who also exploited the coastal fishery, was fiercely opposed by the Inuit to the north and the Naskapi (Innu) in the south.

Confederation and Union – Representatives from Newfoundland attended the final conference in the series beginning

Coast near Gros Morne National Park

Sandra Phinney/Michelin

with the 1864 Charlottetown Conference that ultimately led to Confederation in 1867. However, Newfoundland chose not to join, and postponed the decision. After WW II, the topic once again came up, and a referendum was held in 1948. In March 1949 Newfoundland became Canada's tenth province. A contentious political issue had been a 25-year dispute between Quebec and Newfoundland over Labrador. In 1927 a decision by the Judicial Committee of the Privy Council in London awarded Labrador to Newfoundland, as a protectorate. The boundary was confirmed in the Terms of Union (now the Newfoundland Act), which is enshrined in Canada's Constitution Act of 1982. The official name of the province was formally changed to Newfoundland and Labrador in 2001 by an amendment to the constitution. St. John's-born artist Christopher Pratt designed the provincial flag.

Labrador's Formation – In 1763 the British encouraged the *Unitas Fratrum,* better known as the **Moravians,** to establish a settlement north of the areas frequented by European fishermen so they could convert the Inuit; the Moravians had had some "success" with missionary work in Greenland with the Inuit there. Eventually, over centuries, the northernmost Moravian missions of Killinek (now Killiniq), Ramah, Zoar, Okak and Hebron were closed (the latter two in the 1950s). Many of the missionaries resettled in Nain, Makkovik and Hope-

dale. Since the beginning of the 19C, intermarriage has taken place; descendants formed the Labrador Inuit Association in 1973. In southern Labrador, the intermarriages resulted in what is now known as the Labrador Métis Nation. After Britain took control of Newfoundland, the Hudson's Bay Company also arrived (1863) and dominated the fur trade for about 100 years. The last Hudson's Bay outpost was built in 1923; it is now a museum in North West River.

In 2005 Labrador Inuit ratified a longstanding land claim, originally filed in 1977, with the provincial and federal governments. The result was the beginning of Inuit self-government in the **Nunatsiavut** region of Labrador, which comprises 72,500sq km/28,000sq mi in northern Labrador. Labrador Inuit will own about one-fourth of this land, and have land-use rights in the remainder. The agreement also established the 9,600sq km/3,700sq mi **Torngat Mountains National Park Reserve.** Elections for the legislative assembly were held in 2006, and the presidential election will be held in October 2008.

The Voisey's Bay Nickel Company is investing $3 billon to mine and process nickel from a site discovered in 1993 in Labrador. In 1996 the company announced that Argentia, on Newfoundland's Avalon Peninsula, would be the location of its smelter refinery, but operational headquarters would be located in Labrador, in Happy Valley-Goose Bay.

Collapse of the Fishery – For 500 years the waters of Newfoundland's Banks attracted fishermen to the fish-breeding grounds. By the mid-16C mariners were coming to these fishing grounds by the thousands. An account in 1578 mentioned Spanish, Portuguese, French and English ships in the area in search of cod and whales. Though herring was fished, cod was the traditional catch in the Grand Banks. The boats Newfoundlanders used were called "bankers." Large schooners left the ports to fish the banks for months at a time. When schools of fish were located, actual fishing was done from **dories,** small flat-bottomed open craft stored on deck during the voyage. The catch was either salted on the schooner's deck and stored in the hold ("wet" fishery) or taken ashore and dried on land on wooden racks known as **flakes** ("dry" fishery). From 1945 on, the use of trawlers was the trend, because fish could better be caught en masse. Filleting plants replaced flakes and refrigeration supplanted salting. In 1992, however, it became evident that cod stocks had collapsed due to over-fishing from both Canadian and international fishers, and the Canadian government placed a moratorium on commercial cod fishing; some 40,000 people lost their jobs. Ten years later, stocks had shown no signs of recovery and on April 24, 2003, the fisheries minister announced the closing of the Canadian commercial cod fishery. The social and economic consequences might have been devastating but for the emergence of a far more profitable industry: mineral extraction, particularly oil and gas.

Offshore Oil – Completed in 1997, the **Hibernia oil platform** constructed at Bull Arm is said to be the heaviest offshore oil rig manufactured to date. Secured to its drill site some 315km/200mi out in the Grand Banks, the platform weighs over 1.2 million tonnes/1.3 million tons, heavy enough, it is projected, to withstand collision with the giant icebergs common in these waters. The controversial project, funded with private and public money, is estimated to have cost $6 billion. Production began in 1997; output from one well is about 150,000 barrels of oil a day; new wells are being developed.

In 2002 production began at the **Terra Nova** site, and in 2005 at the **White Rose** site, both some 350km/219mi off the coast. The two sites operate from innovative floating production storage and off-loading vessels that can be moved in case of inclement conditions. White Rose is now bringing in 140,000 barrels a day. Husky Energy Ltd., adjacent to White Rose, will be developing its North Amethyst site to eventually produce 70 million barrels a day, now that it has regulatory approval.

Lifestyle and Food – The population of the province increased in the last half of 2007—the first time in 15 years. Newfoundlanders who had been leaving to find work in the western provinces are now coming home. The biggest change, however, is that the Gross Domestic Product (GDP) per capita went from $10,000 below the national average in 1997 to $10,000 above the average of $46,221 in 2007. Thus, despite the disaster in the cod fishery, the outlook for the province is one of guarded euphoria.

About one-quarter of the island's population resides in the capital city of St. John's; the remainder lives mainly in small coastal fishing villages known as **outports**. Traditionally an outport was any community outside St. John's, but today, with the rise of industrial centres such as Corner Brook, the term is applied to tiny coastal settlements with moored dories and colourful "box" houses. In some outports a small "museum" preserves each community's past. Housed in historic homes or commercial buildings (often with a crafts shop annexed), these collections of donated artifacts are primarily of local interest.

Arctic char, lobster, salmon, snow crab and halibut are favourite seafood dishes, and **squid burgers** are an island peculiarity. A traditional meal is a **Jigg's Dinner** of salt beef, vegetables and peas pudding (split yellow peas baked to a hummus-like consistency).

AVALON PENINSULA

It's been said that Newfoundland and North America begin at the Avalon Peninsula: Cape Spear is the most easterly point on the continent. It was the site of one of the first English settlements in Canada, in 1583. Because of the peninsula's location, the first nonstop trans-Atlantic flight took place from here in 1919, and the first trans-Atlantic wireless signal was received on Signal Hill in 1901. The peninsula lies in the southeast section of the island. On a map, the Avalon Peninsula looks like it is hanging onto the main part of Newfoundland by a thread: this narrow landmass is the 5km/3mi-wide Isthmus of Avalon. At 10,360sq km/4000sq mi, the peninsula is surprisingly large. About half of the province's population lives on this peninsula, the capital city of St. John's being the most populated. Geographically, the peninsula thrusts out into the rich fishing grounds of the north Atlantic. Since the early 1800s, the four bays of the peninsula (Trinity, St. Mary's, Conception and Placentia) have been regarded as the most important of the province's fishing industry. Englishman George Calvert's 18C colony was called Avalon after the mythic area where Christianity was supposedly introduced to England; hence the name of the peninsula. The French and English warred over the island during the 17C and 18C, prompting the French to establish Placentia as the peninsula's capital. Today whale-watching and seabird tours are popular, especially in Witless Bay; indeed, the peninsula's fauna has attracted movie crews for the production of three feature films. Tiny Petty Harbour was chosen as the location for *Orca* (1977), *A Whale for the Killing* (1981) and *Rare Birds* (2001).

St. John's★★★

POPULATION 100,646 – MAP P 235

One of the oldest cities in North America, established in 1583 by Royal Charter from Queen Elizabeth I, the capital of Newfoundland and Labrador sits on the northeast arm of the Avalon Peninsula, facing the expansive Atlantic Ocean. This historic seaport owes its founding to a natural, ice-free harbour that now services an international shipping trade. In 2003, the St. John's Port Authority opened Pier 17, a 4,200sq m/45,208sq ft state-of-the-art facility on the east side

Cabot Tower on Signal Hall

©City of St. John's

of the port. Built as a petroleum support and service centre, the pier boasts the latest in environmental containment and safety systems. Thanks to being considered a safe haven (the port authority is within walking distance of downtown St. John's) and the nearest port-of-call to continental Europe, St. John's attracts cruise ships now on a regular basis; approximately 30,000 passengers came ashore during the summer and fall of 2008. Mineral extraction in Labrador as well as offshore oil are favourably impacting the city's economy: office space is at a premium, and St. John's is experiencing a building boom. While historic sites abound in the city, the modern Johnson GEO Centre, opened in 2002, has put St. John's on the world scientific map and is making the province's geological heritage more accessible to the public.

Information: Tourist Office, Gentara Building, 348 Water St. ☎709-576-8106 or www.stjohns.ca.

▶ **Orient Yourself:** *See map of St. John's.* Visitor information centres are located along St. John's harbour. Water Street and Duckworth Street are main thoroughfares, with shops, restaurants, and services. Several historic attractions cluster around Military Road; the Confederation Building and The Rooms arts and culture centre sit high up above the city. Signal Hill rises to the east of the harbour and is the home of the new GEO Centre.

🅿 **Parking:** Parking meters are in effect year-round Mon–Fri 8am–6pm. Cost is $0.25 for 15min, up to a maximum 2hrs. Extended time meters on Harbour Drive permit parking for 8hrs. Check signs for snow-clearance and street-cleaning.

☺ **Don't Miss:** For an comprehensive overview of the province's art, natural features and human history, visit The Rooms.

🕐 **Organizing Your Time:** Allow 2-3 days. Be sure to see the city at night from Cabot Tower on Signal Hill. Take in a seabird excursion at Witless Bay.

Kids Especially for Kids: Signal Hill's military tattoo and the Johnson GEO Centre.

👣 **Also See:** BONAVISTA PENINSULA, BURIN PENINSULA

A Bit of History

Early Years – According to tradition, **John Cabot** entered the harbour on Saint John's day in 1497. Although he sailed under British colours, Cabot (Giovanni Caboto) was Italian by birth. Whether this claim is true or not, it has been established that, by the turn of the 15C, ships from several European countries were using the harbour as a fishing base. Under charter from Elizabeth I of England, **Sir Humphrey Gilbert** (c.1537-83) sailed to North America, arriving in St. John's harbour in 1583. Finding the crews of several countries assembled in one place, he seized the opportunity to declare Her Majesty's sovereignty and thus is credited with giving England its first possession in the New World. Before his death at sea, Gilbert reputedly joined in the customary celebrations in St. John's of "fishing admiral" elections. Determined to maintain their fishing monopolies, England's West Country merchants opposed settlement of Newfoundland; from 1675 to 1677 a formal ban on settlement was in effect. But gradually people associated with the growing fishing industry began to take up year-round residence.

The Anglo-French Wars – Fear of French expansion changed the attitude of the British government toward permanent settlement. The French had established fortifications at Placentia in 1662 and proceeded to mount attacks on British harbours, especially St. John's. The city fell three times to the French, with the final battle in 1762 at the end of the Seven Years' War, though the city was recaptured soon afterward. These attacks prompted the British to fortify the harbour entrance and Signal Hill, a strategic promontory between the sea and the city, but St. John's was never again threatened.

Practical Information

GETTING THERE AND GETTING AROUND

BY AIR

St. John's International Airport Authority (YYT) is the arrival and departure airport (☎709-758-8500; www.stjohnsairport.com) for several carriers. The airport is served by one taxi company, City Wide Taxi. Taxi rates to hotels in the local area are charged according to zones. **Air Canada** and **Air Canada Jazz,** www.aircanada.ca, www.flyjazz.ca, ☎888-247-2262. **Air Labrador** Head office: 15 Duffy Pl., St. John's. ☎709-758-0002 or 800-563-0342. **Air Saint-Pierre,** www.airsaintpierre.com, ☎877-277-7765 or 011-508 41 00 00. **Air Transat,** www.airtransat.com, ☎866-847-1112. **Continental,** www.continental.com, ☎800-231-0856. **Lufthansa,** www.lufthansa.com, ☎800-563-5954. Provincial Airlines: **St. John's International Airport,** RCAF Rd., Hangar #4. ☎709-576-1800 or 709-576-1666 or ☎800-563-2800. www.provincialairlines.ca Includes **Innu Mikun Airlines**. **Sunwing** (seasonal charter), www.sunwing.ca , ☎877-786-9464. **WestJet,** www.westjet.com, ☎800-538-5696

BY BOAT

Argentia, on the Avalon Peninsula, is the closest town to St. John's that operates a passenger and car **ferry** (from North Sydney, Nova Scotia): ☎800-341-7981. www.marine-atlantic.ca. Argentia is a 90-min drive from the capital city. Newhook's Bus Service takes passengers from the ferry terminal to St. John's: ☎709-227-2552.

Several **cruise lines** now stop in several ports in Newfoundland and Labrador (www.cruisenewfoundland.com).

BY CAR

The airport has six car rental companies on-site. Reserve beforehand if possible for May through September visits.
Avis Rent-A-Car Ltd ☎709-722-6620 www.avis.com. **Budget Car & Truck Rental,** ☎709-747-1234, www.budget.com. **Hertz Rent-A-Car,** ☎709-722-4307 or b709-722-4333, www.hertz.com. **National Tilden,** ☎709-722-4333, www.nationalcar.com. **Thrifty Car Rental,** ☎709-722-6000, www.thrifty.

com. **Enterprise Rent-A-Car Canada,** 835 Topsail Rd., Unit 3, Mount Pearl. ☎709-738-3900, www.enterprise.com. **Discount Car Rental** (350 Kenmount Rd.;☎709-722-6699) and **Rent-A-Wreck** (909 Topsail Rd., Mount Pearl; ☎709-753-1036).

BY TAXI

There are 364 taxis in St. John's (the limit by city law); most drivers know the city (there are many one-way streets in the downtown). Traffic jams are not common, however.
Ann's Taxi & Tours (Conception Bay South. ☎709-834-6666)
Avalon Taxi (190 Water St. ☎709-722-6070)
Bonavista North Transportation Ltd. (1 Macklin Pl. ☎709-579-3188)
Bradbury's Taxi Bay Roberts (13 Queen St. ☎709-754-2635)
Bugden's Taxi Ltd. (266 Blackmarsh Rd. ☎709-726-4400)
Casino Cabs (135 A Campbell Ave. ☎709-579-5999)
City Wide Taxi (5 Adelaide St. ☎709-722-0003)

BY BUS OR SHUTTLE

Bay d'Espoir Bus Service – Head of Bay d'Espoir and St. Albans to Grand Falls-Windsor and St. John's, ☎709-538-3429
Bonavista North Transportation Ltd. – Wesleyville to St. John's, ☎709-536-3044
Thornhill's/Bay d'Espoir Bus Service – Harbour Breton, Head of Bay d'Espoir and St. Albans to Bishop's Falls, Grand Falls-Windsor and St. John's, ☎866-538-3429
Cheeseman's Bus/Taxi Service – Burin to St. John's, ☎709-891-1866
Foote's Taxi – Fortune to St. John's, ☎709-382-0491 or 800-866-1181
Venture Bus Line – Bonavista to St. John's, ☎709-722-4249
Fleetline Bus Service – Carbonear to Holyrood and St. John's. ☎709-229-7600
Newhook's Bus Service – Argentia ferry/Placentia to St. John's, ☎709-227-2552

LOCAL TRANSIT

Metrobus Transit, serving St. John's and Mount Pearl, ☎709-722-9400, www.metrobus.com, 🚌$2.25 or 10 rides for 🚌$20

Wheelway (transit service for the disabled in St. John's area), ☎709-753-2877, www.wheelway.ca

GENERAL INFORMATION

VISITOR INFORMATION

Gentara Building, 348 Water St., St. John's. ☎709-576-8106, www.stjohns. ca. Open year-round Mon–Fri 9am–4:30 pm (Newfoundland Standard Time); also Jun–Sept Sat–Sun 9am–5pm.

ACCOMMODATIONS

For a listing of suggested lodgings, 🕮 *see the Address Book.* Hotels, motels, inns and bed & breakfasts cannot be booked through a central number or website. For a complete list of St. John's accommodations, go online to www.stjohns. ca/visitors/accommodation/index.jsp

LOCAL MEDIA

Daily: *The Independent* (www. theindependent.ca), *The Telegram* (www.thetelegram.com) and *The Globe and Mail* (national newspaper, www.globeandmail.ca). **Bi-weekly:** *The Scope* (www.thescope.ca) free arts & entertainment newspaper.

SPECTATOR SPORTS

St. John's Fog Devils Hockey Club, part of the Quebec Major Junior Hockey League. Games at the Mile One Stadium, New Gower St., St John's. ☎709-754-8282.www.fogdevils.com.

Newfoundland Rock Rugby Team plays at Swiler's Rugby Park, St. John's. ☎709-895-2608. www.rockrugby.ca

Newfoundland Soccer Association and the **Memorial University Seahawks** play at King George V Park. Located at the head of Quidi Vidi Lake in downtown St. John's. ☎709-576-0601. www.nlsa.ca

St. John's Amateur Baseball has senior and junior leagues and plays at St. Patrick's Park (corner of Empire Ave. and Carpasian Rd., St. John's. ☎709-726-7721).

St. John's Memorial Stadium (King's Bridge Rd. at Lake Ave. near Quidi Vidi Lake. ☎709-576-7688) offers sporting and entertainment events. Seating varies: concerts & boxing 4,000; basketball 3,000; ice events 2,500.

ENTERTAINMENT

PERFORMING ARTS

The Arts and Culture Centre Allandale Rd. and Prince Philip Dr., near Memorial University. ☎709-729-3900. www.stjohns.artsandculturecentre. ca/main.asp

Bowring Park Amphitheatre Waterford Bridge Rd., off Rte. 1, St. John's. ☎709-576-8601, Open air theatre with various musical, comedic and theatrical acts, including "Shakespeare by the Sea". Bench seating, with some grass areas. 🕑Open May–Sept.

Concerts Under the Dome Cochrane Street United Church, 81 Cochrane St. ☎709-722-3023 or tickets ☎709-729-3900. www.cochranestreetuc.com

Molson Canadian Theatre at Mile One Stadium New Gower St. ☎709-576-7657. www.mileonestadium.ca Theatrical events.

Pigeon Inlet Productions Various locations in the city with traditional music and dance. ☎888-754-7377. www.pigeoninlet.com

The Resource Centre for the Arts LSPU Hall, 3 Victoria St. ☎709-753-4531. www.rca.nf.ca. Stage productions by the resident RCA Theatre Company.

Spirit Of Newfoundland Productions 6 Cathedral St.,☎709-579-3023 or ☎877-661-3023. www.spiritof newfoundland.com. Comedic dinner theatre with Newfoundland & Labrador-based plays.

CINEMA

Empire Cinemas (Mount Pearl Shopping Centre, 760 Topsail Rd., Mount Pearl. ☎709-364-8527)

Empire Studio 12 (48 Kenmount Rd., St. John's. ☎709-722-5775)

NIGHTCLUBS

Junctions Club – (208 Water St. ☎709-689-2557). Dance club.

Curious – (Holdsworth Court on George St. ☎709-722-6999). Gay club.

Liquid Ice – (186B Water St. ☎709-753-4884) Underground/new music.

Club Etomic – (12-14 George St. ☎709-576-2582). Reggae, hip-hop.
Breezeway – (First Floor, University Centre, Memorial University. ☎709-737-7633). Students, faculty & guests.
Whalen's Pub & Grill – (32 George St. ☎709-722-4900) Sports bar.

TOURS

Adventure Newfoundland (day tours, expeditions). 124 Water St., St. John's. ☎709-722-3524. www.adventurenewfoundland.com Year-round.
Bluestone Tours (helicopter or float plane). 34 Queen's Rd., St. John's. ☎709-754-7544. www.thebluestoneinn.com. ◷Open year-round.
British Island Tours (double-decker buses). 140 Water St., Ste. 303, St. John's. ☎709-738-8687. www.british islandtours.com. Jun–Oct.
Iceberg Quest Ocean Tours (sailing). Pier 7, Harbour Dr., St. John's. ☎709-884-1888. www.icebergquest.com. May–Sept.
O'Boyle's Walking Tours (downtown St. John's) Fairmont Hotel, Cavendish Sq. ☎709-364-6845. www.boyletours.com. Jun–mid-Sept.

SHOPPING

MALLS
Avalon Mall Regional Shopping Centre (48 Kenmount Rd. ☎709-753-7144)
Churchill Square (173 Elizabeth Ave. ☎709-739-6661)
Mount Pearl Square Shopping Centre (760 Topsail Rd. Mount Pearl. ☎709-364-9284)
Torbay Road Mall (141 Torbay Rd. ☎709-754-1990)
Village Shopping Centre (430 Topsail Rd. ☎709-364-7011)
Individual Boutiques
Craft Council Gallery-Devon House (59 Duckworth St. ☎709-753-2749. www.craftcouncil.nl.ca)
Elizabeth Burry Fine Art and Gift Gallery (118 Duckworth St. ☎709-754-7676. www.elizabethsgallery.com)
Nonia Handicrafts (286 Water St., ☎709-753-8062)
Ocean Front Craft (188 Duckworth St. ☎709-726-8868)
Red Ochre Gallery (96 Duckworth St. ☎709-726-6422. www.redochre gallery.ca)

Devastating Fires – In the 19C the capital suffered five fires that virtually wiped out the entire community each time. The first in 1816 was followed by others until the most extensive of all in 1892. A photo taken by Sir Wilfred Grenfell at the time shows the twin towers of the Basilica of St. John the Baptist, one of the few structures still partially standing amid the devastation. Each time, the city was rebuilt, primarily in prevailing architectural styles such as Gothic Revival and, after the 1892 fire, Second Empire, styles still evident in the historic structures of the city today. The rapid expansion of St. John's as a commercial centre during the 19C was reversed each time by the fires.

Confederation and Beyond – St. John's was a wealthy city in the early 20C and during World War II when it served as a base for North American convoys. After the war the Dominion of Newfoundland's decision to enter Confederation resulted in a decline in the city's economy, despite a substantial infusion of federal funds. Its industries collapsed as cheaper Canadian manufactured goods entered Newfoundland. Port activity suffered and St. John's importance as a fish-exporting centre was reduced as major firms abandoned the salt-fish trade for growing wholesale consumer markets. Finally, the 1992 collapse of the commercial cod fishery dealt a blow to area fish-processing plants.

In the 21C, however, the city has found a prosperity underpinned by the province's vast mineral and oil wealth. The huge nickel mine at Voisey's Bay, Labrador, began production in 2005, three offshore oil fields are producing, and mining companies invested $160 million in exploration in 2007. In that same year, the provincial economy eclipsed even that of Alberta—there is now precious little office space available in St. John's and the city is currently undergoing a building boom.

The Old City★★

The city's **site** borders a **harbour**★★ almost landlocked except for a slim passage to the ocean known as **The Narrows.** Only about 207m/680ft wide, this channel is flanked by 150m/500ft cliffs rising on the north side to form Signal Hill. For about 1.6km/1mi, the harbour widens to nearly 800m/.5mi, surrounded by the steep slopes on which the city is built. Parallel to the water, **Harbour Drive** skirts the busy dock where ships from around the world are often berthed. Narrow streets lined with brightly painted wooden houses, topped with flat or mansard roofs, ascend the hills. Perpendicular to them, the main thoroughfares of the old city, **Water Street** and **Duckworth Street,** contain restaurants, shops and banks. Especially colourful, **George Street** is home to several pubs and eateries.

The imposing building on the hillside that reshaped St. John's skyline in 2004 is called **The Rooms** (what compounds of fisheries buildings were once called). Inspired by early Newfoundland architecture, this modern cultural and heritage centre houses under one roof the Provincial Museum, the Provincial Archives, and the Art Gallery of Newfoundland and Labrador. The basement features an ongoing archaeological dig of a 1775 fort, over which the centre was constructed.

The Rooms★★

9 Bonaventure Ave. ⏱Open Jun–mid-Oct Mon–Sat 10am–5pm (Wed & Thu until 9pm), Sun noon–5pm. Rest of the year Tue–Sat 10am–5pm, Sun noon–5pm. ⏱Closed public holidays. ⬤$5. ✕👥☎709-757-8000. www.therooms.ca.

Dominating the hillside above the city, this striking red-roofed group of white buildings opened in 2004 as a state-of-the-art centre of history, culture and art. Its bold architecture is reflective of early Newfoundland fishing rooms where families gathered to process their day's catch. The complex is the combined repository of the provincial museum, provincial archives and provincial art gallery under one roof. It includes an atrium several levels high, a multimedia theatre and a cafe as well as classrooms and an art studio. Offering a broad and insightful introduction to the province, the complex is devoted to Newfoundland and Labrador's history, prehistory, architecture, art and archaeology as well as archival records.

The origins of the museum are multifaceted and colourful, harking back to the city's first newspaper in 1807, mid-19C trade institutes, world fair exhibits and Newfoundland's Geological Survey. Even the site of the new complex is rife with history: the 2004 complex was erected over the remains of former Fort Townshend, a star-shaped citadel built in the mid-1700s to protect Britain's fishing trade. Subsequent tenants were

Duckworth Street

©City of St. John's

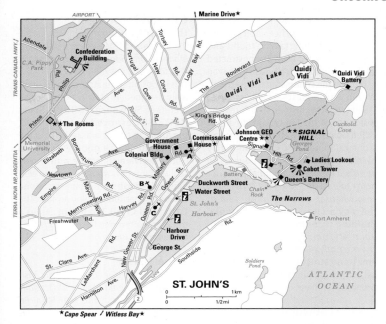

AIRPORT

★ **Marine Drive** ★

Confederation Building

Quidi Vidi

★ **Quidi Vidi Battery**

Quidi Vidi Lake

★★ **The Rooms**

Cuckold Cove

Johnson GEO Centre ★★

★★ **SIGNAL HILL**

Government House

Commissariat House ★

Colonial Bldg.

A

★ **Ladies Lookout**

Cabot Tower

Queen's Battery

B

Duckworth Street

Water Street

St. John's Harbour

Chain Rock

The Narrows

Fort Amherst

C

Harbour Drive

George St.

Soldiers Pond

ATLANTIC OCEAN

ST. JOHN'S

0   1km

0   1/2mi

★ **Cape Spear** / **Witless Bay** ★

the provincial constabulary and the city fire department.

The museum's permanent collection numbers more than one million artifacts covering the archaeology, history and natural history of the province. On Level 3, life after the glaciers retreated is depicted in exhibits exploring 9,000 years of **human occupation,** including Maritime Archaic, Palaeoeskimos, Beothuk and ancestors of today's Innu and Inuit as well as the earliest Europeans to arrive in North America, such as the Norse, Basque fishermen, the British and the French. Among the many artifacts are 7,000 year-old stone tools, 2,000 year-old carved ivory figurines, 500 year-old birchbark containers, European ceramics from the 1600 and 1700s, and an Inuit kayak.

The **natural history** of the province is also explored in the third-floor gallery, including an homage to 30 species of birds in eastern Canada. A giant squid, polar bear, and a rare Newfoundland wolf specimen are on display.

Outside the galleries, in the public spaces, **Fort Townshend** has been re-created as it might have appeared in 1781, with British soldiers and police holding court in what was the first Government House in Newfoundland. Panels also tell the story of the Royal Newfoundland Constabulary since 1870.

On Level 4 the **Art Gallery** showcases Newfoundland and Labradorian works from its permanent collection in a series of thematic installations. A temporary exhibit program is active at the archives, art gallery and museum.

From Level 4, coin-operated *(25 cents)* **viewfinders** provide remarkable views of downtown St. John's and its harbour.

Commissariat House★

King's Bridge Rd. ◷*Open mid-May–Sept daily 10am–5:30pm.* ◉*$3.* ☏*709-729-6730. Off-season 709-729-0592. www.tcr.gov.nl.ca/tcr/historicsites.*

Dating from 1820, this large clapboard house with its tall chimneys was one of the few buildings to escape the 19C fires. Used for many years by the commissariat—the department responsible for supplying the military post of St. John's with non-military provisions—the house also served as the local government pay office. After 1871 it became the rectory for adjacent **Church of St. Thomas (A)**, an elegantly simple edifice (1836) of painted wood. Restored to reflect the 1830s period, the house contains the commissariat offices and kitchen (*ground floor*), entertaining rooms and bedrooms (*second floor*). Reconstructed on the ground, a **coach house** lodges an exhibit on the commissariat's function. Within walking distance (*Military Rd.*) stand two other historic structures: the residence of the lieutenant-governor called **Government House,** a Georgian stone building (1830) surrounded by pleasant grounds (*only the grounds can be visited without appointment;* ⚓*for house tours* ☎*709-729-4494; www.mun. ca/govhouse),* and the former seat of the provincial assembly, the **Colonial Building** (🕐*open year-round Mon–Fri 9am–4:15pm;* 🅿 ☎ *709-729-3065; www.tcr.gov.nl.ca/tcr/historicsites),* a limestone structure with a Neoclassical portico (1850) that now houses the provincial archives.

Basilica Cathedral of St. John the Baptist (B *on map*)

200 Military Rd., corner of Harvey Rd., Military Rd. and Bonaventure Ave. 🕐*Open year-round Mon–Fri 8am–4:45pm, Sat 8am–6pm, Sun 8:30am–12:30pm.* 🕐*Closed major holidays, except for mass.* ♿ 🅿 ☎*709-754-2170. www.thebasilica.ca.*
Situated on the highest point of the ridge above the city, this twin-towered Roman Catholic church has become a landmark, clearly distinguishable from the harbour, Signal Hill and other vantage points. Opened for worship in 1850, the basilica has an ornate interior with statuary and altar carving.

Regatta Day

Each year **Quidi Vidi** (KID-dy VID-dy) **Lake** is the site of St. John's Regatta, the oldest continuously held sporting event in North America (since 1826). Held on the first Wednesday in August (or the first fine day thereafter), the regatta is probably the only civic holiday decided that morning. The local population waits for the cry, "The races are on!" and then crowds the lakeshore to watch competitors row the 2.6km/1.6mi course, the major event of the all-day carnival.

Cathedral of St. John the Baptist (C *on map*)

9 Cathedral St. 🕐*Open early Jun–Sept Mon–Fri 9am–5pm, weekend hours vary.* ⚓*Tours daily.* ☎*709-726-5677.*
This imposing stone structure was originally designed in 1843 by noted British architect Sir **George Gilbert Scott** (1811–78). Destroyed by fire in 1892, the Anglican church was reconstructed only in the 20C, a good example of Gothic Revival architecture with a finely sculpted interior, wooden vaulted ceilings and **reredos,** an ornamental stone or wooden partition behind an altar. The **Cathedral Crypt Tea Room** serves a traditional afternoon tea (*Jul–Aug Mon–Fri 2:30pm–4:30pm*).

Signal Hill★★

🕐*Grounds open year-round daily. Visitor centre open mid-May–mid-Oct daily 10am–6pm; rest of the year Mon–Fri 8:30am–4:30pm.* 🕐*Closed Jan 1, Dec 25-26.* ⚓*$4.* 🅿☎*709-772-5367. www. pc.gc.ca.* 👁*Parks Canada advises that high winds and irregular footing atop Signal Hill can be a dangerous combination: use caution and do not go close to the edge of the cliffs.*
Topped by Cabot Tower, Signal Hill is formed of cliffs rising steeply at the mouth of the harbour. A natural lookout commanding the sea approach, the hill permits splendid views of the city and environs by day and night. Despite its obvious strategic value, Signal Hill was not strongly fortified until the Napoleonic Wars (1803-15). Traditionally used as a signal station to warn of enemy ships, the hill acted in later years as a means to alert merchants to the arrival of their fleets. In 1901 **Guglielmo Marconi** chose the site for an experiment to prove that radio signals could be transmitted long distances by electromagnetic waves. When he reputedly received the letter "S" in Morse code from Poldhu in Cornwall, England – a distance of 2,700km/1,700mi – he made history.
The **visitor centre** contains artifacts, dioramas, audiovisuals and panels on the history of Newfoundland, emphasizing the development of St. John's. Completed in 1898 to memorialize

the quadricentennial of John Cabot's visit to Newfoundland, **Cabot Tower** (🕐 *Jun–Labour Day 8:30am–9pm, Apr–May & Sept–mid-Jan 9am–5pm.* 🕐 *Closed mid-Jan–Mar 31)* also commemorates the diamond jubilee of Queen Victoria's accession. Inside, displays on Signal Hill are complemented by information on communications including a section about Marconi. At the summit of the tower, a viewing platform affords a **panorama**★★★ of the city, the harbour and the coastline as far as Cape Spear, the most easterly point in North America.

A path leads to **Ladies Lookout,** the crown of the hill (160m/525ft) and a vantage point offering views of the surroundings. From **Queen's Battery**—the fortification (1833) that dominates the Narrows—there is a good **view**★ of the harbour. Below is Chain Rock—a white pillar in the Narrows from which a chain was stretched across the harbour entrance in the 18C to keep enemy vessels out. On the other side of the Narrows stand the remains of Fort Amherst (1763), now housing a lighthouse.

In the summer, students in the 19C uniforms of the Royal Newfoundland Regiment perform a **military tattoo** *(Jul–mid-Aug Wed, Thu & weekends 3pm & 7pm, weather permitting;* 💲*$2.50)* consisting of fife-and-drum corps and military drills near the visitor centre. Derived from a Dutch word, tattoo is a bugle or drum signal to call soldiers to quarters at night.

Johnson GEO Centre★★

175 Signal Hill Rd. 🕐 *Open late May–early Oct Mon–Sat 9:30am–5pm, Sun noon–5pm. Rest of the year Tue–Sat 9:30am–5pm, Sun noon–5pm.* 💲*$10.25.* ☎*709-737-7880. www.geocentre.ca.*

Kids This modern, $12 million centre, opened in 2002, was constructed by the Johnson Family Foundation, headed by St. John's-born philanthropist Paul J. Johnson (b.1929), whose interests lie in preserving heritage sites in Newfoundland and Labrador. The centre was built into Signal Hill, whose exposed rock, which is millions of years old, can be seen when visitors enter the centre. The three-storey building has two main floors, but, like an iceberg, 85 percent of the exhibit space lies underground. On the ground level are the lobby, offices and travelling exhibit space; the underground level displays the centre's two permanent exhibits.

Especially appealing to budding geologists, exhibits are interactive and quite sensory. The GEO Theatre's film *(16min)* compels viewers to vicariously experience the power of an earthquake or volcanic eruption. The Titanic Story gives an overview of the famous disaster that happened off Newfoundland's coast. The second permanent exhibit, sponsored by Exxon Mobil, examines the province's oil and gas exploration. An area is devoted solely to geology and its relation to the centre's four themes: the planet, the people, the province and

Johnson GEO Centre on Signal Hill

Sandra Phinney/Michelin

the future. Visitors are ushered into a darkened room, the stellarium, for this latter presentation on the galaxies.

Additional Sights

Quidi Vidi Battery★

Take King's Bridge Rd. Turn right on Forest Rd. When road becomes Quidi Vidi Village Rd., drive 2km/1.2mi to Cuckhold's Cove Rd. Turn right. ⏰Open Jul–mid-Oct daily 10am–5:30pm. ⏤$2.50. ☎709-729-2977. www.tcr.gov.nl.ca/tcr/historicsites.

Built by the French during their occupation of St. John's in 1762, this emplacement, with a Colonial-style wooden house at its centre, stands above the community. In the early 19C the British tried to move fishermen away from the inlet and block the channel since it provided a means of attacking St. John's from the rear. The fishermen refused to budge, so the plan was abandoned and the battery strengthened. Restored to the early 19C period, the house re-creates the living quarters of soldiers stationed there.

Below is the tiny fishing community of **Quidi Vidi,** which has a narrow channel connecting to the larger Quidi Vidi Lake, site of the annual St. John's Regatta.

Confederation Building

Prince Philip Dr. ⏰Open year-round Mon–Fri 8:30am–4pm. ⏰Closed major holidays. Information office on 10th floor. ✕♿🅿☎709-729-2300.

Newfoundland's Parliament and some provincial government offices are housed in this imposing building. Constructed in 1960 and expanded in 1985, the edifice stands high above the city, providing a good **view** from its front entrance of the harbour and Signal Hill. When in session the **legislative assembly** can be observed *(sessions Feb–May Mon–Fri, third-floor visitors' gallery).* Note that the government benches are to the left of the Speaker's chair. Accepted practice elsewhere is for the government to sit on the right. When the Newfoundland Assembly met in the Colonial Building, there was only one fireplace—to the left of the Speaker. The governing body exercised

their prerogative and sat by the fire. The tradition remains.

East Coast Trail

Trail leads south from downtown St. John's; trailhead begins from Fort Amherst. East Coast Trail Assn. 50 Pippy Pl., St. John's. ☎709-738-4453. www.eastcoasttrail.com.

🥾One of Newfoundland's marvels is the utter lack of development along much of the wild and rugged coast. Early settlers migrated to the more placid coves and inlets, leaving the headlands to the terns and gulls. On the **East Coast Trail,** an intrepid hiker can trek southward from downtown St. John's along the edge of the crashing surf for a total, to date, of some 220km/136mi from Fort Amherst in St. John's to Cappahayden on the south shore (another 320km/198mi of trail is under development). There are 18 paths, each with a northern and a southern trailhead; in between are many access points for the trail. Use of ECTA maps is advised for finding the trailheads. Well-suited for day hikes, the trail is interspersed with parking space at access points along the route. Options for walks among wildflowers and memorable vistas are frequent. Guidebooks and maps are available for purchase in many shops around the city or online at www.eastcoasttrail.com.

Excursions

Cape Spear National Historic Site★

About 11km/7mi south; follow Water St. to Leslie St. Turn left at Leslie St. Go over bridge, continue straight after stop sign, following the road (Hwy. 11). ⏰Grounds open year-round. Visitor centre open mid-May–mid-Oct daily 10am–6pm. ⏤$4. ☎709-722-5367. www.pc.gc.ca. ⚠Wear warm clothing. It is colder here than in St. John's.

At longitude 52°37'24", Cape Spear is North America's most easterly point. On clear days there are marvelous **views**★ of the coast and of the entrance to St. John's Harbour. Whales can usually be seen in the waters off the cape seasonally *(May–Sept).*

Address Book

For dollar sign categories, see the Legend on the cover flap.

WHERE TO STAY

$ Roses B&B – *9 Military Rd. ☎709-726-3336 or 877-767-3722. www.theroses bandb.com. 6 rooms.*
Located in the same neighbourhood as the Fairmont Newfoundland, this bed-and-breakfast lodging is within walking distance of downtown and Signal Hill. A good choice for budget accommodations, the Roses consists of four adjacent row houses that have been spruced up for overnight guests. The rooms are bright and pleasantly furnished, some with antiques and original woodwork. Suitable for families, the suites are spacious and have kitchens.

$$ McCoubrey Manor – *6-8 Ordnance St. ☎709-722-7577 or 888-753-7577. www.mccoubrey.com. 6 rooms.*
Situated just across the street from the Fairmont Newfoundland, this pair of 1904 Queen Ann Revival town houses offers good value. Architectural details—such as the double oak mantel in the living room and plaster rosettes on the ceilings—lend an historic air. The innkeepers offer wine and cheese in the afternoons, guest laundry facilities, and all modern amenities. Included in the room rate is a hearty hot breakfast. Four housekeeping apartments are located in nearby buildings.

$$ Winterholme – *79 Rennies Mill Rd. ☎709-739-7979 or 800-599-7829. www.winterholme.com. 11 rooms.* P Spa
Occupying a 1905 Queen Anne Revival house on leafy grounds, Winterholme sits in St. John's Heritage District 15min from downtown. Inside, the magnificent oak woodwork commands your attention; the downstairs parlours are architectural marvels. Varying in size and appointments, guest rooms range in decor from simply furnished (third floor) to mildly decadent (the former billiards room). A full hot breakfast is served in the attractive dining room.

$$$ Fairmont Newfoundland – *115 Cavendish Sq. ☎709-726-4980 or 800-441-1414. www.fairmont.com. 301 rooms.* ✕ & P ⛄ Spa This modern hotel, part of the upscale Fairmont group

of properties, sits on a knoll over the harbour, providing great views of The Narrows. What the hotel lacks in down-home charm, it makes up in top-flight service and attention to detail. Rooms decorated in a contemporary style feature dataports and cordless phones with voicemail. The **Cabot Club ($$$$)** ranks as one of the city's best dining rooms, noted for its seafood dishes and tableside flambés. Less formal fare is available at the on-site Bonavista Café and The Narrows Lounge.

$$$ Murray Premises – *5 Becks Cove. ☎709-738-7773 or 866-738-7773. www.murraypremiseshotel.com. 47 rooms.* & P ⛄. This downtown boutique hotel, which opened in 2001, occupies the second, third and fourth floors of a converted trading house (called "premises" throughout the province). While many of the beams and timbers are old, and some rooms are still tucked under eaves, the space has been given a modern gloss. Luxurious touches abound, such as whirlpool tubs and heated towel racks in guest bathrooms. The lively music scene on George Street is entertaining, but boisterous weekends might take a toll on your sleep. Continental breakfast included.

$$$ Ryan Mansion Heritage Inn – *21 Rennies Mill Rd.* & *☎709-753-7926. www.ryanmansion.com. 6 rooms.*
Completed in 1911, this imposing, three-storey Queen Anne Revival mansion was built by one of the richest men in Newfoundland, James Ryan, whose family had prospered from the fishing industry in the 19C. In 2007 the mansion was opened to the public as an upscale B & B that has the feel of an intimate inn. Built to impress, the main foyer shows off quarter-cut English white oak; the main staircase and mantels on the seven working fireplace were handmade by the same craftsmen who detailed the *Titanic* when it was built in Belfast, Ireland (the inn hosts private dinners that feature the First-Class menu from the *Titanic* served on 24k gold-rimmed china that replicates the original White Star Line china used aboard the ill-fated ship). All guest rooms, some with four-poster

beds, have en suite bathrooms with heated marble floors. Originally built by Ryan's brother, the house next door was purchased in mid-2008 to supplement the accommodation with eight deluxe suites, due to open mid-2009. The furniture for three of the suites was purchased at auction from the Ritz Carlton Hotel in Montreal.

WHERE TO EAT

$ Zachary's – *71 Duckworth St.* ☎*709-579-8050.* **Canadian.** Simple, tasty home-style fare with a regional bias served in relaxed surroundings rules the day here. Expect great value for your dollar. Breakfast, served all day, is the best option, but lunch and dinner are also served. Fish is cooked perfectly, vegetables are served while still crunchy, and Zachary's partridgeberry cheesecake for dessert leaves patrons smiling.

$$ Aqua – *310 Water St.* ☎*709-576-2782. www.aquarestaurant.ca.* **Thai.** Aqua boasts the spare decor and urban sensibility of one of New York City's SoHo restaurants. A much-requested appetizer on the Thai-influenced menu is the blue mussels in basil pomodora sauce; the spring rolls are also popular. Entrées such as the cumin-crusted lamb brushed with a fig glaze indicate the restaurant's electic pairings.

$$ Basho Japanese Fusion Restaurant & Lounge – *283 Duckworth St. A1C 1B8.* ☎*709-576-4600. www. bashorestaurant.com.* **Asian.** This popular dining room and lounge (with an extensive martini list) uses fresh, local seafood and wild game in many of its dishes. The restaurant has gained a reputation as one of the best places to eat in Canada, so reservations are recommended for dinner. Tapas and sushi are the big sellers in the lounge.

$$ Blue on Water – *310 Water St.* ☎*709-754-2583. www.blueonwater.com.* **Canadian.** This boutique hotel (7 guest rooms, **$$**) downtown might be called trendy in another city, but in St. John's, it's considered to be an excellent place to eat as well as sleep. The weekend brunch is a great value: where else could you have banana pancakes with "Screech" [rum] roasted walnuts? The baked lobster is a dinner specialty.

$$ The Celtic Hearth – *300 Water St.* ☎*709-576-2880.* **British/Newfoundland fare.** This is pub food at its friendliest—in a place open 24 hours, year-round, with a fireplace and lots of regulars. The Guinness steak pie is excellent, as are the cod tongues (yes, they really are the tongues of codfish, fried, and surprisingly tasty). Since there are two levels, there is also a higher-priced dinner menu.

$$$ The Cellar – *189 Water St.* ☎*709-579-8900.* **Contemporary.** Popular with local residents, this fine-dining restaurant offers street level or cellar dining, with several semi-private rooms on the lower level. Favourite dishes include blackened scallops with lemon cream, sautéed pork tenderloin with apricots and fruit brandy, and traditional pan-fried cod (when available) with pork scrunchions. A distinctive selection of single-malt scotches helps take the chill off a foggy night.

Walkways from the parking lot lead to the actual point, the visitor centre, an operational lighthouse (☞ *not open to the public*) and the World War II battery where gun emplacements and bunkers remain. The visitor centre features a small display on the function and evolution of lighthouses. Restored to evoke the life of a lighthouse keeper in the 1840s, the domed, square **1836 lighthouse** (🕐*open mid-May–mid-Oct daily 10am–6pm;* 💰*$2.50*) is the province's oldest lighthouse.

The return trip to St. John's *(30km/19mi)* can be made via the villages of Maddox Cove and **Petty Harbour**, the latter a pretty fishing village with fishing shacks and flakes—wooden racks used to dry the fish.

Salmonier Nature Park

12km/7mi south of Trans-Can Hwy. In Holyrood. On Salmonier Line (Rte. 90) on the Avalon Peninsula. 🕐*Open Jun–Labour Day daily 10am–6pm, Labour Day–Thanksgiving daily 10am–4pm.*

 ♿ ☎ *709-229-3915 or 709-229-7888. www.env.gov.nl.ca/snp.*

First opened to the public in 1978, this provincially funded nature park covers 40ha/99acres. Its mandate is to educate Newfoundlanders and Labradorians about the wildlife, plants, insects and natural environment of their province. As it became popular with visitors, as well, the nature paths were turned into wooden boardwalks, accessible to wheelchairs and baby strollers. Along the boardwalks, the animals are viewed in their natural habitats; of special note are three endangered birds: the Peregrine Falcon, the Piping Plover and the Harlequin Duck.

Witless Bay Ecological Reserve★

Embarkation from town of Bay Bulls, 30km/19mi south of St. John's via Rte. 2 to Rte. 10. Then watch for directional signs of your chosen boat tour company to the dock. ⏱Departures May–Sept daily. Round-trip 2hrs 30min. Reservations required. ☜$55. For schedule, contact **O'Brien's Whale & Bird Tours** ✕♿🅿 *☎709-753-4850 or 877-639-4253. www.obriensboattours. com. Departures May–Oct daily. Round-trip 1hr 30min. ☜$47. For schedule, contact* **Gatherall's Puffin and Whale Watch**. *☎709-334-2887 or 800-419-4253. www.gatheralls.com.*

As feeding and nesting sites, the fish-filled waters and shore islands of Witless Bay *(disembarkation on the islands is not permitted; they can be viewed only by boat)* attract thousands of sea birds annually. Three barren islands host the bird population: Great, Green and Gull islands. In summer common murres, greater black-backed gulls, black guillemots and black-legged kittiwakes are plentiful. The **Atlantic puffin** colony here is reputedly the largest on the east coast of North America. Tour boats get as close as possible to two of the rocky isles where hundreds of sea birds skim the water, dive, circle overhead or light in the crevices and crannies of the rocks. An additional highlight of the cruise is **whale watching**★★ *(late spring and summer)*. The reserve is a seasonal feeding area for humpback, minke, pothead and fin whales. Good opportunities to view icebergs at close range may also occur.

Ferryland

71km/44mi south of St. John's via Rte. 2 to Rte. 10. Take Exit marked Colony of Avalon. ♿Visitors must register at the interpretation centre in order to view the archaeological site.

Situated on the southeast side of the Avalon Peninsula facing the Atlantic Ocean, Ferryland grew out of a colony started by Englishman **George Calvert** (c.1580-1632), later Lord Baltimore, in 1621 (his other settlement, now the state of Maryland, was founded 13 years later). Newfoundland's first permanent and enduring settlement, Ferryland is being excavated for remains of the **colony of Avalon.** Evidence suggests the presence of native Beothuks, as well as onshore stations of 16C Basque, Portuguese and Breton fishermen. The site's **interpretation centre** *(☎877-326-5669; www. heritage.nf.ca/avalon)* offers glimpses into 16C and 17C life in the area; artifacts unearthed include cannonballs, gold rings and coins. The excavation site is open *(mid-Jun–mid-Oct)* to visitors who register at the centre.

Marine Drive★

12km/8mi north on Rtes. 30 and 20. Leave St. John's on Logy Bay Rd. (Rte. 30). After 5.5km/3mi, turn right to Marine Dr.

A pleasant drive up the coast through residential areas north of St. John's, the road ascends and descends, affording endless views of the sea, headlands, cliffs, beaches, boats and fields. The **view**★ from **Outer Cove** is especially lovely. At **Middle Cove** there is an accessible beach, good for strolling along the shore.

Conception Bay South

20km/12.5mi west (southwest) of St. John's via Rte. 60. ☎709-834-6500. www. conceptionbaysouth.ca. ♿Note: Rte. 60 from St John's is scenic and follows Conception Bay; if pressed for time, take the Trans-Canada Hwy. and exit at Exit 31.

Incorporated in 1973, this town of 21,000 is composed of nine communities. Visitors are welcome to drop by the **Royal Newfoundland Yacht Club** (incorporated in 1936) at Long Pond; have a picnic at **Topsail Beach,** a provincial day-use park; browse the cafes and shops of town; and admire the scenic views of nearby Kelly's Island, Bell Island and Little Bell Island. Whales and icebergs can sometimes be seen from the shoreline. For scuba divers or those wanting to learn, **Ocean Quest Adventure Resort** (17 Stanley's Lane; ☎709-834-7234 or 866-623-2664; www.oceanquestcharters.com) offers diving lessons, and dive charters to the WWII wrecks off Bell Island; the company's lodge is a building designed and built with divers in mind and has 12 private guest rooms and a common area.

Brigus

About 74km/44mi west of
St. John's via Rte. 60.
Note: Rte. 60 from St John's is scenic and follows Conception Bay; if pressed for time, take the Trans-Canada Hwy. and exit at Exit 31. Follow the Parks Canada signs to Brigus. ☎709-528-4588. www.brigus.net.

Overlooking Conception Bay, this small community is on the map largely because of its ties with history. Today it is a pretty settlement that is believed to have been founded as early as 1612. Census records dating back to 1675 show the presence of some 30 settlers living in Brigus, many of whose residents are of English, Irish and Welsh ancestry.

Its most famous citizen is Capt. **Bob Bartlett** (1875-1946), whose 40 Arctic explorations and feats of daring-do

The village of Brigus

Sandra Phinney/Michelin

made him a household name in North America. Considered a true hero, he rescued stranded members of ill-fated Arctic expeditions in 1914 and 1917, the latter group having been stuck on the ice for four years. Province-wide events in 2009 (www.bartlett2009.com) will celebrate his piloting of American Commodore Robert Peary to within 209km/130mi of the North Pole a century earlier; throughout the year, the last of the Arctic Expeditionary Schooners are stopping at provincial ports to promote the Arctic's riches. Bartlett's family home, **Hawthorne Cottage,** a National Historic Site, is open to the public (corner of South St. & Irishtown Rd.; ⏰open mid-May–Jun & Sept Wed–Sun 9am–5pm, Jul–Aug daily 9am–7pm; 💲$3.95; ☎709-753-9262; www.historicsites.ca/hawthorne.html).

Cupids

About 76km/47mi west of St. John's via Rte. 60. Note: Rte. 60 from St John's is scenic and follows Conception Bay; if pressed for time, take the Trans-Canada Hwy. and exit at Exit 31. Take Rte. 70 (Roaches Line Rd.); turn right at Cupids sign onto Rte. 60. Follow signs to Cupids harbour.

What many historians believe to be the first English colony in Canada will be celebrating its 400th birthday in 2010. **Cupids** was originally called Cuper's Cove when it was established by explorer John Guy in 1610 on behalf of an English society of merchant venturers. The harsher climate and soil (similar to what the French explorers found in 1604 in present-day Nova Scotia) were compounded by attacks by pirates, notably one Peter Easton, a privateer under Britain's Queen Elizabeth I. When James I acceded to the throne, Easton lost his orders but he continued his attacks, especially against the Spanish. Since 1995 an archaeological dig in Cupids has uncovered 110,000 artifacts from John Guy's original homestead. The town's small **museum** (Cupids UC Hall, Seaforest Dr.; ☎709-528-3500) contains some of these artifacts as well as others from subsequent centuries. The excavation site is open to the public (Jul–Aug Mon–Fri).

The Cape Shore★★

MAP INSIDE BACK COVER

Perhaps Newfoundland's most dramatic coastline, the southwest arm of the Avalon Peninsula from Placentia south to St. Bride's delights visitors with its natural wonders and historic sites. Magnificent ocean views and remnants of Europe's territorial struggles await those who travel this isolated shore.

- **Information:** Newfoundland and Labrador Tourism, ☎709-729-2830 or 800-563-6353. www.newfoundlandandlabrador.com.
- **Orient Yourself:** The Cape Shore lies on the southwest arm of the Avalon Peninsula, between Placentia Bay on the west side and St. Mary's Bay on the east side.
- **Don't Miss:** The drive along the Cape Shore provides spectacular views.
- **Organizing Your Time:** Allow one day for a leisurely visit of the sights. Start early and check the weather before heading out.
- **Especially for Kids:** At the St. Mary's bird sanctuary, you can get close to the birds.

Sights

Castle Hill National Historic Site★

In Placentia, 44km/27mi south of Trans-Can Hwy. by Rte. 100. About 8km/5mi from Argentia ferry. ⏱Grounds open year-round. Visitor centre open mid-May–mid-Oct 10am–6pm. ⬤$4. ♿ ☎709-227-2401. www.pc.gc.ca.

This park contains the remains of Fort Royal, built by the French at the turn of the 17C and rebuilt and renamed Castle Hill by the British. Renowned for its commanding position overlooking the small town of **Placentia**, the site affords a **panorama**★★ of the city itself, Placentia Bay and **The Gut**—a small channel that separates the bay from two long, deep inlets.

To protect their interests in the Newfoundland fishery, the French established a small colony called Plaisance in 1662, constructing fortifications at sea level and in the hills.

After the **Treaty of Utrecht** in 1713 confirmed Newfoundland as British territory, the British kept a small garrison at Palcentia until 1811, when it was moved to St. John's. During World War II, construction of a large American base at nearby **Argentia** brought major changes to Placentia. The centre of antisubmarine patrol during the war, Argentia was the site of the famous 1941 offshore meeting between Winston Churchill and Franklin D. Roosevelt that produced the **Atlantic Charter,** a statement of peace goals adopted in 1942 by the United Nations.

An interesting **visitor centre** with dioramas, models and panels describes the French and English presence in the area. Visitors walk uphill to the cannons and scant remains of the fort.

A pleasant pathway through evergreen forests past drystone walls leads to **Le Gaillardin,** a redoubt built by the French in 1692.

Cape Shore Drive★★

46km/29mi from Placentia south to St. Bride's on Rte. 100. ⛽Fuel and food available infrequently. Fog may hamper visibility.

Traversing a rugged, hilly coast, Route 100 is a spectacular ocean drive, providing **views** of beautiful coves, crashing surf and windswept pines. Sparsely populated communities such as picturesque **Gooseberry Cove** *(25km/16mi south of Placentia)* dot the wide inlets of this curving coastline. Colourful flat-topped houses, woolly sheep and an occasional fishing boat anchored offshore are common scenes until the road turns inland at St. Bride's. The landscape then changes to isolated flatlands and pale green hillocks extending to the horizon.

Cape St. Mary's Ecological Reserve★

About 14km/9mi east of St. Bride's. Leave St. Bride's via Rte 100.
Turn right on paved road (turnoff for reserve is clearly marked) and continue 14km/8mi. ◷Open year-round. Mid-May–mid-Aug is best season to view the birds.

Kids Located at the southwest end of the cape, this site has been an official sanctuary for seabirds since 1964. It is one of the largest nesting grounds in North America for **gannets,** relatives of the pelican family. Atop a dramatic shoreline alive with the sights and sounds of an active bird population—over 70,000 birds breed here—its pastoral **setting** is unique. What is especially thrilling is that visitors can get within several feet of the birds. Providing spectacular **views**★ of the rugged coast, a trail from the lighthouse and visitor centre over short-grass hills reminiscent of moors and often covered with grazing sheep leads to **Bird Rock,** the precarious domain of hundreds of gannets. Surrounding cliffs attract throngs of noisy black-legged kittiwakes, common murres and razorbills.

Heart's Content Cable Station★

MAP INSIDE BACK COVER

A little town founded about 1650 on Trinity Bay, Heart's Content is the site of the first successful landing, in 1866, of the **transatlantic telegraph cable.** Its large, natural harbour, protected from the strong winds of the Atlantic Ocean, made the town an ideal candidate for the location of the cable station. North America's major relay site for nearly 10 years, the now obsolete facility was converted into a museum in 1974. The landing was the result of years of work by the New York, Newfoundland and London Telegraph Co., led by American financier Cyrus W. Field. The first attempt to lay a cable in 1858 failed after inaugural messages were sent between Queen Victoria and US president James Buchanan. A second attempt in 1865 also failed. Finally, in the following year, Field successfully used the ocean liner *Great Eastern* to lay the cable between Valencia, Ireland, and Heart's Content, where it joined a cable to New York. Messages initially cost $5 a word, and the station handled 3,000 messages a day. Improved communications technology led to the station's eventual closing in 1965.

⊟ **Information:** Newfoundland and Labrador Tourism. ⓒsee Introduction.
▶ **Orient Yourself:** The town lies at the junction of Routes 74 and 80.
⊜ **Don't Miss:** The 20min film.
◷ **Organizing Your Time:** Allow 1.5hrs to visit the cable station museum.

Visit

58km/36mi north of Trans-Can Hwy. by Rte. 80, Avalon Peninsula. ◷Open mid-May–late Sept daily 10am–5:30pm. $3. ☎709-583-2160 (during season) or 709-729-0592 (year-round). www.tcr.gov.nl.ca/tcr/historicsites.
Displays tell the story of communications, with special emphasis on the impact of the cable. There is a **film** *(20min)* and a special section on the laying of the transatlantic cables, the part played by the *Great Eastern* and the importance of Heart's Content. Costumed guides are on-site for tours of the replica of the first cable office (1866) and operating room. The original equipment can be compared to the complex equipment in use at the station's closing in 1965. In 2004 a new permanent exhibit was unveiled at the cable station site. Titled *Life at Heart's Content Station, 1868-1922,* it provides insight into the lives of those who worked here, as well as the station's impact on the town's physical appearance, which was changed by the addition of many new buildings to house operations and staff.

BONAVISTA PENINSULA

Explorer John Cabot is said to have exclaimed, *O buena vista!* ("good view" or "happy sight") upon seeing for the first time what is now called the Bonavista Peninsula. On the town of Bonavista's harbourfront, a replica can be viewed of Cabot's ship based upon his historic voyage in 1497 from Bristol, England. Indented with coves, bays, arms and sounds, this peninsula, west of the Avalon Peninsula and a bit farther north, stretches northeastward 85km/53mi into the Atlantic Ocean; its width measures between 15km/9mi and 40km/25mi. Picturesque Trinity is the most well-known village on the peninsula. Once one of the most important fishing ports on the island, Trinity possesses an ideal harbour that attracted British naval ships.

Trinity ★★

POPULATION 240 – MAP INSIDE BACK COVER

Situated on a hilly peninsula jutting into Trinity Bay, this charming seaside community has a lovely **setting** with views of the bay, rocks, fields and a small protected harbour. One of the oldest settlements in Newfoundland, the village evokes the feeling of a bygone era with its narrow streets, tiny gardens and colourful "box" houses.

Sufficiently established in 1615, the town became the site of the first Admiralty Court in Canada's history. Sir Richard Witbourne was sent from Britain to settle disputes between resident fishermen and those who crossed the Atlantic just for the season. In time Trinity rivaled St. John's in socioeconomic standing, but it receded in importance when the latter became the provincial capital. Today tourism is a mainstay; it is a popular area for **whale watching** *(departures Jun–Labour Day, weather permitting; 4hrs, including orientation; gear supplied; $75; Ocean Contact Ltd. ☎709-464-3269; www.oceancontact.com)*. **With its roster of pageants, historical plays, dinner theatres and concerts, the highly regarded Rising Tide Theatre is considered a key ingredient of the peninsula's cultural life** *(mid-Jun–mid-Oct; ☎888-464-3377; www.risingtidetheatre.com)*.

Trinity at sunset

Marketa Ebert/©iStockphoto.com

Information: Town of Trinity, 21 West St. ☎709-464-3836. www.townoftrinity.com.

▶ **Orient Yourself:** Trinity sits on the east side of Bonavista Peninsula facing the Atlantic, 74km/46mi northeast of Trans-Can Hwy. by Rte. 230 (south off Rte. 230 5km/3mi).

Don't Miss: A meal at the Village Inn. A performance at the Rising Tide Theatre.

Organizing Your Time: Allow 2 days in Trinity: an overnight stay to enjoy local lodging and dining and a half-day whale-watching excursion.

Especially for Kids: The whale-watching boats are 9m/29ft rubber dinghies, much like Zodiacs. This is an adventure only for older children.

Visit

Located in a restored house overlooking the harbour, the **interpretation centre** has displays presenting the community's history (*open mid-May–Sept daily 10am–5:30pm; ☎709-464-2042 or 800-563-6353; www.tcr.gov.nl.ca/historicsites*). They chronicle Trinity's rise to prominence from the mid-18C to the early 19C as a centre of commerce and society, only to be eclipsed by St. John's in the 1850s. Housed in a seven-room "salt box" dating to the 1880s, the **Trinity Historical Society Museum** contains local artifacts and historical documents (*open Jun–Sept daily 10am–1pm & 2pm–5:30pm; ☎$2; ☎709-464-3599; www.trinityhistoricalsociety.com*). The 1881 **Hiscock House** has been restored to its early-1900s

appearance and contains some original furnishings (*open mid-May–Sept daily 10am–5:30pm; ☎$2.50; ☎709-464-2042 or 800-563-6353*).

In a pastoral setting with the sea in the background, **St. Paul's Anglican Church** (1892) stands as a village landmark. The 31m/102ft clock spire of this large wooden house of worship towers above the town. Distinguished by its detached belfry, the **Holy Trinity Roman Catholic Church** has been in use for over 150 years.

Excursion

Random Passage Site

In New Bonaventure, about 24km/15mi southwest of Trinity, via Rte. 230 west and Rte. 239 south. Open Jul–Aug

Address Book

WHERE TO STAY AND EAT

$$ The Village Inn – *Taverner's Path, Trinity.* ☎709-464-3269. *www.oceancontact.com. 9 rooms.* This quaint inn is housed in a two-storey wooden structure dating to the early 1900s. Wooden floors and brass beds with Newfoundland-made quilts add old-fashioned charm. The sitting area features a fireplace, upright piano, books and games for guests to enjoy. Dining on the premises is a highlight: two **dining rooms ($)** serve home-cooked meals that emphasize fresh seafood and traditional provincial dishes such as salmon, halibut, shrimp, shepherd's pie, and rice and nut roast. For dessert try the figgy pudding with croady sauce. Breakfast, lunch and dinner are served. There's even an on-site pub.

$$$$ Fishers' Loft Inn – *Mill Rd., Port Rexton.* ☎877-464-3240. *www.fishersloft.com. 20 rooms. Rates include breakfast & dinner.* This charming hilltop complex comprises several colourful wooden structures dating between 1850 and 1900. Guest rooms feature handcrafted furnishings and down duvets; all have en suite bathrooms and views of Trinity Bay. A four-course dinner is served at two set seatings in the **dining room ($$)**, which is open to the public (*reservations recommended*). Fresh seafood and vegetables from the inn's extensive kitchen gardens make up the gourmet meals, usually enjoyed by candlelight. The chocolate torte with blueberry coulis is a much-requested dessert. Hearty hot breakfasts include home-grown berries and freshly made baked goods.

daily 10am–7pm. Mid-May–Jun & Sept–mid-Oct daily 10am–5pm. ☎709-464-2233.⟲Contribution requested. www.randompassagesite.com.

In 2000 a dramatic mini-series produced by the Canadian Broadcasting Corp. and shown internationally depicted what life would have been like in a Newfoundland and Labrador outport in the years between 1800 and 1830. The **film set,** a re-created 1800s fishing village, was completely preserved and improved for tourists who have been coming to this unusual attraction ever since. Sundays in summer *(Jul–Sept)* are especially interesting as local actors, writers and singers perform and read local tales and stories.

Trinity to Cape Bonavista

MAP INSIDE BACK COVER

This short driving itinerary takes in the villages and sights of the Bonavista Peninsula's tip, including the cape where 15C explorer John Cabot reputedly fell in love with the view. From Trinity, Route 230 northbound continues inland and returns to the sea at Port Union and Catalina, two fishing communities set along the shore. The drive continues north on Route 230 to Bonavista, and on to the Cape via Route 235. For the return trip, leave the cape by Route 235 south to Amherst Cove to see the west side of the peninsula, along Blackhead Bay; then take Route 237 east across the peninsula to Catalina, where Route 230 heads south to Trinity.

Driving Tour

57km/35mi

▷ *From Trinity, take Rte. 230 northeast to Port Union.*

Port Union
28km/17mi northeast of Trinity, on Rte. 230.

In the first decade of the 20C, independent fishers were scattered around the Bonavista Peninsula. By 1914, largely through the efforts of William F. Coaker (later knighted by the king of England), nearly half the fishermen of the entire (pre-Confederation) province—numbering 20,000—were signed up with the Fishermen's Protective Union (FPU). By 1916 North America's only union-built town was established on the shores of Trinity Bay. The FPU's power waned mid-century, and after a fire in 1945, many of the town's buildings were in a state of disrepair. Since 1999 there has been considerable interest in the history of the town, and the main **factory building** has been restored and opened for tours (🕐*call for opening hours; ☎709-469-2207; www.historicportunion.com).*

One of the buildings nearby housed an influential union newspaper; its offices were used for location shots in the major feature film, *The Shipping News* (2000), starring Judy Dench. The **Port Union Historical Museum** *(1917 Reid Railway Station;* 🕐*open mid-Jun–mid-Sept daily 11am–5pm; ☎709-469-2159)* is a good source of information, as it has much information on Coaker, the FPU and the local railway.

▷ *Follow Rte. 230 through Catalina and continue north. Take Rte. 238 east to Elliston.*

Elliston's Root Cellars
In Elliston, 47km/29mi north of Trinity via Rtes. 230 and 238. ☎709-468-2649. www.rootcellars.com.

The community of **Elliston** has a nice beach, a camping park with all the requisite scenery, and 330 friendly souls. It also has about 135 **root cellars** built in the pre-electricity era, where vegetables (among other food staples) are prevented from freezing in winter and kept cool in summer. To this day some 19 of the cellars are still used by their owners. Most sport a stacked-stone entry with a weather wooden door built into a hillock with vegetation growing on top. In 2000 St. John's Memorial University, working with Human Resources Canada and the local tourism authority, officially declared the town "Root Cellar Capital of the World." In fact, nowadays, the wooden doors built mostly into the hillsides that indicate the existence of yet another cellar are a delight for photographers wishing to document prior-century refrigeration. Stop by the town's visitor centre on Main Street (☎709-468-7080; ⏰open mid-May–Oct daily 9–6pm) to request a tour ($4) of a typical Elliston root cellar, complete with last year's vegetables.

▶ *Return to Rte. 230 and go north to Bonavista.*

Bonavista

This large seaside town is another fishing community, with houses set around an outer harbour protected by a breakwater and a sheltered inner harbour for small boats. Throughout the 16C, European fishing fleets used the harbour. By about 1600 the area had become a British settlement and remained so, despite several attempts by the French to capture it in the 18C.

Mockbeggar Plantation

Roper St. ⏰Open mid-May–Sept daily 10am–5:30pm. $3. ☎709-468-7300.

www.tcr.gov.nl.ca/tcr/historicsites/Mock-beggar.htm.
Situated by the sea toward the cape side of town, the .6ha/1.5acre plantation site includes a storage building and the Bradley House. Restored to the 1930s period, the house contains the personal belongings of prosperous local businessman and senator **Frederick Gordon Bradley** (1888-1966). Born in St. John's, Bradley served as principal of a local Bonavista school before rising in the political ranks to become the first Canadian federal cabinet minister from Newfoundland.

Ryan Premises National Historic Site

Off Rte. 235, in Bonavista.; follow signs to the National Historic Site. ⏰Open mid-May–Oct daily 10am–6pm. ☞$4. ♿ ☎709-468-1600. www.parcscanada.pch. gc.ca/lhn-nhs/nl/ryan/index_E.asp

This is the site where one of the wealthiest families of Newfoundland, the Ryan family, had a huge inshore fisheries supply company in the 19C. International trade was an everyday occurrence here, as the Ryan Premises exported salt cod and other fish to the West Indies and to southern Europe, commonly on board schooners leaving from from Bonavista's harbour. Although **James Ryan Ltd.** withdrew from the fisheries business in the early 1950s, the company did not close until 1978, as it continued to be a

Newfoundland and Labrador Tourism

Cape Bonavista Lighthouse

wholesaler and retailer of various goods. In June 1997, when Queen Elizabeth was visiting, Ryan Premises was re-opened as a National Historic Site after a ten-year refurbishment. Today in St. John's, the former home of James Ryan, the eldest brother in the family and its patriarch, has been turned into a lavish inn in the city's historical district. *See Address Book for St. John's.*

▶ *From town, drive 5km/3mi on Rte. 235, which becomes Church St. Continue past the town hall over the bridge and bear right at the fork.*

Cape Bonavista★

Supposedly named *Bonavista* ("good view") by explorer John Cabot in 1497, the cape is a superb setting, with pound-ing waves, a clear blue sea and interesting rock formations.

A drive through fields with **views** of the sea leads to the remote tip of the cape. A **statue** of Cabot commemorates his first North American landing, though recent research has cast doubt on the authenticity of this claim. Completed in 1843, the **lighthouse**★ has been restored by the provincial government to portray a lightkeeper's living quarters in the 1870s. Exhibits describe the construction and restoration of the lighthouse, the operation of the lamps and the lightkeeper's duties. There are sweeping views of the rocky coast from the lighthouse itself. *Open mid-May–late-Sept daily 10am–5:30pm; $3; 709-468-7444; www.tcr.gov.nl.ca/historicsites.*

BURIN PENINSULA

The doorstep to the once-vast offshore fishing industry in the **Grand Banks, this** barren peninsula of isolated mountain plateaus juts down like a boot into the Atlantic Ocean from the southern coast of Newfoundland between Placentia and Fortune bays. Just off the "toe" are the island remnants of France's once-great empire in North America: Saint-Pierre and Miquelon.

Route 210

MAP INSIDE BACK COVER

The drive on Highway 210 is long and deserted until **Marystown,** situated on Little Bay. Once the largest in the province, its huge shipyard (*inaccessible to the public*), where fishing trawlers are built, has suffered with decline of the industry. South of Marystown, Route 210 crosses the peninsula to the towns of Grand Bank and Fortune before descending to Fortune Bay, providing views of the southern coast of Newfoundland. Just before entering Grand Bank, there is a view of the south coast and Brunette Island. To the west the coast of the French island of Miquelon is just visible, weather permitting.

▪ **Information:** Burin Heritage Tourism Assn. 709-891-2355.
▶ **Orient Yourself:** The peninsula juts down into the Atlantic Ocean from the southern coast of Newfoundland between Placentia and Fortune bays. Route 210 begins at the Trans-Canada Highway near Goobies and heads south some 203km through Marystown before turning west to Grand Banks and south to Fortune.
☺ **Don't Miss:** The Southern Newfoundland Seamen's Museum in Grand Bank. The French island of Saint-Pierre.
◔ **Organizing Your Time:** Allow 3 hours for the drive itself. But an essential part of this trip is a ferry crossing to Saint-Pierre for an overnight stay to enjoy French cuisine and culture (*see Saint-Pierre and Miquelon chapter*).
Kids Especially for Kids: Winterland's EcoMuseum, and the Seamen's Museum.
◔ **Also See:** SAINT-PIERRE AND MIQUELON

Driving Tour

203km/126mi south of Trans-Can Hwy. by Rte. 210.

▶ *From the Trans-Can Hwy., take Rte. 230 south to Marystown.*

Marystown

142km/88mi south of Trans-Can Hwy. on Rte. 210. www.townofmarystown.ca.
This town of under 6,000 residents functions as the service hub for the peninsula. The mainstay of the local economy was the largest shipbuilding facility in the province from the mid-1960s until the 1990s. A 4.5m/15ft statue of the Virgin Mary overlooks the town and harbour from Mary Mount.

▶ *Take Rte. 210 west 12km/7mi to Winterland.*

EcoMuseum★

In Winterland. Museum entrance is .5km/.3mi from intersection with Rte. 222. ⊙Open year-round; phone for hours. ⑆☎709-279-3300. www.k12.nf.ca/she/pgreen/ecomuseum/index.htm.
Kids Winterland is the only village located inland on the Burin Peninsula, and is known for its farming. Since 1998 a group of committed volunteers have developed some 7sq km/2.7sq mi of wetland for conservation. They have built boardwalks (with storyboards along the way), and divided the acreage into four different habitats (wetland, boreal forest, aquatic and barren) in order to educate children and adults about the flora and fauna found in each. This is a true "living museum," which is constantly being upgraded.

▶ *Take Rte. 210 west and then south 43km/27mi to Grand Bank.*

Grand Bank

199km/123mi south of Trans-Can Hwy. on Rte. 210.
An important fishing centre, this community was once the home of the famous "bankers." Some of the houses from that era are examples of the Queen Anne style with their widow's walks—small open rooftop galleries from which women could watch for the return of their men from the sea.

Provincial Seamen's Museum★

54 Marine Dr. ⊙Open late-Apr–late-Oct daily 9am–4:45pm (may open later in summer). ⊙Closed public holidays. ⊙$2.50 ⑆☎709-832-1484. www.therooms.ca/museum/prov_museums.asp. ⊙Note: the museum may be temporarily closed due to a fire.
Kids This branch of the Provincial Museums network features displays on the history of the banks fishing industry. Of particular interest are the photographs of ships and fishing, and **models** of the types of ships used. A large glass-enclosed relief model of Newfoundland shows the banks and the depths of the Atlantic.

▶ *Continue south on Rte. 210 about 8km/5mi to Fortune.*

Fortune

203km/126mi south of Trans-Can Hwy. on Rte. 210.
This fishing community of 2,200 has an artificial harbour. Known as the Gateway to the French islands of St. Pierre and Miquelon, the town sees as many as 20,000 visitors come through its community en route via ferry to the small islands of France lying off the coast. (⊙Note that the ferry does not accommodate vehicles, but there is ample parking in Fortune.) The shale cliffs of Fortune Head have been designated a world ecological reserve because Pre-Cambrian trace fossils have been found there.

Saint-Pierre and Miquelon★
(FRANCE)
POPULATION 6,125– MAP INSIDE BACK COVER

Few people realize that part of France lies off the coast of North America on tiny islands 48km/30mi away by boat from Newfoundland. The two principal islands are Saint-Pierre and the larger Miquelon, connected by a long sandbar to what was once a third island, Langlade. A decidedly continental flavour pervades these rocky and remote shores.

- **Information:** Comité Général du Tourisme, Place du Général de Gaulle. ☎011-508-41-02 00. www.st-pierre-et-miquelon.info or Saint-Pierre et Miquelon Regional Tourism Committee, Pascal Daireaux, B.P. 4274 Saint-Pierre et Miquelon 97500 ☎011-508-41-0200 .
- ▶ **Orient Yourself:** The islands lie 48km/30mi off Newfoundland's southern shore, at the end of Rte. 210 on the Burin Peninsula. 🅟Visitors, including children, must present a valid passport to enter the islands: go online to see all entry requirements in advance of your visit.
- 🕐 **Organizing Your Time:** The islands' time zone is 30min ahead of St. John's and 1hr ahead of Halifax.
- 🌡 **Also See:** BURIN PENINSULA

A Bit of History

Cod fishing was the reason for settlement on these islands. From the early 16C the archipelago was used as a base for Basque and Breton fishermen working the Grand Banks. By the 1763 Treaty of Paris, it became official French territory, but ownership changed repeatedly as France and England fought for hegemony on the continent. Although France was the loser in this battle, it retained these islands as a pied-à-terre for its fishing fleets. During US Prohibition (1920-33), the islands experienced brief prosperity as a "rum-running" centre. Today only tourism adds to income from the fishing industry.

Visit

Saint-Pierre★

From the sea Saint-Pierre appears to be a rugged island of stunted trees and low plants. Upon arrival in the harbour of the island's capital and administrative centre, also named Saint-Pierre, visitors can sense a striking cultural difference

Ile-aux-Marins viewed from on board a ferry

©CRT Saint-Pierre et Miquelon

Practical Information

GETTING THERE

BY BOAT

Passenger ferry from Fortune to Saint-Pierre island: Jul –Labour Day departs from Fortune daily 2:45pm; departs from Saint-Pierre daily 1:30pm. Jun & Sept–mid-Oct departs from Fortune Fri & Sun 2:45pm; departs from Saint-Pierre 1:30pm. 1hr–1hr 35min. Schedule may vary: call to confirm. Winter service varies. One-month advance reservations required. Round-trip ☜$93.50 adult. 🅿 ($10/night) SPM Tours and Lake Travel. ☎709-832-2006 or 800-563-2006 (Canada/US), ☎011-508-41-24-26 in Saint-Pierre. www.spmexpress.net ⚠Warning: the sea crossing can be rough.

BY AIR

Air service from St.John's NL, Sydney and Halifax NS, and Montreal QC, provided by **Air Saint-Pierre.** For information & reservations, contact Air Saint-Pierre ☎1-877-277-7765 (Canada1US) ☎011-508-41-00-00 in Saint-Pierre, or access www.airsaintpierre.com.

CUSTOMS

European and USA citizens must carry a valid passport, which is necessary to transit Canada. Canadian citizens must provide an official ID card with picture and proof of citizenship (birth certificate). Other nationalities must have valid passport and, in some cases, a visa, which can be obtained from the nearest French embassy or consulate.

LANGUAGE

English is not commonly spoken on the islands. Telephone operators and tourist office staffs are bilingual, however.

VISITOR INFORMATION AND ACCOMMODATIONS

Contact in advance the Comité Régional du Tourisme, Place du Général De Gaulle, BP 4274, 97500 St-Pierre-et-Miquelon, ☎011-508-41-02 00. www.st-pierre-et-miquelon.info (click "en" button in upper right-hand corner for English version).

---

from the rest of North America. Lining the waterfront, tall stone buildings house pastry shops, fine restaurants and boutiques stocked with imported goods. The streets are narrow and full of French cars.

At the entrance to the harbour sits **Ile-aux-Marins**★ *(accessible from Saint-Pierre, in front of the tourist office, by 10min ferry ride)*, once a community of over 800 inhabitants, many of whom were active in cod fishing. Villagers progressively abandoned the site for Saint-Pierre. Centred in the old schoolhouse, the **museum** contains a presentation of isle history through artifacts and memorabilia *(Place du Général de Gaule;* 🕐 *open May–Oct Tue–Sat 10am–noon & 2pm–4pm, Sun 2pm–5pm.* ☜*3 euros;* ☎*011-508-41-58-88).* The treeless terrain permits **views** of Saint-Pierre and the remains of one of the more than 600 shipwrecks that have occurred in the archipelago.

Miquelon and Langlade

Boat departures to Miquelon and Langlade available from Saint-Pierre. In summer, daily ferry to Langlade. Transportation by shuttle van to the village of Miquelon is available in summer or may be arranged off-season (🕯contact Cmité de Tourisme above).

Except for the small working town of the same name, the northern island of Miquelon is untouched moorland of soft hills and long beaches. Seals might be seen lying on the sands of **Grand Barachois**, and a variety of sea birds frequenting the shores. The road crosses the isthmus known as the Dune of Langlade, a sandbar formed in part by debris from shipwrecks that have taken place since 1800. Situated at the southern end is the largely uninhabited "island" of Langlade, except for a tiny settlement in the hills above the ferry landing. Along the east side of the dune, a wide beach stretches out in the vicinity of Anse du Gouvernement.

CENTRAL NEWFOUNDLAND

When one is on a small island, there is sometimes a point of highest ground where the view of at least two coasts can be seen. Not so with Newfoundland: when positioned at the heart of the province, visitors might forget they are on an island completely surrounded by water. This chapter begins in the island's heart by exploring Terra Nova National Park and the towns of Gander and Grand Falls-Windsor. Then a driving tour follows the only intraprovincial route, the Trans-Canada Highway (Highway 1), which cuts across Newfoundland's vast interior from east to west before heading south at Corner Brook. Parts of the interior are heavily forested; others are expanses of rocky barrens and boggy peat lands, a legacy of glaciers, as are the multitude of lakes and rivers. Erosion by rivers and glaciers has left odd-looking knobs of rock, known as tolts, rising above the interior's otherwise flat landscape.

Terra Nova National Park ★

MAP INSIDE BACK COVER

Scarred by glaciers of the past, this 396sq km/153sq mi area on the shores of Bonavista Bay is a combination of rolling hills, bogs, ponds and indented coast-line. Deep fjords, or "sounds," reach inland, and in early summer these coastal waters are dotted with icebergs that float down with the Labrador Current. Forests of balsam fir, birch, maple and other trees in the interior are part of the boreal forest of Eastern Newfoundland. The Trans-Canada Highway bisects the park with some good views of the sounds. But visitors must leave the highway to truly appreciate the park's natural beauty. Its varied topography and history of human presence for thousands of years led to Terra Nova's designation, in 1957, as Newfoundland's first national park. Efforts are being made to counter the lack of natural regrowth of the park's forests in recent years, caused very likely from excessive browsing by moose.

- **Information:** Parks Canada ☎709-533-2801. www.pc.gc.ca, or Heritage Foundation for Terra Nova National Park ☎709-533-3145. www.heritagefoundationtnnp.nl.ca.
- ▶ **Orient Yourself:** Terra Nova Park lies on the west side of Bonavista Bay. It consists of a wide swath of land lying along Clode Sound that reaches toward the bay and separates into two large headlands on either side of Newman Sound, with Swale Island between them. The visitor centre sits near the western end of Newman Sound.
- **Don't Miss:** The panorama from Blue Pond Lookout.
- **Organizing Your Time:** Allow one day to enjoy the park. Ask at the visitor centre about interpretive boat tours of Newman Sound, which is home to many bald eagles. A good place for a swim, **Sandy Pond** has a sandy beach, a food concession stand, boat rentals, and a 3km/1.8mi loop trail.
- **Also See:** BONAVISTA PENINSULA

Visit

Open year-round. ☞$5.50/day use fee. Visitor centre open mid-Jun–Labour Day daily 9am–7pm; mid-May–early Jun & Sept–early Oct daily 10am–5pm. Rest of the year Thu–Mon 11am–3pm. Closed Dec–early Jan. ✕&☎709-533-2801. www.pc.gc.ca.

Bluehill Pond Lookout★★

7km/5mi from park's north entrance. Turn onto gravel road and continue approximately 2km/1mi to the observatory platform.

From the lookout platform there is a **panorama**★★ of the whole park: deep inlets, cliffs, rocks, lakes, forests, bogs and hills. To the south Newman Sound and the ocean, scattered with icebergs (in season), can clearly be seen in good weather.

Newman Sound★

12km/8mi from park's north entrance. Take road to the visitor centre and Newman Sound. About 1.5km/1mi to the trail.
The beauty of this sound—a deep inlet with a sandy beach—can be appreciated by walking the trail along its wooded shore. Seasonal wildflowers and tiny seashells complement the setting.

Ochre Lookout

18km/11mi from park's north entrance. Take the gravel road to the tower, about 3km/2mi, where there is an observation deck.
From this lookout tower, another **panorama★** allows visitors to comprehend the vastness of the park. At this height, Clode and Newman sounds are clearly visible, weather permitting.

Terra Nova to Corner Brook

MAP INSIDE BACK COVER

Given the somewhat barren, flat terrain, this 434km/269mi driving tour of Central Newfoundland along the Trans-Canada Highway may seem of long duration, unless you take in the excursions that reach north to the coast with its northerly bays and fishing villages. However, the towns of Gander, Grand Falls-Windsor and Corner Brook offer attractions and amenities for travellers. And the interior's wilderness is home to caribou, moose and other wildlife that you may spot along the way (keep alert for moose along the highway, a real danger for cars). It's best not to rush through, but rather allow three days so as to include local dining and lodging as well as seeing the sights.

▯ **Information:** Central Newfoundland ☎709-533-2801. www.centralnewfoundland.com.

▶ **Orient Yourself:** The Trans-Canada Highway (Highway 1) traverses Central Newfoundland in an east-west direction along a more northerly route.

☺ **Don't Miss:** Gander's North Atlantic Aviation Museum, and if you have time, Barbour Living Heritage Village.

🕐 **Organizing Your Time:** Allow a minimum 2 days to take this drive—3 days if you plan to take in the excursions.

Driving Tour

434km/269mi by Trans-Can Hwy. (Hwy. 1), not including round-trip excursions.

Terra Nova National Park★

☺*see Terra Nova National Park.*

▶ *From the park, follow the Trans-Can Hwy. west toward Gander, some 58km/36mi away. At Exit 24, Rte. 320 leads north to Newton. This is an optional round-trip excursion of 178km/110mi to Newton via Rte. 320 (Exit 24) off Trans-Canada Hwy.*

Barbour Living Heritage Village★

In Newton. 🕐Open mid-Jun–mid-Sept daily 8:30am–9pm. Guided tours (1hr 30min) $7. ☎709-536-3220 or 709-536-2441. www.barbour-site.com/plan. htm. ☺Photographing building interiors is discouraged.

Kids Benjamin Barbour (1809-1891) started a sealing dynasty in Newfoundland and Labrador and his sons and grandsons continued in the tradition of the fishery and related businesses. This charming living village contains two of the original Barbour homesteads and two reconstructed buildings that

©T. Reynolds/Parks Canada

Newman Sound, Terra Nova National Park

house an art gallery, a **dinner theatre** *(Jul–mid-Sept Tue, Wed, Fri & Sat; price varies; reservations recommended)* and a sealers' interpretation centre. The latter educates visitors about what is now a controversial fishery that is still an integral part of the economy in rural Newfoundland and Labrador. A 19C schoolhouse, a fisherman's stage (a building used for codfish preparation and storage), a craft shop and two **restaurants ($$)** are also open in the village.

There are several lodgings available along the shore road (👍see website).

▶ *Return to Trans-Can Hwy. and head west 46km/28mi to Gander.*

Gander

On the Trans-Can Hwy 1. ☎709-651-5900. *www.gandercanada.com.*

Situated on the northeast shore of long, narrow Gander Lake, Gander is a well-known town due to its aviation history. When **Gander International Airport** was built in 1938, it was the largest airport in the world; it was used secretly and extensively during WWII by the Royal Air Force. In the 1950s and '60s, almost every transatlantic flight had to refuel at Gander. Today Gander's airport is the official alternate landing site for NASA's Space Shuttle. It can handle the world's largest aircraft (the Concorde tested here in the 1970s). In the hours

following the terrorist attacks in the US on September 11, 2001, Gander's airport received, one after the other, 39 flights bound for America. Some 6,600 passengers and crew had to be fed and housed for three days until NORAD cleared the air space. The town almost doubled in size that day (Gander's population is 9,650), but in typical Newfoundland fashion, everyone was looked after in terms of food, housing and even entertainment, by local musicians.

Fans of aviation and the aerospace industry can visit the **North Atlantic Aviation Museum** *(on the Trans-Can Hwy between the James Paton Memorial Hospital and the Gander tourist chalet;* 🕐 *open year-round late-Jun–Sept daily 9am–9pm, rest of the year daily 9am–5pm;* ⬢*$4;* ☎*709-256-2923; www.naam. ca)* to see six aircraft on its grounds, as well as several aeronautical displays.

▶ *Continue 43km/27mi on the Trans-Can Hwy. to Notre Dame Junction and take Rte. 340 & Rte. 342 north 14km/9mi to Lewisporte.*

Lewisporte

Off Trans-Can Hwy., via Rte. 340 & Rte. 342 north. www.lewisportecanada.com.

Lying northwest of Gander, this small community of about 3,000 overlooks Burnt Bay, one of the many indentations within larger Notre Dame Bay. Its deep-water port is open year-round. It serves as the departure point for the ferry between Newfoundland and Cartwright and Happy Valley-Goose Bay, Labrador, operated by **Coastal Labrador Marine Services** (☎709-535-0810 or 866-535-256; www.tw.gov.nl.ca/ferryservices/schedules/l-goosebay-cartwright.stm).

▶ *From Lewisporte, return south on Rte. 34 to Rte. 340 and take Rte. 340 north 47km/29mi to Boyd's Cove.*

Beothuk Interpretation Centre

In Boyd's Cove. Off Rte. 340. ◷*Open mid-May–Sept daily 10am–5:30pm, but call to confirm hours.* ☞*$3.* ♿☎*709-656-3114 or off-season 709-729-0592. www.tcr.gov.nl.ca/tcr/historicsites.*

The Beothuk (sometimes spelled Beothuck) were the aboriginal people Europeans would have encountered arriving for the first time in Newfoundland in the 16C. This native group, now extinct, had a fondness for using powdered hematite (a red ochre) that they placed on canoes, artifacts and their own skin; hence, the early appellation the "red Indians," or "redskins." Their belief that all goods were held in common increased hostilities with the early European fishermen, who often found their supplies missing. Mass murder and European diseases greaty diminished the Beothuk population. The last known surviving Beothuk died in St. John's in 1829.

The remains of 11 wigwam-type dwellings have been excavated here. A 1.5km/1mi walking trail connects the centre with the excavated site. It has been determined that the only other region where the Beothuk thrived was the south coast.

▶ *Return to the Trans-Can Hwy. and continue west 47km/29mi to Grand Falls-Windsor.*

Grand Falls-Windsor

Off Trans-Can Hwy., 97km/60mi west of Gander. ☎*709-489-0418. www.grandfallswindsor.com.*

Sitting on the banks of the Exploits River, this town of some 13,500 residents is Central Newfoundland's largest community, the amalgamation of two towns (Grand Falls and Windsor) in 1991. Its economic engine has been the pulp and paper industry. The longest river in the province, the 246km/153mi-long Exploits River is famed for its Atlantic salmon. Since 1985 the **Exploits Valley Salmon Festival** has taken place in the town every year at the peak of the Atlantic salmon run, usually the first weekend in July, with entertainment and food (☞$7/day).

Logger's Life Provincial Museum

At the entrance to Beothuk Provincial Park. ◷*Open mid-May–late-Sept daily 9:15am–4:30pm.* ☞*$2.50.* ☎*709-486-0492. off-season ☎709-757-8023. www.the*

Whale in Iceberg Alley

Newfoundland and Labrador Tourism

Iceberg Alley

Sometimes called "Iceberg Alley," Notre Dame Bay lies about 150km/95mi north of Gander. The fishing village of Twillingate, which overlooks the bay off Route 340, has witnessed some 22 species of dolphin, porpoises and whales drop by annually from May to August. It's not unusual for as many as 5,000 humpback whales to be seen per season. Up to 40,000 icebergs that have "calved" (broken off) from Greenland's ice float southbound along the bay.

The following companies provide upclose tours: **Iceberg Alley Ocean Adventures** *(Baie Vert; departures May–early Oct; ☎709-532-4502; www.centralnewfoundland.com/bview22.php3)*, **Island and Tickle Boat Charters** *(Port Leamington; call for dates and times; ☎709-483-2002; www.oceansidecountrylodge.com)* and **White Star Oceanside Adventures** *(Triton; boat tours and kayaking; Jun–Sept; ☎709-263-2486; www.centralnewfoundland.com/bview662.php3)*. Contact these individual tour operators for sailing times, types of boats and fees.

rooms.ca/museum/prov_museums.asp.
A member of the provincial museums, the Logger's Life museum re-creates a 1920s work camp along the Exploits River. Visitors can see a cookhouse and bunkhouse, a forge, barn, and other structures common to such a compound. On display are examples of loggers' clothing, tools, and utensils of the period.

Salmonid Interpretation Center
At Grand Falls Fishway, 2km/1mi west of downtown off Scott Ave. ◷*Open mid-Jun–mid-Sept daily 8am–8pm.* ☞*$5.* ☎*709-489-7350. www.exploitsriver.ca.*
Located on the Exploits River, this facility showcases the mighty Atlantic salmon, visible through underwater viewing windows and in on-site aquariums. Displays are also devoted to other freshwater fish such as brook trout and eels.

▸ *Continue west on the Trans-Can Hwy. and continue west 211km/131mi to Deer Lake. From Deer Lake, take an optional 76km/47mi round-trip excursion by Rtes. 430 and 422 to Richard Squires Provincial Park.*

Sir Richard Squires Memorial Provincial Park
Off Rte. 422, approximately 38km/24mi north of Deer Lake.
Newfoundland's first provincial park (1954), this scenic expanse along the

Humber River is named in honour of a two-term prime minister (1919-1923 and 1928-1932). Popular with anglers, the park is noted for its Atlantic salmon; during summer *(Jul & Aug)*, a **fish ladder** allows visitors to see salmon leaping their way upstream at 87m/285ft-wide **Big Falls.** Big Falls Trail descends to the falls and Viewpoint Trail leads to a view of the river and its falls *(trailheads off parking lot).*

Corner Brook
52km/32mi southwest of Deer Lake on the Trans-Can Hwy. ☎*709-639-9792. www.cornerbrook.com.*
Newfoundland's second largest city, Corner Brook has a population of some 20,000 people. It was charted by Captain James Cook in 1767 and incorporated in 1956. Located at the mouth of the Bay of Islands, the city lies just 40km/25mi from the Gulf of St. Lawrence. The fishing and pulp and paper industries have brought prosperity, as well as cement and gypsum operations.
Winter activities include cross-country and downhill skiing on **Marble Mountain,** snowmobiling and cat-skiing (a 10-passenger vehicle that goes above the treeline at 762m/2,500ft). In summer the **Family Adventure Park** *(☎709-634-4719. www.familyadventurepark.com)*, has water slides and mini-golf. The **Margaret Bowater Park** *(O'Connell Dr.;* ◷*open Jul–Sept; ☎709-637-1232)* has supervised swimming and a children's play area.

GREAT NORTHERN PENINSULA

Driving Newfoundland's west coast from the northwest tip of the Great Northern Peninsula at St. Anthony to the southwest tip where a ferry arrives at Channel-Port au Basques from Nova Scotia would take more than eight hours. The west coast is not only lengthy, it is also dramatic: besides the scenic coast, the Long Range Mountains are the singular natural feature dominating the west coast. Part of the Appalachians, these flat-topped mountains rise to a maximum height of 815m/2,673ft above sea level southwest of Corner Brook and stretch some 400km/250mi northward from Cape Ray. Farther north along the Great Northern Peninsula, the mountain views are less spectacular since the Long Range summits are smaller and farther inland. The landscape is sparsely forested, with dwarfed spruce and fir, mossy barrens and heath, and dotted with thousands of lakes, locally called "ponds." Between the mountains and the coast lies a poorly drained plain, sometimes high above the sea, with a variety of cliffs, sandy shores and little fishing communities. Two national historic sites—one a World Heritage Site—and a national park make their home on the peninsula.

Gros Morne National Park★★
MAP P 260

Covering 1,805sq km/697sq mi along the west coast of the province's Great Northern Peninsula, this vast, pristine park includes some of the most spectacular scenery in eastern Canada. Designated a UNESCO World Heritage Site in 1987, the park contains geological features that have become a magnet for international scientific research. Consisting of rock more than a billion years old, the cropped **Long Range Mountains**, as well as Bonne Bay's deep fjord and Western Brook Pond are the scenic highlights of the park.

- **Information:** Parks Canada, Rocky Harbour. ☎709-458-2417. www.pc.gc.ca.
- **Orient Yourself:** The park edges the west coast of Newfoundland at the southern end of the Great Northern Peninsula. Route 431 threads the southern part of the park; Route 430 runs along the Gulf of St. Lawrence side from Wiltondale north to Three Mile Rock. Open May through October, the park visitor centre is located near Rocky Harbour. A warm jacket is recommended for the park the entire season, and most especially if you take the Western Pond boat tour.
- **Don't Miss:** A guided boat tour of the fjord gives perspective to the mountains and the park's Discovery Centre.
- **Organizing Your Time:** Allow a minimum 2 days for the park and a week if you wish to hike the trails. For information on accommodations, access www.newfoundlandandlabrador.com. For information on travel during the off-season, contact Gros Morne Gatherings ☎709-458-3605 or 866-732-2759; www.grosmornetravel.com.
- **Especially for Kids:** The park recreation complex, open daily *(late-Jun–Labour Day)*, includes a 25m/69ft indoor swimming pool.

Visit

44km/27mi northwest of Deer Lake. Take Rte. 430 from Deer Lake to Wiltondale, then Rte. 431 to park, 13km/8mi. Open year-round. $9 entry fee (May–Oct). Visitor centre near Rocky Harbour; contact for guided boat tours and trail information (open mid-May–mid-Oct daily 9am, closing hours vary; first two weeks May & late Oct Mon–Fri 9am–4pm; closed Nov–Apr. ☎709-458-2417. www.pc.gc.ca.

Newfoundland and Labrador Tourism

The Tablelands Mountains, Gros Morne National Park

Bonne Bay Area★★

Take Rte. 431 from Wiltondale 50km/31mi to Trout River (food, fuel).
This is beautiful drive along a deep fjord—a glacial trough whose several arms are surrounded by squat peaks of the Long Range Mountains. The road travels westward along the **South Arm** from Glenburnie, offering gorgeous **views**★★ of the bay.

From Woody Point, as Route 431 ascends to the west, the red-brown rubble of a desertlike area known as the **Tablelands** is abruptly visible, a jarring contrast to the lush green of the park. These mountains consist of rock that was once part of the earth's mantle—a magnesium and iron layer surrounding the planet's core—and are evidence of **plate tectonics,** the shifting of the plates within the earth's crust. For a closer look at the Tablelands, stop at the turnoff *(4.5km/2.8 mi from Woody Point),* where a **panel display** describes this unique natural feature. This vantage point offers a striking **view** of the barren expanse. A footpath leads from the parking area into the heart of the Tablelands *(for information on guided hikes, contact the visitor centre).* Beyond the little fishing village of Trout River is the long finger lake called **Trout River Pond** *(tour boats depart Jul–Aug daily 10am, 1pm, 4pm. Jun & Sept 1pm; round-trip 2hrs 30min; reservations required; $25; 709-451-7500 or 866-751-7500).*

Dominating the return drive to Woody Point is the vast bulk of **Gros Morne Mountain** (806m/2,644ft) to the north, the park's highest point. Stop at Parks Canada's new **Discovery Centre** *(open late Jun–Labour Day daily 9am–6pm (Wed & Sun until 9pm), mid-May–late Jun & early Sept–early Oct daily 9am–5pm)* on the south side of Bonne Bay for a look at the geology and ecology of the area.

Water taxi service (no vehicles) from Woody Point to Norris Point may be available. Otherwise, motorists must retrace the route to Wiltondale. From Wiltondale Route 430 travels northeast along **East Arm,** a vantage point for lovely **views**★★ of Bonne Bay, and along Deer Arm.

From Rocky Harbour to St. Pauls

40km/25mi by Rte. 430. Fuel and food available in communities along the way.
Overlooking a wide inlet of Bonne Bay, the small coastal community of **Rocky Harbour** functions as a service centre for park visitors.

On a promontory just north of Rocky Harbour, **Lobster Cove Head Lighthouse** *(open daily in summer)* provides expansive **views**★★ of the town, Gros Morne Mountain, the mouth of the bay and the Gulf of St. Lawrence.

Built on a narrow plain between the sea and the Long Range Mountains, the road affords a pretty drive up the coast past

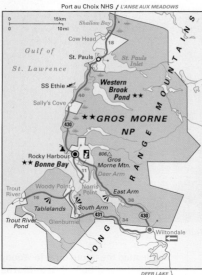

Port au Choix NHS / *L'ANSE AUX MEADOWS*

DEER LAKE

teau where snow remains in crevices even in August. Resembling a fjord because of the towering cliffs, this gorge is not a true fjord because it does not extend to the sea; the pond is freshwater. Bonne Bay is a true fjord.

A trail leads across the boggy coastal plain *(boardwalks over marshy areas)* to the edge of the pond *(3km/2mi walk to boat dock)*. The only way to see the interior of Western Brook Pond is to take the **boat trip** *(departs Jul–Aug daily 10am, 1pm & 4pm; Jun & Sept daily 1pm; round-trip 2hrs; ⌖$45;. ℗3km/1.8 mi walk from parking lot; park pass required; warm jacket recommended entire season; Bon Tours; ☎709-458-2016 or 888-458-2016; www.bontours.ca).*

From the vantage point of the boat at pond level, passengers can appreciate the sheerness of the granite cliffs rising 600m/2,000ft. Impressive waterfalls spill over the towering mountains to the cliff bases below.

After Western Brook Pond, the road follows along the coast with views of the mountains. The road continues to **St. Pauls,** a small fishing settlement at the mouth of a deep fjord. Designated "The Viking Trail," Route 430 exits the park above Shallow Bay and continues north along the coast for another 300km/200mi to L'Anse aux Meadows. The important archaeological site of Port au Choix lies some 135km/84mi north of St. Pauls.

Sally's Cove, a little fishing community. Before the turnoff to Western Brook Pond's trailhead, the rusty remains of the **SS Ethie** shipwreck can be seen on the beach. A small panel describes the fate of the ship's 1919 voyage.

Western Brook Pond★★

29km/18mi from Rocky Harbour.

Western Brook runs through a spectacular gorge (which, in typical Newfoundland understatement, is called a "pond") in the Long Range Mountains before it crosses the narrow coastal plain and reaches the sea. The pond is flanked by almost vertical cliffs that rise to a desolate boulder-strewn alpine pla-

Port au Choix★★

MAP INSIDE BACK COVER

Occupying the Point Riche Peninsula in the Gulf of St. Lawrence, midway up the Great Northern Peninsula, this national historic site—not to be confused with the modern town of Port au Choix—holds the native burial grounds of Newfoundland's aboriginal peoples. To date, the remains of several ancient cultures have been unearthed here, namely the Maritime Archaic, Dorset, Paleoeskimo and Recent Indians, ancestors of the Beothuk.

The first discovery of any evidence that ancient peoples had lived in this area came in 1904 when a local resident found fragments of bone and ivory. Some 25 years later the National Museum of Canada conducted an archaeological survey. Excavations began after WWII in 1949, and between 1960 and 1962 the first of several dwelling sites were unearthed at Phillip's Garden. It has been determined that four native groups lived in this vicinity between 1,300 and 2,000 years ago, including the Maritime Archaic Indian, the Dorset Palaeoeskimo, the Groswater Palaeoeskimo and Recent Indian of Beothuk lineage. In 1970 Port au Choix was designated a National Historic Site of Canada. Archaeological work continued until 2002.

- **Information:** Parks Canada. ☎709-623-2608. www.pc.gc.ca. On-site visitor centre ☎709-861-3522.
- ▶ **Orient Yourself:** Rte. 430, known as the Viking Trail, leads from Gros Morne National Park north to Port au Choix. Port au Choix is located on the coast of the Great Northern Peninsula, on an island in the Gulf of St. Lawrence, 135km/84mi north of St. Pauls and 230km/143mi north of Trans-Can Hwy. by Rte. 430.
- ⏱ **Organizing Your Time:** Allow 2 to 4 hours to visit the national historic site. Services and accommodations are available in St. Anthony, some 200km/124mi north of Port au Choix, at the end of Rte. 430 (www.town.stanthony.nf.ca).

Visit

Open Jun–early Oct daily 9am–6pm. $7.05. ☎709-861-3522. www.pc.gc.ca/lhn-nhs/nl/portauchoix/index_e.asp.

In the **visitor centre,** built in 2001, a film *(12min)* introduces the visitor to the site, its excavations and trails. Interpreters are available to explain the centre's exhibits that showcase the original artifacts, found on-site, of the prehistoric peoples. The limestone bedrock that underpins this area has helped preserve the artifacts through the centuries.

Outside, the first thing one notices is that this is one of the windiest sites in Canada (there is a fair amount of rainfall in the summer months). Fir and spruce trees may appear stunted, due to the strong onshore winds, and none are taller than 4m/13ft. Within the 8sq km/3sq mi site, nearly 50 **rare plants** have been registered. The 8km/3mi Dorset Trail is mostly flat with a steeper walk at midpoint; an easier trail leads to Crow Head, where breathtaking **views**★ are afforded. In 1986 a Dorset Palaeoeskimo burial cave was uncovered here, containing the remains of six bodies. The people are thought to have come from the Arctic on a seasonal basis, especially for sealing, as their finely carved harpoon heads and blades have also been excavated. The trail leads to Phillip's Garden where 50 **house depressions** have been uncovered, believed to be those of the Dorset people, along with thousands of their tools and implements.

The Dorset are thought to have disappeared from Newfoundland about 1,300 years ago, but evidence remains that they survived in northern Labrador up to 600BC. From this vantage point on a clear day, the province of Quebec can be seen, some 96km/60mi away.

Oral Traditions

Visitors to Newfoundland are captivated by the wealth of unusual idioms of its inhabitants. Centuries of isolation have chiselled a character that is independent and humorous. Where else are there settlements named **Stinking Cove,** Useless Bay, **Jerry's Nose,** Cuckold Cove, **Come by Chance** and Happy Adventure, or local terms like *tickle* (a narrow waterway)? Local expressions such as "to have a noggin to scrape" (a very hard task), "to be all mops and brooms" (to have untidy hair) and "long may your big jib draw" (good luck for the future) add colour and humour to everyday conversations. Rich in tradition, Newfoundlanders possess a wealth of legends, weather lore, folk dances and songs that attest to their wry perspective on life. Often parodies of British creations, sea shanties such as "Squid-Jiggin Ground," "Let Me Fish off Cape St. Mary's" and "Jack Was Every Inch a Sailor" record island character and yearnings with relish, melancholy or humour.

L'Anse aux Meadows★★

MAP INSIDE BACK COVER

On a grassy ledge facing Epaves Bay, the remains of the oldest authenticated European settlement in North America are preserved for posterity. This remote site, a National Historic Site of Canada, has been included on UNESCO's World Heritage list as a property of universal value. In 1960 **Helge Ingstad**, a Norwegian explorer and writer, and his archaeologist wife, **Anne Stine**, began a systematic search of the coast from New England northward. Led to a group of overgrown mounds near L'Anse aux Meadows by a local resident, they excavated them from 1961 to 1968. Foundations of eight sod buildings of the type the Norse built in Iceland were uncovered and several artifacts undeniably Norse in origin were found. Evidence of iron working—an art unknown to the North American Indians—was unearthed. Samples of bone, turf and charcoal were carbon-dated to around AD 1000. Experts believe L'Anse aux Meadows was a base for further exploration in search of timber and trading goods. Occupied by about 100 men and women, the camp was probably deserted after five or ten years. Newfoundland's harsh conditions, coupled with the growing accessibility of southern European markets, most likely led to its abandonment.

- **Information:** Parks Canada. ☎709-623-2608. www.pc.gc.ca
- **Orient Yourself:** Lying 453km/281mi north of Trans-Can Hwy. by Rtes. 430 and 436, L'Anse aux Meadows is located on the Great Northern Peninsula, at the farthest northern tip of Newfoundland, opposite Labrador. St. Anthony is the nearest city with food service, accommodations and air service www.town.stanthony.nf.ca.
- **Organizing Your Time:** Allow 3 hours to visit the site. Services and accommodations are available in nearby St. Anthony.

Visit

Open Jun–early Oct daily 9am–6pm. ✎$10.30. ⬧🅿☎709-623-2608. *www.pc. gc.ca.*

In the **visitor centre** displays depict what a Norse settlement might have looked like, but the highlight is the collection of artifacts found on-site. A stirring **film** *(28min)* on the Ingstads' search introduces the visit.

Completely excavated, the site has been preserved as grassy borders that outline the foundations of the original struc-

---

Address Book

WHERE TO STAY AND EAT

$ Tickle Inn – *At Cape Onion via Raleigh.* ☎709-452-4321 Closed Oct–May. ☎709-739-5503 off season or 866-814-8567. *www.tickleinn.net.* 4 rooms. 🅿⬧
This refurbished two-storey 1890s inn is a treat for travellers to this remote peninsula. Guests gather in the dining room for a meal of island favourites such as Newfoundland shrimp and scallops or poached Atlantic salmon, concluding with Northern berry flan. Rates include a deluxe continental breakfast.

$$$$ Quirpon Lighthouse Inn – *Quirpon, off Rte. 436.* ✕🅿⬧ ☎709-634-2285. www.linkumtours.com. 10 rooms. Three meals included. This is a working lighthouse and the inn is the lightkeeper's house (1922) on tiny, uninhabited Quirpon Island. Simply furnished guest rooms occupy two houses. A viewing platform is the perfect spot from which to see the icebergs and the occasional humpback and minke whales who swim by. Breakfast, lunch and dinner as well as brief passage to the island are included in the rate.

Len Klingen/Michelin

L'Anse aux Meadows

tures. The layout of the dwellings, work buildings and a smithy can be clearly distinguished.

Nearby, three **sod buildings**—a long house, a building and a work shed—have been reconstructed.

Inside, wooden platforms that served as beds line the walls. Fire pits are placed at intervals in the middle of the earthen floors. A few animal skins and iron cooking utensils suggest the spartan existence of the inhabitants. Wooden storage chests, barrels and other equipment have been faithfully reproduced. Costumed staff demonstrate Viking skills and perform daily chores necessary for survival.

At the end of "The Viking Trail," **St. Anthony**, a large service centre, is the nearest city *(food, accommodations and air service)* to L'Anse aux Meadows.

At the turn of the 19C, a British doctor, **Sir Wilfred Grenfell** (1865-1940), began his medical missionary work in the area, including Labrador. St. Anthony preserves his memory through the hospital he established, a cooperative craft shop and the house local residents built for him, now the **Grenfell House Museum** (○open Mon–Sun 9am–8pm; ✆$6; &☎709-454-4010; www.grenfell-properties.com).

Vinland

By AD 900 the Vikings (also known as the Norse) from present-day Scandinavia had settled in Iceland, and from there explored Greenland, Baffin Island and beyond. The account of a land sighting by a Greenland-destined ship blown off course inspired Leif Ericsson, then residing in Greenland, to go exploring. About AD 1000 Ericsson landed at a fertile spot and built a settlement for the winter. He named the location "Vinland" for the wild grapes his crew is said to have found there.

This story is preserved in two Norse tales: the Saga of the Greenlanders and the Saga of Eric the Red, which were communicated by word of mouth for hundreds of years before being recorded. Though many scholars have tried to find Vinland, its location is unknown. Once generally thought to be on the southeastern coast of the US because of the grapes, this location was determined to be too far for ships to have sailed in the time suggested by the sagas.

LABRADOR COAST

The Labrador Coast—which encompasses the southeast shore from L'Anse au Clair north to Cartwright—is dotted mainly with small fishing villages. These are permanent communities, most of which have been in existence since the 1800s. Fishermen from various parts of Europe harvested whales, fish and seals from these waters seasonally beginning in the 16C. Since the demise of the cod fishery, these communities now rely on turbot, crab, scallop and shrimp as their principal catch. This coast contains two important attractions of national historic significance, as well as the town of Cartwright, which overlooks Sandwich Bay. Sitting at the southern end of Labrador, L'Anse-au-Clair is the first village encountered once visitors cross the Quebec border from the Blanc-Sablon ferry terminal. The southeastern portion of Labrador lies within the **Boreal Shield,** where fir and spruce forests are prevalent, along with lakes, wetland and upland areas. Caribou, lynx and black bear are found in the boreal interior. Along the coast, whales, seals, seabirds—and icebergs may be spotted.

Labrador Coastal Drive★

MAP INSIDE BACK COVER

After a stop at the Gateway Visitor Centre in L'Anse-au-Clair (*a stop is essential to help plan any self-guided journey in this region*), **visitors will find that the road is paved to Red Bay and its National Historic Site. Beyond Red Bay, the route continues to Cartwright as a gravel road.** *Ensure that you have adequate supplies in your vehicle, as the drive from Port Hope Simpson to Cartwright is in the interior with no settlements along the way.*

- **Information:** Gateway to Labrador Visitor Centre in L'Anse au Clair. ☎709-931-2013. www.destinationlabrador.com. ◷Open Jun–Oct daily 9:30am–5:30pm. Also www.labradorcoastaldrive.com.
- ▸ **Orient Yourself:** The Labrador Coastal Drive is an actual region of Labrador and is referred to as such. It is an alternate designation for one of Labrador's four representative districts (ridings) for the provincial assembly.
- ◷ **Organizing Your Time:** This drive is accessible by taking the seasonal drive-on, drive-off ferry from St. Barbe on the northwest coast of Newfoundland (☎866-535-2567 *in province;* ☎709-724-9173 *outside; www.labradormarine.com*) to the port town of Blanc-Sablon, Quebec. The day passage on the *MV Apollo* ferry takes about 90min, and reservations are essential. Rental cars are available in the area for ferry passengers crossing the Strait of Belle-Isle without a vehicle. Depending on how one arrives, 2 days may be ample to see parts of the southern coast.

Driving Tour

414km/257mi via Rte. 510 from L'Anse au Clair northeast to Cartwright.

L'Anse-au-Clair

Stop at the Gateway to Labrador **Visitor Centre** (*opening hours above*) for maps, and information on the region, including accommodations and car services. Housed in a community church edifice,

restored to its 1909 appearance, the centre also has exhibits on area history and natural history.

L'Anse-Amour
23km/14mi east of L'Anse au Clair.
This village is the site of a **burial mound** that is considered to be the oldest funeral monument in the western world; it held the remains of a 7,500-year-old Maritime Archaic adolescent. The tall-

Address Book

WHERE TO STAY

$ Beachside Hospitality Home B&B – *9 Lodge Rd., L'Anse-au-Clair.* ☎*709-931-2338. 3 rooms.* Upon arriving in southeastern Labrador from Newfoundland, this is the first B & B to be seen and would make a good home base if your trip is confined to the south coast of Labrador. Breakfast is included in the rate, and in the evenings traditional accordion music is played. Walking paths lie nearby.

$ Bradley's B&B – *Happy Valley-Goose Bay.* ☎*709-896-8006. www.bbcanada. com/bradleybb. 3 rooms.* Within walking distance to mostly everything in Goose Bay, this B & B offers a complete breakfast and en suite bathrooms.

$ Campbell's Place – *Port Hope Simpson.* ☎*709-960-0269. 4 rooms.* Comfortable and clean guest rooms in this newly built home provide a good base for exploring the nearby coastal area. Each room has a private bath.

$ Harbourview Bed & Breakfast – *37 Main Rd., Cartwright.* ☎*709-938-7325. 1 room, 1 apartment.* This small, cozy bungalow is located in the historic part of Cartwright and is conveniently located. Breakfast is included in the rate.

$ P.J.'s Inn by the Lake – *606 Tamarack Dr., Labrador City.* ☎*709-944-6002. www.pjsinnbythelake.com. 6 rooms.* This newly renovated B & B has a lake view. All guest rooms have Internet access and private baths. Free pick-up at the airport included.

$$ Battle Harbour Heritage Properties – *25 Oliver's Pond Rd., Portugal Cove-St.Philip's.* ☎*709-921-6325. www.battleharbour.com. 13 units in 5 buildings.* Stay for a night or for two weeks. This island village is a place to get away from the stress of urban living. Much is available, from a licensed dining room to a general store (to stock up on provisions to make your own meals) and the best selling points are that there are no phones, TVs or cars on the island. It's easy to pretend you're back in the mid-19C.

est lighthouse in Atlantic Canada is also located here, the 33m/109ft-high **Point Amour Lighthouse** (○*open May–Oct daily 10:30am–5:30pm;* ✆*$3;* ☎*709-931-2013; www.pointamourlighthouse.ca)*; those who climb the 128 steps to the top are rewarded with a **panorama**★★ of the surroundings.

In the nearby village of West St. Modeste, the **Labrador Straits Museum** (○*open mid-Jun–Sept Mon–Sat 9:30am–5:30pm;* ✆*$2;* ☎*709-931-2067)* contains reproductions of artifacts from the burial mound.

Point Amour Lighthouse

C. Robbins/Labrador Straits Historical Development Corporation

Practical Information

GETTING THERE

BY AIR

🎧 *For airline phone numbers and websites, see Practical Information at the beginning of the Newfoundland and Labrador chapter.*

Commercial air carriers provide daily flights to Labrador with arrivals at Blanc Sablon, Goose Bay and Wabush. (Note that Goose Bay is part of the amalgamated community of Happy Valley-Goose Bay.)

To **Blanc-Sablon:** Daily flights to Blanc-Sablon, Quebec, on Air Labrador and Provincial Airlines from St. John's and Montreal. Situated just west of the Labrador border, Blanc-Sablon is a short drive from Labrador.

To **Goose Bay:** Daily flights on Air Canada Jazz, Air Labrador and Provincial Airlines from St. John's (via Deer Lake), Montreal (via Wabush) and Halifax.

To **Wabush** (Labrador City): Daily flights on Air Canada Jazz, Air Labrador and Provincial Airlines from Montreal and St. John's (via Goose Bay).

Airports

Quebec: **Blanc-Sablon Airport (YBX)** ☎418-461-2514. www.tc.gc.ca/quebec/en/airports/lourdesdeblancsablon.htm Labrador: **Goose Bay Airport (YYR)** ☎709-896-5445. www.goosebayairport.com. **Wabush Airport (YWK)** ☎709-282-5412. www.tc.gc.ca/atl/en/air/airports/wabush/menu/htm Newfoundland: **St. John's International Airport (YYT)** ☎709-758-8500. www.stjohnsairport.com. **Deer Lake Airport (YDF)** ☎709-635-3601. www.deerlakeairport.com

CAR RENTAL

Budget Wabush Airport, 1 Airport Rd. Wabush; 210 Humber Ave., Labrador City; Goose Bay Airport and 141 Hamilton River Road, Goose Bay ☎800-268-8900. (within Canada). www.budget.com.

National Wabush Airport, 1 Airport Rd. Wabush, and 210 Humber Ave., Labrador City. Goose Bay Airport and 141 Hamilton River Road, Goose Bay. ☎800-227-7368. www.nationalcar.com Also search www.destinationlabrador.com for "auto rent/lease."

BY BOAT

Reservations not required but recommended. Check in required at dockside 2hrs prior to departure. Disabled travellers requiring boarding assistance and/or information on facilities available should notify Ticket Agent. Schedules subject to change without notice. Confirm sailing times by calling in advance.

Ferry from Newfoundland to Labrador: Lewisporte to Goose Bay via Cartwright (vehicles permitted): early Jun (pending ice conditions) to late-Sept; 🎧always call to confirm that the ferries are running. Departs Lewisporte Fri 12:01pm; departs Goose Bay Sun & Tue 5pm. $118, or $312.25 with vehicle. ☎709-535-0810 or 866-535-2567. www.tw.gov.nl.ca/ferry services. Departs St. Barbe, Newfoundland for Blanc-Sablon, Quebec (vehicles permitted): mid-Apr–mid-Jan; 🎧$7.50 per person, one way. With vehicle $22.75, one way. Duration 1hr 45min. Departure times vary; check the website. ☎709-535-0810. www.tw.gov.nl.ca/ferry services. 🎧Always call to confirm schedule.

BY TRAIN

Service from Sept-Isles, Québec to Labrador City on Québec North Shore & Labrador Railway. Times vary; ☎709-944-8205.

GETTING AROUND

BY BOAT

Passenger ferry service (no vehicles). Reservations not required but recommended. Check in required at dockside 2hrs prior to departure. Disabled travellers requiring boarding assistance and/or information on facilities available, please notify Ticket Agent. Schedules subject to change without notice. Confirm sailing times by calling the phone number.

Service to Charlottetown, Norman Bay, Williams Harbour, Port Hope Simpson on the MV *Challenge One* early Jun–Nov. 🎧$8–$17.50 one way. ☎709-729-2300. www.tw.gov.nl.ca/ferryservices/schedules.stm

Service to Goose Bay, Rigolet, Cartwright, Black Tickle and ports north to Nain on the MV *Northern Ranger* early

Jun–mid-Nov. ⊗ $14–$142 one way. ☎709-535-0810 or 866-535-2567 during business hours only. www. tw.gov.nl.ca/ferryservices/schedules. stm. Note: the ship has not been built for tourist-class luxury. Available cabins sell out months in advance. Reservations essential.

Cruises

Check these websites for touring cruises that include Labrador: www.cruise northexpeditions; www.adventurenew foundland.com; www.alvoyages.com; www.peregrineadventures.com.

BY AIR

To North Coast (Nain): daily flights from Goose Bay via Air Labrador and Provincial Airlines (Innu-Mikun).

BY CAR

From Baie Comeau, Quebec, the 598km/370mi **Route 389** heads northeast to Labrador City: about half of the distance is paved, the remainder is gravel. **Route 510,** known as Labrador Coastal Drive, is a paved, single-lane road linking communities from L'Anse-au-Clair northwest to Cartwright; from Red Bay to Cartwright, the road is gravel. Known as the Trans-Labrador Highway, **Route 500,** a gravel road, leads 526km/326mi from Happy Valley-Goose Bay in Central Labrador west to Labrador City.

Car rental companies are located at some airports. ⓒ*See GETTING THERE above.*

Road Regulations – ⓒ*See Practical Information at the beginning of Newfoundland and Labrador above.* In Labrador cell phone use is not permitted while driving a vehicle.

GENERAL INFORMATION

VISITOR INFORMATION

Destination Labrador, 379 Hamilton River Rd., Happy Valley-Goose Bay. ☎709-896-6507. www.destinationlabrador.com. Open seasonally, visitor centres in Labrador are located at: L'Anse-au-Clair ☎709-931-2013; Goose Bay ☎709-896-3489; and Labrador City ☎709-944-7631.

ACCOMMODATIONS

For a listing of suggested lodgings, ⓒ *see the Address Book.* Hotels, motels, inns

The Pitcher Plant, Newfoundland and Labrador's provincial flower

Newfoundland and Labrador Tourism

and bed & breakfasts cannot be booked through a central number or website. To search for accommodations by category, go online to www.destination labrador.com/guide/find_accommoda tions.htm.

CLIMATE

Labrador is located in the easternmost part of Canada, and separated from Newfoundland by the Strait of Belle Isle. The climate is more Arctic than Atlantic: winters are cold, with temperatures of -10° to -15°C/5°F; summers are short and cool, especially along the coast due to the cold Labrador Current. Average temperatures along the coast in July are 8°C/46°F to 10°C/50°F. Some areas of southern Labrador may be snow-covered for six months of the year and eight months in the far north. Labrador's mean annual precipitation is 1000mm. In Central Labrador winters are cold (-17°C/1.4°F in January) and summers pleasantly warm: mean temperature for July is 16°C/60.8°F.

RECREATION

Lakes abound and hundreds of rivers thread Labrador, making it ideal for **fishing,** especially for brook trout, northern pike and Atlantic salmon. For a list of outfitters, visit www. destinationlabrador.com. Some 16 designated **hiking** trails varying in length from 3km/1.8mi and longer can be found in Coastal, Central and West Labrador. **Geocaching** with a GPS

Newfoundland and Labrador Tourism

Snowmobiling is popular in Labrador

is popular; access www.geocaching.com for more information. Labrador has two **golf** courses: a brand-new 18-hole course at the Tamarack Golf Club in Labrador City (☎709-955-3007; www.tamarackgolfclub.ca) and a 9-hole course at the Amaruk Golf Club (☎709-896-2112) in Happy Valley-Goose Bay. Winter activities such as **snowmobiling** begin in November on Labrador's many groomed trails. In the Upper Lake Melville region near Happy Valley-Goose Bay, groomed trails are expected to be connected with the coast and West Labrador to create hundreds of kilometres of linked trails throughout Labrador and eventually to join Quebec's trail system. With some 25km/15mi of groomed trails, West Labrador opens the **cross-country**

skiing season in November; by the end of December the coast's 5km/3mi of groomed trails are in use. **Snowshoeing** is popular (*Nov–Apr*).

Downhill Skiing Venues:
Menihek Nordic Ski Club, Labrador City ☎709-944-5842. *Oct–Apr. www.home.crrstv.net/menihek/index.htm.* 40km cross-country trails. Canada's cross-country team practices here.
Smokey Mountain Ski Club, Labrador City ☎709-944-2129. www.fancey.com/smokey/index2.html.
Birch Brook Nordic Ski Club, Happy Valley-Goose Bay. www.birchbrook.com. 30km of ski trails Jan–Apr.
Ski Mont Shana, Happy Valley - Goose Bay ☎709-896-8162. 7 trails; vertical drop of 52m/169 ft. 2 lifts.

Red Bay National Historic Site★
About 80km/50mi northeast of L'Anse au Clair. ◷*Open Jun–Oct daily 9am–6pm.* ✑*$7.* ☎*709-920-2051. www.pc.gc.ca/lhn-nhs/nl/redbay.*

In the late 1500s, whale oil was one of the most valuable exports from the New World to Europe. Basque and French fishermen in whaling galleons would come to this bay, then called Butus, and hunt right and bowhead whales. They also used another type of vessel, an 8m/26ft-long *chalupa,* in the pursuit, killing and towing of the great mammals. In 1978 underwater archaeological research was undertaken in Red Bay harbour: three Basque whaling galleons

and four chalupas were found, one of which is on display at the site; all were remarkably well-preserved and serve as examples of 16C shipbuilding methods. The **interpretive centre** exhibits 16C whaling tools, household items and even clothing preserved from that time period.

Battle Harbour National Historic District★★
On Battle Island near Mary's Harbour, 174km/108mi north of Red Bay.
A passenger boat (☎709-921-6948) takes visitors from the mainland to Battle Island; departs from Battle Harbour's private wharf (Main St., Mary's Harbour) daily at

11am & 7pm. ☎*709-921-6216.* ⊜*$9 for boat.* ◷*Open mid-Jun–mid-Sept. www. battleharbour.com. An alternate 1hr passage to Battle Harbour is available through Jones Charters & Tours (*☎*709-921-61216 or 709-921-6325, mid-Jun–mid-Sept daily at 11am & 6pm, returning at 4pm & 9am;* ⊜*$50;* ☎*709-921-6325).*

Designated a national historic district in 1997, this island site, with its more than two dozen structures, preserves nearly 200 years of Labrador's fishery trade and coastal community life. The village grew out of a base for cod-processing operations established in the early 1700s by English merchants. Its location north of French fishing territory attracted Newfoundlanders seeking unharassed waters.

After 1820 accelerated growth led to the building of medical, religious and educational facilities typically expected of a major city. Beginning in 1992 all the wooden buildings, including the fish-processing plant—the sole intact example of a mercantile fishing "room"—were restored, and 500 artifacts from village life were put on display. The Gothic Revival church is the oldest extant Anglican church in Labrador. For a trip back in time, visitors can be accommodated overnight on-site in a B & B or cottage managed by the Battle Harbour Historic Trust (◖*see Address Book*).

Port Hope Simpson
About 49km/30mi north of Mary's Harbour.

A logging and boatbuilding community of about 530 people, this port town is the largest community in southeastern Labrador. It makes a good base for exploring the nearby villages. **Alexis Hotel Tour Planning** (◷*open year round;* ☎*709-960-0228*) can assist with one-day or multi-day activity tours.

Cartwright
About 211km/131mi north of Port Hope Simpson.

With a population of around 600, this community on Sandwich Bay was founded in 1775 by Capt. **George Cartwright**, a fish and fur trader. The town's sheltered harbour is attractive, but Cartwright residents erected cannons on **Flagstaff Hill** (they are still there) to intimidate privateers.

In 1837 the settlement was sold to the Hudson's Bay Company, the dominant fur-trading firm in Canada at the time. A major employer today in Cartwright is a crab-processing plant.

The town is the terminus for Route 510, and a **ferry** that originates in Lewisporte, Newfoundland, stops in Cartwright en route to Happy Valley-Goose Bay (◖*See Practical Information*).

Aerial view of Battle Harbour National Historic District

©J. McQuarrie/Parks Canada

CENTRAL LABRADOR

Central Labrador acts as a transportation hub for this part of Labrador. Of its four main communities—Happy Valley-Goose Bay, Mud Lake, North West River and the Innu town of Sheshatshiu—the largest town, Happy Valley-Goose Bay, has both a commercial airport and an international air base, as well as ferry services to Newfoundland and other parts of Labrador.

Built during World War II, the **5 Wing Goose Bay airbase** is home to an allied military partnership for flight training and tactical exercises; it employs 500 civilians. Most government offices are also located in the town. Throughout much of the year, the Northern Lights, or **aurora borealis,** can be seen in the skies. Pocketed with lakes, the landscape is topped by spruce and pine forests and riven by streams and rivers. Along immense Lake Melville's eastern shore, the Mealy Mountains dominate the area south and east of Happy Valley-Goose Bay.

Happy Valley-Goose Bay ★

POPULATION 7,572 – MAP INSIDE BACK COVER

Located almost in the middle of Labrador on the Churchill River, the prosperous town of Happy Valley-Goose Bay is ideally situated for growth. The mining operations of Voisey's Bay Nickel Company, under development in the region, lie 356km/221mi to the north; the town serves as a supply and logistics centre for the company. If another hydro-electric station on the Lower Churchill River is built 80km/50mi away (the proposal is under review), Happy Valley-Goose Bay will again be the closest business centre. Forestry is big business here as well, and there are high hopes for tourism once the new road to Cartwright has been completed (the Trans-Labrador Highway between Cartwright Junction and Happy Valley-Goose Bay is scheduled to open in 2009).

- ℹ **Information:** Visitor Centre, 365 Hamilton River Rd. ☎709-896-3489. www.destinationlabrador.com. ⏱Open Jun–Oct daily 9:30am–5:30pm. This chalet-style building is located at the corner of Loring Dr. & Hamilton River Rd. Town of Happy Valley-Goose Bay, 212 Hamilton River Rd. ☎709-896-3321. www.happyvalley-goosebay.com.
- ▶ **Orient Yourself:** Hamilton River Road (Rte. 520) is the main thoroughfare and intersects Route 500. Happy Valley sits at the east end of the community; Goose Bay lies in the west. Goose Bay airport is just north of the town.
- ⏱ **Organizing Your Time:** Three days should be adequate for exploring the town, North West River and Sheshatshiu.
- Kids **Especially for Kids:** The model trains and preserved wildlife at the Northern Lights Building.

Sight

Northern Lights Building
170 Hamilton River Rd. ⏱*Open year-round Tue–Sat 9am–5pm.* ☎*709-896-5939.* This crowded, eclectic emporium has something for everyone. Kids will enjoy looking at the lifelike displays of Labradorian wildlife, such as the black bear,

lynx and loons, as well as the large collection of **model trains** (*lower level*) from the 1940s and '50s.

Adults may want to look at artifacts from the Northern Lights **Military Museum,** also on-site, where memorabilia from the Royal Newfoundland Regiment is featured, among other displays.

View from Sunday Hill of sunset over Little Lake

Osmich/Wikimedia Commons

Excursions

Birch Brook Nordic Ski Club

13km/8mi north on Rte 520, towards North West River. 10 trails totalling 35km/ 22mi. ⏰ Open May–Oct daily. www.birch brook.com.

In the late spring and summer, the cross-country ski trails that have been maintained by volunteers for over 20 years are opened as well-marked hiking trails. A chalet with a wood stove, picnic tables and even a sauna are available to hikers who purchase a day pass. Three hiking trails are recommended (Rabbit Run, Brook Trail-Scotts Run and The Loop), and maps are available at the Labrador North Chamber of Commerce tourist booth in Happy Valley-Goose Bay *(169 Hamilton River Rd. ☎709-896-8787).*

Muskrat Falls

27km/17mi west of Goose Bay on Rte. 500 (Trans-Labrador Hwy.).
Local tour operators (Churchill River Boat Tours ☎709-896-0936 or Break Away Adventures ☎709-896-9343) offer guided tours to the falls. A visit can be self-guided, but⛰by experienced hikers only, since the trail is not marked.

For outdoor enthusiasts who enjoy challenging hiking conditions, this trek to the 15m/49ft-high falls in the middle of a spruce and pine forest is a definite must. The trail is unmarked, and there

are no amenities after the car is parked, so it is advisable to have insect repellent, water, hiking shoes or boots, food and a camera.

North West River

42km/26mi north by Rte 520.
The oldest community in Central Labrador, North West River was founded as a French trading post in 1743. When Labrador came under British control 20 years later, the Hudson's Bay Company (HBC) chose North West River as a hub of its fur-trading activity. Housed in a former HBC building, the **Labrador Heritage Society Museum** *(Portage Rd., ⏰ open Jun–Oct daily 10am–6pm; ⬛$2. ☎709-497-8858; www.labheritage. ca/home/7)* features displays themed around the fur-trapping trade that flourished in this area for 300 years. Upon entry, the company store (1923) looks as if it has just opened, with groceries lining the shelves behind the cashier; furs are laid out as if ready to be traded. The trapper gallery showcases the implements and clothing the hunters would have used, including antique snowshoes and seal-skin leggings.

For a true vantage point of Lake Melville, Grand Lake and the Mealy Mountains, go to **Sunday Hill Lookout** *(Sunday Hill Rd.)* at the highest point of North West River.

Aerial view of airbase, Goose Bay

Sheshatshiu Innu First Nation

43km/27mi north on Rte. 520. www.innu.ca
The name of this Innu community of 1,200 people literally translates to "narrow place by the river." Prior to becoming a permanent village, the site was the summer camp of the First Nations people, the place where they spent the months after hunting and gathering in the wilderness during winter and spring. Now there are several businesses, a church and a school in the community. This visit would be of interest to anyone wanting to see firsthand a small native community.

LABRADOR WEST

One of Labrador's four political divisions, Labrador West includes the mining towns of Labrador City and Wabush, as well as Churchill Falls, site of the second largest hydro-electric station in North America. This is an area that is at once heavy into industry but surrounded by northern Canadian forests, lakes and rivers. It is big snow country, and residents enjoy the winters cross-country skiing, snowshoeing, skating and snowmobiling. Most of the land lies in the Taiga Shield, which means that it is comprised of spruce and pine forests, wetlands, rolling hills, lakes, streams and peat bogs. Wildlife here includes black bears, grizzly bears, moose, wolf and caribou.

- **Information:** Labrador West Tourism Development Corp., 1365 Rte. 500, Gateway Complex, Labrador City. Open year-round Mon–Fri 9am–5pm. ☎709-944-5399. www.labradorwest.com.
- ▶ **Orient Yourself:** Churchill Falls is 292km/181mi west of Happy Valley-Goose Bay on Rte.500. From Churchill Falls west to Labrador City is 249km/154mi by Rte. 500. Wabush is only 6km/3.7mi southeast of Labrador City. These distances may seem longer than they are due to the dirt roads and the long stretches of wilderness driving.
- **Organizing Your Time:** Allow 2 days to see the sights, given the great distances between cities.

Sights

Churchill Falls Hydro Generating Facility★

Town of Churchill Falls. Visit by 3hr guided tour only, year-round daily 9am, 1:30pm & 7pm. Tours restricted to those 8 yrs of age and older and must be booked in advance by calling the town office ☎709-925-3335 Mon–Fri 8am–noon & 1pm–4:30pm.

It wasn't until 1839 that a nonindigenous person saw the Churchill River's 75m/245ft waterfall. After World War II, a study showed the huge hydro-electric possibilities of harnessing the power of the falls and the river.

Construction of the facility started in 1966, and by 1969 the town was coming into being. In 1971 one of the largest underground powerhouses in the world began generating power for Hydro Québec and the northeastern US.

The power plant collects and stores water in a reservoir that has an area of 5,700sq km/2,200sq mi.

Iron Ore Company of Canada & Wabush Mines★

Labrador City. Tours Jul–Aug Wed. & Sun 1:30pm depart from the Gateway Labrador complex, 1365 Rte. 500, Labrador City. ☎$5.70. ☎709-944-7631. www.labradorwest.com.

Operating Canada's largest iron-ore mine, the Iron Ore Company of Canada has been in business since 1962 and has produced more than one billion tonnes of crude ore with an iron content of 39%. At this site, known as the Carol Project, trucks that are incredibly large (250-tonne) can be seen among other giant-sized mining equipment that is regularly used.

Crystal Falls Hiking Trail

Fermont Hwy. (Rte. 389), Labrador City. Open Jun–Nov. ☎709-944-7631. www. labradorwest.com

Here's a place for photographs as well as exercise: a hiking trail that leads to the top of Crystal Falls. The one-kilometre-long trail is strewn with sub-arctic flora. From the falls, the view of the towns and rural areas is excellent.

LABRADOR NORTH

The vast expanse that is northern Labrador has only 3,400 residents, mostly Inuit and Kablunângajuit (people of mixed Labrador Inuit and European ancestry). They reside primarily along the coast in the communities of Rigolet, Makkovik, Postville, Hopedale and Nain. The nickel deposits found around Voisey's Bay are closest to Nain. Ferries and aircraft bring freight and passengers to and from these villages. Tour operators and guides are often the preferred arrangement for travel to this remote region. Within Labrador North, the area called Nunatsiavut is now an Inuit-governed territory (see A Bit of History). Within **Nunatsiavut** lies the wild and unforgiving 9,600sq km/3,700sq mi **Torngat Mountains National Park Reserve,** where only the most experienced trekkers come on their own. Northernmost Labrador sits within the Arctic Cordillera ecozone. This is a land of fjords and valleys created by glaciers of ages past. Plant life is limited, and the waters are ice-covered for most of the year. Arctic fox, hare and wolf survive in the Torngat Reserve.

- **Information:** Destination Labrador, 379 Hamilton River Rd., Happy Valley Goose Bay. ☎709-896-6507. www.destinationlabrador.com.
- ▶ **Orient Yourself:** Ferries (some of which are only seasonal) and small planes are the only modes of transportation to these communities. Nain is the northernmost community and is the location of the Torngat Mountains National Park office.
- **Organizing Your Time:** Allot 4 days minimum because of time consumed in getting here and getting around.

Wilderness Cruising

Two adventure-tour operators handle expeditions into the most remote parts of Labrador, including the Torngat Mountains National Park Reserve. **Linkum Tours,** based in Corner Brook, Newfoundland (☎709-634-2285or 877-254-6586; www.linkumtours.com), has summer tours of the park directed by Inuit guides; a 16m/55ft fishing vessel serves as home base. The two guided summer trips along the northern Labrador coast and into the park sponsored by **Wildland Tours** (124 Water St., St. John's; ☎709-722-3123 or 888-615-8279; www.wildlands.com), called Polar Bear expeditions, are sold out a year in advance. Because of the small number of people these tours can accommodate, reservations should be made far in advance.

Sight

Torngat Mountains National Park Reserve

Map of Principal Sights. Park Office in Nain. 🕐*Park open year round, but because of weather, visits are recommended only in late spring and summer.* ☎709-922-1290. www.pc.gc.ca/pn-np/nl/torngats/natcul/index_e.asp

This reserve really is the untamed wilderness, arctic-style, even if indigenous peoples have been in the region for thousands of years. There are two main landscapes: the rugged and coastal Torngat Mountains and the George Plateau, a bedrock plain accentuated with river valleys. Glaciation has clearly left its marks: drumlin fields (streamlined hills formed by moving glaciers), erratics (rocks transported from great distances by glacial action) and eskers (narrow ridges of sand and gravel deposited by melting glaciers) cover the craggy tundra.

As a national park of Canada, the reserve only recently came into existence (in 2005), and as of mid-2008, there are no fees to enter the park, nor any businesses operating within the park. Everyone who enters it must register (and later de-register) with the park office. Air and boat charters are available from Nain; inquire at the park office for names of local operators.

Once inside the park, the only limit to outdoor activities is one's imagination, although hunting is forbidden. Camping ("no trace" camping: all garbage must be taken out of the park), fishing, hiking, skiing and mountain climbing are the most common forms of activity in the park. Other visitors may choose to view the park via helicopter, small plane, sailboat or motorboat: these charters can also be arranged by local operators in Nain. Alternatively, professional tour guiding companies can plan your trek into Torngat Mountains Park (🕐*see Wilderness Cruising sidebar*).

Torngat Mountains and the Iron Stand coastline

©Parks Canada

For the best little places, follow the leader.

Looking for the latest news on today's best hotels and restaurants? Pick up the Michelin Guide and look for the Bib Gourmand and Bib Hotel symbols. With 45,000 addresses in Europe, in every category and price range, the perfect place to dine or stay is never far away.

A better way forward

The following abbreviations are used to indicate the provinces: NB, NS, NL and PE.

INDEX

INDEX

INDEX

WHERE TO STAY

INDEX

WHERE TO EAT

MAPS AND PLANS

LIST OF MAPS

COMPANION PUBLICATIONS

MAP 583 NORTHEASTERN USA AND EASTERN CANADA

MAP 585 WESTERN USA AND WESTERN CANADA

- Large-format maps providing detailed road systems; includes driving distances, interstate rest stops, border crossings and interchanges.
- Comprehensive city and town index
- Scale 1:2,400,000
  (1 inch = approx. 38 miles)

NORTH AMERICA ROAD ATLAS

- A geographically organized atlas with extensive detailed coverage of the USA, Canada and Mexico. Includes 246 city maps, distance chart, state and provincial driving requirements and a climate chart
- Comprehensive city and town index
- Easy to follow "Go-to" pointers

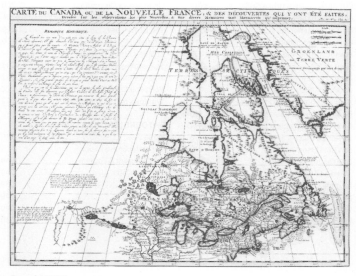

Canada (1719)

Historic Urban Plans

LEGEND

★★★ **Highly recommended**
★★ **Recommended**
★ **Interesting**

Sight symbols

Recommended itineraries with departure point

Church, chapel – Synagogue		Building described
Town described		Other building
AZ B Map co-ordinates locating sights		Small building, statue
Other points of interest		Fountain – Ruins
Mine – Cave		Visitor information
Windmill – Lighthouse		Ship – Shipwreck
Fort – Mission		Panorama – View

Other symbols

Interstate highway (USA)	US highway	Other route
Trans-Canada highway	Canadian highway	Mexican federal highway
Highway, bridge		Major city thoroughfare
Toll highway, interchange		City street with median
Divided highway		One-way street
Major, minor route		Pedestrian Street
15 (21) Distance in miles (kilometers)		Tunnel
2149/655 Pass, elevation *(feet/meters)*		Steps – Gate
△6288(1917) Mtn. peak, elevation *(feet/meters)*		Drawbridge - Water tower
Airport – Airfield		Parking – Main post office
Ferry: Cars and passengers		University – Hospital
Ferry: Passengers only		Train station – Bus station
Waterfall – Lock – Dam		Subway station
International boundary		Digressions – Observatory
State boundary, provincial boundary		Cemetery – Swamp
Winery		Long lines

Recreation

Gondola, chairlift		Stadium – Golf course
Tourist or steam railway		Park, garden
Harbor, lake cruise – Marina		Wildlife reserve
Surfing – Windsurfing		Wildlife/Safari park, zoo
Diving – Kayaking		Walking path, trail
Ski area – Cross-country skiing		Hiking trail

Sight of special interest for children

Abbreviations and special symbols

MP Marine Park	NP National Park	NF National Forest
NHS National Historic Site		PP Provincial Park
Visitor centre:	Local - 🅱	Provincial - 🅱
16 Yellowhead Highway		Subway station (Montreal)

All maps are oriented north, unless otherwise indicated by a directional arrow